DATA
PROCESSING
FOR
BUSINESS

DATA PROCESSING FOR BUSINESS

GERALD A. SILVER
Los Angeles City College

JOAN B. SILVER

HARCOURT BRACE JOVANOVICH, INC.
New York Chicago San Francisco Atlanta

Cover photo by Linda Lindroth

Library of Congress Catalog Card Number: 72–90642

ISBN: 0–15–516804–5

Printed in the United States of America

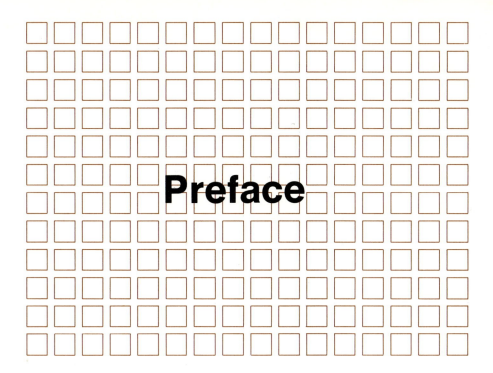

Preface

The phenomenal growth of electronic data processing shows no sign of subsiding. Already an integral part of countless business operations, EDP is finding increasing use in government, health sciences, and education. Perhaps in the near future an understanding of EDP will be as basic to education as a knowledge of reading, writing, and arithmetic.

Designed for a first course in data processing, this book is a contemporary view of computer technology and languages. It deals with fundamental concepts, terminology, and theory in logical order, moving from the simple to the complex. Excessive detail has been avoided in favor of broad coverage of central topics.

Data Processing For Business is divided into eight parts.

Part One, Introduction, discusses the general subject, defines important terms, and surveys data processing methods and trends.

Part Two, Unit Record Processing/Electrical Accounting Machine Processing, introduces the fundamentals of unit record processing and treats the basic terminology of the punched card.

Part Three, Computer Hardware, considers input, processing, storage, and output methods. Chapter 8, in particular, concentrates on numbering and coding systems, conversions, and elementary mathematical operations.

Part Four, Solving a Problem with the Computer, explores computer problem solving, algorithms, logic, and flowcharting. The discussion begins with simple flowcharting rules and elementary algorithms and proceeds from

v

structuring problems for the computer through coding, running, debugging, and documentation.

Part Five, Computer Software, opens with an elementary treatment of operating systems, which lays the groundwork for understanding the design and function of compilers and their relationship to the computer. COBOL and FORTRAN are treated in separate chapters. Another chapter describes such languages as PL/I, RPG, BASIC, and Assembler.

Part Six, Business Systems, explores business systems and the organization of the data center.

Part Seven, Teleprocessing and Computer Utilities, covers two rapidly growing elements of data processing.

Finally, Part Eight, Applied Business Systems, presents nine case studies, which can be used as springboards for discussion or for a review of the concepts covered in the preceding chapters.

Each chapter is followed by a list of key terms; a glossary appears at the back of the book. Exercises follow each chapter to aid the student in evaluating his progress. Some of the exercises broaden the learning experience by requiring that the student go into the field to interview people or to observe computers and businesses.

Cartoons and anecdotes are used throughout the book to present the ideas, thoughts, and commentary of people who feel strongly about data processing and to remind the student that in data processing people are as important as machines.

A textbook is not the product of one or two individuals. We wish to thank the firms and organizations that graciously provided assistance. The people who reviewed the manuscript also deserve our thanks: Jerry Ardissone, Oakland Public Schools; William J. Billeter, College of San Mateo; Leonard J. Garrett, Temple University; and Robert Ripley, San Diego City College.

It is our hope that this book will make learning data processing an enjoyable and fascinating undertaking.

GERALD A. SILVER
JOAN B. SILVER

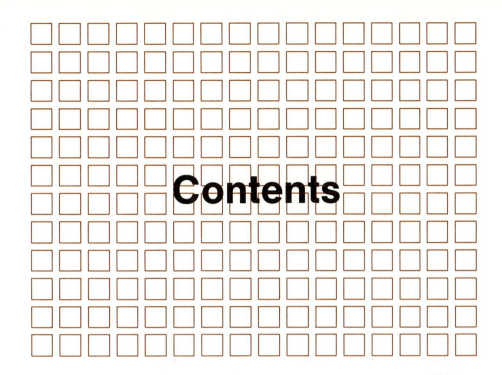

Contents

DATA
PROCESSING
FOR
BUSINESS

PART ONE

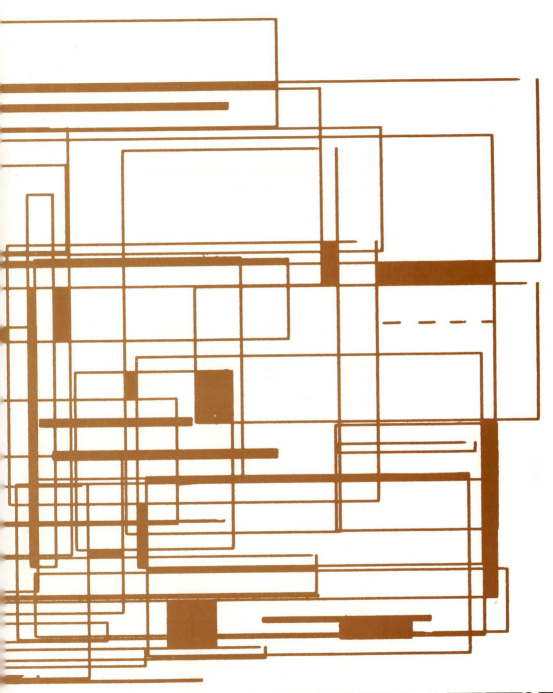

INTRODUCTION

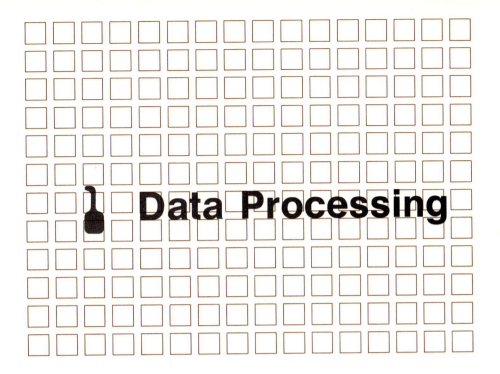

1 Data Processing

Deep in a concrete vault in the heart of a city is a giant electronic brain. It monitors the movements of all citizens. It controls every transaction. It establishes the policies of the government. It decides which families may have children, and whether they will be male or female. The lights of the machine flicker and, in an instant, a force equal to the brainpower of 10,000 scientists is brought to bear on a single problem. A million medical records are sorted in three seconds. And the vital statistics of 200 million people are stored in a one-inch deep, cold cube. . . .

It is 1823 in England. The "keeper of the monies" records the day's sales, "108 shillings." The light of the candle plays across his handwritten letters and documents as he works long into the night. With his new adding machine, a handsomely engraved device composed of gears, wheels, and cogs, he can do up to a dozen addition problems in an hour. He is excited—it will also multiply—and with patience, he can learn to divide. . . .

Of course the two examples above represent extremes. Today's world of data processing lies somewhere between science fiction and the quill pen. By definition, data processing is the restructuring or reordering of data, by man or machine, to increase its usefulness and value. It involves classifying, merging, sorting, retrieving, calculating, transmitting, summarizing, or reporting. In electronic data processing, high-speed electronic computers are used to process data, print out reports, or transmit information.

In 1970, 80,000 computers were in use in the United States, and from 30 to 50 more were being added each business day.[1] (See Figure 1.1.) These computers process millions of calculations each minute and help control the marketing, manufacturing, and distribution of a vast quantity of goods and services.

Thousands of engineers, analysts, programmers, computer operators, installers, and others are employed in data processing. The need for such services is expected to double by 1975. In the next decade it will be a rare business or organization which will not in some way rely on modern data processing.

Clearly, electronic data processing has become a vital part of American business. This book will explore the machines, equipment, services, and personnel engaged in this dynamic new industry.

WHAT ARE COMPUTERS?

Broadly defined, a computer is any device that computes, calculates, or reckons. Thus the abacus, adding machine, and slide rule are all forms of computers.

The definition of a computer has become more limited in contemporary usage. A computer is now defined as an electronic device that processes data, is capable of receiving input and output, and possesses such characteristics as high speed, accuracy, and the ability to store a set of instructions for solving a problem.

Computers are electronic devices composed of switches, wires, motors, transistors, and integrated circuits, assembled on frames. The frames form components such as typewriters, line printers, card readers, card punches, magnetic tape drives, and central processing units. These components are wired together into a network called a computing system. The entire system is often called, simply, a computer.

A computing system can read data from hundreds of punched cards in one minute, or type out information at the rate of hundreds of lines per minute. It can store millions of letters or numbers, ready for retrieval.

Computers can perform a variety of mathematical calculations, ranging from simple adding and subtracting to solving complicated math equations which involve thousands of steps. They can repeat a complicated calculation millions of times without error.

Computers can print out whole paragraphs of text matter, write letters, draw pictures, or plot curves and draw graphs. They can sort data, merge lists, search files, and make logical decisions and comparisons.

A computing system may range in size from rather small desk top devices with limited capability to huge machines occupying several large rooms. It

---

[1] *Datamation,* July 15, 1970, p. 40.

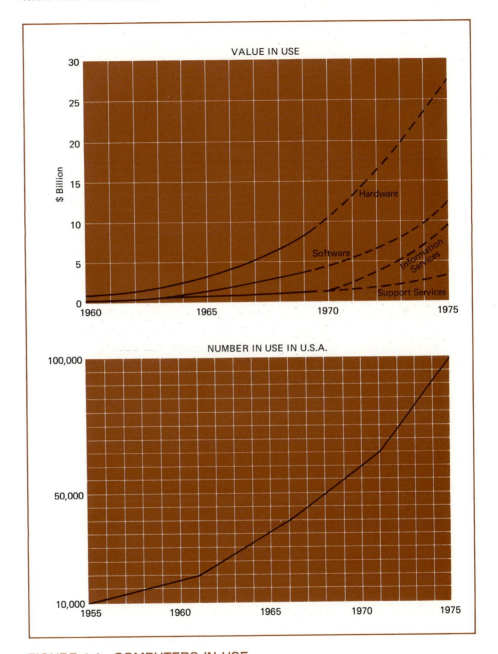

FIGURE 1.1   COMPUTERS IN USE

may be constructed as a single, integral device, or as a group of machines, remotely connected, but functioning as a unit. The individual parts may be located within the same building or scattered across the country, connected by telephone lines.

Computers can be characterized by their function. Special-purpose computers are built to solve one kind of problem, such as processing airline reservations or controlling a metalworking machine. General-purpose computers can be used for many business, scientific, educational, social, and other applications. These machines are not limited to one type of problem, but lend themselves to the solution of many.

Computers may be generally characterized by the way in which they receive and process data. Some systems process numeric values represented by discrete electronic pulses; others process data of a continuous nature.

Analog computers process data input in a continuous form. Data, such as voltage, resistance, temperature, and pressure, is represented in the computer as a continuous, unbroken flow. In engineering and scientific applications, where quantities to be processed exist as wave forms, or continually rising and falling voltages, pressures, etc., analog computers are very useful. They are not suitable for processing business data, which usually occurs as a discrete quantity. Output from analog computers is usually displayed on cathode ray tubes or plotters. A cathode ray tube converts electric signals into visual forms, much like an ordinary television set. A plotter converts electric signals into lines or a graph on a page.

Digital computers process data in the form of discrete letters or numbers and are, therefore, more useful in business applications. The output is on line printers, typewriters, card punches, or paper tape punches in a form convenient for business such as typed reports or paychecks. This book is concerned with the digital computer.

The differences between digital and analog computers may be further illustrated by comparing how an increase in temperature is noted by an engineer and an increase in inventory is noted by a businessman. The increase in temperature, say from 68 to 69°, is not abrupt and may be represented as a continuum. The best way to input this information is by using an increasing electrical voltage, analogous to the rise in temperature.

To the businessman, an increase in the number of units of an item in stock is represented by a discrete number. His inventory total may increase from 105 to 106 units, but not from 105 to $105\frac{1}{2}$ units. Similarly, employees increase in units of one, a paycheck is a discrete amount, and a sales price is quoted as a specific number. This kind of business data is best input to the computer using common numbers or alphabetic characters.

WHY STUDY DATA PROCESSING AND COMPUTERS?

For a number of reasons a knowledge of the role, capacity, and limitation of data processing is of value to everyone. In fact, it is almost impossible to go through a day without encountering data processing in some form. Government, industry, schools, hospitals, the courts, etc. all use data processing in some way. The character and development of modern business

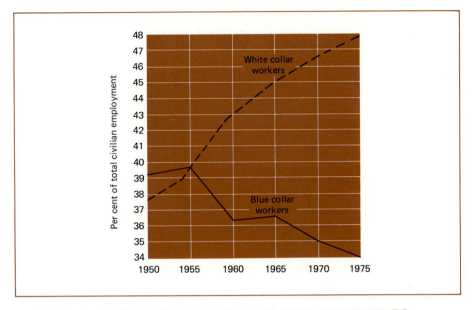

FIGURE 1.2   WHITE COLLAR AND BLUE COLLAR WORKERS
              IN THE LABOR FORCE

is influenced by data processing. Business decisions depend on the quality and accuracy of available data.

Data processing is a growing industry and the source of many jobs. Blue collar workers are decreasing in number. In 1965 they made up approximately 37% of the civilian labor force, by 1975 only 34% will be blue collar workers. On the other hand, the need for white collar workers continues to grow, and by the same year they should account for 48% of the labor force (a 3% increase in ten years). (See Figure 1.2.) Many of these workers will be employed in data processing. In fact, it has been estimated that by 1980 one million people will be employed in electronic data processing.

Important Terms   Throughout this book, important terms and vocabulary will be introduced and explained. Here are some basic terms which you should understand.

DATA (INFORMATION).   Data is useful knowledge, or information of value to an individual or a business. It is factual material used as a basis for discussion or decision, or for calculation or measurement. Data may consist of reports, letters, facts, figures, records, or documents with which a business can operate.

In a narrower sense, data consists of numbers or letters which may be processed or reordered by man or machine to increase its value or utility. (Although ''data'' is technically the plural of ''datum,'' it is commonly used as a singular form.) The terms data and information are used interchangeably in this book. Some writers prefer to define data as facts, and information as knowledge derived from data.

COMPUTER PROGRAM.　A computer program is a series of instructions or statements recorded in a form acceptable to a computer. These instructions direct the computer through a series of steps to solve a problem. Programs are written by individuals, called programmers, who understand the nature of the problem to be solved and who can communicate with the computer.

An important feature of the modern computer is its ability to store a program. The program is entered into the computer and stored. Then the data is fed in. This arrangement greatly increases the usefulness and general-purpose nature of the machine, since the same program can operate on many sets of data.

WHO USES ELECTRONIC DATA PROCESSING?

Electronic data processing was originally developed for scientific and mathematical applications and is still widely used in these disciplines. Because of the specialized nature of early computers, they were impractical for business usage. However, the introduction of general-purpose machines and simpler programming languages greatly increased the computer's utility. Computers are now indispensable tools of business.

Business Needs
Electronic data processing, or the use of computers, is growing, because it is capable of meeting a need of modern business firms—the accurate, efficient handling of vast amounts of data. What are the demands faced by business that create this need?

1. NUMBER OF TRANSACTIONS.　The growth in size and number of business firms naturally increases the number of business transactions. The computer, with its high capacity and speed, can process thousands of records or business calculations per minute, and with far greater efficiency than any previous method.
2. COST.　Competitive pressures have led many firms to adopt computerized methods of data processing. In the past, sales could be written up longhand, orders filled by hand, and the bills and records of the transactions prepared by longhand. However, with a large number of transactions the cost of hand labor precludes this method.
3. ACCURACY.　Another pressure on the business firm is the requirement of strict accuracy in many areas. The firm must make decisions, perform calculations, and plan production with precision. A business decision involving millions of dollars may rest on a few pieces of data. Calculations themselves must be performed accurately. An error of only a fraction of a

cent per transaction may not seem too critical, but it is disastrous when one or two million transactions are involved.

With electronic data processing thousands of calculations can be processed with virtually no errors. The error level in a modern computer is about one error per ten million calculations. No known device matches this performance.

4. SPEED. The pace of modern business necessitates the fast flow of data. Decisions must often be made on short notice, or immediately following a transaction. For example, the stock market and the export and import industry rely heavily upon prompt data flow. The computer can process data at speeds unequaled by other means. Data can be moved within a computer in billionths of a second, and complete reports can be printed out in a matter of minutes.

5. SELECTIVITY. Businessmen demand greater selectivity in the ways data is reported. The computer can reorder a collection of data into many different forms. One program can list the sales from the previous day's activities in chronological order. With a few modifications of the program, the computer will categorize the same list by type of merchandise sold, by salesman, by amount, or by location.

6. INFORMATION. Good decision making is imperative in business, and good decisions require comprehensive and complete information. This information must often be related to previous experience. Many business managers rely heavily upon ratios, cost comparisons, and time comparisons.

For example, a study of manufacturing costs may require the review of data from hundreds of previous jobs and comparisons between many elements in each job. Unless these comparisons can be made quickly and economically, their value may be lost by the cost of the effort to obtain the data.

One large restaurant chain compares weekly food, linen, labor, and other operating costs for each of their several hundred restaurants. Costs that are out of order are immediately apparent. Such things as theft of linen goods and inefficient or profitless operation are detected before serious losses occur.

7. RECORD KEEPING. There is a growing need to record transactions at the instant they occur, not hours or days later. Passenger reservations for a 400-seat airliner are valued at thousands of dollars. Because unsold seats are an economic loss to the airline, the airline clerk must know the availability of seats at all times.

Often a sale can be made if current stock, price, or delivery data is available. The lack of data may cost a sale. On the other hand, a sale made on the basis of insufficient credit data may cause a firm to lose thousands of dollars.

The computer can process and record thousands of transactions as they occur. Real time processing means data is processed and recorded at the moment the physical transaction occurs. Batch processing, on the

THE MAN WHO ALMOST INVENTED THE COMPUTER

Charles Babbage had two loves: machines and mathematics. His studies at Cambridge in the early 1800's gave him the opportunity to investigate the principles of mathematics, science, and mechanics. His sizable inheritance gave him the means to pursue his lifelong dream—the development of a calculating machine.

He envisioned a machine that could prepare complex arithmetic tables with a precision and speed far beyond the ability of the human mind. But could he build such a machine? In 1822, the Royal Society persuaded the government to grant him £1,500 to begin his work. He labored eight years without success on the project, and repeatedly requested more money. He himself invested £6,000 trying to perfect the machine he called the "Difference Engine."

Then he dreamed of another device that could perform calculations on data read from punched cards. He abandoned his plans for the Difference Engine in favor of this even more complex device he called the "Analytic Engine."

Building the Analytic Engine proved far more frustrating than the Difference Engine. Babbage returned again and again to the drawing board to change his designs and plans. During the next several years he tried more than 400 different plans and modifications for his Analytic Engine.

When he approached the government for additional funds, he met with such strong opposition that he abandoned the project. After 21 years in engineering and investigating the world's first digital computer, Babbage had to admit defeat. His dreams, far ahead of the ideas and the mechanical technology of his time, were not to come true in his lifetime.

But Babbage's efforts were not all in vain. He wrote several treatises including "The Decline of Science" and "On the Economy of Machinery and Manufactures." His work laid the foundation for the first unit record machines. Three decades after his death, Herman Hollerith relied upon many of his ideas to invent the first successful unit record processing equipment.

other hand, means data is collected in groups and processed several hours or days after the physical transaction. With proper equipment, a computer can perform both real time and batch processing. Such a procedure can mean more sales, better utilization of productive resources, and reduction of credit loss.

8. SERVICE.   As businesses grow, it is harder for them to provide individualized service to customers. This problem is alleviated, and sometimes even eliminated, with data processing. With the support of high-speed data processing equipment, firms can better service their customers. A department store with 25,000 open accounts must give thorough consideration to each customer each month. Returned merchandise, payments, and charges must be posted promptly and accurately. Without electronic data processing, it would require many clerks, working full-time, to maintain the accounts.

9. MECHANIZATION.   It is said "machines should work and people should

think.'' Many businessmen believe that the human resource should be applied to those tasks for which humans are uniquely qualified. Routine transactions, calculations, and processing of data should be done by machines, thus freeing people for more creative activities. Electronic data processing allows this.

Business Applications

What are some specific uses for computers in business? A representative sampling of current business applications is given below. These and others are considered in greater detail in later chapters.

SALES FORECAST AND CONTROL. The computer can prepare an estimate of future sales, called a sales forecast, from sales data. It can be programmed to read historical sales data and calculate trends. With this data, the marketing department can make predictions about coming business cycles—useful information in planning advertising campaigns, stocking retailers, tooling up assembly lines, and contracting with suppliers.

PAYROLL. The computer can process a firm's payroll. It can be programmed to read source documents, calculate earnings, deductions, and withholdings, and print out paychecks. Computerized payroll systems can handle hourly or salaried payrolls and commission payments; they can process salaries on a weekly, monthly, or other basis.

ORDER POINT CALCULATION. The computer can calculate usage and print out a list of goods and the quantities that must be ordered in advance, based on a review of order times and consumption. It can forecast errors, set safety stock levels, and aid in planning production.

"SAD CASE THERE....BRILLIANT COMPUTER MAN—TOOK A SIX WEEK'S VACATION AND FELL TOO FAR BEHIND IN HIS FIELD"

© Datamation®

BUSINESS MANAGEMENT.   The computer can provide reports and data for management. Inventory, sales analysis, credit analysis, and other operating ratios can be calculated.

GENERAL LEDGER.   A comprehensive accounting system can be put on the computer by using electronically stored ledgers in the machine. The computer can print out journal entries, taxes, reports, profit and loss statements, and balance sheets.

PERSONNEL MANAGEMENT INFORMATION.   The computer can provide management with data on the composition of its personnel. It can print out information on job classifications, personnel capabilities, and employees by department, by salary schedule, or by both.

COST ACCOUNTING.   The computer can print out an analysis of production costs. It can be programmed to perform routine cost accounting tasks with budgeted hourly costs on individual machine rates and overhead figures. It can analyze a production job according to the number of hours required on each machine and in each department, calculate return on investment and profit, and print out a selling price.

MANUFACTURING INFORMATION CONTROL.   The computer is used in the manufacture and production of goods. It can provide ordering, warehousing, and cost data, based on part numbers or bills of lading.

The computer can schedule work for an assembly line based upon labor available by shift. It can print out a list of equipment and material needs for the line for a given day and predict output. The same machine can then report the number of units produced and provide follow-up cost data.

BANKING.   The computer is used in the finance, credit, and collection industry. It can process deposits, commercial and consumer loans, and revolving charge accounts for banks and department stores. It can prepare credit card statements. It can maintain trust accounts and even handle the firm's own payroll.

MODELING AND PLANNING.   The computer can also be used to simulate business ventures. Actual business conditions can be analyzed and reduced to mathematical terms and the problem fed to the computer. Then different sets of trial data are fed in and the computer prints out results. The firm is spared the time and expense of actually testing the real thing.

Suppose a manufacturer wants to produce a food product of specific nutritive value. Assume it is not to exceed a given cost, nor a given number of calories per pound. Further assume it must contain certain specified vitamins and a given amount of protein. It is difficult to decide the proper formula if there are many ingredients which can be combined to make the food product. The best combination of components to produce the desired result at the lowest cost must be determined. By using a mathematical technique called *linear programming,* the computer can print out a list of ingredients and quantities which most closely meets the manufacturer's requirements.

Size of Installations

Large business firms rely heavily upon electronic data processing. Airlines make ticket reservations, insurance companies handle claims, and large department stores process billing and collections. Manufacturers control assembly lines by computer, railroad companies locate freight cars by computer, and oil and gas companies control the manufacture of their products by computer.

These applications are often complex and require large systems like the one shown in Figure 1.3. Computers such as these, leasing at a cost of from $20,000 to $100,000 per month, are capable of storing millions of pieces of data and can process thousands of instructions per second. Large-scale users may tie computer facilities located at several places across the country into a nationwide network.

FIGURE 1.3 LARGE COMPUTER INSTALLATION

FIGURE 1.4   MEDIUM-SIZED COMPUTER INSTALLATION

FIGURE 1.5   SMALL COMPUTER INSTALLATION

Computers are also widely used by firms with from 100 to several thousand employees. Firms of this size, such as loan companies, sales organizations, manufacturers, trucking companies, or insurance companies, use electronic data processing to prepare invoices, handle accounts receivable and payable, and customer credit, and provide management with marketing data, records, and forecasts.

Machines suitable for this level of need are shown in Figure 1.4. They are capable of processing hundreds of instructions per minute, but may be more limited in speed and capability than the large computers. Leasing costs range from $10,000 to $20,000 per month.

Improvements in equipment design have brought about lower cost computers, which can be leased for $2,000 to $10,000 per month. (See Figure 1.5.) Another development is the minicomputer, small desk top computers costing $5,000 to $25,000. (See Figure 1.6; see also Figure 6.9.)

Terminals, such as the one shown in Figure 1.7, bring the power of the computer to even the smallest firms. These typewriter-like devices are located in business establishments and are connected by ordinary telephone lines to computers at a remote location. Remote computer terminals, discussed in more detail in Chapter 22, lease for as little as $35 per month, plus the charges for computer time and line charges.

FIGURE 1.6   MINICOMPUTER

FIGURE 1.7 PORTABLE DATA TERMINAL

In 1970 approximately 50,000 remote terminals were in use in retailing establishments. It is predicted that by 1980 approximately 800,000 of these terminals will be in use.[2] (See Figure 1.8.) Such terminals can be used by food, department, and discount stores to handle credit authorization.

DATA FLOW IN BUSINESS

A business enterprise is dependent upon the efficient flow of data, both internally and externally. Accurate, prompt, and complete data is essential in the decision-making process. Business executives must have adequate data to properly direct the operations of the business enterprise. The manufacturing, marketing, and distribution departments need data for production and shipment of goods.

[2] *Computer Decisions,* November 1970, p. C7.

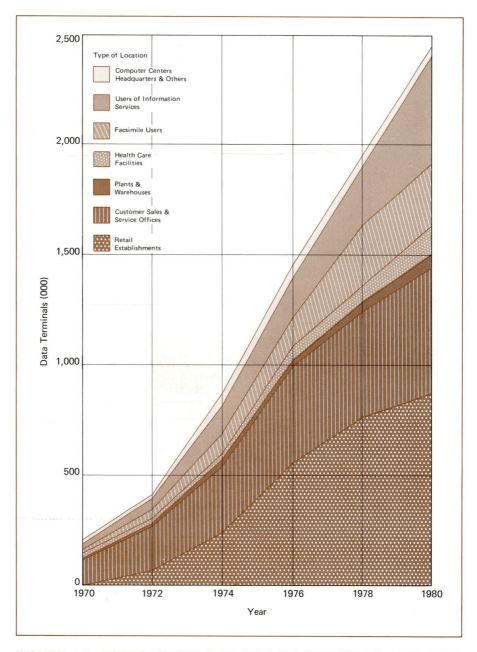

Type of Location

- Computer Centers Headquarters & Others
- Users of Information Services
- Facsimile Users
- Health Care Facilities
- Plants & Warehouses
- Customer Sales & Service Offices
- Retail Establishments

Data Terminals (000)

Year

FIGURE 1.8   FORECAST NUMBER OF DATA TERMINALS, 1970–1980

A business enterprise is illustrated in Figure 1.9. The firm is in the center of the diagram, surrounded by the groups with which it interacts. Data flows back and forth between the center—the firm—and the peripheral elements—

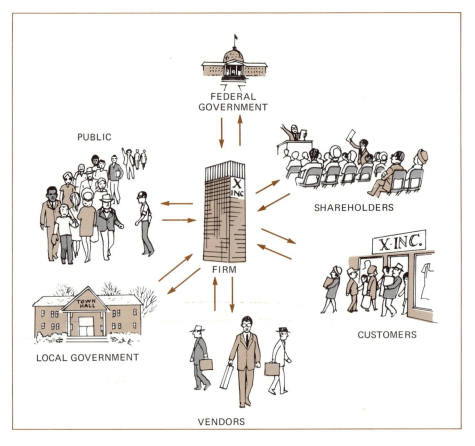

FIGURE 1.9 EXTERNAL DATA FLOW

the vendors, customers, government, and the public. This kind of communication is called external data flow. Some examples of external data flow are reports on employee withholding and unemployment, tax reports, earnings reports, specifications to vendors, and sales orders.

Internal data flow takes place within an organization and can be divided into two groups called vertical and horizontal data flow. (See Figure 1.10.)

In an organization, data flows in a vertical direction from a foreman to line employees, or from the president to branch managers. Data may also flow from employees in lower echelons to their supervisors or to the president of the company.

Data also flows horizontally between personnel on the same level of the organization. For example, the head of manufacturing may supply salary information to the head of the payroll department. Or an employee on the shipping dock may sign for goods and supply data to a clerk in the purchasing department.

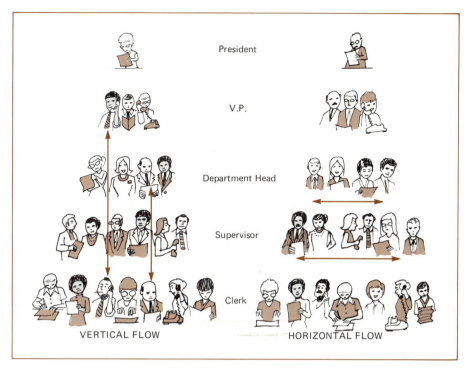

President

V.P.

Department Head

Supervisor

Clerk

VERTICAL FLOW   HORIZONTAL FLOW

FIGURE 1.10   INTERNAL DATA FLOW

Time Factor To be of optimum value to an organization, certain data must be available at specific points in the business cycle. A system of processing data must take the time element into account. The storage and retrieval of data for representation is an important function of data processing. The accuracy and thoroughness of data processing are of little value to a firm unless the results it produces are presented at the correct times and places. For example, data on the credit standing and reputation of a prospective customer must be in the hands of the sales department prior to a sale. Credit data delivered after the transaction may be little consolation for the sales manager who has extended credit to an account incapable of repayment.

Data Cycle Data being processed goes through three steps called the data cycle, as shown in Figure 1.11. They are data input, data processing, and data output.

DATA INPUT. Data input involves converting data from source documents into a form acceptable to processing by computer or other means. Source documents are the original records of a transaction. These records, often written in longhand (such as employee time cards, sales orders, and memos) must be converted and transferred to punched cards for entry into the system.

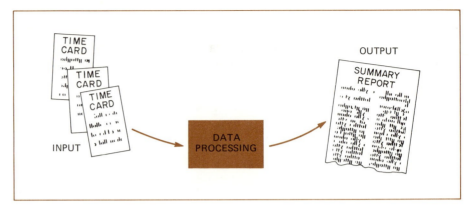

FIGURE 1.11   THE DATA CYCLE

(Other means of entering source documents will be covered later in the book.)

DATA PROCESSING.   During data processing, the data is changed in form, order, or structure to increase its value or utility. Sales orders for the week may be totaled. A list of employees may be classified by department. A sales commission may be calculated. Data may be stored for later retrieval and presentation.

DATA OUTPUT.   In the data output phase, the results of the previous steps are made available in a form of maximum use to the business firm. It is not enough that data be input and processed. It has little value until it is reported, summarized, or in some way communicated to the businessman. Output consists of printing forms, statements, or reports, or in the display of results on a visual device that resembles a television set.

KEY TERMS   Data
Information
Data cycle
Input
Source documents
Output
Computer
Electronic data processing
Analog computers

Digital computers
Program
External data flow
Internal data flow
Real time processing
Batch processing
Minicomputer
Terminals

EXERCISES
1. Give four reasons why a study of data processing is of value.
2. What is the difference between an analog and a digital computer?
3. Diagram the data cycle of a particular business firm. List source documents, processing requirements, and output.
4. Define the term "computer." Explain how the usage of this term has changed.
5. What is a program? Write a set of ten instructions which tell, step-by-step, how to perform a task such as balancing a checkbook or determining monthly payments on a loan.
6. Diagram the vertical data flow in your college. Show kinds of information which flow vertically and the individuals involved.
7. Diagram the horizontal data flow in a firm or organization with which you are familiar. Show the kinds of information which flow horizontally and the personnel involved.
8. Why is the time factor important in data processing? Give several examples of the effect of the time factor on the value of data.
9. The demands on the business enterprise are discussed in this chapter. Select a business firm with which you are familiar and give examples of how these pressures affect it.
10. Only a few of the many applications of data processing have been studied in this chapter. Visit a business firm which does not have electronic data processing. List at least three applications of electronic data processing which would be of value to that firm.
11. Name four types of businesses that process data and might be able to use terminals.
12. What are the trends in the labor force regarding white and blue collar workers?
13. Select a business firm to study. Interview its owners or employees. Draw a simplified diagram of its external data flow. (See Figure 1.9.) (Show the firm at the center, and list the names of the firms and organizations with which it interacts.)

2 Trends in Data Processing

A study of data processing shows that in the past, years, even centuries, elapsed between the introduction of new inventions. Today, the gap has closed. New machines, new methods, and improved systems enter the industry daily. (See Figure 2.1.) Advancements in data processing technology may be divided into two categories:

1 hardware developments
2 software developments

Hardware technology is defined as machines, devices, mechanisms, or physical equipment used to process data. An output printer, a computer terminal, and the machines illustrated in the previous chapter are examples of data processing hardware.

Software technology is defined as programs, computer languages, series of actions, codes, concepts, and theories used in data processing. A computer program giving instructions for the steps involved in preparing and printing out employees' checks is an example of software. The language used to communicate with the computer and a diagram of the flow of business information in a firm are also software.

Computers and some of the other data processing equipment could not be used without adequate software. Early software was crude or very limited. Computer languages were difficult to understand and to learn, and no

	DATA PROCESSING HISTORY
1980	
1970	FOURTH GENERATION, Monolithic circuits, cryogenics
	Integrated circuits
	Magnetic tape and disk, Minicomputer, audio response unit
1960	THIRD GENERATION, multiprogramming, teleprocessing, OCR, MICR
1950	SECOND GENERATION, transistor
	FIRST GENERATION, ENIAC, stored program
	EAM Processing
1900	Monroe Calculator
	Hollerith code
	Key-driven multipliers
	Felt's comptometer
	Babbage's Analytical Engine and Difference Engine
1800	Jacquard punch card loom
1700	
	Leibnitz's Calculator
	Pascal's numerical wheel calculator
1600	Slide rule (analog computer)
1500	
1400	
	Double-entry bookkeeping system
1300	
PAST	Abacus
	Decimal system
	Finger counting

FIGURE 2.1 DATA PROCESSING HISTORY

systems were available to efficiently schedule jobs for the computer. Much of the growth and change in data processing in the last decade has been in the area of software.

This chapter will trace important developments and trends in both hardware and software technology.

DEVELOPMENTS IN HARDWARE

Throughout history, man has used his creative powers to invent and develop devices and systems to help him in his tasks. The manipulation, processing, and recording of data is no exception.

The human fingers were the first devices used to process data. This readily accessible, but limited, means of counting and calculating formed the basis for the decimal numbering system. Later, crude methods such as piling rocks or gathering sticks were used to indicate larger quantities and added another dimension in mathematical computation.

The abacus was one of the first mechanical devices man developed to process data. Although its origin is uncertain, it was used by many civilizations, including the early Chinese and Romans. It is still in use today in many parts of the world.

The oriental abacus consisted of a frame and rods. Beads strung along the rods represented quantities. Addition and subtraction and other arithmetic operations were performed by manipulating the beads. The Romans moved pebbles, called calculi, in slots to perform computations. (See Figure 2.2.) The abacus is the first known example of a digital computer.

In 1617 John Napier invented the device, later called Napier's bones, shown in Figure 2.3. Napier's bones are rods with numbers, representing logarithms, engraved upon them. By rotating the rods, they could be made to perform division and root extraction.

The development of the slide rule was an early example of an analog computer. This device appeared in several forms throughout the seventeenth century. Gunter's Scale, shown in Figure 2.4, was one such example. It was approximately two feet long and was used to perform multiplication.

In 1642 Blaise Pascal successfully built an adding machine. This primitive device, shown in Figure 2.5, performed calculations by means of wheels and cogs indexed to represent varying quantities.

In 1671 Gottfried Leibnitz completed a multiplying machine called the Leibnitz Calculator, shown in Figure 2.6. It operates on the principle of the stepped reckoner and pin wheels, features still found in some mechanical desk calculators.

The next major step in the evolution of data processing was the development of a device completely unrelated to early calculators and slide rules. In 1801 in France, Joseph Marie Jacquard perfected an automatic system for weaving patterns into fabric. He used cards with punched holes to guide the warp threads on his loom, shown in Figure 2.7. The holes in the card controlled the pattern that was woven into the fabric. The Jacquard card illustrated in Figure 2.8, was the forerunner of the cards used in unit record systems today.

FIGURE 2.2   ROMAN ABACUS

FIGURE 2.3   NAPIER'S BONES

FIGURE 2.4   GUNTER'S SCALE

FIGURE 2.5

PASCAL'S NUMERICAL

WHEEL CALCULATOR

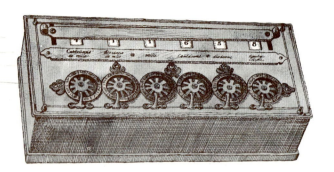

FIGURE 2.6   LEIBNITZ CALCULATOR

FIGURE 2.7 JACQUARD LOOM*

*Letter references have been dropped in the discussion.

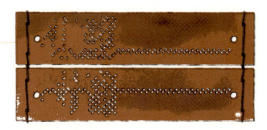

FIGURE 2.8 JACQUARD CARDS

FIGURE 2.9

BABBAGE'S

DIFFERENCE ENGINE

FIGURE 2.10 FELT'S COMPTOMETER

FIGURE 2.11 HOLLERITH'S ACCOUNTING MACHINE

About ten years later in England, a visionary mathematician began work on a calculator that would perform extremely complex arithmetic functions and calculations. Charles Babbage spent most of his life and fortune attempting to build his "Difference Engine." Figure 2.9 shows the portion which he completed in 1833. Later, he abandoned this machine in favor of a more complicated one, called the "Analytical Engine," which would perform arithmetic functions on data read in from punch cards. Neither device was ever completed because of the limited technology of the day.

Charles Babbage has earned his place in the history of data processing as the man who attempted to construct the first complex computer. The hundreds of drawings and plans he left have served as inspiration and education to the inventors and mathematicians who came after him.

Although a century would elapse before man would successfully build such a complex computer, many small steps were taken during the next few decades. The era of industrialization and mechanization had begun. American inventors were actively pioneering new machines and devices. Many of these are the forerunners of our modern desk top calculators. This era saw the beginning of companies such as Burroughs, Baldwin, and Monroe.

Nineteenth century inventors successfully developed machines that performed some of the operations Babbage envisioned for his Analytical Engine. In 1887 Dorr Felt patented a "comptometer." This machine, shown in Figure 2.10, was the first calculator able to perform carries and opened the way for adding multidigit numbers.

In 1890 Herman Hollerith successfully combined the concepts of Jacquard's cards and data recording and manipulation. He devised a coding system which could be punched into cards to represent data. Figure 2.11 shows the machine he built to read and manipulate data read in from the cards. This system was used to process the 1890 Census in one fourth the time it had taken to do the 1880 Census. The Hollerith coding system became the standard data representation method for the unit record system.

Hollerith left the Census Department to manufacture and sell his data processing machine. The company he founded is now known as the International Business Machines Corporation, or IBM—a leader in the production of electronic data processing machines.

Birth of the Computer

In 1944 Howard G. Aiken, a physicist at Harvard University, brought Babbage's dream to fruition. Aiken perfected the first general-purpose computer, the Automatic Sequence Control Calculator, Mark I. The Mark I was an electromechanical device composed of numerous telephone relays, and rotating mechanical wheels. Punched paper tape and, later, punched cards provided data input.

Shortly after the Mark I was introduced, Dr. John W. Mauchly and J. Presper Eckert developed a prototype computer called the ENIAC, the Electrical Numerical Integrator and Calculator. It differed from Aiken's computer in that it used vacuum tubes instead of telephone relays and, therefore, operated much more rapidly than the Mark I. The ENIAC differs in hardware and appearance from the modern computer, but is the same in concept. It has earned the title of computer because it was fully electronic in nature and had no moving parts.

Next came the development of the internally stored program—a concept basic to modern computers. Princeton mathematician John von Neumann designed a machine, the Electronic Discrete Variable Automatic Computer (EDVAC), which would accept and store a set of instructions (or program).

Previously, all computers were programmed by physically soldering wires to terminals to direct the circuitry. Some devices used wiring boards, which were replaceable panels, containing circuitry permanently wired to perform a sequence of operations. Early computer capabilities were thus greatly limited because each program or sequence of steps required physical wiring and changing programs was a slow, cumbersome, and inconvenient process.

Von Neumann's stored program concept replaced the inconvenient wiring board with instructions read into the machine on punched cards. These instructions directed the machine to carry out a sequence of steps. The internally stored program gives the computer much of its power. The advantages of the internally stored program are

1. The computer can be reprogrammed by entering instructions from another set of cards, instead of by rewiring or using wiring panels.
2. The program may be written and tested before the actual data is available.
3. The machine is self-directing and a human operator does not have to guide each step.

In the past several decades, there have been many significant innovations in computers. These include a reduction in size of equipment and an increase in storage capacity and speed of operation. There have been so many innovations that computers have been grouped into categories, called generations.

FIRST GENERATION. First-generation computing systems were composed of tubes and relays, but had the ability to store a program internally. They received their input data via paper tape or cards. The machines were large and often unreliable because of the many vacuum tubes involved. First-generation machines date to the later 1940's. They proliferated in use in the mid 1950's.

SECOND GENERATION. The introduction of the transistor led to smaller, more dependable, and faster machines. Second-generation computing systems were characterized by greater speed, storage capacity, reduction in physical size, and a reduction in cost. Data was input by paper and magnetic tapes, or, most often, by punched cards. The late 1950's and early 1960's saw the introduction and proliferation of these machines.

circuit **THIRD GENERATION.** Development of new manufacturing techniques and the microtransistor led to improvements in computer design. The third-generation computing systems, characterized by further reduction in size and lower cost, introduced improved methods of storing data. Data could now be input by magnetic tape or from optical or magnetic images printed on a page. The third-generation machines were distributed during the latter 1960's.

evolution **FOURTH GENERATION.** Fourth-generation machines appeared in the 1970's, utilizing new technology such as cryogenics (deep cold), integrated circuitry, and monolithic circuits. Physically they are characterized by new types of terminals and new kinds of computers, such as portable minicomputers. Many new programs for the general user will be developed.

The 1970's is the era of teleprocessing, time sharing, readily available terminals, and ready-made software. These are discussed in later chapters.

Storage Devices   First- and second-generation computers used punched cards for data input and had limited storage capacity. Faster, more efficient, and larger capacity means of data input, output, and storage were needed. Two methods of storage and input were developed: magnetic tape and magnetic disk.

MAGNETIC TAPE. Magnetic tape is commonly used for storing and recording data for large computers. (See Figure 2.12.) It allows large amounts of data to be stored in a comparatively small volume. Tape can be fed to a computer much faster than punched cards, is more economical, and can be stored conveniently. A $\frac{1}{2}$-inch-wide ribbon of tape, similar to $\frac{1}{4}$-inch tape used on home tape recorders, is coated with iron oxide and spooled on reels of varying length. Data is placed on tape by magnetizing small areas of the coating. These areas represent bits of data. It is a process similar to recording information on a home tape recorder except that digital data is encoded.

All data is stored on the tape in the same sequence in which it was recorded. To access data, the computer searches the data in sequence for the desired information. Thus, this storage medium is called sequential access storage.

MAGNETIC DISK. Magnetic disks offer high speed and are convenient to store. (See Figure 2.13.) Several disks, resembling ordinary phonograph records, are assembled into a conveniently carried disk pack. The top and bottom of each disk in the pack is coated with iron oxide. Data is magnetically recorded on the disks as they are spun at high speed.

A disk pack can store up to several million characters in a system called random access storage. Data can be accessed without searching in sequence. With magnetic tape, the entire tape must be searched to locate a particular piece of data, but data can be retrieved directly from the moving disk. A single character, or group of characters, can be retrieved from or recorded on the revolving disk in a fraction of a second.

FIGURE 2.12   TAPE STORAGE DEVICE

FIGURE 2.13   DISK STORAGE DEVICE

PRINCIPAL METHODS OF PROCESSING DATA

Data processing methods, as well as equipment, have gone through a process of evolution. Generally these changes reflect new equipment design and capability.

There have been three stages in the development of data processing methods. They are

1. manual'
2. unit record
3. electronic data processing (computers)

They are best evaluated by contrasting methods of input, output, and processing.

Manual Method   The manual method was the first means employed to process data. Many small business firms still use it. With this method, pencils, adding machines, an abacus, or similar devices are used to process data.

DATA INPUT.   Input involves procedures such as writing in data on forms, or typing in figures.

DATA PROCESSING.   Data processing is done mentally, or with paper and pencil, adding machine, or desk calculator. Sorting, merging, and classifying are performed by hand; examples are totals run up to figure gross pay, account balances or credits due a firm, placing employee timecards in sequence by department, or sorting orders by sales personnel.

DATA OUTPUT.   Data output is by pencil and paper, or typewriter. Examples include writing a receipt or paycheck longhand, or typing a balance sheet, ledger card, or report.

ADVANTAGES.   Advantages include simplicity, ease of implementation, and low cost of processing small amounts of data. Since complicated equipment and systems are not involved, changes can be made easily and the method is flexible.

LIMITATIONS.   The manual method is slow, inaccurate, and costly when a moderate or large volume of data is involved. It is difficult to standardize procedures and reporting. Manual data processing is also limited by the speed of the human hand and eye. A human may also introduce errors into the system because individuals are subject to illness, varying rates of speed, and boredom.

FIGURE 2.14 UNIT RECORD EQUIPMENT

√Unit Record Method Later a second method of data processing evolved from Herman Hollerith's system of coding data on punched cards. (See Figure 2.14.) It relies upon human operators and electromechanical devices to process data. It is sometimes called the EAM (electrical accounting machine) process.

In the unit record system, punched cards are used to store data. Data from each transaction is punched on a separate card, hence the term "unit record." These unit records form the basis for a system which manipulates, processes, and outputs data.

DATA INPUT. Information to be processed by this method is entered into the system from punched cards. The data is punched into the cards by a keypunch machine (explained later) in the Hollerith code.

DATA PROCESSING. The manipulation of data involves sorting, collating, or merging of decks of punched cards, or the calculation of figures from data input on punched cards. These operations are done by machines which physically move the cards about. Calculations are performed by electromechanical devices which store values in counters.

DATA OUTPUT. Output is on an accounting machine which prints out the results of calculations on a sheet of paper. These may be reports, forms, or similar documents. Summary data or the results of calculations may also be punched on cards.

ADVANTAGES. Advantages include simplicity, relative low cost of equipment, and reliability. The system uses ordinary punched cards for storing and transmitting data. Punched cards are easily filed, mailed, stored, or written upon by hand. Unit record accounting is practical for the small to medium business firm. Its accuracy and speed far exceeds that of the manual method.

LIMITATIONS. For the large firm, this method has several disadvantages. First, the cost of processing thousands of punched cards precludes their use for high volume processing. Second, punched cards are bulky to store and are subject to damage and mutilation. In addition, programs for this method are stored externally; wiring boards are usually used, and operators must connect jumper wires to direct the machine.

Electronic Data Processing— EDP (Computers)

Computers were a natural and logical outgrowth of the unit record system. (See Figure 2.15.) As companies grew, it became inefficient to move punched cards through machinery to perform the data processing cycle. New methods were clearly needed to input, store, and output data.

FIGURE 2.15 ELECTRONIC DATA PROCESSING METHOD

√ DATA INPUT. It became necessary to develop additional methods of data input to feed information to the computer. Manual and unit record methods required a duplication of effort. All data to be input had to be recorded on source documents. Then the data on the source documents had to be converted to a form acceptable to the system—keypunched into a punched card.

Developments in hardware in recent years eliminate this double effort. Machines accept and convert data from magnetic tape, paper tape, and several new methods. Mark sense, optical character recognition (OCR), and magnetic ink character recognition (MICR) are now used to input data for many business applications.

1. *Mark Sense.* Mark-sense recognition devices sense the presence of a pencil mark on a card. They convert these marks into punched holes in the card, ready for input to the computer system. Data to be entered into the system is recorded by filling in appropriate bubbles with an Electrographic pencil. (See Figure 2.16.)

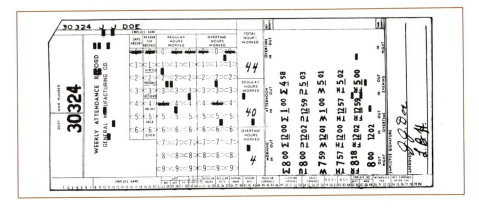

FIGURE 2.16 MARK-SENSE CARD

2. *OCR.* Optical character recognition devices are capable of reading printed, typewritten, or handwritten characters. (See Figure 2.17.) Using a technique similar to the electronic beam in a TV tube, these devices can recognize the shape of a character. They scan the character, breaking it down into areas.

OCR machines can read sales documents, typewritten records, or printed pages. (See Figure 2.18.) They convert these into electronic pulses, which can be sent to the computer. Because data from source documents can be transmitted directly to the computer, keypunching is eliminated.

3. *MICR.* Magnetic ink character recognition devices rely on the magnetic characteristics of special inks rather than the optical image for recognition. (See Figure 2.19.) Data to be input must be printed with special magnetic

1234567890

OCR-A

IS AVAILABLE IN UPPER CASE AND WITH COMPATIBLE LOWER CASE AND SHOULD BE USED IN APPLICATIONS THAT ARE PRIMARILY HUMAN FACTORS INSENSITIVE.

The compatible lower case extends the available character set.

OCR-B

With lower case provides good human com-patability with some compromise for ease of machine reading. It is recommended for applications that are human factors sensitive.

ELITE

When maximum interchange with humans is a requirement, an elite face can be utilized with utmost efficiency, for the total man/machine system.

FIGURE 2.17 OPTICAL CHARACTERS

inks. The MICR machine (shown in Figure 2.20) converts the magnetic ink form into an electronic pulse which can be sent to the computer. An example is the account number printed at the bottom of many checks, such as that shown in Figure 7.10.

DATA PROCESSING.   Once the data is entered in the computer, it is manipulated by electronic means. Data within computers is represented by electric signals, called pulses. These pulses are moved about within the computer in microscopically small circuits, and calculations are performed in billionths of a second.

DATA OUTPUT.   Various methods of output characterize modern computers. Output can be on high-speed line printers, punched cards, video devices such as a cathode ray tube, or by spoken word from an audio response unit. (These devices will be explained in more detail later.)

FIGURE 2.18 OPTICAL CHARACTER SCANNER

FIGURE 2.19 MAGNETIC INK CHARACTERS

FIGURE 2.20 MAGNETIC INK CHARACTER READER

ADVANTAGES.   Several advantages of the computer have already been touched upon in the previous chapter. These include high reliability, processing speed, accuracy, and low cost per unit of processing. For large firms, the computer is the most practical of the three means for processing data. Teleprocessing and terminals are bringing computers to many new users. These developments are described in the next section.

LIMITATIONS.   Disadvantages relate more to the size of the firm using the computer, than to an internal weakness in the device itself. The installation cost of a computer is fairly high. Large computers may cost millions of dollars to purchase, or thousands of dollars per month to lease. Cost may preclude its use for many medium and small users.

Second, although computers are ideal for solving repetitive problems, they are generally not efficient for single-time problems. It may often be easier for a single problem to be solved by pencil and paper, than by computer. It could cost $1,000 to solve a $1 problem.

A third limitation is the nature of the problems that can be solved. Computers can only solve problems stated in quantitative terms. They cannot solve problems which cannot be reduced to precise numbers or values.

NEW COMPUTERIZED METHODS

Growth of Terminal Usage

Many firms cannot afford to lease or buy their own computer, but still need the convenience and cost savings of EDP. To fill this need, terminals came into use in the 1960's.

COMPUTER TERMINALS. A computer terminal is a device, located at a location different from that of the central computer, that allows the user to gain access to the computer. Data is transmitted to the computer, processed, and returned through the terminal. Communication links, such as telephone or telegraph wires, microwave transmission, or leased wires, tie the terminal to the central computer.

Coined by IBM, the term *teleprocessing* refers to the terminals, communication links, and programs which facilitate the remote processing of data. Because it has shortened the time gap between the receipt of data and the delivery of results, reports, or solutions to problems, teleprocessing has had a strong influence on computer usage. The 1970's should show a greater dependency upon remote terminals and teleprocessing by banks, large and small retailers, and manufacturers.

APPLICATIONS. Terminals can be used, for example, by large and small retailers to handle accounting, bookkeeping, and credit, by insurance companies to process claims, and by hospitals to process patients' records.

In many instances, terminals make practical the processing of data which could not be done profitably or quickly enough at central locations.

Airlines can process ticket reservations from several local offices, hotels can record room reservations, and an auto leasing company in Los Angeles can use teleprocessing to have a car waiting for a customer's arrival in New York. Banks and savings and loan associations can use specially designed terminals to process passbooks, withdrawals, mortgage payments, or to prepare money orders.

A major use of teleprocessing is in file maintenance. Many businesses maintain master files for accounts, inventories, and payrolls, on magnetic disks. File maintenance involves updating an account with debits, credits, items taken from stock, reservations closed, tickets sold, etc. Terminals provide an ideal means of updating master files immediately from the field.

A business executive at his desk can query the master file to learn financial conditions or sales volume. Warehousemen can check the current inventory of parts or supplies, and salesmen can check the current credit balance and status of accounts. With teleprocessing, these people obtain immediate access to the master files.

TYPES OF TERMINALS. Many different types of terminals are available to meet differing business needs. Some terminals print out typewriter-like copy,

COMPUTERS ON ELECTION NIGHT

On November 4, 1952, two automatic computers (UNIVAC on CBS and Monrobot on NBC) made their television debuts for the purpose of computing political trends.

The main part of the problem assigned UNIVAC was to make hourly estimates of the numbers of states to be carried by each candidate, the total electoral vote, and the total popular vote. Several mathematical methods using early election returns of previous years were tried and found lacking; finally one was chosen. As the deadline approached, eight comptometer operators and six programmers were working on the problem, and everyone was putting in 60 to 120 hours per week. The final program was checked out early in the evening of November 4.

At 9:15 that night, UNIVAC calculated the first complete set of predictions. The automatic printer typed out the following:

. . . UNIVAC PREDICTS
—WITH 3,398,745 VOTES IN—

	STEVENSON	EISENHOWER
STATES	5	43
ELECTORAL	93	438
POPULAR	18,986,436	32,915,049

Many of the men could not believe the result, as it was contrary to a great many predictions. So they agreed to change the "national trend factor" that the machine had computed, from "a 40% shift to the Republicans" to 4%, and required the machine to recompute.

At 9:54, the prediction using the arbitrary 4% trend factor was made: Stevenson 263 electoral votes, Eisenhower 268; and this was released over television. It soon became clear that the 40% trend factor was much closer to the truth. At 10:32, with the 40% factor, UNIVAC predicted Stevenson 155 electoral votes, Eisenhower 376; General Draper of Remington-Rand appeared on TV to "explain." Not long afterward, Stevenson conceded.

The general public became more aware of electronic computer machinery in one night than they would have in several years of usual development and advertising. Here was first-class evidence of what automatic machinery for handling information could do. Here was evidence of the vast amount of work in preparing a program. Here was a lesson that once a program was correct, it was important that people not tamper with it. Here was evidence of the troubles of dealing with inaccurate, unchecked data. And all of this evidence was presented to an audience of millions—an audience that could notice oversights and mistakes and yet be intrigued by this new device.

SOURCE Adapted from "Automatic Computers on Election Night," Eugene F. Murphy and Edmund C. Berkeley, *Computers and Automation*, December 1967, p. 26.

others display images on a video screen (cathode ray tube), some punch out cards or paper tape, and still others record on magnetic tape.

1. *Hard-Copy Terminals.* The first terminals were patterned closely after the Teletype terminals. (See Figure 2.21.) These machines, resembling typewriters, can feed information to a computer and type out results. They are "hard-copy" terminals, because they generate a print out resembling a

page from a typewriter, rather than an image on a cathode ray tube, or "soft copy."

To input data from a hard-copy terminal, the operator strikes a key that sends an electronic pulse over telephone lines to the computer and also prints the character on the platen of the typewriter. After the data is entered, it is processed and the results are sent back to the terminal.

Some hard-copy terminals such as the Teletype Keyboard Send and Receive (KSR) can only enter data through the keyboard. The Teletype Automatic Send and Receive (ASR) can also punch and send data via paper tape. When the latter is used, the data on the tape is sent through the terminal to the computer.

2. *Tape and Card Terminals.* A second major group of terminals handle data from punched cards or magnetic tape.

Data returned from the computer to the terminal is punched into cards, rather than printed out on a typewriter. Some punch results on paper tape, or record it on magnetic tape. Although these forms of output are not as

"You know, the only thing this house lacks is the warmth of an old-fashioned fireplace."

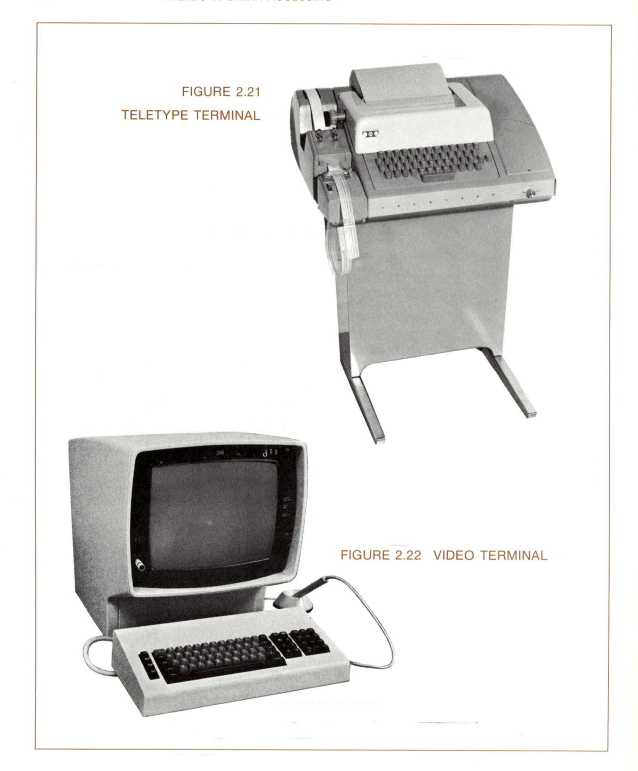

FIGURE 2.21
TELETYPE TERMINAL

FIGURE 2.22   VIDEO TERMINAL

easily read, they are valuable because the data is in a medium that can be used by other machines.

3. *Video Terminals.* The CRT or video terminal is a fast, low-cost means of querying the master file and displaying data. (See Figure 2.22.) A video terminal looks much like a television set on top of a keyboard. Data is displayed on the screen and sent to the computer. Results, in the form of drawings, graphs, or charts, are displayed on a cathode ray tube. Since no hard copy is generated, the display of new data erases the old, unless some provision is made to save the data or copy the screen.

The advantages of video terminals are speed, low cost, and display capacity. Hundreds of characters can be displayed on a screen at one time, as well as lines, graphs, and curves.

4. *Audio Response Terminals.* The audio response terminal was designed to output verbal results. Data is entered in the computer by keyboard or other means. However, results of the processing are not printed on a page, nor displayed on a screen, but given as words spoken in English over a telephone.

Audio response terminals store recorded statements of the human voice, such as sentences, balances, telephone numbers, stock levels, or credit ratings. The computer will select the appropriate phrase or word and construct a verbal message. New messages or different text may be recorded as required.

Gaining Access to a Computer

Originally, the same individual programmed, operated, and, in fact, sometimes built a computer. During the late 1940's and early 1950's, a computer operator had to be a "jack of all trades." Only those who understood the internal mechanisms of the computer could write programs. Today, such knowledge is no longer necessary to use the computer effectively in business.

OPEN SHOP. Early computer installations were operated by an open shop or "hands-on" arrangement. In "hands on," programmers operate the computer as well as write the program. Today only a few computer installations allow hands-on usage, and usually only on the smaller machines. Although it is convenient for many programmers, this arrangement tends to be inefficient because work cannot be grouped or scheduled to increase productivity.

A problem with hands-on usage is the difficulty in maintaining security in the computer area. Important business records, documents, files, and confidential data are often accessible in the room. This exposes confidential records and vital information to anyone in the center.

CLOSED SHOP. Most computer installations now maintain a closed shop or "hands-off" arrangement. Programmers must submit their programs to a control clerk who, in turn, gives it to a trained, supervised operator.

The advantages of this arrangement are that only qualified operators have access to the machine and that tight security can be maintained in the computer area. In addition, since like work can be grouped and run in batches, output is increased and rush work can receive preference.

TELEPROCESSING.   A third method of gaining access to a computer is by a remote terminal. Remote terminals (mentioned earlier) have become important means of accessing computers. In one sense, they give each user his own "open shop," located at his desk or office, and provide him with a staff of professional operators to process his job. The next decade should see great expansion in the use of remote terminals and teleprocessing.

DEVELOPMENTS IN SOFTWARE

Evolution of Programming Languages

Software for data processing has passed through many phases of evolution, moving from crude numbering systems, such as Roman numerals, to modern computer languages, such as COBOL and FORTRAN. One of the earliest numbering systems involved Roman numerals. Later two significant developments improved man's ability to manipulate data: the concepts of the zero and the adoption of the Arabic numbering system. Man's understanding of the mathematical laws also expanded. Long division, logarithms, square roots, trigonometric functions, and countless other advances have their place in the continuing development of computer software.

These early mathematical discoveries represent milestones in man's development of software. However, the real breakthroughs which have facilitated *man-machine communications* occurred during the last several decades, when computer languages were introduced.

MACHINE LANGUAGE.   A problem must be communicated to a computer in a language which it understands. The original method of communicating with computers was by machine language. In this language all instructions are coded in 0's and 1's (zeroes and ones).

Early computer programming could be done only by computer engineers who were familiar with the internal mechanisms of the machine. Programming in machine language was time consuming and tedious and, therefore, impractical for modern business usage. Another drawback is that each computer has its own language and programs written for one machine usually will not run on another type of machine or that of another manufacturer.

ASSEMBLER LANGUAGE.   Another language, called Assembler, developed from improvements in computer design and a further study of *man-machine communication*. In Assembler language, instructions are given to the computer in symbols or abbreviations, called *mnemonics*. These mnemonics, such as ADD, OR, and PACK, tell the machine to perform certain functions.

Assembler language is much easier for the programmer than machine language because he can work with symbols rather than 0's and 1's. However, since the computer operates in machine language, the abbreviations must be translated. Special programs are required to perform the function of translating Assembler instructions into machine instructions. In Assembler, an instruction must be given for each minute step or operation in the program.

PROBLEM-ORIENTED LANGUAGE (POL). Since people prefer to communicate in a language that closely resembles their own, new languages were needed. Languages that stressed problem-solving features and eliminated many of the programming details required in machine and Assembler languages were designed.

Instructions written in these problem-oriented languages must be translated into machine language before the computer can execute them. This is done by a *compiler,* a complex program written by a manufacturer or user. A different compiler is used to translate each problem-oriented language into machine language.

One of the important advantages of problem-oriented languages is that each instruction written by the programmer need only give the broad steps, such as read a card or compare values. The compiler will translate each broad step into many minute steps to direct the computer through the action specified.

One of the first of the problem-oriented languages was developed during the late 1950's. This language, called FORTRAN (FORmula TRANslating System), has become one of the major languages in use today. Programs written in FORTRAN can be run on most computers with a FORTRAN compiler with little or no modifications. This language and others are explained more fully in later chapters.

The second major language to appear was COBOL (COmmon Business Oriented Language), which has become widely used for business programming. COBOL is still undergoing improvements and changes.

During the past several years, many new languages have come into use. They have such exotic names as RPG, SNOBOL, BASIC, ALGOL, SIMSCRIPT, PL/I. Each has its advantages and limitations. But without these languages it would be difficult for the programmer to communicate with computers.

Operating Systems

As the volume of work thrust on computers increased, it was essential to develop better methods of scheduling work and assigning line printers, terminals, and card punches for each program.

Early computer programs were set up and run one at a time, while the operator stood by to handle errors and problems. It he detected an error, he stopped the computer. This procedure was satisfactory as long as only a few programs had to be run.

But as the volume of work increased and the cost of computers rose, the need for a better method became imperative. Special programs, called *operating systems,* were written to replace the human attendant in scheduling work. These programs are discussed later in the book. Operating systems start programs, stop them when they do not run properly, and deal with error conditions and interruptions efficiently without stopping the computer.

Multiprogramming

Improvements in operating systems further expanded the computer's utility by allowing multiprogramming; that is, several programs can be processed simultaneously, by sharing the computer's available resources.

A bank can use its computer to service data entered from remote teller terminals while it also prepares the payroll. Both functions can be manipulated at the same time by a system of slicing the computer's time into fractions of a second.

Time Sharing

Time sharing of computers developed to enable many users to share the cost and burden of one large installation. Any one user could not afford to lease or buy the computer by himself, but with time sharing, he may enjoy the benefits of modern EDP.

Time sharing has become an important part of business data processing and has necessitated the development of new software, programs, operating systems, and hardware. Many firms have been established to provide time sharing services to business establishments. These firms buy a computer and sell time on it. A client gains access to the computer by telephone and enters data and programs through remote terminals. The client receives a monthly bill for his share of time.

Time sharing firms offer their customers many other services, including systems design and programming. They may also have ready-made programs which can handle many common business problems stored on the computer. Such programs may deal with interest, stocks and bonds, capital investments, costs analysis, or mathematics and statistics. A user dials the computer firm from his personal terminal, calls out the required programs, and enters in his data.

Proprietary Programs

One of the newest areas of software expansion is proprietary software. Proprietary software is a program written by a firm for sale or lease. Many companies now provide computer users with package programs at a fixed price or monthly rental. The programs include personnel management, systems, report writers, file maintenance routines, and account billing. This decade should see a growth in the numbers and types of firms offering ready-made programs.

KEY TERMS

Hardware	Magnetic ink character recognition
Software	(MICR)
Analytical Engine	Teleprocessing
Jacquard system	Hard-copy terminals
Hollerith code	Video terminals
ENIAC	Open shop
Stored program	Closed shop
Computer generation	Machine language
Magnetic tape	Assembler language
Magnetic disk	Problem-oriented language
Sequential access storage	Compiler
Random access storage	FORTRAN
Manual method	COBOL
Unit record	Operating system
EAM process	Multiprogramming
Optical character recognition	Time sharing
(OCR)	Proprietary program

EXERCISES

1. Explain the differences between hardware and software.
2. What were the major developments in data processing techniques prior to 1900?
3. What is a stored program? What are the advantages of using one?
4. Outline the major developments in the first, second, and third generations of hardware. What generation are we presently in?
5. Define sequential access storage and random access storage. List the ways in which they are different.
6. Describe three data processing tasks that are profitable for the small firm to do manually.
7. What are the advantages of electronic data processing over unit record?
8. How do OCR methods of data recognition differ from MICR?
9. Define teleprocessing, and draw a diagram of a teleprocessing system with its terminals.
10. What advantages do hard-copy terminals have over video terminals?
11. Write a sentence that might be stored in an audio response terminal. Underline the words or numbers in the sentence which the computer will vary, depending on the individual problem it is solving.
12. How does machine language differ from Assembler language?
13. What are the advantages of POL's?
14. What is time sharing? List six applications for remote time-sharing users.
15. What kinds of services do proprietary software firms offer?

PART TWO

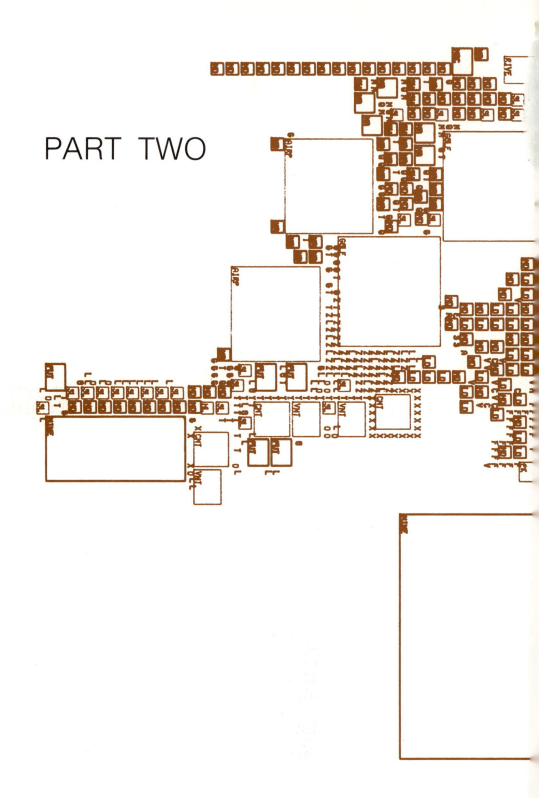

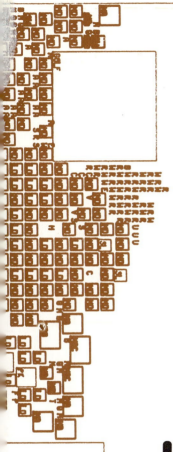

UNIT RECORD PROCESSING

ELECTRICAL ACCOUNTING MACHINE PROCESSING

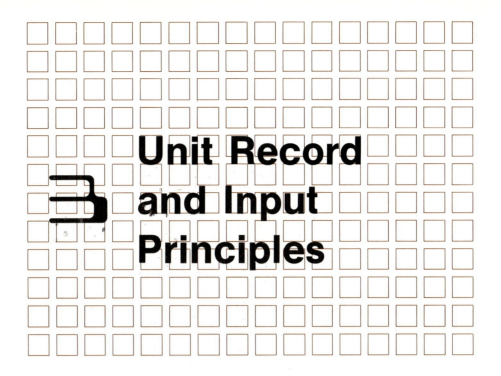

Unit Record and Input Principles

3

Dr. Herman Hollerith, Census Bureau statistician, faced a dilemma. It would soon be time for the 1890 Census, and the United States population had increased greatly in the last decade. How could his office tabulate, summarize, and report the data before it became obsolete? With the existing manual methods, the job would take so long that the results would be meaningless.

Hollerith turned to the principle used by Joseph Marie Jacquard to direct his weaving machine. As mentioned in Chapter 2, cards with holes punched in them were used to control the patterns of the loom. Hollerith adapted the punched-card principle to record and process statistical data. He was able to complete the 1890 Census in $2\frac{1}{2}$ years, a record for the time.

This marked the beginning of the punched-card method of data processing. This mode of processing is called unit record, electrical machine accounting, or just "punch card" processing.

From 1930 to 1960, electrical accounting machine (EAM) was the major method of processing data for large firms. It is still used today by many companies.

To develop and produce unit record equipment, Hollerith originally formed the Tabulating Machine Company, which, after a series of mergers, evolved into the International Business Machines Corporation, or IBM. Today IBM is one of the world's largest manufacturers of unit record and computer data processing equipment.

EAM CYCLE

The EAM cycle consists of three phases: input, processing, and output. In the first phase, data is input to the system by keypunching or recording data on cards. The second phase involves processing. That is, cards containing data are sorted, collated, duplicated, and manipulated in various ways. The final phase is output. Output consists of converting information on cards into a form more convenient and useful to a business firm. This information may be listed on a printing device, the total accumulated during processing printed on a page, etc.

Data processing systems can be classified by the way in which individual records are handled and processed. It is convenient for people to refer to lists, journals, rosters, and reports where data is all on the same form. The element common to these forms is that many items are grouped on the same document, called a collective list. Some examples of collective lists are

1 method of D.P.

1. a roster of a class, listing names of students and test scores.
2. a typed list of accounts receivable, showing firm names and balances due.
3. a stock list, containing the names, description numbers, and quantities of parts in stock.

2 method of D.P.

A second method of processing and handling data is by unit records. Here data concerning individual items is kept on separate records. Collective lists, rosters, or journals are not maintained. Machines can more readily locate single cards, remove an item from a group, or update a record that is not physically tied to other records.

In the unit record system, data from source documents is punched on cards. The cards are then fed into machines for further processing. Processing involves the physical movement of cards through the machines to merge groups, sort, perform calculations, etc. The output, or reporting of results, is done by an accounting machine, which prints data on a sheet of paper. (See Figure 3.1.) Data may also be output on a calculating punch machine, which punches data onto other cards.

Unit Record System

The unit record system is based on the principle that each punched card or record contains data or information about only one item. A unit record may contain several pieces of data, but all refer to the same item. Some examples are

1. a student's name, ID number, and test score.
2. a salesman's name, employee number, and sales for the month.
3. a part name, description, stock number, and quantity left in stock.
4. a paycheck and stub, issued to one employee, showing his name, employee number, deductions, and net salary.

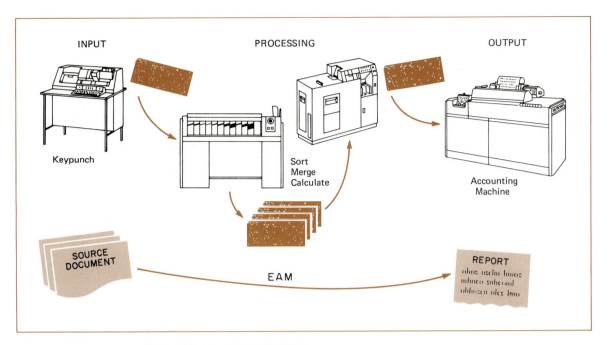

FIGURE 3.1 EAM CYCLE

ADVANTAGES. Since only one transaction is recorded on each card, data on one record can easily be changed or updated without disturbing the other records. A test grade for a student can, for example, be added, inventory for a part adjusted, or a name deleted from a group.

This method of data processing is fast and efficient for small to moderate amounts of data. Punched cards are convenient to handle, as well as easily mailed, written or typed upon, or filed. Equipment costs are moderate, and machine operators can be trained easily.

LIMITATIONS. An ordinary punched card holds a maximum of 80 columns of data. If the data on a transaction requires more than 80 columns, several cards must be used. The use of more than one card to store data negates the main advantage of a unit record system.

The punched cards can jam in machines, tear, or be mutilated. If holes are not properly punched, or have been tampered with, errors occur. Punched cards are not reusable and, at about $1.00 per thousand, are relatively expensive. In addition, storage becomes a problem when thousands of cards are involved.

Since large numbers of cards move relatively slowly through machines, the unit record system is impractical for processing files containing hundreds of thousands of cards. (Time intervals involved in processing data are usually measured in seconds or thousandths of a second (milliseconds) in the unit record system. In electronic data processing, they are measured in millionths of a second (microseconds) or billionths of a second (nanoseconds).) Further, processing systems which depend on the physical movement of cards are prone to error. Cards may be lost, misfiled, damaged, etc.

PUNCHED CARDS

The Hollerith Card

In referring to the punched card, several terms are used synonomously, such as

- IBM card
- Punched card
- Tab card
- Unit record
- Data card

The standard punched card shown in Figure 3.2 is described below.

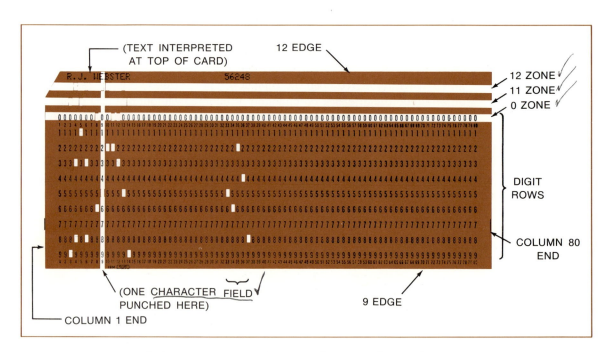

FIGURE 3.2   THE STANDARD PUNCHED CARD

FORMAT. Each card is $3\frac{1}{4}'' \times 7\frac{3}{8}''$ with corner cut and is available in a variety of colors, printed forms, or with a colored stripe for identification.

The face of each card contains 80 ~~vertical~~ ~~columns~~. Each column is made up of 12 punch positions and can record one alphabetic or numeric character. Columns are often labeled from 1 to 80, for ease of identification and keypunching. A punch position is the location of one hole punched in a card. Each alphabetic or numeric character has its own combination of punch positions. A punch position is sometimes called a bit (the shortened form for binary digit). A group of bits (punch positions), are combined to form each character.

A row is a horizontal group of punches across the card. Each row contains 80 possible punches. Digit rows are labeled 0 through 9 with the tenth row (row 9) at the bottom of the card. The numbers that label the rows may or may not be printed on the card.

A zone is one of three horizontal rows across the top of the punched card, which overlap and include the digit row zero. The row at the top of the card is the "12 zone"; the one below it is the "11 zone," sometimes called the "X punch"; the third row is the "0 zone." Zones are usually not labeled.

A field is one or more columns reserved for related information. Fields can range from 1 to 80 columns in width. For example, a five-digit identification number punched in columns 33 through 37 of a punched card is in a five-column field. A name up to 20 letters long in columns 1 through 20 occupies a "20-column field."

The top edge of the card, nearest the 12 zone, is called the 12 edge. The bottom edge of the card, nearest the 9 row, is called the 9 edge. The left edge of the card, nearest column 1, is called column 1 end. The right edge of the card, nearest column 80, is called the column 80 end.

Punched Card Codes

Modifications of the Hollerith coding system are used for punching alphabetic and numeric information onto cards. One character, a letter, number, or symbol is printed in each column, using a unique combination of holes for each letter, symbol, or number. Numbers from 0 to 9 are represented by punching the corresponding digit in that column. Alphabetic letters require two punches per column, one in zone 11, 12, or 0, and one in digit rows 1 to 9. Special characters, such as *, /, +, may require a combination of three holes per column.

HOLLERITH CODE. Figure 3.3(A) shows the Hollerith code for alphabetic characters. (There is no advantage in memorizing this code, since the keypunch machine automatically punches the proper holes when a key is struck.)

EBCDIC. Most keypunch machines in use before 1965 used the 12-bit Hollerith code. In 1965 IBM introduced the 029 Keypunch, which uses a modification of the Hollerith code called the Extended Binary Coded Decimal Interchange Code (EBCDIC). EBCDIC is described in more detail in Chapter 8. The major difference between these two codes is in the punch combinations for the special characters. Figure 3.3(B) shows the punched

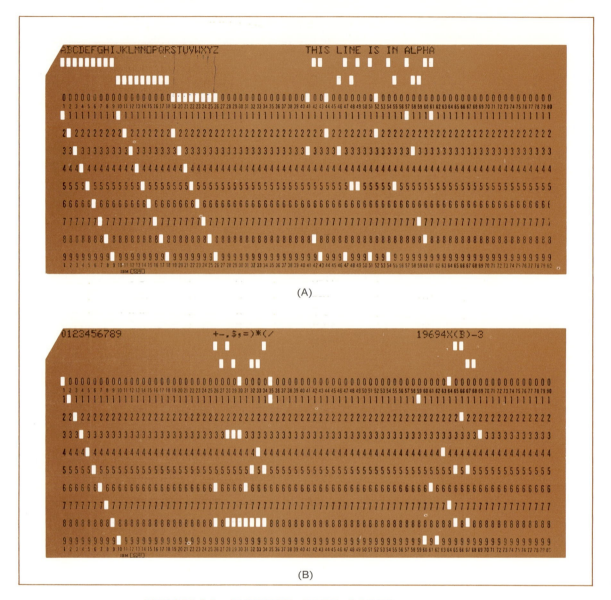

FIGURE 3.3   PUNCHED CARD CODES

holes for numbers 0 to 9 and the special characters in EBCDIC. The combinations for the alphabetic and numeric characters are the same in both codes. Table 3.1 lists the combination of holes which make up the codes for the alphabetic, numeric, and special characters on the 029 Keypunch.

SYSTEM/3 PUNCHED CARD CODE.   In 1971 IBM introduced a 96-column

TABLE 3.1   IBM 029 KEYPUNCH CODE

Key Number	ALPHABETIC		NUMERIC	
	Card Code	Graphic	Card Code	Graphic
1	11-8	Q	12-8-6	+
2	0-6	W	0-8-5	−
3	12-5	E	11-8-5	)
4	11-9	R	12-8-2	¢
5	0-3	T	0-8-2	0-8-2
6	0-8	Y	12-8-7		
7	12-1	A	none	none
8	0-2	S	0-8-6	>
9	12-4	D	8-2	:
10	12-6	F	11-8-6	;
11	12-7	G	11-8-7	¬
12	12-8	H	8-5	'
13	0-9	Z	none	none
14	0-7	X	0-8-7	?
15	12-3	C	8-7	''
16	0-5	V	8-6	=
17	12-2	B	11-8-2	!
18	11-5	N	12-8-5	(
19	11-7	P	12	&
20	0-1	/	0	0
21	0-4	U	1	1
22	12-9	I	2	2
23	11-6	O	3	3
24	11-1	J	4	4
25	11-2	K	5	5
26	11-3	L	6	6
27	11-4	M	7	7
28	0-8-3	'	8	8
29	12-8-3	.	9	9
33	11	–	11	−
40	8-4	@	8-3	#
41	0-8-4	%	0-8-3	,
42	11-8-4	*	11-8-3	$
43	12-8-4	<	12-8-3	.

punched card shown in Figure 3.4 for use in their System/3 computers. Up to 96 columns of data can be punched onto a single System/3 card by using a coding system in which varying combinations of six punch positions (bits) encode each character. The card is relatively small ($2\frac{5}{8}''\times 3\frac{1}{4}''$); only 32 columns of information can be punched across it. Therefore, three layers, or

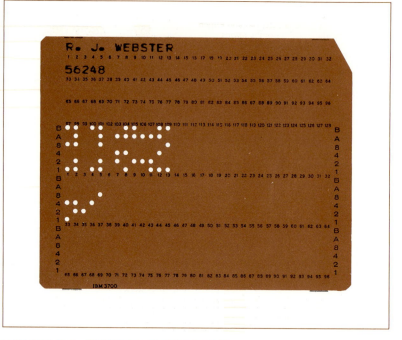

FIGURE 3.4 SYSTEM/3 IBM CARD

tiers, are used to encode the 96 characters. (See Figure 3.5.) Columns 1
through 32 of data are punched onto the first tier, columns 33 through 64 are
punched onto the second tier, and columns 65 through 96 onto the third tier.
In the same way, the printed information is interpreted (printed) across the
top of the card in three rows. The top portion containing the printed
information is called the print area, and the lower portion is called the punch
area.

FILE ORGANIZATION AND TERMINOLOGY

The principles of file organization and maintenance are basic to all forms of
data processing, including computers and unit record. A file is a collection of
two or more records in the same category. (See Figure 3.6.) A group of
cards, each containing the name of a student and his test score, is a file.
Files used in business include, for example, personnel lists, lists of accounts
receivable and payable, parts lists, inventories, sales for the day, lists of
back-ordered items, and lists of goods out to bid.

Files can contain fixed-length records or variable-length records. A
fixed-length record contains a predetermined or standard number of columns
of data. The length may be set deliberately for consistency or convenience, or
determined by the physical limitations of the record. The standard punched

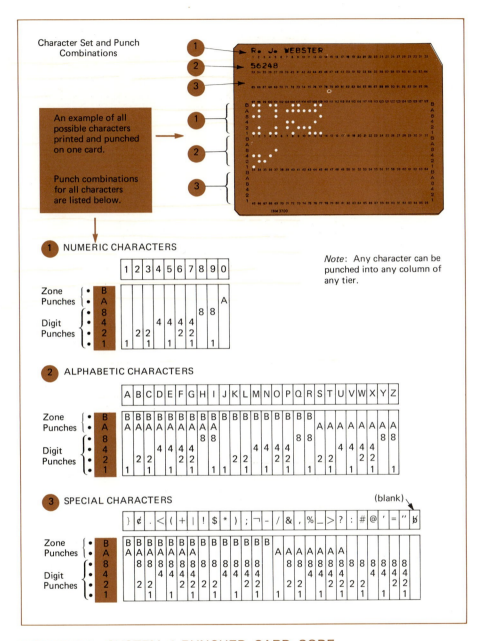

FIGURE 3.5   SYSTEM/3 PUNCHED CARD CODE

card is a fixed-length record, since it holds a maximum of 80 characters. System/3 IBM cards, limited to 96 columns, are also fixed-length records.

Variable-length records are limited only by the amount of data that applies to each transaction. Ordinary punched cards are usually too limited to hold

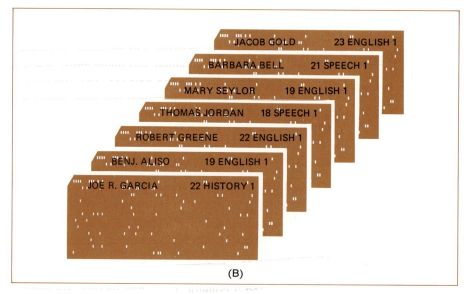

FIGURE 3.6 (A) RECORD   (B) FILE

variable-length records. Magnetic tape, however, which is discussed in Chapter 10, is an excellent media for variable-length records.

Each punched card requires the same amount of storage space regardless of the number of characters punched onto it. Variable-length records do not waste space at the end of each record and are, therefore, more efficient than fixed-length records.

Types of Records

L.R.,

Records can be classified by content as well as by length. A logical record contains all of the data related to a single item. It may be a payroll record for an employee, or a record of all of the charges made by a customer in a department store. Since a logical record has no size limitation, it must often be shortened or condensed if it is to fit on a punched card.

MR.,

A master record contains information or data of a permanent or semipermanent nature. Master records may contain all available data on an item, even though only a small amount of it may be used at one time. Selected data may be copied from the master record. An example of a master record is a stock card giving a part's name, size, quantity in stock, supplier, costs, order point, etc.

DR.,

A detail record contains selected data copied from the master record or original data that will be added to the master record to bring it up to date. An example of a detail record would be one containing an account name, number, and the amount charged that day. A detail record that contains new information, such as payments to be posted, is sometimes called an activity record.

SR.,

A summary record contains data that has been summarized, condensed, or reported from other records. For example, a summary card could be prepared from a file containing 100 detail cards. Each detail card contains the title of an account and the balance. The 100 detail cards in the file could be entered into a calculating punch machine, which would add the individual balances and punch the cumulative total on a card to produce a summary record.

File Maintenance

Much of the work in data processing is keeping files current. To be of value, the information in personnel, cash flow, manufacturing data, and sales and warehousing files, etc. must be current.

File maintenance involves such tasks as posting debits and credits to accounts, adding new names to personnel lists and removing inactive ones, revising hourly employee records, and changing the number of exemptions on an employee's payroll record.

In unit record processing, file maintenance is usually performed on a machine called a collator. Individual records are pulled from files and corrected. New cards are inserted, or revised cards are merged on the collator.

Record Layout

The layout of cards in the unit record system must be carefully planned to hold the maximum amount of data and facilitate processing. Personnel who lay out new records must consider several factors.

Color is frequently used to differentiate files. For example, a red card could be used for accounts payable, a blue card for accounts receivable, a green card for personnel records, etc. Cards with colored stripes printed across their faces can also be bought and used to differentiate files. For example, a yellow-striped card may be used for data from the Los Angeles branch, a green stripe from the Chicago branch, and a purple stripe from the New York branch.

Record layout also involves determining the number, type, and sequence of fields used for recording data. The card designer attempts to use these elements, as well as codes, to place as much data as possible in the 80 columns of a card.

The designer first carefully studies the data to be punched into the card to determine the number and types of fields needed. The order in which the fields appear is important for accuracy and ease of keypunching. Often this sequence will be determined by the design of the source document. It is easier and faster to punch data into a card in the same order in which it appears on the source document. Finally, the designer draws a layout, showing where the fields will be located.

Figure 3.7 illustrates a card layout with eight fields. The fields are labeled and reserved for selected data. The first three fields contain alphabetic data and the last five, numerical and coded data. To make it easy to identify data and differentiate fields, forms can be printed directly on the cards in a variety of colors.

Coding Methods

So that maximum information can be recorded on a single card, data is often represented by codes made up of letters, numbers, or a combination of them. For example, a two-digit code system for state names would obviously require a narrower field than if the names were spelled out. The codes used for recording data should not only be convenient to use and easy to interpret, but also expandable so that more items can be added to the list.

The fifth and sixth fields in Figure 3.7 illustrate the use of codes. In the fifth field, column 55, a single digit is keypunched to indicate type of account. In this case, code is used not only to save columns, but also to facilitate later sorting of cards by account type.

In the sixth field, columns 59 and 60, a two-character alphabetic code identifies the products purchased by the account. The two-column code saves many columns.

Some commonly used types of codes in unit record systems are

1. SEQUENCE CODE. In a sequence code, each item is assigned a number in sequence, beginning with 1. For example, the departments in a business firm could be coded as follows:

CODE	DEPARTMENT
1	Accounting
2	Advertising
3	Personnel
4	Production
5	Sales
6	Shipping

2. MNEMONIC CODE. Mnemonic codes rely upon either mnemonics

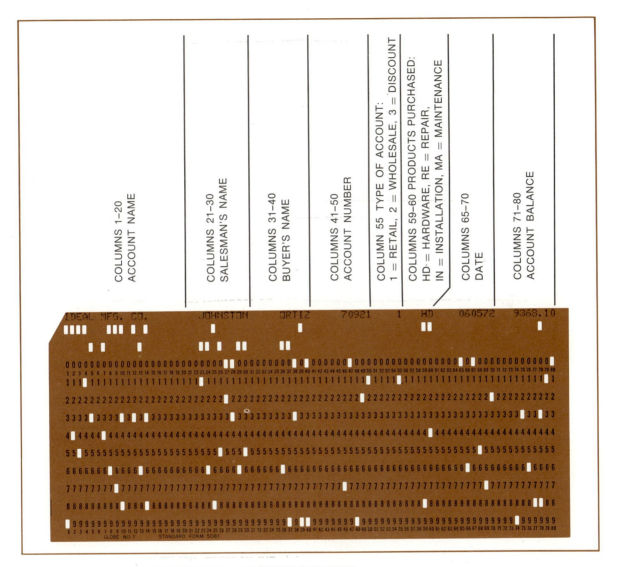

FIGURE 3.7 RECORD LAYOUT

(memory devices) or the sound of words. For example, a mnemonic code for a list of automobile names could be developed as follows:

CODE	AUTOMOBILE
CV	Chevrolet
CA	Cadillac
FO	Ford
OL	Oldsmobile
DO	Dodge

ROUND VERSUS RECTANGULAR

"Mr. Hollerith, you've got to do something! The Census results will be outdated before they're ready . . . ."

Herman Hollerith of the U. S. Census Bureau knew that something did indeed have to be done. The 1890 Census was about to begin, and the U. S. population had passed the 60-million mark. It would take so many years to do the job with the present manual tabulating and calculating methods that the results would be meaningless before they were obtained.

Hollerith investigated many ideas and inventions. Finally, he discovered a system Joseph Jacquard had developed to weave patterns into fabric. Jacquard used cards containing codes in the form of punched holes to control a machine. Hollerith realized that if the holes in a card represented data, a machine could tabulate the information by sensing the hole combinations.

Since holes came in different sizes and shapes, Hollerith made several decisions of historic import without being aware of it. He designed his system to punch rectangular holes across the face of a card in a single tier, or row. This, it seemed to him, was the most efficient and practical means of recording data.

What finally emerged from his efforts was a punched card, a coding system, and a punched card machine. Each time the operator pressed a key, the machine punched a combination of rectangular holes into the card, in serial order.

Hollerith's system worked, and the 1890 and 1900 Census were processed in record time. But Hollerith wasn't satisfied. He envisioned his fantastic data coding system being used by businesses throughout the country. In 1896, he formed the Tabulating Machine Company (later known as IBM) to manufacture and sell his invention.

In the meantime, James Powers replaced Hollerith in the Census Department. This brash young man had his own ideas and believed that the system needed several important improvements. First, the rectangular holes had to go. So Powers built his own punch card machine, which punched 90 round holes in several tiers in cards. It also had a mechanism to store the keystrokes. After the operator keyed all the characters, the machine punched them into the card simultaneously.

Power's machine was very successful and before long he founded the Powers Accounting Machine Company (later known as UNIVAC Division of Sperry Rand).

The battle was on! Hollerith stressed the advantages of rectangular holes; Powers the virtues of round holes. Throughout the 1920's and 1930's, the giants, IBM and UNIVAC were locked in a marketing struggle. By the late 1950's, the marketing strategy of IBM proved superior. The rectangles pulled ahead and emerged victorious. Cards with 80 rectangular holes punched in a single tier became the industry standard.

In 1970 UNIVAC introduced a new series of keypunch machines to punch rectangular holes in a standard 80-column card. Powers had been repudiated. It seemed that Hollerith had been right.

But the conflict wasn't over yet. IBM was planning a new series of electronic equipment, envisioned as the most up-to-date, modern punched card computer system on the market. Their new system would need the most efficient, practical, and advanced punch coding system that could be created. IBM engineers searched, investigated, and experimented.

Almost the day that UNIVAC announced their decision to go rectangular, IBM introduced their new System/3 Computer. It accepts only cards with 96 round holes, arranged in three tiers and punched simultaneously.

Was James Powers right after all?

3. SIGNIFICANT-DIGIT CODE. Meaning can be assigned to each digit or position in a group of characters to develop a significant-digit code. Strings of letters or numbers can be built into an efficient, compact coding system, allowing more data to be recorded in fewer columns. For example, a code to record dollar volume, salesman, and type of account could look like this:

CODE	DOLLAR VOLUME	SALESMAN	TYPE OF ACCOUNT
10 SM W	$10,000	Smith	Wholesale
35 GR R	35,000	Green	Retail
18 CH D	18,000	Chester	Discount

"ONLY ONCE IN EVERY GENERATION IS THERE A COMPUTER THAT CAN WRITE POETRY LIKE THIS."

Data Input
Methods

Originally, all data input to a unit record system was punched onto cards by keypunch machines. Although keypunch machines are still widely used, the past several decades have seen the development of other methods of inputting data such as those illustrated in Figure 3.8.

Some common means of unit record data input are keyboard to punched card, Port-A-Punch, and mark-sense cards.

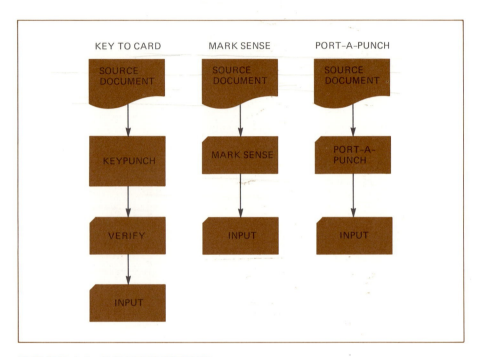

FIGURE 3.8   INPUT SYSTEMS

KEYBOARD TO PUNCHED CARD.   Keypunch operators punch data directly from keyboards onto cards. Keypunch machines include the standard 80-column ones, such as the IBM 029, the IBM 059 Verifying Machine, the Univac 1710 Verifying Interpreting Punch, the IBM 129, and for System/3 cards the IBM 96-column machines, such as the IBM 5496 Data Recorder. *IBM 029 Keypunch.* The IBM 029 Keypunch was introduced to punch cards for the IBM/360 Computer. The Model 029 is a refinement of the earlier 024 and 026 keypunches, many of which are still in use today. The 029 differs from earlier versions in improved styling, operating features, and wider character set on the keyboard, and different punch combinations.

Figure 3.9 shows the main parts of the 029 Keypunch. This machine feeds cards from a hopper to a punching station. Here the card moves under a set of punch dies. As keys are pressed, the dies punch the appropriate code into

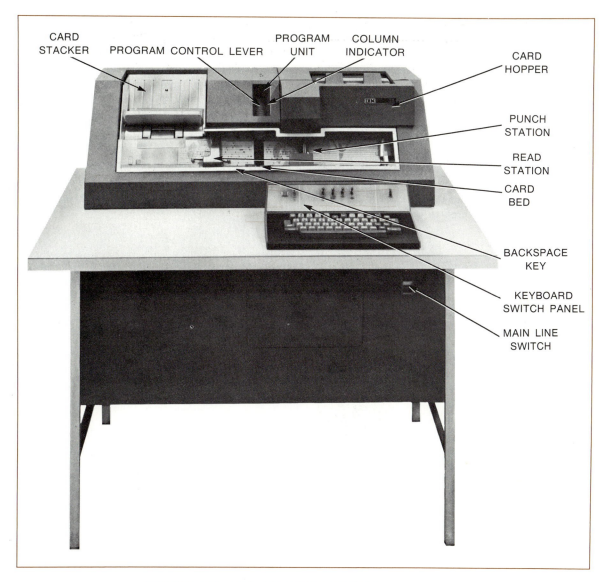

FIGURE 3.9   IBM 029 CARD PUNCH

the card and the corresponding character is printed at the top. As the punching proceeds, the card moves from right to left under the punch station.

Next, the card moves to the reading station. This station is used for duplicating cards. A series of contacts sense the holes punched in the card and transmit this information to the punching station where a duplicate field or card can be punched without rekeyboarding. From the reading station, the card moves to the card stacker.

A switch panel located just above the keyboard enables the operator to control the movements of the cards from the keyboard. The switches control automatic feeding of cards, skipping columns, tabbing, and shifting.

There are several different keyboard arrangements available on the 029 Keypunch. The most common layout includes both alphabetic and numeric characters. Another arrangement includes only numeric keys.

IBM 059 Verifying Machine.   The IBM 059 Verifying Machine, shown in Figure 3.10, is used to verify the accuracy of the data punched onto cards from original source documents.

The purpose of verifying is to see that the original data has been accurately punched onto the card. This necessitates keyboarding all data twice, once to keypunch it and once to verify it. Verification is an essential step to ensure accuracy of data input.

FIGURE 3.10   IBM 059 VERIFYING MACHINE

Univac 1710 Verifying Interpreting Punch.   The Univac keypunch, shown
in Figure 3.11, combines automatic printing, punching, and verifying in a
single machine. All data to be input is first keyboarded. However, instead of
each keystroke punching a code onto a card, the data is entered into a
memory device within the machine. After all data has been typed into
storage, and verified by rekeyboarding, the machine automatically punches
data onto a card. This is done without operator attention, or while data for
the next record is being keyboarded.

Core storage allows the keypunch operator to verify the work in one pass.
Data is entered from the keyboard, and the card image is held in core
storage. Data is again keyboarded for verification. If the keystrokes match, a
card is punched out. If an error is detected, the operator backspaces and
enters the correct data.

FIGURE 3.11   UNIVAC 1710 VERIFYING INTERPRETING PUNCH

IBM 129 Card Data Recorder.   The IBM 129 Card Data Recorder resembles the 029 Keypunch, but has an additional feature for storing data. (See Figure 3.12.) As each character is keyboarded, it is stored in the input storage system. Errors are erased by backspacing and typing the correct character. After the entire line has been keyboarded, it is transferred into an output storage section and then punched into the card. While the card is being punched, the operator is free to keyboard information for the next card into the input storage system. In the 029 machine, data is punched directly into the card as each key is pressed. In the 129, the data is stored until the entire line has been keyboarded and then rapidly punched into the card automatically.

FIGURE 3.12   IBM 129 CARD DATA RECORDER

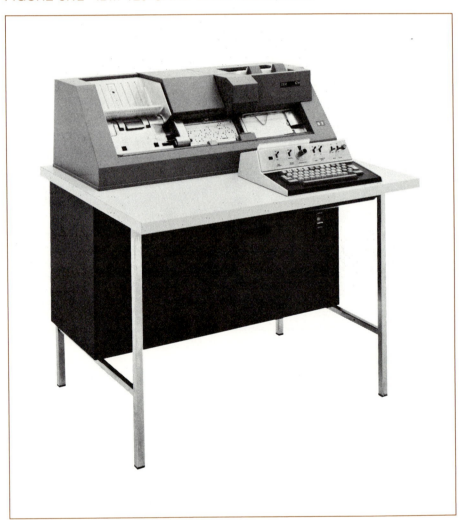

IBM 5496 Data Recorder. The IBM 5496 Data Recorder is designed to punch data into the System/3 IBM card. (See Figure 3.13.) The machine is composed of a desk, keyboard, card hopper, and stacker. As keys are pressed on the machine, the data is recorded in an input storage section. Just as in the IBM 129, characters can be corrected by backspacing and striking over. After the entire line has been keyboarded, the data is automatically punched into the card.

FIGURE 3.13   IBM 5496 DATA RECORDER

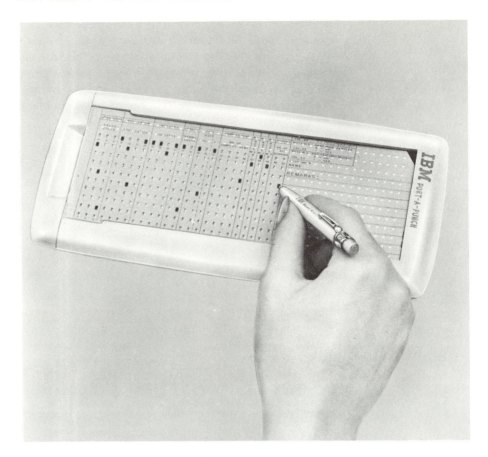

FIGURE 3.14   IBM PORT-A-PUNCH

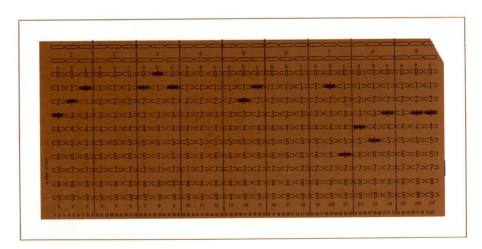

FIGURE 3.15   MARK-SENSE CARD

IBM Port-A-Punch. The IBM Port-A-Punch can be used to code data onto specially die-cut IBM cards. (See Figure 3.14.) The card is inserted into a hand-held plastic holder and characters are recorded by punching out appropriate holes in the card with a stylus. Using this method of input, source documents can be prepared in the field with simple equipment. For example, a salesman can carry a Port-A-Punch in his briefcase and enter data directly into IBM cards in his customer's office.

Mark-Sense Cards. Another method of inputting data to unit record systems is with a mark-sense card. (See Figure 3.15.) To record data, the user fills in a bubble (outlined area) with an Electrographic pencil, which leaves a residue of graphite on the surface of the card. Cards that have been mark-sensed are fed through an IBM 519 Reproducing Punch. (See Chapter 5.)

Sensing brushes on this machine detect the thin graphite coating on the surface of the card and actuate a set of punch dies. The dies punch holes in the appropriate rows and columns of the card. This method is a convenient, simple way of entering numerical data onto cards without using keypunch equipment. Data such as test scores, prices, order numbers, and stock inventory can be entered directly on cards in the field. Source documents prepared in the field on mark-sense cards reduce the need for verification.

KEY TERMS

Unit record
Punched card
EAM cycle
Column
Row
Zone
Field
12 edge
9 edge
Column 1 end
Column 80 end

Hollerith code
EBCDIC
File
Port-A-Punch
Mark sense
Keypunch
Verify
System/3 card
Sequence code
Mnemonic code
Significant-digit code

EXERCISES

1. Prepare a collective list for use in
   a. your school
   b. a business establishment
2. Mark the following unit record data on three unused punched cards.
   a. The first unit record card should show a student's name, ID number, and test score.
   b. The second unit record should list an automobile by brand, date of manufacture, whether two or four door, and color.
   c. The third unit record should show an account name, number, payment for the month, and a field for returned items.

3. What are the differences between unit records and collective lists? What are the disadvantages of the unit record?

4. Obtain an unused punched card. Draw a pencil line through columns 20, 40, and 60 and through rows 2, 4, and 8. Label the edges of the card to show the 9 edge, 12 edge, column 1 end, and column 80 end.

5. Obtain some used punched cards that have not been interpreted (that is, the English equivalent is not printed at top of each column). To understand how the Hollerith code works, decipher the text on these cards.

6. Obtain six unused punched cards. Assume they are physical records belonging to a file named "Employee Vacation Periods." Mark in appropriate data for each of six employees.

7. Prepare an unused punched card as a master record. Prepare a detail record on another card, using selected data from the master record.

8. Prepare four detail cards, each containing a product and amount in stock. Prepare a summary record from the detail cards.

9. If a machine is available, keypunch a group of cards with your name, address, city, and phone. Put one item on each card in columns 1 to 20.

10. If a machine is available, keypunch your records from Exercises 2, 6, or 8.

11. Obtain an unused Port-A-Punch card. Carefully punch out your school ID number, age, and social security number. Mark the fields.

12. Obtain some unused mark-sense cards. Using an Electrographic pencil, enter your age, social security number, and school ID number.

13. Develop a single-column sequence code for eight groups of office furnishings and supplies.

14. Develop a two-character mnemonic code for 12 cities located in your state.

15. Develop a significant-digit code giving part name, year of manufacture, and supplier.

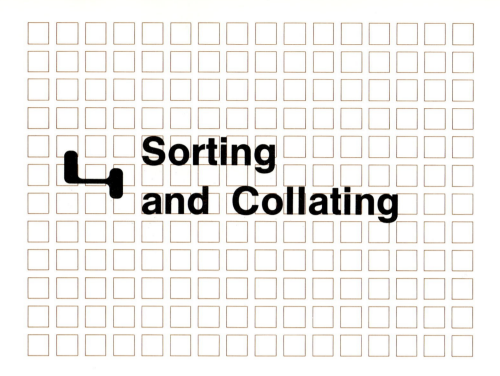

Sorting and Collating

The process of reorganizing data to increase its usefulness includes sorting and collating. Such steps as classifying and arranging data into groups, selecting a specific record from a file, combining several files into a single file, matching records in files, or detecting blank columns in a record are all part of sorting and collating.

In this chapter we consider the principles of sorting and collating. Two unit record machines, the sorter and the collator, are described.

All operations that can be performed by machine can also be done manually, but may take longer and may not be as accurate. A human operator can detect blank columns in a card, match cards, or sort or sequence them. A human operator can classify and sequence about ten cards per minute and sort about 100 cards per minute. Unit record equipment is faster, processing up to 2,000 cards per minute. Many medium and large business firms use computers and unit record equipment to perform such tasks.

Both unit record and manual methods rely upon the physical movement of cards from station to station for processing. Computers use data converted into electrical pulses and move these pulses at speeds measured in nanoseconds.

BASIC SORT, SEARCH, CHECK, AND MERGE ROUTINES

Over the years certain routines have been developed in data processing. Files are maintained by adding new records and removing or deleting old ones. Certain records are selected from files for special handling, such as mailing past due notices to delinquent accounts. The processes of merging, selecting, matching, etc. follow the same basic concepts whether performed by hand or machine.

Sorting   NUMERICAL SORTING. Numerical sorting is the rearrangement of records so that numbers in the same field on each record are put in numerical order. Before sorting, a file may be in no specific order. A sort may be ascending (lowest number at the beginning and highest at the end) or descending (highest number at the beginning and lowest at the end). Figure 4.1 is an example of a sort in ascending order.

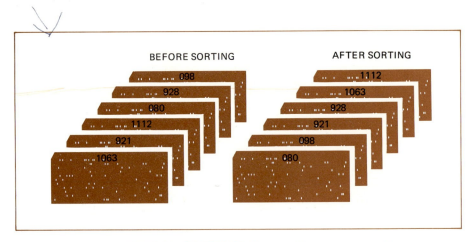

FIGURE 4.1 NUMERICAL SORTING (Ascending sequence)

Files are sorted according to a specified field on each record. For example, a file of records may be sorted by account number, date account opened, current balance, or date payment due.

A file can also be sorted into subgroups. For example, a certain file contains student records, giving age, name, and test score. These records are to be placed in order first by age and then by test score within each age group by descending sorts. (The first field to be ordered is called the major sort field. The second field to be ordered is called the minor sort field.) To achieve the required subgroups, the file is first placed in numerical sequence (descending) by sorting the minor sort field, test score. Then it is again sorted by major field, student age. The result will be the record of the oldest student at the top of the file, with the remaining ages in descending order.

Within each age group, scores are sequenced with the highest score on top and the others in descending order.

ALPHABETIC SORTING. Alphabetic sorting is the processing or rearrangement of files into alphabetical order. Before sorting, a file or records may be in random order. After sorting, the file begins with the letter A and moves through to Z.

A file can be alphabetized by employee name, geographic location, job description, part name, or by any alphabetic data field. Figure 4.2 is an example of a file arranged alphabetically by part name.

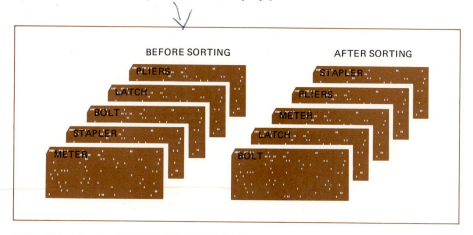

FIGURE 4.2 ALPHABETIC SORTING

Alphabetic sorting is often used in conjunction with other data processing operations on a file. For example, a file of student records containing names and test scores could be grouped by test score and then, within each test score, alphabetized by name. To do this, first the minor (alphabetical) field is sorted and then the major (numerical) field is sorted.

The computer is the most efficient means for performing alphabetic sorts. Sorting by hand is time consuming and tedious. Sorting by unit record machines is also a slow process; a unit record file must pass through the sorter several times before it is correctly alphabetized.

Grouping   Grouping is the procedure of bringing together like records in a file. Before grouping, records in the file are in no specific order. After grouping, records containing like data are arranged next to each other.

For example, a file of business expenses can be grouped by the name of the department which incurred the expenses. (See Figure 4.3.) Before grouping, records containing the expenditures and department names are in random order. After grouping, all records are arranged in small groups, one composed of office expenses, another manufacturing expenses, another shipping expenses, and finally sales expenses. Files can be grouped by other

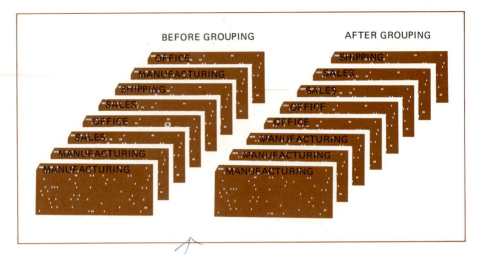

FIGURE 4.3 GROUPING

categories, such as name of individual, month, store where sold, or product line.

Merging   Merging is the operation of combining two files into a single file. Before merging, two separate files exist, each in the same sequence. After merging, all of the cards from the previous two files are contained in one file in alphabetic or numeric sequence. Figure 4.4 is an illustration of merging.

There are many reasons for merging files. A master file containing the account name and balance may be merged with records containing account name and monthly payments made. After merging, one file exists with each payment record (activity record) placed behind the master record. An updated file of new master cards can then be prepared from this merged file.

MERGING WITH SELECTION. The process of merging with selection is similar to merging in that two files are combined. But, in addition, records from one file without corresponding matches in the other file are pulled out, or selected, as the merging operation takes place.

Before merging, there are two files, each in the same alphabetic or numeric sequence. A record in one file may or may not have a match in the other file (matching data in a specified field, i.e., account number, catalog number). After merging with selection, three files are present: the merged file with matched sets of records (one behind the other) and two selected files. Each selected file contains records without a match from one original file. (See Figure 4.5.)

Merging with selection can be used to determine if all parts of a set are ready for distribution or mailing. For example, suppose a credit card and a statement of account card are to be mailed to each customer. In no case is a credit card or a statement of account card to be mailed out alone. The two

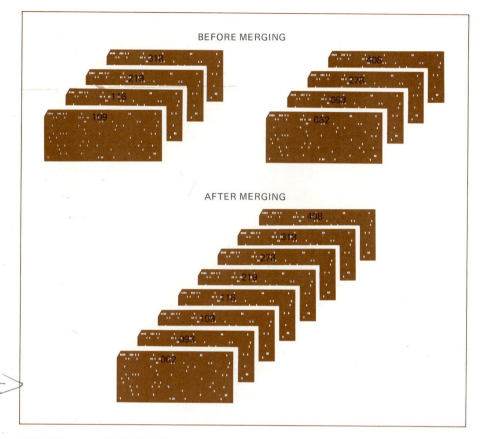

FIGURE 4.4 MERGING

files, one with credit cards and the other with statement of account cards, are merged with selection. After merging, the paired set of credit cards and statement of account cards is ready for further processing. Any unmatched cards have been put aside into two separate groups.

Checking   MATCHING. Matching is a checking procedure in which records from two files are compared for matching data, but are not merged. Before matching, two files are present. Each may contain records without a match in the other file. After matching, the two files remain as separate entities. However, all records without matches are pulled aside. (See Figure 4.6.)

Matching and merging with selection are similar procedures, but differ in the way they rearrange the files. Matching results in four files: two containing records in corresponding order and two with selected records. Merging results in three files: one with matches physically paired and two with selected records.

Matching may be used to determine whether all records that should be in a file are there. This is particularly important when working with master files.

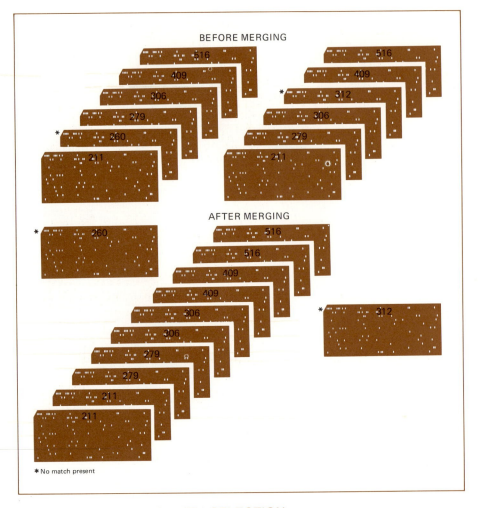

FIGURE 4.5 MERGING WITH SELECTION

For example, suppose the billing department prepares monthly statements for account customers from a master file in the credit department. If a record in the monthly statement file has no match in the master file, it must be put aside for special handling. Conversely, all customers listed in the master file should receive current statements of account. If a monthly statement record has been lost or has not been prepared, the matching process would detect it by putting aside the master record.

CHECKING SEQUENCE. The procedure of checking sequence is used to check a file for sequential order. Each record in the file is compared with the one ahead of it. If a record is out of sequence, the machine stops. Files may be checked for either numeric or alphabetic sequence. (See Figure 4.7.)

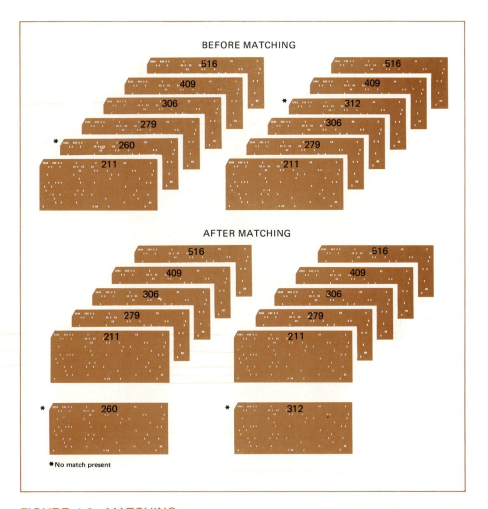

FIGURE 4.6   MATCHING

Files are not physically rearranged; errors are flagged. If sequence checking is being done manually, the operator merely switches records that are out of sequence. If a machine is being used, the device stops to allow the operator to correct the situation. After sequence checking, one file remains with all cards in the proper order.

Sequence checking is often done before further processing. Suppose, for example, mailing labels are to be pasted on envelopes containing personally addressed letters. Before labels are pasted on, the operator must be sure that they are in the same order as the envelopes.

BLANK-COLUMN DETECTION.   Blank-column detection is the procedure of checking records in a file for blank columns in a specified field.

Before blank-column detection, one file is present. Some records may

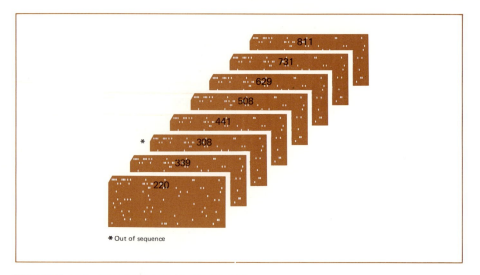

＊Out of sequence

FIGURE 4.7   CHECKING SEQUENCE

have blank columns in certain fields due to mechanical failure, oversight, error, or because no data was entered in the record. After detection, those records that contain blank columns are identified, flagged, or pulled aside, depending on the device used. Figure 4.8 illustrates blank-column detection.

For example, suppose that employee paychecks are being prepared from master payroll records stored on punched cards. Each master record contains the name of the employee, gross pay, deductions, and net pay amount. Assume that a card with some missing information has found its way into the master record file. It would not be desirable to mail a paycheck with the amount left blank. Therefore, the fields in the master file are checked to see that no blank columns are present.

SINGLE-COLUMN SELECTION. Single-column selection is the process by which records punched with a predetermined code are removed from a file. Before selection, there is one file of records. After selection, the original file is basically unchanged, except that the desired records have been removed, or selected.

Single-column selection is used for many purposes. It can be used to divide a file into two groups: male or female; over or under 21; tenured or nontenured; delinquent or nondelinquent, etc. This is easily done by reserving one column on a record for a code symbol—usually an X punch in the 11 zone. The presence of the X punch indicates one condition; its absence, another. In Figure 4.9, single-column selection is used to pull aside records that refer to one part of an assembly.

Single-column selection can also divide a file into several groups. For example, accounts can be classified by industry group. Manufacturing plants could be given the code "1," retailers "2," wholesalers "3," etc. By the

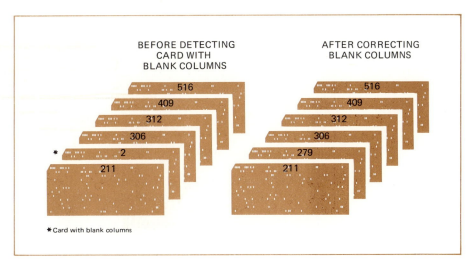

FIGURE 4.8   BLANK-COLUMN DETECTION

FIGURE 4.9   SINGLE-COLUMN SELECTION (X punch selection)

A GIANT STEP BACKWARD

A giant step backward has been taken. A computer has been fired and replaced with people.

George Gustafson, executive secretary of the State Teacher Preparation and Licensing Commission of California, fired the machine and switched to human beings. The move cut teacher credential processing time by 900% from an average 95 days to 10.

Gustafson described his demodernization program as "converting credential processing from a complex and costly automated system to a streamlined, fully manual operation."

In other words, "It was easier to do it by hand. We got rid of a million and a half dollars worth of computer. We pulled the plug and sent it back to IBM."

Although the computer was unable to hold its job, Gustafson is the last person to pick on the unemployed machine. He said it was a "good worker, it just couldn't compete with people."

SOURCE   "Humans Replace Computer in Teacher Credential Office," *Los Angeles Times*, January 18, 1972, part I, p. 3.

single-column selection technique, records relating to retailers (2) could be easily pulled aside.

Searching   Searching is the process of checking through a file to locate a specific record. Both alphabetic and numeric searches may be made. The data in the

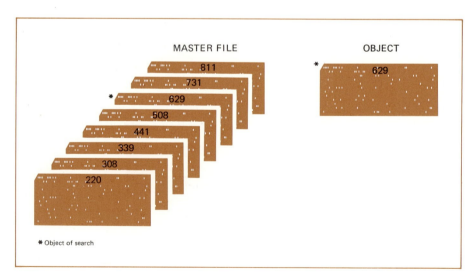

FIGURE 4.10   SEARCHING

alphabetic or numeric field being sought, called the object of the search, must be known in advance.

A file may or may not contain the object of the search. After the search, the file remains intact, and the object of the search has either been found or is known not to be present in the file. (See Figure 4.10.)

Searches for alphabetic data and multicolumn numeric fields are usually performed by collators or on computers, using search programs.

MANUAL METHOD OF SORTING AND COLLATING

Before the advent of unit record equipment, all sorting and collating was done by hand. Individual pieces of data were transcribed onto cards or

sheets of paper and these, in turn, were sorted, classified, or rearranged. If a specific piece of data was needed, it was simply pulled from the file (selected) by hand.

The manual method is still satisfactory for processing small amounts of data. It is faster to manually select a required card from a small file than to use machines or computers. But this method is slow, tedious, and inefficient when thousands of punched cards or records must be sorted in a short time.

COLLATING AND SORTING MACHINES

Two types of unit record machines, called collators and sorters, are extensively used to perform the procedures just described. However, these machines are practical only when processing small or moderate amounts of data. When millions of punched cards must be sorted, or huge files merged or searched, it is often more practical to use the power and efficiency of electronic computers.

Sorting Machines   Several pieces of equipment sort punched cards. Among them are the IBM 82, 83, and 84 Sorters and the UNIVAC 1720 Sorter which are similar in operation. Basically, their function can be described as follows: a card is fed into the sorter, the sorter senses its hole combination and guides the card through a chute into a receiving pocket. These machines will sort numeric or alphabetic data, detect blank columns, or select cards from a file.

IBM 82, 83, AND 84 SORTERS.   These machines are motor driven and contain a card hopper, column indicator, switches, sort brush (or photocell), and 13 receiving pockets. (One pocket exists for each row position in a column, and one is labeled ''R'' for reject.) These machines sort from 450 to 2,000 cards per minute. The Model 84 Sorter is designed to handle alphabetic sorting more efficiently than Models 82 and 83.

To operate the sorter the stack of cards to be sorted is placed in the hopper, the column selector switch is set, and the machine is started. (See Figure 4.11.) Cards are fed one at a time to the sorter brush. As the card moves between the sorter brush and a metal contact roller, the hole punched in one column is sensed and a chute selecting mechanism is activated. The proper chute is brought in line and the card moves through it to one of the 13 receiving pockets.

The specific chute a card follows is determined by the hole punched in the column being read. If a hole is present in punch position 1, the card will be guided through chute 1 and dropped into pocket 1. A hole in punch position 2 will cause the card to drop into pocket 2, etc.

The cycle continues—a card is fed, sensed, guided through the chute, and dropped into a pocket—until all cards have been sorted. The operator then removes the cards from the pockets in this order: nines at the bottom, eights

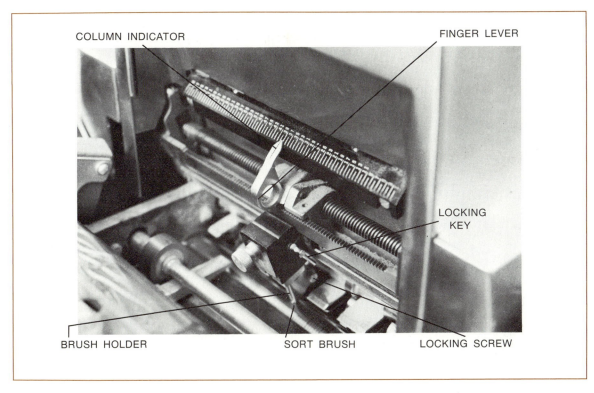

FIGURE 4.11   SORTER BRUSH AND COLUMN INDICATOR

on top, sevens next, etc. If no hole is present in the card, or if an incorrect punch combination is present, the card will drop into the reject pocket.

The machine can sort only one column at a time. The sorter has only one reading brush, which the operator must physically locate directly over the column to be sorted.

UNIVAC 1720 SORTER.   The UNIVAC 1720 Sorter is similar in design to the IBM Sorters and can sort, sequence, and column select punched cards. (See Figure 4.12.) The cards are sensed or read electronically by a photocell, at a rate of 1,000 cards per minute. The machine has a six-digit counter similar to an odometer to count the cards fed to each pocket and can also do blank-column detection.

How the Sorter Performs Numeric Sorts   Multicolumn numeric sorts require as many passes through the machine as there are columns. This is called a reverse digit sort. If a two-column numeric field is to be sorted, the file must be run through the machine twice. First the right-hand column is sorted, then the reading brush is readjusted, and the left-hand column is sorted. A six-column number would require six passes through the sorter.

Figure 4.13 illustrates a file of five cards to be sorted. Each card contains

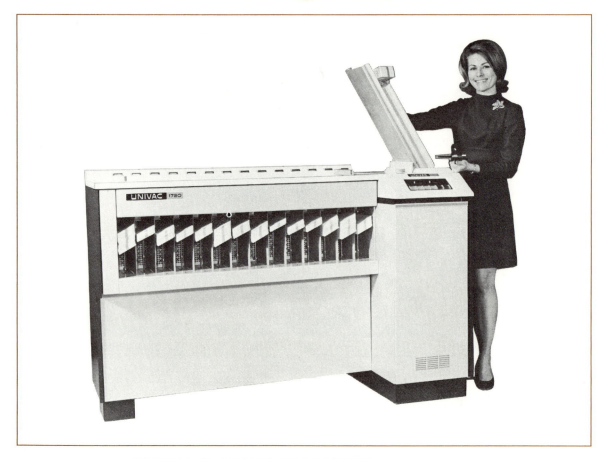

FIGURE 4.12   UNIVAC 1720 SORTER

FIGURE 4.13   REVERSE DIGIT SORT

BEFORE SORTING	FIRST PASS 1's POSITION	SECOND PASS 10's POSITION	THIRD PASS 100's POSITION	FOURTH PASS 1,000's POSITION
3829	3829	9782	3829	9782
1336	3209	1336	9782	6634
9782	1336	6634	6634	3829
6634	6634	3829	1336	3209
3209	9782	3209	3209	1336
	↑	↑	↑	↑

a four-digit number and requires four passes through the machine. The cards are carefully aligned (jogged) and placed in the hopper of the machine. The column selector indicator is set to the rightmost column (the units position). The machine is started, and the cards are automatically fed from the hopper and passed under the brush. The hole punched in that column is sensed or "read," and the card is dropped into the appropriate pocket.

Then the cards are removed from the pockets (nines on the bottom, eights next, etc.), aligned, and replaced in the hopper. The column selector is reset over the next column to the left (the tens position). The machine is started again, and the cards are sorted into pockets. They are again removed, aligned, and placed in the hopper. The column indicator is reset to the third column on the left (the hundreds position), and the cards are sorted. Again the cards are removed from the pockets, aligned, and placed in the hopper to sort the last column (the thousands position). When the cards are removed from the pockets after the last sort, they are in numerical order.

How the
Sorter Performs
Alphabetic Sorts

Alphabetic fields may also be sorted on these machines. However, they require two passes per column, one for the digit rows and one for the zone rows. A 20-column alphabetic field would require 40 passes through the machine. The sorter is not efficient for handling large alphabetic fields and has largely been superseded by computerized sorting techniques.

Collating
Machines

Collating machines perform several operations, including merging, merging with selection, matching, and detecting blank columns. They are often used in conjunction with computers and other unit record equipment to prepare files for further processing.

IBM 85 AND 87 COLLATORS. The IBM 85 Collator is shown in Figure 4.14. The IBM 85 Collator processes numerical data, and the 87 Collator processes numeric, alphabetic, and special characters. They have two card hoppers for feeding cards from two files simultaneously and four receiving card pockets, numbered 4, 3, 2, and 1 from left to right.

One card hopper is called the primary hopper, and the file placed in it is called the primary file. The other is called the secondary hopper, and cards stacked in it are referred to as the secondary file. Cards can be fed from each hopper at the rate of 240 per minute, or a total of 480 cards per minute from both hoppers.

Cards fed from the primary hopper pass under two sets of brushes, called the primary sequence brush and primary brushes. Each set has 80 brushes, permitting the machine to read the punches in all 80 columns of a card at one time. Cards from the secondary hopper pass through one set of 80 brushes, called the secondary read brushes.

A wiring control panel is used to direct the machine. This board has many rows of hubs or terminals. These terminals are wired together in different combinations to cause the machine to perform various collating jobs.

FIGURE 4.14   IBM 85 COLLATOR

How the Collator
Merges Cards

To merge two files on the collator, the control panel is removed and jumper wires are inserted into the hubs which direct the machine to merge the two files. The control panel is replaced, the master cards are loaded into the primary hopper, the detail cards into the secondary hopper, and the machine is started.

The first card from the primary hopper is read, the first card from the secondary hopper is read, and their values compared. Three relationships can exist between the data read from these cards:

❶ The value on the primary card is greater than the one on the secondary card.

❷ The value on the primary card is equal to the one on the secondary card.

❸ The value on the primary card is less than the one on the secondary card.

If the value of the primary card is less than or equal to the secondary card, it is dropped into the receiving pocket (usually pocket 2) and the secondary card is held at the read station. If the value of the primary card is greater than the secondary, the secondary card is dropped into the pocket and the primary card is held at the read station.

The machine then feeds the next card to the primary or secondary brushes, whichever is empty. Both values are again read and compared, and the lower one dropped into pocket 2.

This procedure continues until all cards in the two files have been read, compared, and dropped into the receiving pocket in the proper order. The final result is one file in numerical order. If there is more than one card with the same number, the master card comes first, followed by the related detail card.

HOW THE COLLATOR MERGES WITH SELECTION.   Suppose two files are to be merged; however, the cards without matches are to be pulled aside. The two files are loaded into the collator, one in the primary hopper and the other in the secondary hopper. The control panel is appropriately wired to cause the machine to merge with selection, and the machine is started.

First it reads the value on the primary card and compares it to the secondary card. If the primary card is less than the secondary, the primary card is dropped into receiving pocket 1. If they are equal, both cards are dropped into pocket 2, the merging pocket. If the secondary card is less, it is dropped into pocket 3 or 4. New cards are fed, sensed, and compared. The procedure continues until both files are processed.

The end result is that pocket 2 contains the newly merged file of matched cards. Pocket 1 holds unmatched cards from the primary file, and pocket 3 or 4 holds the unmatched cards from the secondary file.

How the Collator Performs Matching

The files to be matched are sequenced and placed in the primary and secondary hoppers of the machine. The control panel is appropriately set up, and the machine is started. Cards are fed from both hoppers, compared, and dropped into one of four pockets. The matched primary cards go into pocket 2, and the secondary cards into pocket 3. Unmatched primary cards fall into pocket 1, and secondary cards into 4. At the end of the run, there are two matching files, one in pocket 2 and the other in pocket 3. Cards without matches are in pockets 1 and 4.

KEY TERMS

Numerical sorting	Merging
Ascending sort	Merging with selection
Descending sort	Matching
Major sort field	Checking sequence
Minor sort field	Blank-column detection
Sequential sorting	Single-column selection
Alphabetic sorting	Search
Grouping	Reverse digit sort

EXERCISES

1. Label a deck of 25 punched cards with the numbers from 10 to 34. Shuffle the cards and then sequence them in descending numerical order.

2. Prepare 25 punched cards as follows: label five cards PENS, five PENCILS, five ERASERS, five PAPER, and the last five CLIPS. Number each of the groups with the numbers 1 through 5. After shuffling all the cards, perform a minor and major sort, using the alphabetic data as the minor field and the numeric data as the major field.

3. Shuffle the same deck as in Exercise 2 and re-sort, using the numeric data as the minor field and the alphabetic data as the major field.

4. Prepare a deck of 26 punched cards with the numbers from 1–26. Shuffle the deck and split it in half. Sequence each half numerically, then merge the two files.

5. Perform a matching procedure using the decks from Exercises 1 and 4.

6. Perform a checking sequence routine using the deck from Exercise 1.

7. Perform a checking sequence routine using the deck from Exercise 4.

8. If a machine is available, keypunch a deck of 30 cards with five-digit numbers. Place an X punch in column 80 on every fifth card. Shuffle the deck. Separate all cards with an X punch.

9. Use the same deck as in Exercise 8. Shuffle. Do a reverse digit sort manually, carefully following the procedure described in Figure 4.13.

10. If a sorter is available, perform Exercise 9 on it.

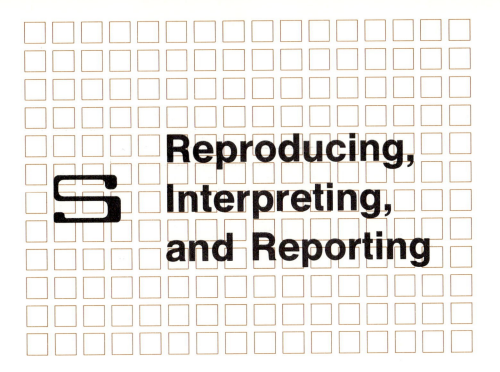

Reproducing, Interpreting, and Reporting

Reproducing is the process of duplicating records or files. Punched holes in one set of cards are sensed and punched into another set of cards. Data may be copied by punching into one or more new cards, punching detail cards from master cards, translating mark-sense to Hollerith codes, or end printing.

Interpreting is the process of decoding holes in a punched card into graphic, readable symbols printed on the face of a card, or into large numbers on the end of a card.

Reporting is the process of restructuring and manipulating data, and outputting it in a form which increases its usefulness. Both arithmetic calculations and graphic rearrangements are used to manipulate data. The resulting data may be outputted as printed forms, statements, and other hard documents.

In this chapter the principles of reproducing, interpreting, and reporting are considered. The devices that perform these functions, the reproducing punch, interpreter, and accounting machine, are described.

BASIC REPRODUCING, INTERPRETING, AND REPORTING ROUTINES

Copying data from one record to another is an important job in data processing. EAM operators frequently prepare duplicate sets of records, punch detail cards from master cards, convert mark-sense to Hollerith codes, or decode punched data into readable characters. They prepare bills, invoices, statements, purchase orders, and other forms. Some common operations performed in the EAM department are described here.

Reproducing   80–80 REPRODUCING.   80–80 reproducing is copying all data from one deck of punched cards into another deck. (See Figure 5.1.) Data from each original record is punched into a duplicate record in exactly the same order and position. The term "80–80" means that all 80 columns on the original cards are copied.

duplicating

Before 80–80 reproducing, one file of punched cards is present with data punched in any of the 80 columns across each record. (Each record in the file may contain different data.) After 80–80 reproducing, two files are present: one the undisturbed original, the other an exact copy of the original. In this operation, the punches and blanks are copied exactly. The characters

FIGURE 5.1   80–80 REPRODUCING

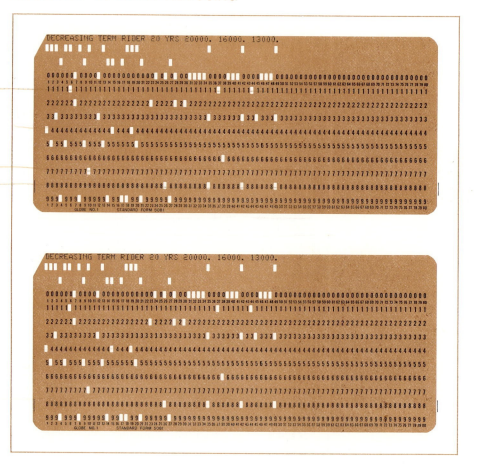

at the top of the card are printed in a second operation, called interpreting.

The 80–80 reproducing operation is a convenient way to duplicate decks as a protection against loss or damage. Also, important computer programs, sets of data, etc. are often copied 80–80 and the duplicate filed. Frequently used punched cards, such as control cards and job order cards, are often copied on the reproducer for accuracy and to save time. Rekeypunching may introduce errors. Copies of files or data sets may be sent to different departments in a business.

FIELD-SELECTED REPRODUCING.   Field-selected reproducing is the copying of only selected columns of data, say from a master file, onto new punched cards. (See Figure 5.2.) As many columns as are necessary may be copied from the master to detail cards, or from detail to detail cards.

Before field-selected reproducing, one deck is present with up to 80

FIGURE 5.2 FIELD-SELECTED REPRODUCING

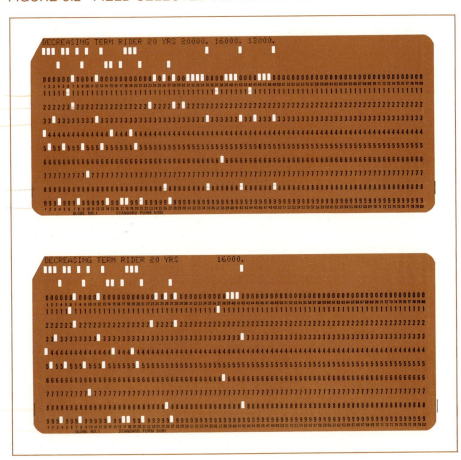

columns of data on each record. After field-selected reproducing, two files are present: the undisturbed original deck and a deck with only certain selected columns reproduced in each record.

Field-selected reproducing is useful when confidential business data is on master records. For example, suppose cards in a master file contain a part number, description, confidential wholesale price, and supplier name. Information from this file is needed for warehouse inventory control. The original file is field-selected reproduced to create a detail file listing only the part number and description. This second file can be distributed to the warehouse area without fear of disseminating confidential company information.

SELECTIVE REPRODUCING. Selective reproducing is the reproduction of only specified records in a file. All or part of the data on a record may be copied, but only from certain cards in the file. (See Figure 5.3.)

An X punch (zone 11 punch) in one of the columns of a record is often used to indicate the records that should be reproduced or skipped in selective reproducing. For example, before selective reproducing, one file is present. The file contains some records that are not to be reproduced. These cards do not have an X punch. After selective reproducing, two files are present: one the undisturbed master file, the other with copies of only those cards with an X punch.

OFFSET REPRODUCING. Offset reproducing is the punching of data from selected columns in a master record into different columns on the detail

FIGURE 5.3 SELECTIVE REPRODUCING

FIGURE 5.4 OFFSET REPRODUCING

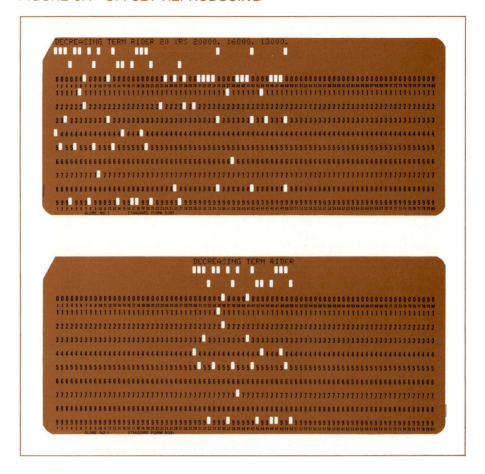

record. Offsetting means that data is copied onto a detail card in a different position from that on the original record. (See Figure 5.4.)

Before offset reproducing, one file that contains data in several columns is present. After offset reproducing, two files are present: one the original undisturbed file, the other with some or all of the same data, rearranged into new column positions.

Offset reproducing is used to shift data from one column to another. Computer programs may be written to process only data from specified columns on a record. For example, if a program has been written to read the price of a product from columns 1–10 on a record, the information on the data set must agree. Suppose though, that the data cards to be processed by the program have the price punched into columns 21–30. This may be the result of an error in keypunching, or for convenience in processing by another program or department.

The price data from columns 21–30 must be offset punched into columns 1–10 on a new deck of cards. This new file is now ready for the computer. It is often easier to rearrange data by offset reproducing than to rewrite an existing program or to rekeypunch the data into the correct columns.

GANG PUNCHING. Gang punching is the copying of data from one master card onto one or more detail cards. Two common types of gang punching operations are

1. *Single Master-Card Gang Punching.* In this operation, a single master card is reproduced many times. (See Figure 5.5.) Before gang punching, only one master record is available. After gang punching, a file of cards exists, each card in it a duplicate of the original master record.

duplicating

In practice, EAM equipment performs this function by a series of punch and copy operations. First the master card is read and the data copied onto the first detail card. The first detail card is then advanced to the reading station and becomes the image to punch the second detail card. The cycle continues, with each card being a duplicate of the one previously punched.

FIGURE 5.5 SINGLE MASTER-CARD GANG PUNCHING

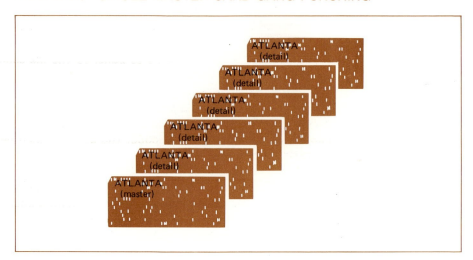

2. *Interspersed Master-Card Gang Punching.* In this operation, a file of master cards is to be reproduced. One or more copies of each master card may be made. The results will be a file consisting of groups of cards. Each group will be a master card, followed by one or more detail cards. (See Figure 5.6.)

Detail cards do not have to be exact duplicates of the master card. Data copied by gang punching may be 80–80 reproduced, field selected, or offset reproduced.

FIGURE 5.6 INTERSPERSED MASTER-CARD GANG PUNCHING

MARK SENSING. In mark sensing, information penciled on the face of a punch card is translated into holes punched into the same card. Mark sensing is a data input method in which Electrographic pencil marks on a record are read and punched directly into the same record. (See Figure 5.7.)

Before mark sensing, a file of cards marked with Electrographic pencil is present. After mark-sense punching, a single file remains, with data punched into the cards in the Hollerith code. The data can then be read by the machine for further processing.

END PRINTING. End printing is a form of reproducing and interpreting in which selected numbers punched into a card are printed in large display numbers on the edge of the same card, or on a new card. End printing can be done in numbers $\frac{1}{4}$-inch high and in either of two positions on the end of the card. Up to eight numerical characters can be printed on one line. (See Figure 5.8.)

Before end printing, a single data file with numerical information punched in one or more fields is present. After end printing, the numerical information from the fields is printed in $\frac{1}{4}$-inch letters on the edge of the card.

It is much easier to read numerical information which has been end printed on records than the original small type from a keypunch machine or interpreter. Stock cards, identification numbers, part numbers, etc. are often end printed.

For example, end-printed cards with part numbers in large type may be placed in plastic boxes near the bin where the parts are stored in a

FIGURE 5.7 MARK-SENSE PUNCHING

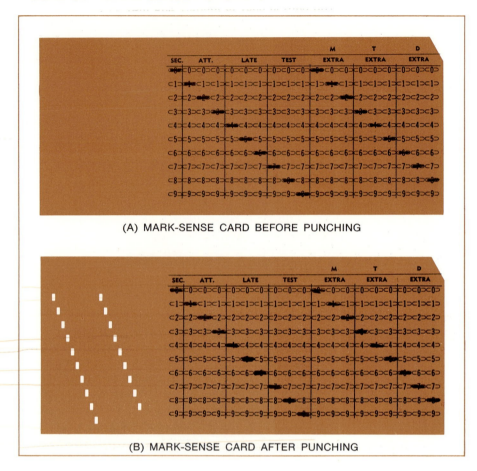

(A) MARK-SENSE CARD BEFORE PUNCHING

(B) MARK-SENSE CARD AFTER PUNCHING

FIGURE 5.8 END PRINTING

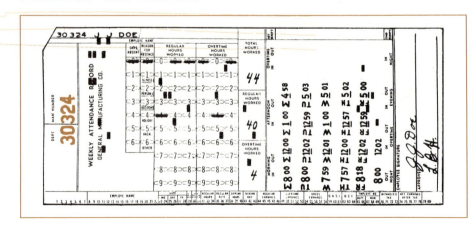

warehouse. When a part is taken from stock, the warehouseman pulls a card. The card is easy to identify and may be pasted on cartons or attached to shipments.

Interpreting

Interpreting is the translation of symbols. Interpreting involves reading the hole combinations in a card and printing their graphic representation or English language equivalent on the card as shown in Figure 5.9.

Before interpretation, cards in a file are punched with a code. No letters, numbers, or symbols are printed on the face of the card. It is difficult and time consuming for someone to decipher the data on these cards. After interpretation, the graphic equivalent of the punched data is printed on the face of the card. Interpreting may be done in various positions on the face of a card.

FIGURE 5.9   INTERPRETING

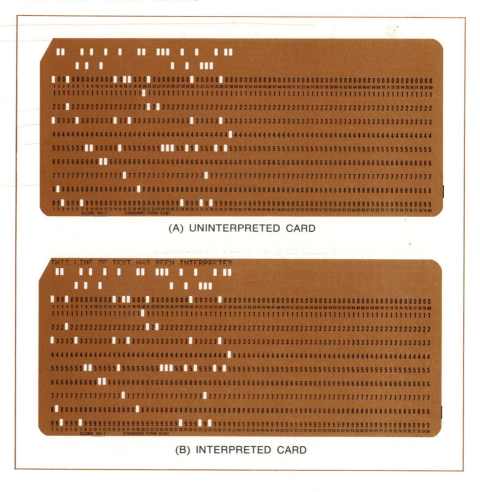

(A) UNINTERPRETED CARD

(B) INTERPRETED CARD

Reporting   Reporting is the outputting of data in the form of statements, invoices, paychecks, printed forms, and other hard documents. The data being outputted may be the original data fed to the machine, or the result of processing performed on this data. Processing of data is usually done arithmetically or by restructuring its order or arrangement.

CALCULATING.   Calculating is the manipulation of data by arithmetic means. It involves finding sums, figuring balances, paychecks, interest, etc.

Before calculating, various data from other processes are present. Hours worked, costs of goods, stock levels, sales figures, etc. are all forms of input data. Calculations must be performed on them to make them usable for preparing paychecks, invoices, statements, etc.

Prior to the introduction of the computer, calculating was done on EAM machines. Today, most of this processing is done on computers because of their greater capacity, flexibility, speed, and efficiency.

LISTING (DETAIL PRINTING).   Listing is a form of reporting in which data is read from a punch card and printed out on a sheet of paper. All or part of the data on a record may be read and printed on the page. A print out of all 80 columns is referred to as an "80–80 listing."

Before listing, a file of punched cards is present (they may or may not be interpreted). After listing, the file itself is unchanged, but a readable print out of each record in the file has been generated.

Listing is used to check the accuracy of files—source documents can be compared with the listing. It is also a convenient way to check sequence of records and to verify that none have been omitted.

PRINTING.   Printing is another form of reporting in which invoices, statements, bills, or other documents are prepared from input data. Printing is usually done on data resulting from some type of restructuring or manipulation.

Printing may be done on continuous pin feed forms, carbon forms, NCR papers, snap-apart or multipart forms. Pin feed forms are long sheets of paper folded in accordion fashion. Pin holes, small holes similar to sprockets on film, are punched along the edges of the paper to facilitate feeding through the machines and to ensure proper positioning. Carbon and snap-apart forms can be separated after printing, and the copies distributed as needed.

REPRODUCING, INTERPRETING, AND REPORTING MACHINES

Reproducing, interpreting, and reporting are done on specially designed EAM machines. In addition, a limited amount of interpreting and reproducing can be done on some keypunch machines.

Reproducing
Machines

The IBM 514 and 519 Document Originating Machines dominated the market for reproducing functions until computers became available. These machines, often called reproducing punches, repro punches, or, simply, punches, are still widely used and are found in many computer installations for short-run work.

IBM 519 DOCUMENT ORIGINATING MACHINE.   This machine, shown in Figure 5.10, has two feed hoppers, two card pockets (called stackers), and an automatic card feeder. The IBM 519 can process up to 100 cards per minute and will punch, gang punch, end print, compare, and mark-sense punch.

FIGURE 5.10   IBM 519 DOCUMENT ORIGINATING MACHINE

The machine is motor driven and contains a removable wiring control panel. Short jumper wires are connected to hubs on the panel, shown in Figure 5.11, in various combinations to program the different reproducing and checking functions.

The machine has two major sections as illustrated in Figure 5.12: the read unit and the punch unit. A card hopper in the read unit feeds cards through a set of Read X control brushes (RX brushes), two sets of sensing brushes, and into the card stacker. The six RX brushes sense the X punches (11 zone) in the cards being fed. The first set of 80 sensing brushes, called the reproducing brushes, reads all 80 columns of a card. If a hole is present in a column, the brush makes an electrical contact. Current is passed through the contact and is fed to a terminal on the wiring panel. The second set of 80 brushes, the comparing and transcribing brushes, is used for verifying accuracy and for end printing.

The punch unit contains the punch station, two or three sets of brushes and a print unit. A hopper in the punch unit feeds cards past brushes and punch dies to the punch stacker. The PX brushes read X punches for special handling. The punch dies duplicate the impulses coming from the brushes in the read unit and punch the proper code into another card. Next a set of 80 gang-punching and interpreting brushes check the accuracy of the new card.

FIGURE 5.11   WIRING CONTROL PANEL, IBM 519 DOCUMENT
             ORIGINATING MACHINE

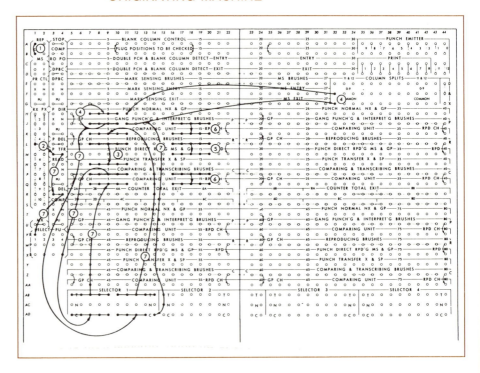

FIGURE 5.12   IBM 519 DOCUMENT ORIGINATING MACHINE
COMPONENTS

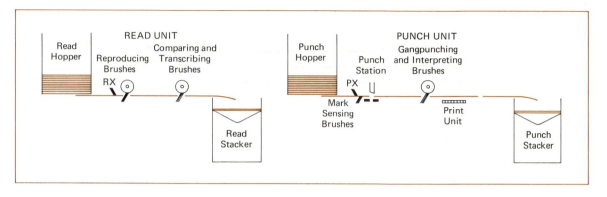

(On machines capable of doing mark-sense punching, an additional set of 27 brushes is present in front of the punch dies.) The print unit is used for end printing.

The sets of brushes and punch dies can be connected in various combinations to cause the machine to punch, gang punch, compare, etc. The specific column arrangement is determined by the jumpers placed on the wiring control panel.

The wiring control panel has several dozen rows of terminals, one for each brush and punch die on the machine. Any punch die can be coupled to any sense brush. Thus, a column in a master card can be offset punched into any other column.

Reproducing on the Reproducing Punch.   To perform 80–80 reproducing on the IBM 519, the wiring control panel is removed and jumper wires inserted in the appropriate hubs to tie the reading and punching units together. The brushes in the read unit sense the holes in the master card and feed the information through the wiring control panel to the punch dies. There, holes matching those in the master card are punched in a new card. Then, the master card passes through the set of comparing and transcribing brushes in the read unit and, at the same time, the duplicate passes through the set of gang-punching and interpreting brushes in the punch unit. These brushes compare the punches and verify the accuracy of the new card.

As the cycle continues, a card from the read hopper moves past the read brushes. At the same time, a new card from the punch hopper is fed under the set of dies. At a signal from the read brushes, the dies punch the new card, which is then compared with the original for verification. The master card is dropped into the read stacker and the duplicate into the punch stacker.

Selected field reproducing is accomplished in a similar manner, except that only a limited number of punch dies are coupled to the read brushes. If offset punching is to be done, brushes from one column are wired to punch

COMPUTER KEEPS TIRELESS WATCH OVER THE SEAS

On a small island in New York Harbor, a computer keeps a tireless watch over merchant ships plying the oceans of the world. Operated by the U.S. Coast Guard on Governors Island, the electronic system continuously monitors an average of 1,800 ships of all nations. The installation is called AMVER, for Automated Merchant Vessel Report system. Its mission: to make travel on the high seas as safe as possible. The service covers the Atlantic, Pacific, and Indian Oceans.

In the event of an emergency at sea—a foundering ship, an injured crewman, a fire—AMVER's computer can print out, in minutes, a list of nearby ships. The list, called a surface picture or SURPIC, can include such information as which of the nearby ships have doctors aboard and which are headed in the direction of the emergency.

Sixty nations take part in AMVER's search-and-rescue operations. When a ship leaves port, it notifies the Coast Guard in New York of its departure, intended course, and final destination. This information is stored in the computer. While underway, the ship files position reports regularly and, if it cruises more than 25 miles off its planned course, it sends special "deviation reports."

If the ship should need assistance, it notifies the nearest search-and-rescue agency, which relays the information to AMVER. Then the computer goes to work, printing out a SURPIC of the ship's area. The SURPIC information is radioed to the search-and-rescue agency that relayed the distress signal, and marine or airborne rescue parties are quickly dispatched.

SOURCE   Abstracted from "Tireless Watch Over the Seas," *Data Processor*, Vol. XI, No. 1, February 1968, p. 18.

dies from a different column. Since any read brush can be connected to any punch die, data can be punched into any column in the duplicate card.

End Printing on the Reproducing Punch. Records to be end printed must, of course, first contain numerical data punched into the card. The wiring control panel is removed and jumper wires connected to activate the end-printing mechanism.

End printing is done on a printing unit that has eight print wheels, each engraved with the numbers 0 to 9 and a blank. As cards are fed from the hopper, they are sensed by the brushes which activate the print wheels. The wheels print the number on the end of the card and it is dropped into the stacker. The cycle continues until all cards in the hopper have been end printed. Cards can be fed through either the read or the punch unit for end printing.

Mark-Sense Punching on the Reproducing Punch. For mark-sense punching, the control panel is wired so that impulses picked up by the mark-sense read brushes from the input data cards are amplified and fed to the punch dies. Cards to be mark-sense punched are fed from the hopper, sensed, punched, and dropped into the stacker. The thin coating of pencil lead on the surface of the card serves as a carrier for a weak electrical current. The cycle continues until all cards are processed.

Summary Punching on the Reproducing Punch. Summary punching is the process by which a total accumulated by an accounting machine is punched into cards by a reproducing punch connected to the accounting machine. This feature is not available on all 519 Document Originating Machines.

Before summary punching, one file that contains a number of records to be totaled, summarized, or otherwise mathematically manipulated is present. After summary punching, two files are present: the undisturbed original file in the accounting machine and in the reproducer a summary file containing one or more totals prepared from the master file. (See Figure 5.13.) Summary punching techniques are used in accounting systems to keep updated records on, for example, account balances, stocks, and inventories.

Double Punch and Blank-Column Detection. Occasionally, an error may occur and a file with data punched into the wrong columns run through an EAM machine. This will cause errors in further processing. The double punch and blank-column detection feature is available on some 519 Document

"It says the economy will slow down
after the 21st when Mercury retrogrades
in Scorpio."

FIGURE 5.13 SUMMARY PUNCHING

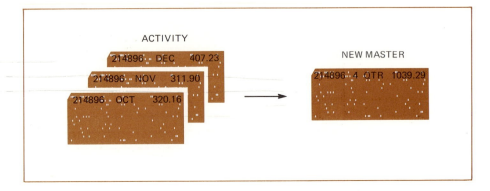

Originating Machines. With this feature, the machine will stop and a signal light will go on if any record has multiple punches in one column, or blank columns in a field that should contain punches.

Interpreting Machines

Interpreting can be done on a keypunch, on the IBM 557 Interpreter, or on a similar machine.

IBM 029 CARD PUNCH, MODEL C AND UNIVAC 1710 VERIFYING INTERPRETING PUNCH.
Both of these machines were designed primarily as keypunch machines, but can be used to interpret cards. The Model C Keypunch can operate in one of two modes for interpreting. It can punch data into cards and interpret at the same time. Or, when activated by a switch on the keyboard, it will read prepunched cards and print out the graphic representation of the data punched in each column.

The UNIVAC 1710 Verifying Interpreting Punch can also interpret as it keypunches or interpret alone. This machine will also interpret only selected columns on a record. From 40 to 60 cards per minute can be interpreted.

Generally, interpreting on a keypunch is a slow process since the letters are printed serially (one at a time). On the interpreting machine, they are printed parallel (all at one time). A maximum of 80 characters is printed by a keypunch, across the 12 edge of a card, on a single print line.

IBM 557 ALPHABETIC INTERPRETER.
This machine, illustrated in Figure 5.14, has a single card hopper, card stacker, counter, print line dial, and wiring control panel. The IBM 557 is motor driven and automatically moves cards from the card hopper past two sets of brushes: the read brushes and the proof brushes. Each set contains 80 brushes, one for each column on the punch card. After passing the proof brushes, the card moves under a set of 60 type wheels.

The type wheels contain alphabetical, numerical, and special characters. As the card passes the type wheels, it is struck from behind by a set of

FIGURE 5.14 IBM 557 ALPHABETIC INTERPRETER

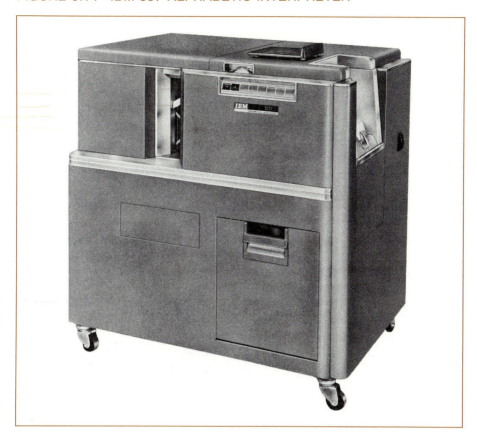

hammers, which force it against the type wheels. A fabric ribbon placed between the card and the print wheel provides inking. After printing, the card moves on a conveyer belt to the card stacker.

The Interpreter can print data in any of 25 horizontal positions across the face of a card, as illustrated in Figure 5.15. (Thirteen positions have been printed.) The print wheels and the read brushes can be wired into different arrangements. Print wheels for one column can be connected to the read brushes from a different column. For example, data punched into columns 20–30 of a card can be printed above columns 40–50 or 60–70.

The Interpreter will print only 60 characters on a line. Figure 5.16 illustrates the difference in spacing and type size of interpreting done by the keypunch and the IBM 557 Interpreter. If all 80 columns of data are to be interpreted on one card, two passes must be made through the machine. On the first pass, the first 60 columns of data are printed along the 12 edge. The cards are removed from the machine, aligned, and reinserted in the hopper. The print line dial is reset to horizontal position below the first, and the cards

FIGURE 5.15 INTERPRETER PRINTING POSITIONS

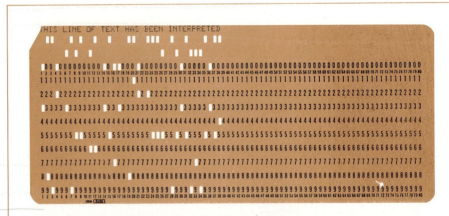

FIGURE 5.16 SPACING ARRANGEMENTS

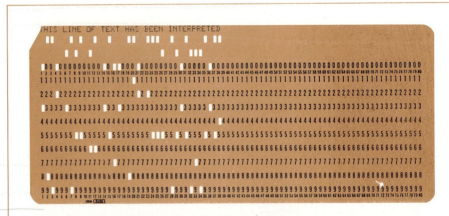

(A) IBM 029 CARD PUNCH (PRINTS 80 CHARACTERS ACROSS ONE LINE)

(B) IBM 557 INTERPRETER (PRINTS 60 CHARACTERS ACROSS ONE LINE)

fed through again. <u>On this second pass, the last 20 characters are printed</u> <u>on a second line, below the first.</u>

The Interpreter is a flexible machine. The wiring panel can be adjusted so that the machine will repeat print. In this operation, a master card with punched data is fed into the machine. All succeeding cards run through will contain the same data (interpreted, but not punched) as that on the master card. This is a convenient way to prepare information cards, notices, memos, and similar documents, where repetitive copy is desired. The IBM 557 Interpreter can also be used to prepare many business documents such as ledger cards, loan cards, deposit slips, and postcards.

Calculating and Reporting Machines

Although largely replaced by card-oriented computer systems, such as the IBM 360/20 and UNIVAC 9200, some unit record machines are still used for calculating and reporting tasks. The IBM 402 and 407 Accounting Machines, IBM 604 and 609 Calculators, and the UNIVAC 1004 Electronic Card Processing machine are examples.

IBM 407 ACCOUNTING MACHINE.   This machine, illustrated in Figure 5.17, is designed to do listing and printing on forms and reports. It has a card hopper, card stacker, and printing assembly. The printing assembly has 120 print wheels with 47 characters on each. The machine can print 18,000 characters per minute and process 150 cards per minute.

FIGURE 5.17   IBM 407 ACCOUNTING MACHINE

The accounting machine has a paper feeding mechanism for handling pin feed continuous forms. Paper tape carriage control mechanisms control vertical spacing and positioning of the print line on the forms.

A limited amount of calculating can be done on the machine, mainly addition and subtraction. Some machines have up to 112 counter positions to store data for printing. These counters are electromechanical devices, rather than solid-state (transistorized) devices.

Listing on the 407 Accounting Machine. To list a file of punched cards, the wiring panel is removed and jumper wires inserted for an 80–80 listing. The cards are then placed in the card hopper and a roll of continuous pin feed paper positioned in the carriage. The data from the first card is read, decoded, and printed on a single horizontal line. The next card is read and listed on the next line. (See Figure 5.18.) The cycle continues until the last card has been processed.

FIGURE 5.18 LISTING ON THE IBM 407 ACCOUNTING MACHINE

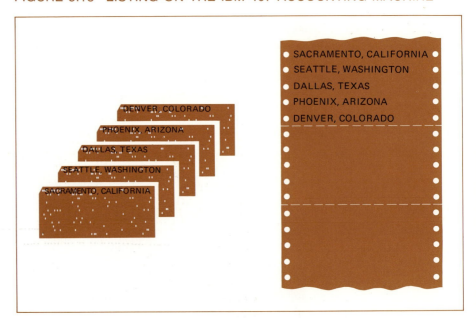

KEY TERMS

Reproduce
Interpreting
Reporting
80–80 reproducing
Field-selected reproducing
Selective reproducing
Offset reproducing
Gang punch

Single master-card gang punching
Interspersed master-card gang punching
Mark-sense punching
End printing
Reproducing punch
Summary punch
Double punch and blank-column detection
80–80 listing

EXERCISES

1. Keypunch a deck of ten cards with data in all 80 columns, divided into five or more fields. If a 519 Document Originating Machine is available, do an 80–80 reproduction of your deck.
2. Select two fields from the deck used in Exercise 1. Prepare another deck with only these two fields reproduced.
3. Reproduce the deck used in Exercise 1, transposing the first and second fields.
4. Obtain some blank mark-sense cards and an Electrographic pencil. Mark sense alphabetic and numeric data on the cards. Run them through the reproducing punch and compare the hole combinations.
5. If a 557 Interpreter is available, interpret the deck reproduced in Exercise 1. If a 557 Interpreter is not available, use a keypunch to interpret the deck.
6. If a 407 Accounting Machine is available, list the cards prepared in the previous exercises.
7. Develop a sample inventory updating system on unit record cards. Keypunch master and detail cards for this system.
8. List three instances in which it is more advantageous to input data by mark sensing rather than by keypunching.
9. Lay out and keypunch a master card that contains confidential price data and part descriptions. Then keypunch a detail card for warehouse use, omitting the confidential information.
10. If a data center is available in your school, prepare a list of unit record equipment available in the center.
11. Design and lay out a form which requires data to be interpreted on several horizontal printing positions on the card.

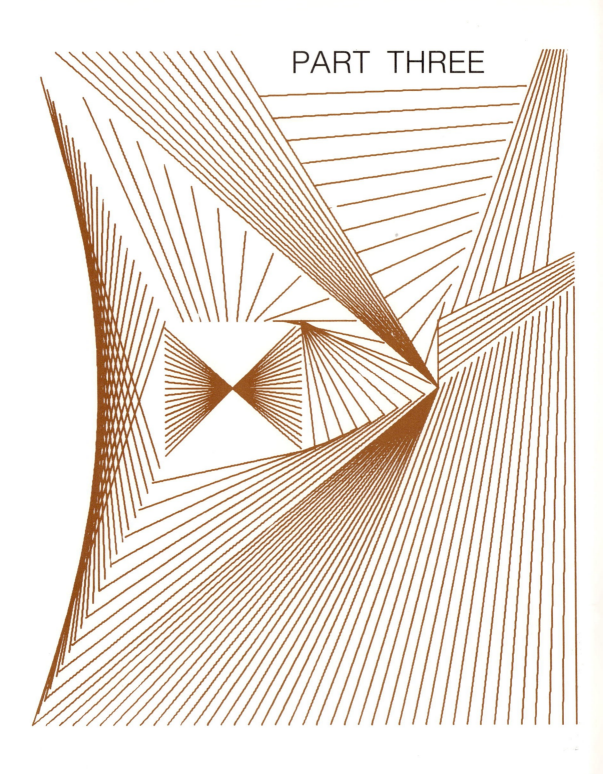

PART THREE

COMPUTER HARDWARE

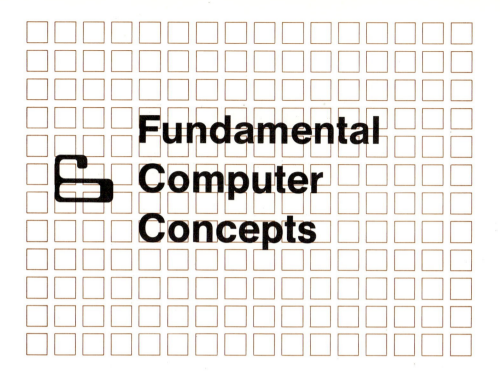

Fundamental
Computer
Concepts
6

A system is a group of related parts that function as a unit. A change in the condition of one element in the system usually affects one or all of the other elements.

The human organism is one of nature's most perfect systems. The senses, memory, logic, mobility, etc. are elements of the total system. Working as a unit, they create an active, integrated, functioning person who is capable of sensing the environment, grasping a problem, structuring a solution, and, finally, affecting the environment. The components of this system could be called input, processing, output, and memory. (See Figure 6.1.) Input is through the five senses. Processing and memory occur in the brain. Humans can remember hundreds of events, places, people, and facts. But memory is not an unlimited, totally dependable resource; some things are harder to remember than others, or are easily confused. Therefore, people take notes, make up lists, look up facts in tables or charts, and keep records. These are called external memory aids.

Man is capable of goal setting and self-direction. He can select a goal and coordinate his entire capacity to move toward it. Activities and actions are planned and performed, behavior patterns are tested and adjusted, until the goal is reached. The human organism is capable of feeding its own output back into the system for reprocessing. As a result, behavior can be changed, corrected, and adjusted to more accurately direct actions toward the goal.

119

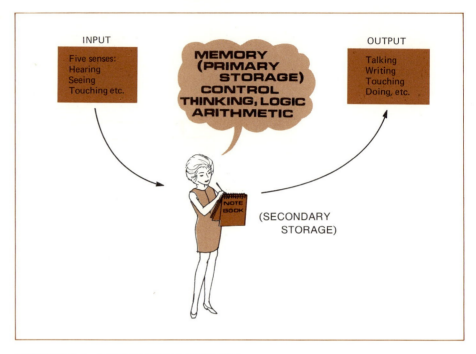

FIGURE 6.1   THE HUMAN SYSTEM

THE COMPUTER SYSTEM

Computers are also systems and are similar in many ways to the human organism. Input, processing, output, and storage are also elements of the computer system, and the system is capable of logical deductions and, to a limited extent, self-direction. Figure 6.2 is a block diagram illustrating these functions.

There are, of course, major differences between the two systems. Computers are incapable of long-range planning, generalizing from seemingly unrelated data, "intellectualizing," or "deep philosophical" thinking. However, the ability of the computer to function in business data processing compares favorably with man's. In fact, in some areas the computer far surpasses its creator. For example, computers can perform arithmetic computations much faster than man.

The computer inputs data via a card reader, tape reader, or other input device. It processes information in its central processing unit (CPU), where it performs mathematical calculations and makes logical decisions. The computer is self-directing to the extent that it can follow a set of instructions, process data and output on paper, punch cards, or record on magnetic tape or other output device, without human intervention. When it exceeds its

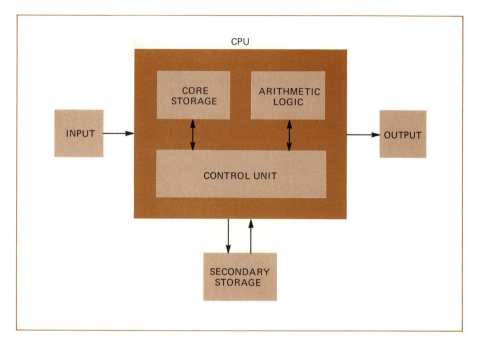

FIGURE 6.2   THE COMPUTER SYSTEM

internal storage capacity, it may call in external storage devices. Figure 6.3 illustrates the relationships of the parts of the system.

COMPUTER SUBSYSTEMS

Each part of the computer is itself a subsystem, which functions as part of the larger system. The major subsystems that can make up a computer are

- Input
- CPU
- Secondary storage
- Output
- Telecommunications

Input System In sending telegraph messages by Morse code, the telegraph operator converts words into a string of dots and dashes, which are sent over the line. Similarly, the input system of a computer reads data in the form of holes on punched cards or paper tape or from magnetized areas on magnetic tapes or disks and converts it into electronic pulses. It then transmits these pulses through wires to the CPU for processing. In a computer, each pulse is called

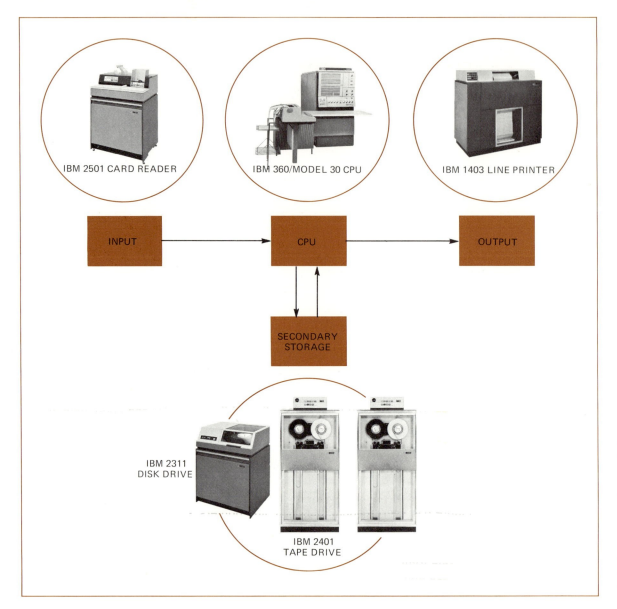

FIGURE 6.3   PARTS OF A COMPUTER SYSTEM

a *bit* and represents one piece of data. Groups of bits (pulses) are used to represent numbers, letters, or words. (Bit combinations or codes used are discussed in Chapter 8.)

    A computer input system may have only one device for reading punch cards or it may have several devices, each handling a different input media.

Large installations often have several card and tape units. The most common modes of computer input are :

CARD READER. It reads the holes in a punched card and converts them to electronic pulses.

MAGNETIC TAPE READER. It reads the magnetized bits on magnetic tape and converts them to electronic pulses.

MAGNETIC DISK DRIVE. It reads magnetized bits on a magnetic disk and converts them to electronic pulses.

PAPER TAPE READER. It reads holes punched into paper tape and converts them to electronic pulses.

OPTICAL CHARACTER AND MARK-SENSE READER. It senses handwritten, typewritten, or printed character forms, or pencilled-in bubbles on a page and converts them to electronic pulses.

CONSOLE TYPEWRITER. It converts keystrokes from a typewriter into electronic pulses.

Central Processing System

The most complex and powerful part of the computer is the central processing unit (CPU) or processor. The major functions of the CPU are

1. To control the overall operation of the computer and coordinate its parts.
2. To perform arithmetical calculations and make logical decisions.
3. To store the programs and data being processed (primary storage).

The relationship of the CPU to the input and output devices is shown in Figure 6.4. Card readers, punches, line printers, etc. are wired to the CPU. Data may flow between the input and output machines and register and core primary units. The control unit performs a switching activity directing the flow of data from core storage and registers to the input/output units. (Core storage and registers are devices which store strings of electronic pulses during processing; they are discussed in detail later.)

PHYSICAL APPEARANCE. As shown in Figure 6.5, the CPU resembles the other components of the computer system in size and appearance. Often a desk and typewriter unit, called the console typewriter, is attached. On the control panel, or console, at the front of the CPU are sense lights, buttons, and switches. The sense lights show the status of the machine at all times and indicate the contents of some of the storage locations.

The CPU is sometimes called the mainframe. The related input and output devices—such as card readers, line printers, and punches—which provide the

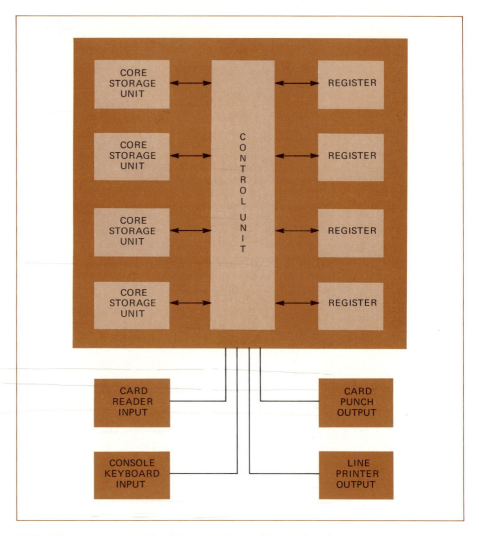

FIGURE 6.4   RELATIONSHIP OF THE CPU TO I/O

CPU with outside communications are called peripheral devices. Peripherals are any associated input or output devices used with a computer, but not including the CPU. The abbreviation I/O is often used to refer collectively to input and output devices.

Internally, the CPU is usually a solid-state device composed of transistors, wires, and integrated and monolithic circuits. (A monolithic circuit consists of many microscopic electronic components manufactured on a small piece of glass or crystal. See Figure 6.6.) It also contains several thousand minute magnetic storage devices that hold the program and the data for processing. The circuitry is designed to move, store, and manipulate data electronically

FIGURE 6.5 CPU CONSOLE

and has no moving parts—only the electronic impulses move about inside the CPU. Its major parts are diagramed in Figure 6.7. The functions of these parts are discussed below.

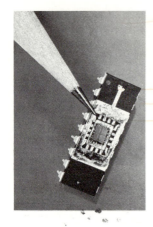
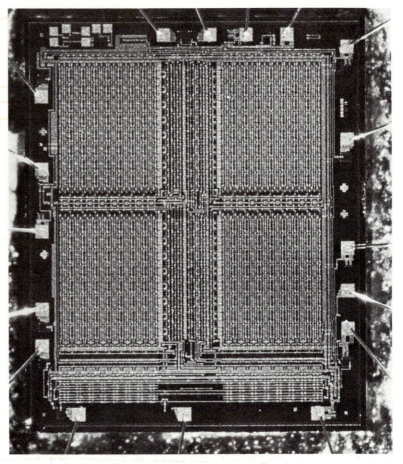

FIGURE 6.6 MONOLITHIC STORAGE CIRCUIT

Functions of the CPU

CONTROL.   Part of the CPU circuitry is designed to monitor and supervise the operation of the entire computer. It calls upon the card reader, line printer, tape drives, etc. The control unit provides a system for storing and remembering the instructions in programs and opens and closes circuits which feed data to and from storage.

The control unit is similar in function to the central switchboard at the telephone company, or in a large business establishment. Control is effected through the wires that connect all parts of the system to the central control board.

Another aspect of the control function of the CPU is governed by the problem program. The problem program is written to solve a specific, local problem. This program is entered into the computer, usually with the related

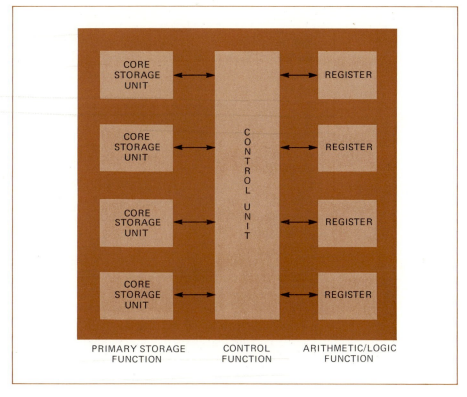

FIGURE 6.7   CPU

data, and instructs the machine to perform mathematical calculations, read data cards, write information on the line printer, store data, etc. The problem program is often called the program deck and the collection of data to be processed is called the data set or data deck.

ARITHMETIC AND LOGIC.   Another section of the CPU is designed to perform mathematical calculations, compare numeric and nonnumeric values, and make decisions. (These jobs are done with sophisticated electronic circuitry, called gates and registers.) Both arithmetic and logical decisions can be made. For example, the computer can branch to one of three circuits, or paths, depending on whether the value being tested is greater than, equal to, or less than another value.

Arithmetic is performed by reading numbers into temporary holding stations called registers. Numbers from several registers may be added, subtracted, or operated upon. After calculations are completed, data is either returned to computer storage or output.

PRIMARY STORAGE.   Primary storage, often called core storage, is another function of the CPU. This section of the CPU is composed of millions of magnetic storage devices—magnetic cores, flux rings, or cores printed on thin film.

Primary storage is a reusable, fast storage medium, directly accessible by the control unit. Primary storage capacity varies from one computer to another, ranging from as few as 4,000 bytes to over several million bytes. A byte is a group of bits (pulses) which form a character—number or letter. Under normal conditions, one alphabetic character, or two numeric characters, are stored in a byte. Primary storage is sometimes divided into parts, or sections, as shown in Figure 6.7. Thus the control unit can allocate parts of its core capacity to different tasks, and each part can function without interfering with the others. On some computers, core is expandable—additional storage units can be purchased as the need arises. Primary storage is most often used for storing data which must be called in frequently, such as the program under execution and the data being operated upon.

Secondary Storage System

Because the primary storage capacity of most computers is limited, the CPU calls upon its secondary storage system to handle and store large amounts of data. This supplementary storage capacity is usually provided by tape and disk drive systems. Secondary storage allows billions of additional characters or pieces of data to be stored until needed.

Most computers systems use a combination of primary and secondary storage media. Data can be fed to and from primary storage in only a few billionths of a second. In secondary storage, on the other hand, it takes several thousandths of a second to retrieve a piece of data. Secondary storage is used for large files of data which need not be accessed continually, such as accounts receivable, accounts payable, inventory, and payroll records.

Output System

The output system is designed to report the results of calculations and processing from the CPU. Reporting and outputting may be done on a line printer, card punch, a cathode ray tube, or audio unit. The objective of the output system is to convert electronic pulses from the CPU into documents, cards, or a visual display, giving the results of the processed data in a usable and permanent form. The form of the output is chosen for suitability for input into other machines, or for easy readability and comprehension by people. The most common modes of computer output are:

LINE PRINTER. Electronic pulses from the CPU are converted into readable characters on a printed page.

CARD PUNCH. Electronic pulses are converted into a code on a punched card.

MAGNETIC TAPE DRIVE. Electronic pulses are recorded as magnetized areas on magnetic tape. This tape may be stored or used as input data into other machines.

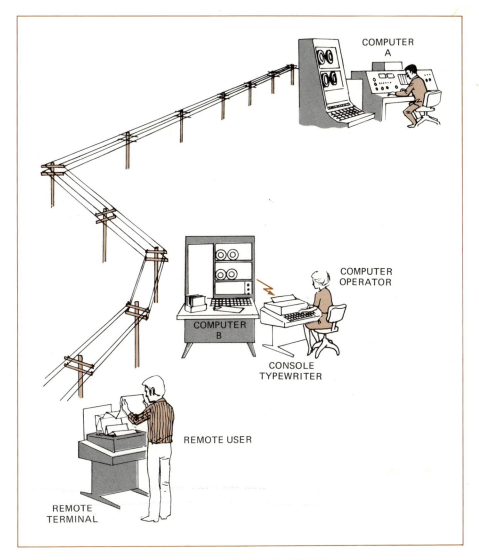

FIGURE 6.8   TELECOMMUNICATIONS NETWORK

MAGNETIC DISK DRIVE.   Electronic pulses are stored as magnetized areas on a magnetic disk. The disk can be stored or placed on another computer.

PAPER TAPE PUNCH.   Electronic pulses are converted into holes punched in a roll of paper tape.

AUDIO RESPONSE DEVICE.   Electronic pulses are converted into spoken

THIS IS A RECORDING . . .

The story may be apocryphal, but reportedly the ultimate in computer confrontation occurred here.

A computer was programmed to report its own malfunctioning to a serviceman. The equipment went on the blink one night and called the serviceman, who had moved. The telephone company's computer responded with a recorded message that the telephone was disconnected. The computer broke the circuit and redialed the disconnected number, and the telephone replied again with the recorded message. And the computer broke the circuit . . .

SOURCE Abstracted from "What Hath Babbage Wrought Department," "Hello, Hello, Good-by, Good-by . . . ," Henry G. Owen, *Modern Data*, May, 1971, p. 54.

words or audio responses. These responses are stored on tape. The unit is equipped with a tape or drum head, amplifier, and loudspeaker.

VIDEO OR CATHODE RAY TUBE (CRT). Electronic pulses are converted into a graphic display on a cathode ray tube. Drawings, illustrations, and tables can be displayed.

CONSOLE TYPEWRITER. Electronic pulses from the CPU are converted into typewritten characters on the typewriter attached to the console.

PLOTTER. Electronic pulses are converted to graphic designs, plots, or line drawings on a sheet of paper.

Output is an essential step in the data processing cycle. Unless output is provided to the user in some way, the cycle has little value.

Telecommunications System

Another subsystem of the computer can be a telecommunications network, shown in Figure 6.8. Telecommunications networks vary in complexity and purpose from one computer to another. They are not always tangible devices, such as a card punch, but often are a network of wires, codes, and messages. Telecommunications systems have two real uses: first, they may enable two or more computers to be tied together into a unit, increasing the available CPU power and capacity. This is called a multiprocessing system (see Chapter 22). Second, they facilitate communication between the machine and its users. They allow remote users to access the system, both to transmit data to the CPU and to receive data from it. The following are typical computer communications systems and their functions:

MULTIPROCESSING. The CPU's of two or more machines can be tied together to increase available primary storage capacity. In this arrangement, several processors are employed under an integrated control to execute programs.

REMOTE COMMUNICATIONS. Data can be transmitted between the CPU and remote terminals, permitting access from distant points. Telecommunications systems are in the form of telephone and telegraph lines and microwave transmission systems.

MODERN COMPUTER SYSTEMS

The systems described below are typical of general classes of systems in industry. Since improvements and changes in design are frequently made in computer systems, these examples should be considered only as illustrations representative of general classes.

"You'll be all right as long as you remember it's just another tool."

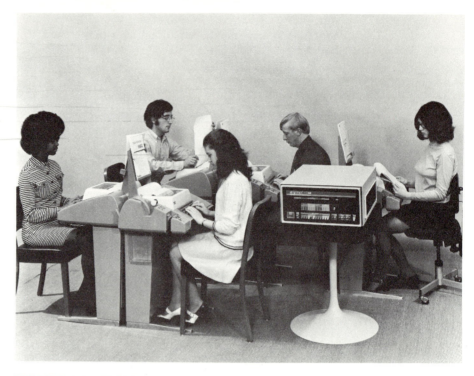

FIGURE 6.9   DIGITAL EQUIPMENT CORPORATION, PDP-8/e

PDP-8, Digital Equipment Corporation

The computer shown in Figure 6.9 is a general-purpose minicomputer. It is a desktop device, $10\frac{1}{2}'' \times 19'' \times 24''$ and weighs about 100 pounds. The principal input/output device is an ASR 33 Teletype Terminal and several may be connected. Primary storage capacity is 4K (1K equals 1,024 characters) bytes. The computer can be programmed in BASIC and COBOL languages. The complete system, including one or more teletype terminals, costs approximately $13,000.

Varian 620/L, Varian Data Machines

The Varian 620/L is a minicomputer approximately 21 inches wide. Primary storage is 4K bytes. The central processor can be connected to paper tape, magnetic tape, or card readers, and can service a line printer or digital plotter. Programming for the Varian 620/L can be done in Assembler, FORTRAN IV, BASIC, and RPG IV languages. Basic system price is $10,000.

System/3, IBM Corporation

Figure 6.10 shows a small, general-purpose computer, with 8K bytes of primary storage capacity. The basic system includes a central processing unit, line printer, data recorder, and multifunction card unit. A magnetic ink character reader, disk storage drive, and video display terminal can be added. The System/3 is a card-oriented computer which processes the 96-column IBM card. Programming can be done in Assembler and RPG II

FIGURE 6.10   IBM CORPORATION, SYSTEM/3

FIGURE 6.11   SPERRY RAND, UNIVAC 9200 SYSTEM

languages. The System/3 has several utility programs to perform sorts, merges, and other card manipulating functions. Monthly rental costs range upward from $1,000. A card sorting machine is available (IBM 5486) which will sort up to 1,500 cards per minute.

UNIVAC 9200, Sperry Rand Corporation

The computer in Figure 6.11 is a small, card-oriented computer. Monthly rental costs begin at $1,000. Main storage has 8K bytes and is expandable. The system includes a card reader which can read 400 cards or punch 200 cards per minute. A ball printer will print up to 250 lines per minute. The system will also support paper tape units and an optical document reader. Programming for the 9200 may be done in RPG, Assembler, COBOL, and FORTRAN languages.

System/360, Model 30, IBM Corporation

The computer shown in Figure 6.12 is a medium-sized, general-purpose computer system. It consists of a central processing unit with console, line printers, card readers and punches, and disk storage drives. Up to 64K bytes may be held in primary storage. Many additional disk drive devices, magnetic tape drives, printers, card readers, and video display devices can be connected. The system leases for approximately $12,000 per month and can be programmed in COBOL, FORTRAN, RPG, Assembler, PL/I, and other languages.

FIGURE 6.12   IBM CORPORATION, SYSTEM/360, MODEL 30

System B3500, Burroughs Corporation

The system illustrated in Figure 6.13 is a medium-sized, general-purpose computer designed for many different business, engineering, and scientific applications. It can hold up to 500K bytes in primary storage. A large number of input/output units, including card readers, punches, paper tape readers, line printers, optical character readers, and magnetic ink character readers may be attached. Additional secondary storage devices, including magnetic tape or disk devices may be connected. Programming may be done in FORTRAN, COBOL, Assembler, and RPG languages. The system leases for $18,000 and up per month.

Sigma 9, Xerox Data Systems

Sigma 9, shown in Figure 6.14, is a large, general-purpose computer system which provides time-sharing capability for as many as 128 users simultaneously. The primary memory will hold up to two million bytes of data. Many different kinds of input/output units and secondary storage units may be connected simultaneously to the system, including line printers, magnetic tape and drum storage, graphic display devices, and even remote batch terminals. The Sigma 9 can be programmed in many languages including COBOL, FORTRAN, BASIC, and Assembler. The monthly rental price varies with the particular system installation, but may run more than $100,000

FIGURE 6.13   BURROUGHS CORPORATION, SYSTEM B2500/B3500

monthly. The Sigma 9 is the largest of the Xerox systems and provides the maximum storage capability and processing speed.

UNIVAC 1110, Sperry Rand Corporation

The UNIVAC 1110, shown in Figure 6.15, is one of the largest, most flexible systems in operation and has a basic primary storage capacity of 65,000K bytes, expandable to many millions. The system includes a central processor that can support numerous input/output devices, including card readers, punches, video display terminals, and even complete remote job entry systems. From these remote processing terminals, jobs may be entered as cards and the results received back on high-speed line printers. The system supports time sharing and multiprogramming. Programming may be done in many languages, including COBOL, FORTRAN V, and Assembler.

PROBLEM SOLVING

The human organism and the computer differ in the methods they use to solve a problem. Generally, humans attempt to solve problems in an "all-at-once" fashion. They don't spell out all the procedures before actually beginning to execute them and often carry out the first steps before structuring the last. There are advantages to this procedure. The plan for solving a problem becomes intermixed with and responsive to the results. This kind of activity allows humans to solve problems rapidly with creativity and insight.

Computer Problem Solving

The computer cannot solve a problem in this way; it must first be given a clear, explicit set of instructions. It must be told where to find the required information, what logic to use, what calculations to perform, and in what form to output the answer.

A computer programmer studies the problem or procedure the machine is to process and prepares a plan of action called a flowchart. He decides which steps the machine must take to reach the results and specifies the form of input and output. He then converts this plan of action into a set of steps in a programming language.

These instructions are prepared for input to the computer by keypunching into cards or paper tape or by recording on magnetic tape. The set of instructions, ready for input, is called a source program, program, a program deck or a problem program. The source program is entered into the computer via an input device which converts it to electronic impulses.

Computers can only process data in machine language (1's and 0's). Instructions coded in any other language must be translated into machine language for processing. This is done with a compiler or assembler. This translated set of instructions is called an *object deck* or *object module*.

The compiler is a program written by a manufacturer to translate instructions into the machine language for the computer. The compiler is

FIGURE 6.14   XEROX DATA SYSTEMS, SIGMA 9

FIGURE 6.15   SPERRY RAND, UNIVAC 1110

capable of generating many lines of detailed instructions in machine language from each coded statement. A separate compiler is required for each language and each variation of a language.

An assembler program is used to translate Assembler language into machine language. Each type of computer has its own Assembler language and, therefore, its own assembler program. Assemblers are less complicated than compilers and usually are capable of generating only one line of machine language for each line of code. This, of course, requires the programmer to spell out many more processing details in writing his program.

Compilers vary in size and the amount of CPU primary storage they use. For example, the compilers for FORTRAN can use as few as 12,000 bytes or more than 40,000 bytes. Since a different compiler is required for each language, most computer installations have several available.

COMPILATION.   The CPU calls a compiler for the particular language from secondary storage, and loads it into core storage. The compiler checks each coded instruction to see that it follows the rules for that language, uses proper punctuation, spelling, etc. All acceptable instructions are translated into machine language and stored on a disk or cards. This process is called compilation. Usually the machine will print out each instruction on the line printer, noting any errors. If no coding errors (or only minor ones) are present, and all instructions in the program have been translated and stored, the problem program is said to have compiled and is now ready for execution.

EXECUTION.   Execution is the final step in processing the problem. It is the phase in which the CPU follows the step-by-step instructions in the stored program. As directed, it will read in data from the card reader or tape or disk drive, print out headings on the line printer, perform mathematical calculations, make logical decisions, rearrange data, control movement of data between secondary and primary storage, and output results.

Most problem programs involve operating on a collection of data. For example, a program that prepares a company's payroll operates on the file of employees' payroll records. This file is the data set. When running the job, the data set is entered in the computer after the problem program has been compiled and loaded. The combination of a problem program and one or more data sets is called a job.

One problem program can execute on many data sets consecutively. This is an important advantage of the computer. Once written, the program can be saved and used dozens of times. For each run, the program is entered into the computer followed by the data set.

Stored Program   It is the computer's ability to follow the instructions of the stored problem program without further human intervention or direction that gives it a degree of self-direction. But it is limited to following the steps in the program. It cannot examine its own output, decide something is wrong, and change the procedure it is following.

This ability has advantages and disadvantages. If the programmer has made an error in procedural logic, the results outputted by the machine may be incorrect, sometimes without the programmer realizing it. On the other hand, once a program is known to be logically sound and accurate in coding, the programmer is assured that the procedural steps and level of accuracy will not vary from one run to another.

The stored program has other major advantages. A program can be written and tested before the data to be processed is available. The programmer uses symbolic names to refer to the quantities he will manipulate in his program. For example, his instructions could tell the computer that the values punched in columns 30–35 of the records in the card reader would be the amount an employee has earned, referred to as EARN in his program and that the employees' deductions, called DEDUC, would be found in the third field of each record on a magnetic tape. He could then instruct the computer to subtract DEDUC from EARN and print out PAY on the check form in the line printer. The use of symbolic names gives the computer a great deal of power and flexibility.

KEY TERMS

System	Primary storage
Input	Mainframe
Processing	Peripheral equipment
Output	I/O
Memory	Problem program
Hardware	Data deck
Software	Core storage
Central processing	Secondary storage
unit (CPU)	Telecommunications
Subsystem	Compiler
Console	Assembler program

EXERCISES

1. Draw a schematic diagram showing the related parts of the computer. Show input and output.
2. List five common external memory aids used by humans.
3. How does software differ from hardware?
4. What do all computer input systems have in common?
5. What do all computer output systems have in common?
6. Draw a schematic diagram showing the relationship of the parts of the CPU.
7. How does primary storage differ from secondary storage?
8. What is the function of the telecommunications system?

9. How do the steps a computer might use in solving a problem differ from those an individual might use?
10. What is the function of the compiler?
11. Select a simple mathematical or business problem, such as calculating the annual interest on a savings account. Perform the calculations manually and list the steps you take.
12. Study a running program provided by your instructor or other source. Identify the problem program and data set, if one is present.
13. Select several documents. List the ways in which data from these documents could be inputted to a computer.
14. Define peripheral device and CPU and explain how they differ in function.
15. What kind of data is usually stored by a CPU in its primary storage?

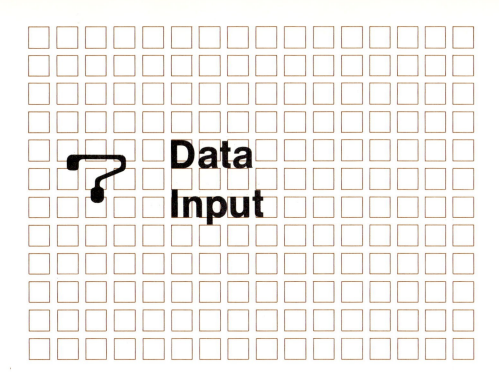

Data Input

The function of the computer's input system is to convert data into a form that can be processed by the central processing unit. Data input machines convert the holes in paper tape or cards, the magnetic areas on tape, or the optical images on forms into direct-current pulses. These pulses are routed to the CPU through a system of buffers, control units, and channels.

DATA INPUT MACHINES

On-Line Input Devices Modern computers receive data from a variety of input devices, such as card readers, paper and magnetic tape readers, optical character readers, and console typewriters. All are wired directly to the CPU and transmit electronic images, or pulses, of the data from a record. On-line input means that data from the record enters the CPU directly from the input device. (See Figure 7.1.) The electronic pulses leave the input devices one at a time, forming a pulse train.

Timing is important in data entry. Data must be made available to the CPU at the proper points in the processing cycle. Control units regulate the timing of the input and output machines, removing this burden from the CPU. Their standard wiring arrangement permits different I/O devices to be coupled to the CPU, or more than one input device to be connected. (See Figure 7.2.)

141

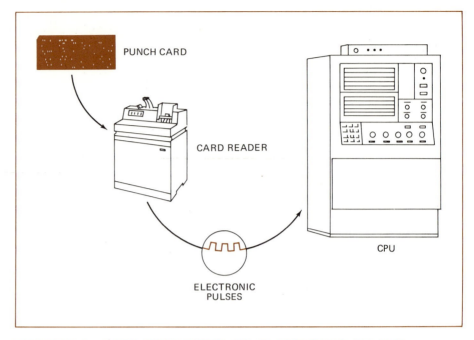

FIGURE 7.1   DATA CONVERTED TO ELECTRONIC PULSES

FIGURE 7.2   CONTROL UNIT

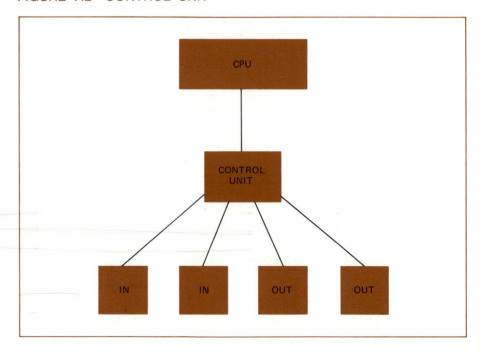

Control units either stand alone as a separate unit or are part of the CPU. They are signaled by the input device when the data is ready for input. Upon receiving another signal from the CPU, they feed in the data in phase, at the proper speed.

Examples   Below are examples of typical on-line input devices.

IBM 2501 CARD READER.   This machine, shown in Figure 7.3, converts data from punch cards to electronic pulses. It is equipped with a card hopper, read station, photocells, a light source, and a card stacker. The machine will read 1,000 cards per minute. The card hopper holds 1,200 cards and feeds one card at a time from the bottom of the stack. It is linked to the CPU by a control unit.

A signal from the control unit initiates the reading cycle. An electric motor drives the card feeding mechanism. First, a card is moved from the hopper

FIGURE 7.3 IBM 2501 CARD READER

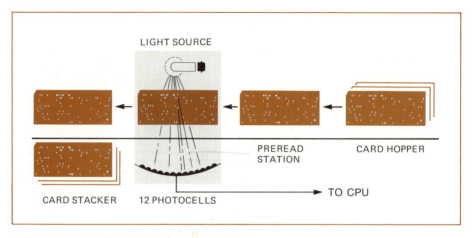

FIGURE 7.4 IBM 2501 CARD PATH

and positioned in a preread station. (See Figure 7.4.) The card then moves to the read station, where one column at a time is read. A light source focuses a beam on the column at the read station. The light beam passes through any holes present in that column and activates one or more of the 12 photocells (corresponding in position to the rows and zones of the column) beneath it. As each photocell is activated, it creates an electronic pulse. If no hole is present in the column, no light passes through, and no photocells are activated.

The columns are read serially, character by character, until all columns across the card have been read. The machine is equipped with an error-detection check. It will determine if cards are properly punched, if columns contain too many punches, or if punches do not agree with a valid card code.

This machine is representative of the photocell type of card reader. Other card readers use sensing brushes to generate pulses. These sensing brushes make electronic contact with a roller below the card, through the holes punched in the column.

IBM 2671 PAPER TAPE READER. This device (and the IBM 2822 Paper Tape Reader Control), shown in Figure 7.5, is designed to convert holes in paper tape to electronic pulses, and to relay these to the CPU. The machine reads data from paper tape at up to 1,000 characters per second.

The IBM 2671 feeds the tape past a photoelectric device which senses the holes in the tape and converts them to electronic pulses. Several different codes are used for punching data into paper tape. (Figure 8.9 shows the code used on the eight-channel paper tape. Details of data representation and other codes are discussed in another chapter.)

FIGURE 7.5   IBM 2671 PAPER TAPE READER AND
            IBM 2822 PAPER TAPE READER CONTROL

IBM 1287 OPTICAL CHARACTER READER.   This optical input device,
illustrated in Figure 7.6, is representative of optical character reader (OCR)
machines. It reads data optically and converts it to electronic pulses. The IBM
1287 is designed to read handwritten or printed numbers and special
characters from checks, orders, cash register tapes, adding machine tapes,
utility bills, telephone bills, tickets, etc.
   The IBM 1287 reads data from a page that can vary in size from $2\frac{1}{4}'' \times 3''$
to $5\frac{9}{10}'' \times 9''$. About 550 documents, size $2\frac{1}{4}'' \times 3''$, can be read in one
minute. It can also read cash register and adding machine tapes up to 200
feet long at the rate of 3,300 lines per minute.
   Documents to be scanned move from the document hopper, past a
separator mechanism to the aligner, and then to the read station. (See Figure
7.7.) After a document has been read, it is sent to one of the three stackers.
   The aligner positions the document for entry into the reading station. The
document moves into the read station, where it is again positioned and
scanned with a beam of light from a cathode ray tube. As the beam moves

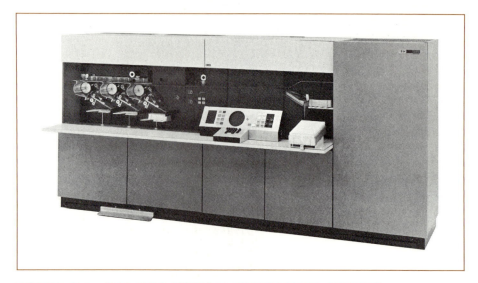

FIGURE 7.6   IBM 1287 OPTICAL CHARACTER READER

FIGURE 7.7   ELEMENTS OF AN OPTICAL CHARACTER READER

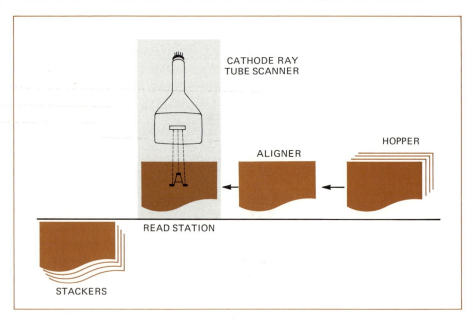

FIGURE 7.8   HANDWRITTEN CHARACTERS READ BY IBM 1287

back and forth across the page, images on the document reflect varying amounts of light. Light from an image is reflected back to a sensing mechanism which detects minute differences. These differences are converted into electronic pulses to be input to the CPU.

IBM 1287's that read cash register and adding machine tapes have input and take-up spindles to hold the rolls of tape. The tape is threaded from the input spindle, through the reading chamber, and onto the take-up spindle. The machine scans six inches of tape at a time.

Figure 7.8 illustrates handwritten numeric characters the 1287 can read optically. This is a convenient means of recording data in the field without keypunching. The salesclerk, secretary, or stock clerk can write each character in a separate block on specially printed forms, observing a few simple rules for letter shaping.

In addition to handwriting, the machine can read typewriter faces and several printed optical character type fonts. The machine can be programmed to read selected areas on a bill or order form. It can read a price column, skip down to the total, read a printed form number and then a handprinted message.

FIGURE 7.9 IBM 1419 MAGNETIC INK CHARACTER READER

IBM 1419 MAGNETIC INK CHARACTER READER. Figure 7.9 illustrates a device designed to read data printed in magnetic ink on a page. It can read magnetically inscribed checks, deposit slips, bills, etc. The machine is equipped with a document hopper, read station, and 13 document stacking pockets.

Up to 1,600 documents can be read per minute and sorted into one of the 13 receiving pockets. The machine will read documents of different sizes and thicknesses, such as a collection of checks from many different banks.

Documents to be input must be printed using special magnetic ink and a specific type style. Figure 7.10 shows the layout of the check form approved by the American Banking Association.

As the documents containing data to be inputted move through the IBM 1419, they are scanned for the special ink images. The magnetic images on the page affect a magnetic field in the machine and are recorded as electronic impulses ready for input.

IBM 1052 PRINTER-KEYBOARD. Another common group of computer input devices are the printer-keyboards, or console typewriters. The IBM 1052, shown in Figure 7.11, is representative of keyboard-to-electronic-pulse input devices.

FIGURE 7.10   APPROVED CHECK FORM

ALICE and GARY GOLDMAN
1281 Blair Avenue
Long Beach, New York

No.

T

1-679
260

19

PAY TO THE
ORDER OF

$

DOLLARS

The Merchants Bank of New York

757 THIRD AVENUE
NEW YORK, N. Y.

⑆0 260⑈0679⑉: ⑈6 012345⑉

FIGURE 7.11   PRINTER KEYBOARD   *Console typewriter (slow)*

Console typewriters are usually located on the console table and attached directly to the CPU. The keyboard is similar to that of an ordinary typewriter and has rows of numbers, letters, and special characters.

The IBM 1052 includes a pin feed platen which feeds paper up to $13\frac{1}{8}$ inches wide. It prints at about 15.5 characters per second.

A group of status lights on the machine inform the operator of its readiness to receive input data. As keys are struck, the machine converts each keystroke to electrical pulses, which are fed to the CPU, and simultaneously types the message on the platen.

The console typewriter is the operator's means of communicating with the computer. The operator uses it to direct the function of the CPU and to receive messages from it. It is a means of outputting as well as inputting data. This permits communication between the CPU and the operator regarding a program, computer status, data input for a program, or instructions on how to handle an error condition.

The IBM 1052, however, is a very slow means of data input and is usually reserved for small amounts of data. It is sometimes used to input single lines of data. For example, in updating a file, a record can be found and typed out on the console typewriter by the CPU. Then the operator can type a corrected line and instruct the machine to replace it in the file.

Off-Line Input Devices
Off-line input devices record data first onto magnetic tape or disk from a keyboard. Then the tape or disk is placed on an on-line input device, and the data is transmitted to the CPU. Key-to-magnetic-tape and disk systems are a fast, economical means of off-line data input.

Examples
Below are some examples of typical off-line input devices.

DATA ACTION MAGNETIC DATA INSCRIBER. Data is recorded on magnetic tape from a machine similar in appearance to a keypunch. However, this machine records on a cartridge of magnetic tape, instead of on punched cards. A plastic cartridge encloses and protects the tape, and provides for easy handling. Cartridges can be easily stored and are reusable. This key-to-tape system is shown in Figure 7.12.

As keys are depressed, 20 characters per inch are recorded on magnetic tape. As each character is typed, it is displayed on a screen before the operator. An end-of-record mark separates variable-length records, which may be as long as 720 characters. A record counter keeps track of the number of records entered on each tape.

To verify data, the tape is backed up to the beginning and the source document rekeyboarded. An error is corrected by backspacing and rekeyboarding.

TAPE POOLER. Data recorded on magnetic tape cartridges at 20 characters per inch must be condensed to 800 to 1,600 characters per inch for input to a computer. A tape pooler, shown in Figure 7.13, is a specialized machine

FIGURE 7.12 KEY-TO-TAPE SYSTEM

FIGURE 7.13 TAPE POOLER

ECOLOGY:
MAN AND THE COMPUTER

A computer with a long memory is short-ening the time it takes to get vital river in-formation to flood-conscious residents of the Ohio River Valley.

As each storm approaches, the computer races through its electronic memory, re-lates current observations to historical in-formation, and pinpoints potential flood areas. In minutes it can provide accurate and timely river forecasts and flood warn-ings to the millions of people who live near the banks of the Ohio and its tributaries.

Previously, a hydrologist assigned the task of predicting a flood wave had to use complex charts and tables to determine the combined impact of tributaries on the main stream. And he then had to write his an-swers in longhand.

The continuous flow of new data is com-bined with the cumulative rainfall history of 2,000 previous storms over the river basin to produce an index of soil moisture—a critical element in flood forecasting. A complete river report is transmitted by teletypewriters to offices throughout the river basin for dissemination to the public.

SOURCE   Abstracted from "Silver Lining in the Smog" *Data Processor*, February 1968, p. 15.

that converts widely spaced characters on a magnetic tape cartridge to tightly spaced characters on magnetic tape. The tape pooler can handle variable-length records up to 720 characters per record.

CMC18 KEY PROCESSING SYSTEM.   The CMC18 Key Processing System, shown in Figure 7.14, is a keyboard-to-magnetic-disk system. Data is entered onto magnetic disk packs from one or more keyboards. The disk pack is then placed on an on-line disk drive for input to the CPU.

Up to 32 keyboard units, called keystations, can be connected directly to one disk storage drive and operated simultaneously through a control unit. Each keyboard operator has full control of data input and works independently of the operators at other keystations.

Keyboarding source documents directly onto a disk eliminates the need for a pooler to condense the characters for computer input. As many as seven million characters can be stored on a single disk pack.

THE PROBLEM OF SINGLE ACCESS

Early computers had only one input and one output device. A pair of electrical wires connected to the CPU served as the route for both the input and output pulses. (See Figure 7.15.) To feed in data, the input device (usually a tape reader) was connected by a switch to these wires. When the time came to print out data, the switch disconnected the input device and connected the wires to the output unit. This set of wires was called an I/O channel.

"EVER WONDER WHAT WE MAKE HERE?"

FIGURE 7.14   KEY-TO-DISK SYSTEM

FIGURE 7.15   SINGLE I/O CHANNEL

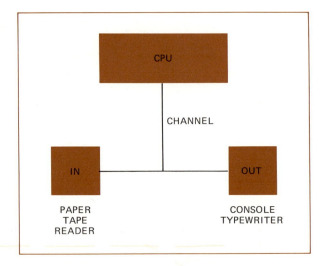

With only one input and one output device to serve, a single I/O channel was sufficient. But the amount of data that could be processed was limited by the speed of the I/O devices. As computers became more complex, the CPU became capable of processing data much more rapidly than the data could be transmitted. But because the CPU was idle while data was being read into storage, much of the increased processing capacity was wasted.

This input bottleneck can be illustrated as follows. A business office served by only one elevator is located on the tenth floor of a large metropolitan office building. Regardless of the number of employees and the speed at which they work, only those customers that gain access to the tenth floor by the single elevator can be serviced. If more elevators are installed, more customers can enter and leave, increasing the throughput. An even greater volume of transactions can be processed if a system of scheduling is available. In fact, some office buildings employ individuals to regulate elevator traffic.

Multiple Inputs
To increase input/output capability, computer designers developed a multiple I/O system. At first several devices, such as tape or card readers, were wired to the CPU through a single channel. Each device was switched in and out of the system manually, by a selector switch. (See Figure 7.16.) The number and variety of devices connected to the system increased the computer's flexibility, but did not improve throughput. The total number of jobs read in or out was still limited by the single channel.

Computer engineers then added more input and output channels between

FIGURE 7.16 MULTIPLE INPUT WITH SELECTOR SWITCH

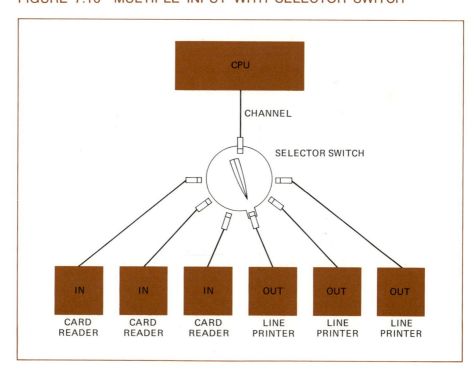

the CPU and the I/O devices. Figure 7.17 shows a CPU with four channels. Two card readers are permanently connected to channels 0 and 1. Two line printers are permanently connected to channels 2 and 3.

FIGURE 7.17   MULTIPLE CHANNELS
(SIMULTANEOUS OPERATION)

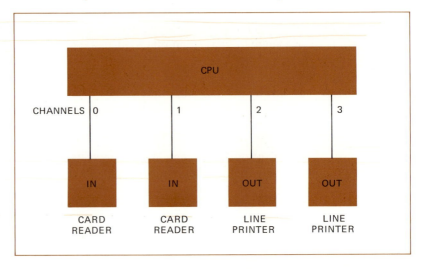

All channels can operate simultaneously, allowing the computer to receive the data from more than one job at a time. The input channels can be feeding in data from different jobs, while the output channels are printing out the results of previous jobs. The CPU keeps the data from one job from being intermixed with that from another. This system greatly increases the throughput.

The next step was to have each channel serve more than one I/O device for increased flexibility. This way, two tape readers (or card reader and tape reader) could input data at one time. And a line printer and a tape drive (or two line printers) could output simultaneously.

omit

Channel Address

As the number of input and output devices on a system increased, a problem of identifying each unit arose. The mechanical selector switch was replaced by an electronic switching arrangement and an addressing system. Each I/O unit on the system is given a unique number, called a channel address, composed of channel number, control unit number, and device number.

The CPU in Figure 7.18 has 15 I/O devices, located on four separate channels. Each channel contains a control unit between the CPU and the input/output device. The function of the control unit is described later. Each channel has a number (0 to 3), each control unit has a number (0 to 1), and each I/O unit is referred to by an alphabetic character (A to C) or a number (such as 181).

The specific address for a given unit is composed of its channel number, control unit number, and device number. Figure 7.18 identifies several devices on the system by these addresses.

FIGURE 7.18   CHANNEL ADDRESSING

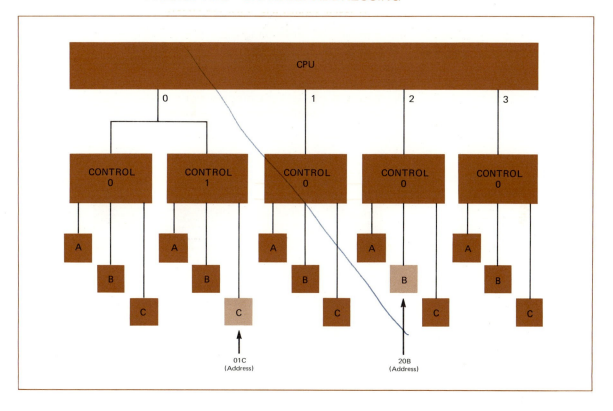

For example,

CHANNEL	CONTROL UNIT	DEVICE NUMBER
0	1	C
2	0	B

This system of addressing allows a programmer to identify which of several hundred devices connected to a CPU he wants to use. He can also reassign devices to meet the needs of his program.

Channel Scheduler

The channel scheduler is a system used by a computer to keep track of which input/output devices are busy and what jobs are waiting to use them. It also starts the input and output operations. When the end of the file is reached or an error is detected, it will stop the input/output operations. If the channel scheduler detects an error, it will try to correct it, print out an error message on the console, or terminate the job without processing it. Then it will start the next job waiting in line.

Queuing   A system can become overloaded if its input/output or storage devices have more jobs assigned to them than they can handle. When the entire system is in use, the channel scheduler places waiting jobs in a line until a device is available. It has provisions for keeping track of jobs and processes them on a first-come, first-served basis. This waiting line is called a queue.

Sometimes several jobs being processed at the same time will specify the same I/O device, while others wait unused. This slows down throughput. The channel scheduler may override the programmer's device specification and adjust I/O assignments to suit the load. It electronically connects input and

waiting line for overloading

FIGURE 7.19   CHANNEL SCHEDULING (BEFORE)

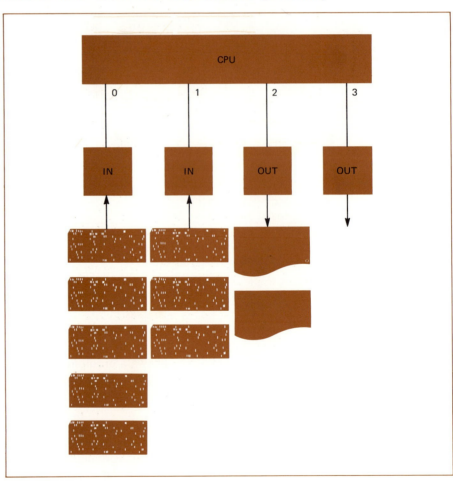

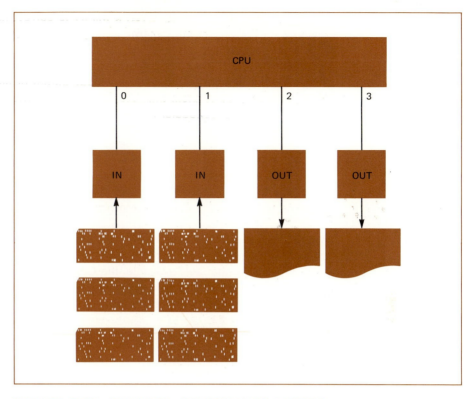

FIGURE 7.20   CHANNEL SCHEDULING (AFTER)

output devices to the channels to allow maximum utility of the channels and the CPU.

In these instances, the channel scheduler is performing the same function as an elevator scheduler in a busy office building who routes passengers to different elevators. He sees that some cars are going up, some down, that none are idle while people wait, and that none leave only partly full during peak hours. He also adjusts the load for morning and evening conditions.

Figure 7.19 shows ten jobs to be input and output. Five jobs are waiting to be input to channel 0, three to channel 1. Two jobs are waiting to be output on channel 2, while channel 3 is idle. The channel scheduler can override the I/O address specified by the programmers and assign the loads to gain maximum throughput. In this case, it could assign one of the input jobs from channel 0 to channel 1; one of the output jobs from channel 2 to channel 3. (See Figure 7.20.) The output and input channels now have balanced loads.

FIXED CHANNELS.   A fixed channel is permanently assigned to a given group of input or output devices. In Figure 7.21 two input devices and two output devices are permanently wired to the four channels. They cannot be changed unless the system engineer and installers rewire the system.

FLOATING CHANNELS. Floating channels are not permanently wired to a single group of devices. They can be assigned to any group of devices depending upon the demands of the system. This arrangement greatly increases the I/O throughput.

Suppose, as in Figure 7.21, four jobs are to be input to the system. With fixed channels, the two input channels have waiting lines (queues), while the two output channels remain idle. If the channels were floating, as in Figure 7.22, all four channels could be assigned to input duties. As a result, data could flow to the CPU from four input devices at one time. After processing, the same four channels could be reassigned to output duties.

Overlapping   Just as throughput increases when several I/O devices operate at once, it also increases when all portions of the CPU function at once. With several input and output channels available, the CPU can input, process, and output data simultaneously. This is called overlapping.

To illustrate the principle of overlapping, suppose that three jobs are to be run as in Figure 7.23.

FIGURE 7.21   FIXED CHANNELS

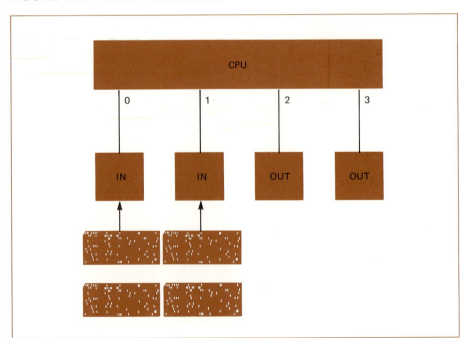

FIGURE 7.22 FLOATING CHANNELS

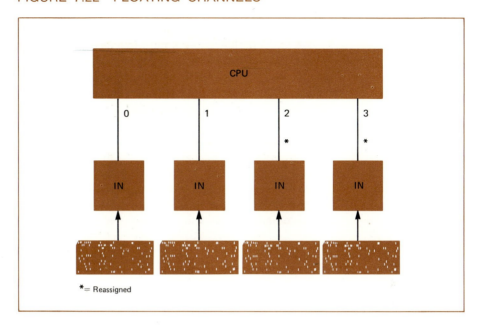

*= Reassigned

FIGURE 7.23 OVERLAP PROCESSING

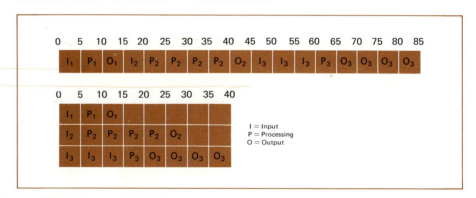

I = Input
P = Processing
O = Output

	Input time	Processing time	Output time	Total time per job
Job 1	5 min	5 min	5 min	15 min
Job 2	5 min	20 min	5 min	30 min
Job 3	15 min	5 min	20 min	40 min
		Total time to run all three jobs:		85 min

Without overlapping it would take a total of 85 minutes to run the three jobs. Job 1 would require 15 minutes to input, process, and output; job 2, 30 minutes; and job 3, 40 minutes.

Overlapping allows the input, processing, and output to be carried on at the same time. Assume a computer has three floating channels. At the start, all three channels are assigned to input. Jobs 1, 2, and 3 are read in simultaneously during the first five minutes. During the second five minutes, the computer begins to process jobs 1 and 2, while it is still inputting job 3.

During the third five minutes, the scheduler assigns one of the channels to output data. While the computer outputs job 1, it continues processing job 2 and inputting job 3. During the next five-minute period, the computer opens the first channel for other jobs, continues to process job 2, and begins processing job 3. The total time required to process the three jobs is only 40 minutes. Further, after the first 15 minutes, one channel has been opened to receive other jobs; after 30 minutes. the second channel is open.

THE PROBLEM OF DIFFERENT SPEEDS

Because of their physical nature, input devices convert data to electronic pulses at different speeds.

Since electromechanical devices, such as line printers, card punches, card readers, and console typewriters, physically move cards or activate mechanical printing mechanisms, they transmit or receive only a few hundred characters per second. This speed is too slow for direct transmission to the CPU.

Devices which read, write, and record characters electronically are high-speed units. They transmit or receive several hundred thousand characters per second, and, therefore, can transmit data directly to the CPU. These devices are discussed in detail in Chapter 10 and include magnetic tape drives, magnetic disk drives, data cell storage devices, and drum storage devices.

The differences in speeds of input/output devices present several input problems. A CPU manipulates data at a high rate of speed. Data coming from all input devices must enter the CPU at the same speed. Buffering and multiplexing are two techniques which have been used to resolve these problems.

Buffering   One method of reconciling the differences in speed between input units is to use a buffer between the input device and the CPU. The buffer is a storage unit that saves up a group of characters (bytes) coming from a slow input device. When sufficient data is accumulated, it is fed from the buffer to the CPU in a burst at high speed. Burst input speed (hundreds of thousands of bytes per second) equals the speed at which most CPU's are designed to manipulate data.

Buffers are usually composed of core storage systems, which hold data electronically. They may be physically located within the input device or within the CPU. (See Figure 7.24.)

Buffering increases computer efficiency. Suppose four card readers are feeding data to a computer with four channels. Each could be connected directly to a separate channel. But this would tie up all channels, and only a relatively small amount of data would enter the CPU because of the slow speed of the card readers.

A better arrangement would be to provide buffering for each card reader and tie all four to one input channel. When a buffer has received all the data from one record, it is switched on-line and transmits it to the CPU. As a result, all four card readers can operate simultaneously, with buffers holding data until the line is open. (See Figure 7.25.) This leaves the other three channels open for other input/output tasks.

Multiplexing   Another method of compensating for differences in speed between input devices is to multiplex, or interleave data. Bytes of data coming from several input devices are interleaved, one after the other. In buffering, one or more records are held in storage and fed to the CPU in a burst. In multiplexing, data is picked up one byte at a time from several input devices, in turn. Both allow a maximum amount of data to be fed over a single channel, increasing throughput.

FIGURE 7.24   PHYSICAL LOCATION OF BUFFERS

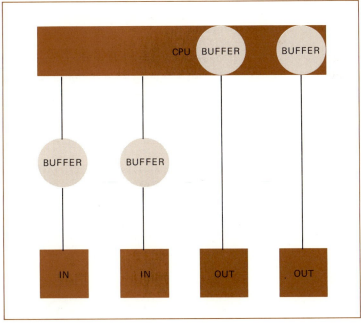

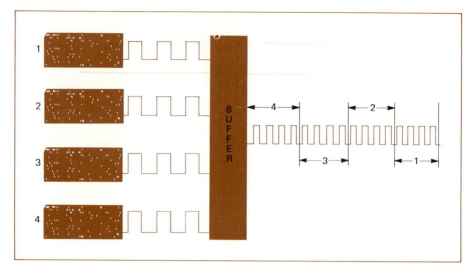

FIGURE 7.25   BUFFERING FOUR CARD READERS

Suppose data from four slow devices are to be fed to a CPU designed to receive data at high speed. The data can be buffered and sent in bursts from each card reader, or they can be multiplexed. In either case, only one channel is required. If it is to be multiplexed, one character at a time is transmitted from each of the card readers. Once in the CPU, the multiplexer separates each byte, and the original records are reconstructed in separate storage areas.

Types of
Channels

Third-generation computers are designed with two types of I/O channels: multiplexer and selector. Computers may have more than one of each type. Figure 7.26 illustrates a CPU with two multiplexer and two selector channels. Each channel has a control unit to time the input of data and to serve as a standard coupling for the I/O devices.

MULTIPLEXER CHANNEL.   Multiplexer channels feed data from slow input devices to the CPU at the rate of 170,000 bytes per second. Each multiplexer channel can service up to 256 separate input or output units. This allows dozens of card readers, punches, or terminals to operate at the same time.

From a programming standpoint, each of the devices on the multiplexer is an independent unit, with its own address. The arrangement is similar to a telephone party-line system. Each input device has its own portion of the multiplexer channel, called a subchannel. Even though many units share a channel, each can be stopped, started, and called by a program independently.

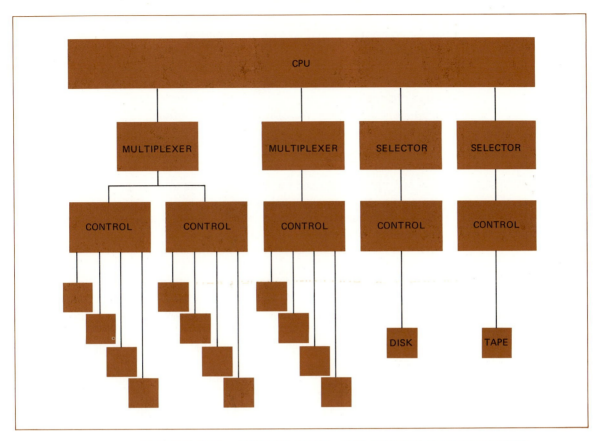

FIGURE 7.26   MULTIPLEXER AND SELECTOR COMPUTER
CHANNELS

SELECTOR CHANNEL.   Selector channels feed data from fast devices
directly to the CPU. They are usually used with magnetic tape and disk
drives. Only one unit can be coupled to a selector channel at a time. Data is
fed to the CPU at the rate of 312,000 bytes per second. Selector channels
are also used to link the CPU's of more than one computer for direct
transmission of data between them.

DATA INPUT

KEY TERMS   I/O Channel   Control units

Channel address   Multiplex

Channel scheduler   Multiplexer channel

Queue   Selector channel

Fixed channels   Pulse train

Floating channels   On-line input

Overlap   Off-line input

Buffer

EXERCISES

1. Explain the system used for detecting holes in a punched card and converting them to electrical pulses.
2. How are characters converted from the printed page to electrical pulses by the Optical Character Reader?
3. What is the disadvantage of using the printer-keyboard to feed data in and out of the computer?
4. Draw a sketch of a simple computer, showing one access channel.
5. What are I/O channels? What function do they serve?
6. Copy Figure 7.18. Label the channel addresses for each component on the system.
7. What is channel scheduling, and how does it improve computer throughput?
8. Explain the difference between fixed and floating channels. Which has the most advantages?
9. What is overlapping, and how does it improve computer throughput?
10. Why are slow input devices a problem for the CPU? List four slow and four fast devices.
11. Define the term buffering. How is it used in the computer system?
12. Define multiplexing. How does it differ from buffering?
13. Visit your data center on campus and list all input and output devices on the system. Categorize each according to its input speed.

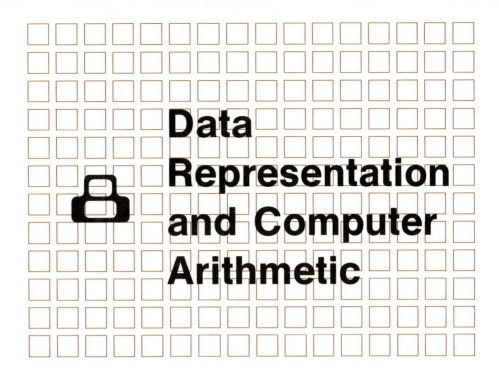

Data Representation and Computer Arithmetic

In written communication, it is necessary to use symbols in place of actual objects or events. The use of symbols makes it easier to process data. Data can be represented as numbers (0, 1, 2, 3, 4, 5, 6, 7, 8, 9). Each number is the symbol of a certain quantity. The alphabet is another way of representing data. Each combination of symbols has a specific meaning. For example, by convention the symbols *Jane Smith* form a name, which represents a person.

In electronic data processing, data is represented by coding systems that can be converted to electronic pulses for manipulation by a computer.

EARLY DATA REPRESENTATION

Man's first attempts to represent data probably consisted of using fingers, rocks, or sticks. To add two and two, he might, for example, have raised two fingers on one hand, and then two on the other. Four raised fingers then represented the sum of the objects he was counting.

Each rock, stick, or finger represented one object or thing. Since he had few objects or things to count, this simple system was adequate. The skins of 100 animals could conveniently be represented by 100 sticks.

This early numbering system was based on two principles: First, each unit represented only one object (1). For example, two units had to be used to

167

represent two objects (11); ten to represent ten objects (1111111111). Second, only two states could be represented: an object existed (1) or it did not (0).

As man's needs changed, this crude system of data representation became inadequate. A shorthand method of representing larger numbers was needed.

Numbering systems developed which used different symbols to represent quantities of more than one. For example, consider the Roman system, shown in Figure 8.1, which uses letters as symbols. An I represents one unit, and III represents 3. But a V represents 5 units; an X, 10 units; and a C represents 100 units.

FIGURE 8.1   USE OF SYMBOLS TO REPRESENT OBJECTS

OBJECTS	ROMAN NUMERAL SYSTEM	DECIMAL SYSTEM
○	I	1
○ ○	II	2
○ ○ ○	III	3
○ ○ ○ ○ ○ ○ ○ ○ ○ ○	X	10

But since man could conveniently remember and use only a limited number of symbols, the next step was to devise a system where the position of the symbol gave it a different value. This led to the development of numbering systems that used bases and place values.

The base of a numbering system is the number of states it recognizes. For example, a system with ten states (0, 1, 2, 3, 4, 5, 6, 7, 8, 9) is called base 10. A system with four states (0, 1, 2, 3) is called base 4.

Place value is that value assigned to a symbol according to its position or place in the number. (See Figure 8.2.) It is an important concept; it greatly increases the flexibility and capacity of a numbering system.

Place value is a multiple of the base of a numbering system. In base 10, the rightmost position or the symbol before the decimal (or reference) point is equal to the symbol times 10^0 or one. (In fact, any number to the zero power (n^0) equals one.) The position to its left is equal to the symbol times 10^1 or 10: the next, the symbol times 10^2 or 100 (10×10); the next position, the symbol times 10^3 or 1,000 ($10 \times 10 \times 10$), etc.

FIGURE 8.2   PLACE VALUE

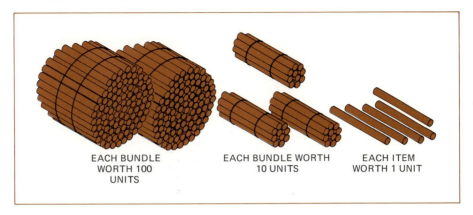

EACH BUNDLE
WORTH 100
UNITS

EACH BUNDLE WORTH
10 UNITS

EACH ITEM
WORTH 1 UNIT

BASE 10 SYSTEM

Our common numbering system, with ten states, is base 10 or the decimal system. Ten different symbols represent the states: 0. 1, 2, 3, 4, 5, 6, 7, 8, and 9.

The decimal system also uses place value. In the following example, each digit in the number 345 has a different place value.

10^2	10^1	10^0
100	10	1
3	4	5

The value of each digit depends upon its position with respect to the other digits. The number in the right-hand column (5) represents five units. This is the units, or ones column. The number 4 is in the tens column and represents 10×4, or 40 units. The number in the left column (3) is in the hundreds column and represents not 3 units, but 3×100 or 300 units. It is the place value which determines the actual quantity a numeral represents.

Looking at it another way, we see that the number 345 is the same as

$$
\begin{array}{rr}
3 \times 100 & 100 \\
 & 100 \\
 & 100 \\
4 \times 10 & 10 \\
 & 10 \\
 & 10 \\
 & 10 \\
5 \times 1 & 1 \\
 & 1 \\
 & 1 \\
 & 1 \\
 & \underline{1} \\
 & 345
\end{array}
$$

The decimal system needs only three digits to represent the quantity instead of a string of 345 ones—a definite improvement over the system of early man!

In the decimal system of representation, the following place values and symbols are used:

Place values

10^5	10^4	10^3	10^2	10^1	10^0
Hundred thousands	Ten thousands	Thousands	Hundreds	Tens	Ones
100,000	10,000	1,000	100	10	1

Symbols used

0, 1, 2, 3, 4, 5, 6, 7, 8, 9

It is interesting to speculate about what would have happened had man been born with only eight, or as many as twelve fingers. In all likelihood, his numbering system would be quite different.

If he had only eight fingers, man's numbering system might be base 8 and look like this:

Place values

8^4	8^3	8^2	8^1	8^0
4,096	512	64	8	1

Symbols used

0, 1, 2, 3, 4, 5, 6, 7

Not having a need for a ninth or a tenth state, he probably would not have created the symbols for 8 and 9.

Had he been born with 12 fingers, his system might be base 12 and look like this:

Place values

12^4	12^3	12^2	12^1	12^0
20,736	1,728	144	12	1

Symbols used

0, 1, 2, 3, 4, 5, 6, 7, 8, 9, Ψ, ξ

With twelve instead of ten states to represent, he would have designed additional symbols to represent them.

Although the decimal, or base ten, system can be used, the base 2 (binary) and base 16 (hexadecimal) systems have been found to be more efficient in data processing.

BINARY REPRESENTATION

Early computer engineers designed machines that used the decimal system. But since these computers had to be able to represent and store all ten states present in this system, they proved to be complicated and inaccurate.

There was a need to represent data in a form compatible with computer hardware capabilities. Computers, in fact most electronic devices, are inherently "two-state" machines. Switches, relays, lamps, diodes, memory cores, etc. are either off or on, charged or not charged, conducting or not conducting. Therefore, a numbering system with only two states is the most efficient for the machine. Binary representation is ideal because it is based on only two conditions: on or off. And two symbols represent these states: 1 and 0.

Each storage unit of the computer is capable of representing only one of two possible states, "1" or "0." But to have any value, a numbering system must represent more than two numbers. By connecting storage units in series, positions for place value are created, and larger numbers can be represented. Thus, any number that can be represented as a decimal can be represented as a binary number, and all mathematical operations, such as addition, subtraction, and multiplication, can be performed upon it.

Place Values   The binary numbering system uses place values to represent numbers larger than its base, just as the decimal system does. Each place value is a multiple of 2 (the base) and increases in magnitude as it moves to the left. The first eight binary place values are

	2^7	2^6	2^5	2^4	2^3	2^2	2^1	2^0
...	128	64	32	16	8	4	2	1

The following table gives some examples of binary numbers and their decimal equivalents.

128	64	32	16	8	4	2	1	DECIMAL EQUIVALENT
0	0	0	0	0	0	0	1	1
0	0	0	0	0	0	1	1	3
0	0	0	0	0	1	0	1	5
0	1	0	0	0	0	0	1	65
1	0	0	0	0	1	1	0	134
1	1	1	1	1	1	1	1	255

With the eight place-value positions above (each capable of only two conditions), any number from 0 to 255 can be represented. Larger numbers can be represented by adding more place values. The number of numerals that can be represented is doubled each time a place value is added.

To a human, the binary system appears inconvenient and awkward. It requires many more place-value positions to represent a number than does the decimal system. But an electronic device can manipulate these long strings of binary bits both efficiently and rapidly.

Binary Mathematics   Any mathematical operation can be performed on numbers stored in the computer in binary representation. The principles involved are very similar to those used in manipulating decimal numbers. Although it is unnecessary for you to become proficient in binary mathematics, you should have some understanding of the process. Here are some fundamental rules for binary mathematical operations.

BINARY ADDITION.   Addition of binary numbers is performed in a manner similar to adding decimal numbers. Follow these rules:

1. Zero plus zero equals zero (0 + 0 = 0)
2. Zero plus one equals one (0 + 1 = 1)
3. One plus zero equals one (1 + 0 = 1)
4. One plus one equals zero with one to carry (1 + 1 = 10)

The following is an example of binary addition. The result is given below with the decimal equivalent to the right.

$$
\begin{array}{cc}
0\ 1\ 1\ 1 & 7 \\
+0\ 0\ 1\ 1 & 3 \\
\hline
1\ 0\ 1\ 0 = 10
\end{array}
$$

Begin from the right-hand side and add each column of digits. Place the sum below the line, just as in decimal addition. Remember, if the sum of any two digits in a given column exceeds 1, a carry must be made.

Step 1. Add 1 + 1. The sum is greater than 1 and the answer is 0 with 1 to carry.

Step 2. Add 1 + 1 + 1. This results in 1 with 1 to carry.

Step 3. Add 1 + 1. Again, 0 is below the line and 1 is carried.

Step 4. Add 1 + 0. The answer is 1.

The resulting binary number, 1010, is the sum. This is how it looks expressed by place value and converted to its decimal equivalent:

$$
\begin{array}{c}
8\ 4\ 2\ 1 \\
\hline
1\ 0\ 1\ 0
\end{array}
$$

which is the same as

$$
\begin{aligned}
\text{one group of 8 units} &= \quad 8 \\
\text{one group of 2 units} &= \underline{+2} \\
& \quad 10 \text{ decimal units}
\end{aligned}
$$

Here are several other examples of binary addition:

8 4 2 1		16 8 4 2 1		8 4 2 1	
0 1 0 1	5	0 1 0 1	5	0 1 1 0	6
+1 0 1 0	10	+1 1 1 1	15	+0 1 1 1	7
1 1 1 1 = 15		1 0 1 0 0 = 20		1 1 0 1 = 13	

BINARY SUBTRACTION.   Binary subtraction is performed by following these rules:

1. Zero minus zero equals zero ($0 - 0 = 0$)
2. One minus one equals zero ($1 - 1 = 0$)
3. One minus zero equals one ($1 - 0 = 1$)
4. Zero minus one equals one, with 10 borrowed. ($0 - 1 = 1$ with 10 borrowed)
5. Binary 10 (decimal 2) minus one equals one ($10 - 1 = 1$)

The following is an example of a subtraction problem. As before, the result is given below with its decimal equivalent to the right.

	8 4 2 1	
Minuend	1 1 0 1	13
Subtrahend	−0 1 0 0	4
Difference	1 0 0 1 = 9	

Step 1. $1 - 0 = 1$. Subtract zero from one, the answer is one.
Step 2. $0 - 0 = 0$. Zero minus zero equals zero.
Step 3. $1 - 1 = 0$. One minus one equals zero.
Step 4. $1 - 0 = 1$. One minus zero equals one.

The result is binary 1001, or decimal 9.

Here is another example.

	8 4 2 1	
Minuend	1 0 0 1	9
Subtrahend	−0 1 1 1	7
Difference	0 0 1 0 = 2	

Step 1. $1 - 1 = 0$. One minus one equals zero.

Step 2. $0 - 1 = 1$ and a borrow. To subtract one from a zero it is necessary to borrow from the next place value. In this case, the next place value is a zero; therefore we must borrow from the next one (the eights place value). To do this we transfer one group of eight units to the fours place-value position. This is equivalent to two groups of fours.

$$8 \ 4 \ 2 \ 1$$
$$0 \ 10$$
$$\cancel{1} \ \cancel{0} \ 0 \ 1$$

Now we want to transfer one group of four units to the twos place value. This will leave one group of four units at the fours place value.

```
          8  4  2  1
             1 10
          0  1̶0̶
          1̶  0̶  0̶  1
       −  0  1  1  1
          0  0  1  0
```

Now we have one group of four units in the twos place value. This is equivalent to two groups of two units. According to Rule 5, $10 - 1 = 1$, so we place a 1 beneath the line.

Step 3. $1 - 1 = 0$. At the fours place-value position, one minus one equals zero.

Step 4. $0 - 0 = 0$. Zero minus zero equals zero.

The answer is binary 0010, which equals decimal 2.

It is obvious that binary subtraction can become very complicated; therefore the computer uses another method, called subtraction by the twos complement.

In a computer, a series of transistors or other devices can easily be changed from one state to another (from conducting to nonconducting, for example). Thus, it is an easy matter to convert a string of ones and zeroes to their opposite, or complement string. For example,

```
    0 1 1 0    0 1 0 1    becomes
    1 0 0 1    1 0 1 0,   its complement
```

This feature makes it convenient to perform subtraction using the twos complementary addition method. By this method, the subtrahend is converted to its complement and added to the minuend. Then a binary 1 is added to the units position to give the answer.

Let's work the second subtraction problem by the twos complement method:

```
    1 0 0 1    9
   −0 1 1 1    7
    0 0 1 0 = 2
```

Step 1. Binary 0111 (the subtrahend) is converted to its complement, 1000.

Step 2. The number 1000 is added to the minuend 1001, giving 10001.

Step 3. The "1" in the highest place value is carried around and added to the units position, giving the answer 0010, a decimal 2. (This is called an end-around carry.)

```
    1 0 0 1         1 0 0 1
   +1 0 0 0        +1 0 0 0
   1 0 0 0 1        1 0 0 0 1
                         → 1
                    0 0 1 0
```

In an example using numbers as small as 9 and 7, this method may appear to be overly complicated and not worth the effort. But in dealing with numbers involving long strings of binary bits, it makes more efficient use of the computer.

BINARY MULTIPLICATION AND DIVISION.   Multiplication is actually a shorthand way of doing a series of addition problems. 3×7 is the same as adding three sevens or $7 + 7 + 7 = 21$. And $50 \times 3,891$ is the same as adding 3,891 fifty times. Both equal 194,550.

Division, of both decimal and binary numbers, is a shorthand method of doing a series of subtraction problems. $30 \div 10 = 3$ is the same as subtracting 10 from 30 three times. And $135 \div 25 = 5$ with a remainder of 10, whether it is done by the traditional method, or as a series of subtraction problems.

The computer performs multiplication as a series of addition problems and division as a series of subtraction problems. This is more efficient for the machine and it can use the same circuitry set up for addition and subtraction. The mechanics of these processes are performed internally by the computer without operator intervention or instruction. The programmer has only to supply the values to be operated upon.

Converting Binary and Decimal Numbers

The CPU performs arithmetic calculations on binary data. Usually, however, data is entered into the computer in decimal form. The CPU will automatically convert numbers from decimal to binary for processing, and reconvert the results to be output in decimal form.

Occasionally, however, a programmer must know how to make this conversion. Many tables and charts are available which give the equivalent binary and decimal values. Or, since the principles involved are fairly simple, the programmer can learn to do it himself.

DECIMAL TO BINARY CONVERSION.   There are two common methods of converting decimals to binary numbers. One is a system of division and the other involves regrouping the units under the new place values.
Division By Two.   One way to perform decimal-to-binary conversion is by dividing the decimal number by 2. For example, here is how the binary equivalent of 71 would be found:

$$
\begin{aligned}
71 \div 2 &= 35 + 1 \\
35 \div 2 &= 17 + 1 \\
17 \div 2 &= 8 + 1 \\
8 \div 2 &= 4 + 0 \\
4 \div 2 &= 2 + 0 \\
2 \div 2 &= 1 + 0 \\
1 \div 2 &= 0 + 1
\end{aligned}
$$

$$1\ 0\ 0\ 0\ 1\ 1\ 1$$

In this system, the remainders from each of the divisions form the binary equivalent of the decimal number.

Regrouping Units. A second way to convert a number from one base system to another is to regroup the number of units according to the new place values. As an example, we will convert decimal 48 to a binary 48. We will need binary place values large enough to represent 48 units (the first six place values)

32	16	8	4	2	1

We can regroup 32 of the 48 units by placing a "1" under the place-value position which represents 32 units.

This still leaves 16 units to be regrouped. There is a binary place value representing 16 units, so we write a "1" under it, and fill in the place values to the right with zeroes:

32	16	8	4	2	1
1	1	0	0	0	0

$$
\begin{array}{rl}
48 & \text{units} \\
-32 & = 1 \text{ group of 32 units} \\
\hline
16 & \text{units} \\
-16 & = 1 \text{ group of 16 units} \\
\hline
0 &
\end{array}
$$

The binary representation of 48 units is 110000.

Other examples:

Decimal 73 is expressed as binary 1001001.

64	32	16	8	4	2	1
1	0	0	1	0	0	1

$$
\begin{array}{rl}
73 & \text{units} \\
-64 & = 1 \text{ group of 64 units} \\
\hline
9 & \text{units} \\
-8 & = 1 \text{ group of 8 units} \\
\hline
1 & \text{unit} \\
-1 & = 1 \text{ unit} \\
\hline
0 &
\end{array}
$$

Decimal 101 is expressed as binary 1100101.

64	32	16	8	4	2	1
1	1	0	0	1	0	1

```
101    units
−64  = 1 group of 64 units
 37    units
−32  = 1 group of 32 units
  5    units
 − 4  = 1 group of 4 units
  1    unit
 − 1  = 1 unit
  0
```

BINARY TO DECIMAL CONVERSION.   Converting from binary to decimal numbers involves adding the number of units represented by each binary place value.

As an example, let's convert binary 1110101 to its decimal equivalent. First determine the place value of each digit in the binary number. Then sum the number of units they represent.

64	32	16	8	4	2	1
1	1	1	0	1	0	1

```
There is one group of   64  units
There is one group of   32  units
There is one group of   16  units
There is one group of    4  units
There is one group of    1  units
                       117  decimal units
```

Binary 1110101 is equivalent to decimal 117.

BCD Numeric Code

Although binary representation of numbers is efficient for use by the computer, it is awkward and inconvenient for us to use. It is easier for us to read and understand numbers that more closely resemble the decimal place-value system.

A modified form of the binary numeric system was developed, called the Binary Coded Decimal Numeric Code (BCD). In this system, only the binary codes for the numbers 0 to 9 are used. Four binary digits are required to express these values.

DECIMAL	BINARY (BCD)	DECIMAL	BINARY (BCD)
0	= 0000	5	= 0101
1	= 0001	6	= 0110
2	= 0010	7	= 0111
3	= 0011	8	= 1000
4	= 0100	9	= 1001

A decimal number is expressed by translating each digit in the number to its binary code. For example, decimal 213 would be expressed as

2   1   3
0010 0001 0011

(The pure binary representation of decimal 213 is 1101 0101.)
Decimal 5,168 would be expressed in BCD as

5   1   6 8
0101 0001 0110 1000

Decimal 1,009 would be expressed in BCD as

1   0   0 9
0001 0000 0000 1001

HEXADECIMAL REPRESENTATION   *Base 16*

Although the BCD system increases the flexibility and ease of programming numeric data, it does require more computer space to record each number. Four binary digits are necessary to express the ten values of the BCD system but in this system there are six unused combinations of four digits. These unused combinations represent empty storage space in the computer.

Another numbering system, hexadecimal representation (hex), was developed. This system, using a base 16, incorporates the convenience of the BCD system with the full storage capability allowed by using all code combinations of pure binary.

Strings of binary bits, representing a number, are divided into groups of fours. A group of four zeroes and ones has 16 possible combinations: the 16 states of the hex numbering system. The first ten states have the same values and symbols as the decimal system. The last six states are represented by the first six letters of the alphabet.

Table 8.1 lists the symbols required to represent the first 16 numbers in the decimal, hexadecimal, binary and BCD systems.

Each hex place value is expressed in binary by one group of four digits. Therefore, a hex number with two place values requires eight binary digits and one with three place values, 12 binary digits. For example,

HEX	BINARY	DECIMAL
A5	1010 0101	165
2E7	0010 1110 0111	743
F00	1111 0000 0000	3,840

TABLE 8.1   VARIOUS NUMBERING SYSTEMS

DECIMAL	HEX	BINARY	BCD	
0	0	0000	0000	0000
1	1	0001	0000	0001
2	2	0010	0000	0010
3	3	0011	0000	0011
4	4	0100	0000	0100
5	5	0101	0000	0101
6	6	0110	0000	0110
7	7	0111	0000	0111
8	8	1000	0000	1000
9	9	1001	0000	1001
10	A	1010	0001	0000
11	B	1011	0001	0001
12	C	1100	0001	0010
13	D	1101	0001	0011
14	E	1110	0001	0100
15	F	1111	0001	0101

With only 16 combinations to remember, programmers can easily refer to large binary numbers by their hex names, such as

$$0010\ 1111\ 0001\ 1110\ 1100 = 2F1EC = 193{,}004$$
$$2\quad\ F\quad\ 1\quad\ E\quad\ C$$

and

$$1110\ 0010\ 1110\ 0000\ 1101\ 1010\ 1011 = E2EODAB = 237{,}899{,}179$$
$$E\quad\ 2\quad\ E\quad\ 0\quad\ D\quad\ A\quad\ B$$

Conversion of large binary numbers to the decimal system is simplified. The hex name for the binary number is determined. Then the hex number is converted to the decimal number. Conversion from decimal to binary is also simplified by first converting the number to hex and then to binary. The computer, of course, makes this conversion automatically.

The listings of information which computers print out about a program after it has unexpectedly stopped are usually in hex. To understand them requires a knowledge of hex and the ability to convert data between the decimal and the hex systems. A knowledge of hex conversion is also necessary for writing programs in some languages, such as Assembler.

Appendix B illustrates the relationship of hexadecimal, decimal, and binary numbers. A close look at the three systems will indicate the efficiency of the hex numbering system.

HEXADECIMAL TO DECIMAL CONVERSION. Conversion between the two systems is most easily accomplished by using a table such as Table 8.2. This table will convert hex numbers up to eight place values or positions. The place values are numbered from 1–8, right to left, along the bottom of the table. Each place value is a multiple of 16, the base, and represents these units:

8	7	6	5	4	3	2	1
268,435,456	16,777,216	1,048,576	65,536	4,096	256	16	1

A hex 1 in position 3 means there is one group of 256 units in a number. An A in that position means there are 10 groups of 256 units in the number, or 2,560 decimal units. A hex B in position 2 means there are 11 groups of 16 units or 176 (11 × 16) decimal units, etc.

The table provides a convenient method of simplifying the conversion of hex and decimal numbers. The decimal value of each hex position is found and added to give the equivalent decimal number.

Here are several examples of hex to decimal conversion, by using the place values above.

1. HEX 1CB3 = DECIMAL 7,347
   hex 3 in position 1 = 3 × 1   =   3 in decimal
   hex B in position 2 = 11 × 16   =   176 in decimal
   hex C in position 3 = 12 × 256   = 3,072 in decimal
   hex 1 in position 4 = 1 × 4,096 = 4,096 in decimal
                                      ─────
                                      7,347

2. HEX 1010 = DECIMAL 4,112
   hex 0 in position 1 = 0 × 1   =   0
   hex 1 in position 2 = 1 × 16   =   16
   hex 0 in position 3 = 0 × 256   =   0
   hex 1 in position 4 = 1 × 4,096 = 4,096
                                     ─────
                                     4,112

3. HEX 14BBB = DECIMAL 84,923
   hex B in position 1 = 11 × 1   =   11
   hex B in position 2 = 11 × 16   =   176
   hex B in position 3 = 11 × 256   = 2,816
   hex 4 in position 4 = 4 × 4,096 = 16,384
   hex 1 in position 5 = 1 × 65,536 = 65,536
                                       ──────
                                       84,923

DECIMAL TO HEXADECIMAL CONVERSION. A reverse procedure will convert decimal numbers to hexadecimal values, also by using Table 8.2. It is basically the process of rearranging the units represented by a number into new groups corresponding to the place values of the hex system.

TABLE 8.2 HEXADECIMAL TO DECIMAL CONVERSION

HEX	DEC	HEX	DEC	HEX	DEC	HEX	DEC	HEX	DEC	HEX	DEC	HEX	DEC	HEX	DEC
0	0	0	0	0	0	0	0	0	0	0	0	0	0	0	0
1	268,435,456	1	16,777,216	1	1,048,576	1	65,536	1	4,096	1	256	1	16	1	1
2	536,870,912	2	33,554,432	2	2,097,152	2	131,072	2	8,192	2	512	2	32	2	2
3	805,306,368	3	50,331,648	3	3,145,728	3	196,608	3	12,288	3	768	3	48	3	3
4	1,073,741,824	4	67,108,864	4	4,194,304	4	262,144	4	16,384	4	1,024	4	64	4	4
5	1,342,177,280	5	83,886,080	5	5,242,880	5	327,680	5	20,480	5	1,280	5	80	5	5
6	1,610,612,736	6	100,663,296	6	6,291,456	6	393,216	6	24,576	6	1,536	6	96	6	6
7	1,879,048,192	7	117,440,512	7	7,340,032	7	458,752	7	28,672	7	1,792	7	112	7	7
8	2,147,483,648	8	134,217,728	8	8,388,608	8	524,288	8	32,768	8	2,048	8	128	8	8
9	2,415,919,104	9	150,994,944	9	9,437,184	9	589,824	9	36,864	9	2,304	9	144	9	9
A	2,684,354,560	A	167,772,160	A	10,485,760	A	655,360	A	40,960	A	2,560	A	160	A	10
B	2,952,790,016	B	184,549,376	B	11,534,336	B	720,896	B	45,056	B	2,816	B	176	B	11
C	3,221,225,472	C	201,326,592	C	12,582,912	C	786,432	C	49,152	C	3,072	C	192	C	12
D	3,489,660,928	D	218,103,808	D	13,631,488	D	851,968	D	53,248	D	3,328	D	208	D	13
E	3,758,096,384	E	234,881,024	E	14,680,064	E	917,504	E	57,344	E	3,584	E	224	E	14
F	4,026,531,840	F	251,658,240	F	15,728,640	F	983,040	F	61,440	F	3,840	F	240	F	15
	8		7		6		5		4		3		2		1

For example, look at the steps involved in converting the decimal value 32,184 to its hex equivalent:

1. Find the decimal number on the table equal to or almost as large as the number being converted. In this case, it is 28,672 in position 4. The hex equivalent is 7 _ _ _. The number will contain four place values, and the leftmost digit is a hex 7. This means the decimal number contains 7 groups of 4,096 units (7 × 4,096 = 28,672).

2. Now subtract 28,672 from 32,184 since these units have been regrouped. This leaves 3,512 units.

$$\begin{array}{r} 32,184 \\ -28,672 \\ \hline 3,512 \end{array} \qquad 7\,\_\,\_\,\_$$

3. The closest decimal value to 3,512 is 3,328 in position 3. Its hex equivalent is D _ _. 3,512 contains 13 groups of 256 units, with 184 units still left to be regrouped. The hex number now looks like this:

$$\begin{array}{r} 3,512 \\ -3,328 \\ \hline 184 \end{array} \qquad 7D\,\_\,\_$$

4. Decimal 176 is the closest value to 184 and its hex equivalent is B _, with 8 units left. The number is now

$$\begin{array}{r} 184 \\ -176 \\ \hline 8 \end{array} \qquad 7DB\,\_$$

GEORGE BOOLE, MATHEMATICAL WIZARD

What a disappointment George Boole turned out to be. He had been such a promising mathematician as a youth. At 16, he became an assistant master in a private school and founded a very successful school by the time he was 20. A brilliant teacher, he was later made Professor of Mathematics at Queen's College, Cork, Ireland, a post he held for the rest of his life.

He began his investigation in experimental mathematics while at Queens College. A fantastic new scheme came to him—a system of mathematics and algebra that was a perfect plan of logic using only ones and zeros. He envisioned sets and subsets, unions, intersections, universals, and complements. It all fit together nicely.

In 1847 he wrote a statement describing his new system and in 1854 he published his monumental work on Boolean algebra, but it brought him only frustration and disappointment. No one cared or even pretended to be interested. One colleague asked him why he wasted his time developing a new system when a perfectly good decimal system already existed. And besides, who would want a primitive system using only ones and zeros?

Librarians had such trouble cataloging his writings that even they wished he hadn't strayed from the beaten track. (Where would you put "An Investigation of the Laws of Thought, on Which Are Founded the Mathematical Theories of Logic and Probabilities"? under philosophy? mathematics? logic?) In December of 1864, George Boole died, leaving a mathematical system no one wanted.

For almost a century Boole's work lay unused. Then in the late 1940's, scientists and engineers created a device capable of processing decimal numbers. But it kept adding two and two and getting five. What was needed was a system of mathematics based on ones and zeros—a system suitable to the on-off states inherent in computer hardware. Then an engineer came upon a rare work—Boole's treatises. It was the perfect match, a mathematical system apparently custom-made for the modern computer.

Today, almost every digital computer in the world performs its mathematical computations in circuitry based on Boole's scheme. From kindergarten to college, students are studying new math. And, for the modern twentieth-century computer technologist, the most important mathematical scheme that exists is the Boolean system of algebra.

5. Eight decimal units are equal to 8 hex units, and these are added to give the final answer. The decimal number 32,184 is equal to a hex 7DB8. Some other examples are

```
DECIMAL      12,431 = HEX 308F
             12,431
            −12,288 = 3 _ _ _
           ─────────
              143
             −128 =    08 _
           ─────────
               15
              −15 =         F
           ─────────
                0    3 08 F
```

```
DECIMAL 10,396,652 = HEX 9EA3EC
        10,396,652 =
        −9,437,184 =        9 _ _ _ _ _
       ────────────
          959,468
         −917,504 =         E _ _ _ _
       ────────────
           41,964
          −40,960 =         A _ _ _
       ────────────
            1,004
             −768 =         3 _ _
       ────────────
              236
             −224 =         E _
       ────────────
               12
              −12 =              C
       ────────────
                0         9EA3EC
```

© Datamation®

ALPHABETIC CODING SYSTEMS

The coding systems discussed up to this point represent only numeric data, since any system using four bits can only represent 16 different characters. (Hex represents 16 numbers and BCD represents ten numbers and has six unused combinations.) But a coding system using five bits is able to represent 32 characters; and one with six bits, 64 characters, etc. Such systems allow for coding of alphabetic data and special characters, such as $, +, and (.

Several codes have been developed, many based on the BCD coding system, to convert alphabetic and special characters to binary bits that can be processed by the computer. Each coding system is designed to meet certain needs. For example, some are for transmitting data over telephone lines, others for storage of data within the CPU. Modern coding systems are able to represent as many as 256 different characters.

Terminology has developed describing specific aspects of coding systems. Intelligence bits are those bits that are part of the code for a character. Some codes include extra bits, used for accuracy control. The BCD code, for example, has four intelligence bits. A six-bit code might have five intelligence bits and one bit for checking accuracy.

In the early years of telegraph transmission, paper tape was used to feed data. The code combination for each character was punched across the width of the paper tape. The row of holes formed by each punch position across the length of the tape was called a channel. There were as many channels as there were bits in a code.

Paper tape codes commonly have from five to eight channels. A channel may contain intelligence or control bits, but never both. Those with intelligence bits are called intelligence channels.

Tracks are similar to channels, except they are related to magnetic rather than paper tape. Magnetic tape may have from seven to nine tracks depending on the code used.

Provisions for maintaining accuracy, called parity checks, have also been developed and included in some of the codes.

Parity Check   Early in the development of data transmission and coding systems, a serious problem arose. It was not uncommon for a bit to be lost in transmission because of a mechanical or electronic failure. (See Figure 8.3.) If the loss went undetected, the character received on the other end of the line was incorrect. By the same token, if an extra bit found its way onto a tape or into the transmitted signal, incorrect data resulted.

To prevent this from happening, the parity system was developed to detect errors in coding. Each character, or byte, is composed of a different combination of bits. Some characters have an odd number of bits turned on

FIGURE 8.3   LOST BITS (NO CHECK BIT PRESENT)

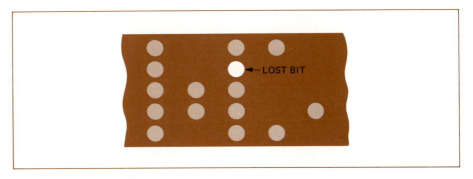

and some an even number. For example, these code combinations have an odd number of bits turned on

$$1 = 0001$$
$$7 = 0111$$
$$8 = 1000$$

these have an even number

$$6 = 0110$$
$$5 = 0101$$
$$3 = 0011$$

To use the parity system, an extra bit, called a check bit, is added either to all the combinations with an odd number of bits on, or to all the combinations with an even number on.

EVEN PARITY.   Even parity codes place a check bit with each uneven byte to make the sum of the bits even. (See Figure 8.4(A).) It is transmitted only with characters composed of an uneven number of bits. Thus, all characters transmitted will have an even number of bits. The check bit is generated along with the other bits required to make up the code for the character. It is transmitted to and from the computer along with the character code. If a bit is lost (or added) in transmission, the system is designed to detect this. An uneven number of bits received in a code string composed of even bits will signal an error.

ODD PARITY.   Odd parity codes punch an extra check bit with code combinations that have an even number of bits. (See Figure 8.4(B).) Thus, all characters transmitted will have an odd number of bits. Odd and even parity are similar in nature. They are both designed to signal an error in the event data is lost or added.

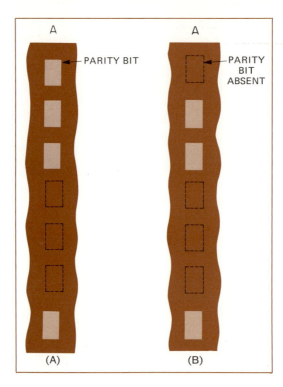

FIGURE 8.4 (A) EVEN PARITY (LETTER A, SEVEN-BIT CODE) (B) ODD PARITY (LETTER A, SEVEN-BIT CODE)

LONGITUDINAL PARITY. Longitudinal parity is used for checking accuracy when recording and transmitting on magnetic tape. In this form, all characters in a track are tallied along the length of the tape. At the end of each track a check bit is added to maintain even or odd parity. (See Figure 8.5.) Longitudinal parity can be even or odd and can be used in addition to the parity system used to check each byte.

FIGURE 8.5 LONGITUDINAL PARITY

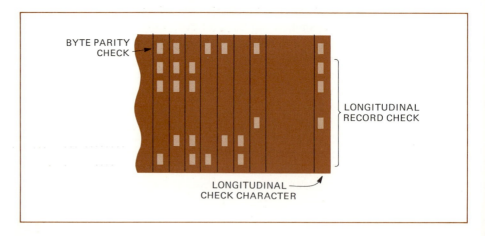

Data
Transmission
Codes
The following codes are used to transmit data between the CPU and input and output devices, and between CPU's of different computers. Some codes are limited in the number of characters they can transmit; some do not contain parity checks.

BAUDOT PAPER TAPE CODE.   This code, shown in Figure 8.6, was developed by a French engineer, Jean Baudot, for use in telegraph communication. It has five intelligence channels. Two sets of 32 characters allow a total of 64 characters to be transmitted. A special combination of characters, called shift codes, identifies each set. The Baudot code has no parity check. A row of small sprocket holes in the tape does not contain data, but is used to drive the tape through a tape feeder.

FIGURE 8.6   BAUDOT PAPER TAPE CODE

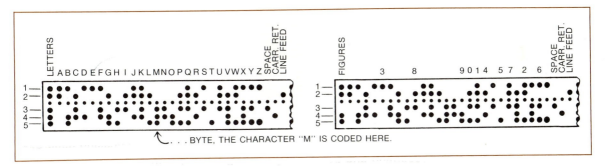

BINARY CODED DECIMAL ALPHAMERIC CODE.   This code is sometimes called the Binary Coded Decimal Interchange Code (BCDIC). It is shown in Figure 8.7 and is an extension of the BCD numeric code. It contains seven tracks: six for intelligence, one for the parity check bit. The tracks are numbered 1, 2, 4, 8, A, B, C. This code can transmit 64 different characters and was used on early computer systems, such as the IBM 1401.

FIGURE 8.7   BCD ALPHAMERIC CODE
(SIX-BIT, SEVEN-TRACK CODE)

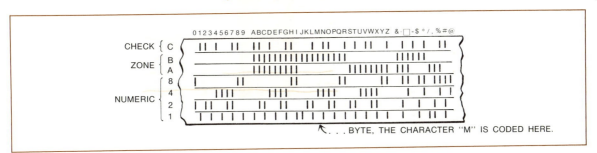

TWX PAPER TAPE CODE.   This code, shown in Figure 8.8, is an extension of the Baudot five-channel code. It consists of eight channels. Six are intelligence channels, the seventh is for the parity check, and the eighth is an end-of-line control bit. This code is used extensively by telegraph and teletype users. With the proper decoding device, these tapes may be used for computer input.

FIGURE 8.8   TWX PAPER TAPE CODE
(SIX-BIT, EIGHT-CHANNEL CODE)

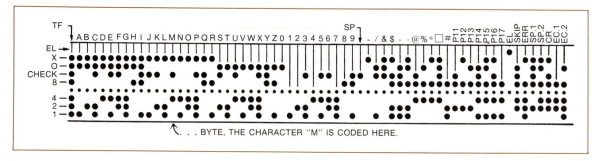

. . . BYTE, THE CHARACTER "M" IS CODED HERE.

AMERICAN NATIONAL STANDARD CODE FOR INFORMATION INTERCHANGE (ASCII).   This code, shown in Figure 8.9, consists of seven intelligence channels and an eighth check-bit channel. The channels are numbered C, B1, B2, B3, B4, B5, B6, B7. It resembles the TWX code, but makes more efficient use of the channels. Since it uses the seventh channel for intelligence instead of control, it can represent 128 characters. (This code was formerly referred to as USASCII, United States of America Standard Code for Information Interchange.) One of the two most widely used codes for transmitting data to computers, ASCII is also used for data transmission between many terminals and CPU's.

FIGURE 8.9   AMERICAN NATIONAL STANDARD CODE FOR
INFORMATION INTERCHANGE (SEVEN-BIT,
EIGHT-CHANNEL CODE)

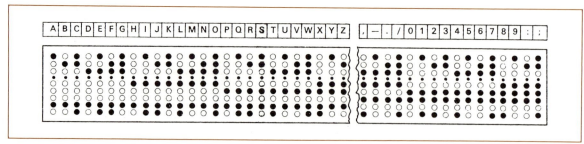

EXTENDED BINARY CODED DECIMAL INTERCHANGE CODE (EBCDIC).

This code, shown in Figure 8.10, is an extension of the ASCII code. It has nine tracks: eight for intelligence and one for check bit. It is capable of representing 256 characters. It allows both upper- and lower-case characters, many special symbols, and control characters to be transmitted. EBCDIC coding system was originally used by IBM in its 360 series computers. It is one of the two codes most widely used for data transmission.

FIGURE 8.10   EXTENDED BINARY CODED DECIMAL INTERCHANGE CODE (EIGHT-BIT, NINE-TRACK CODE)

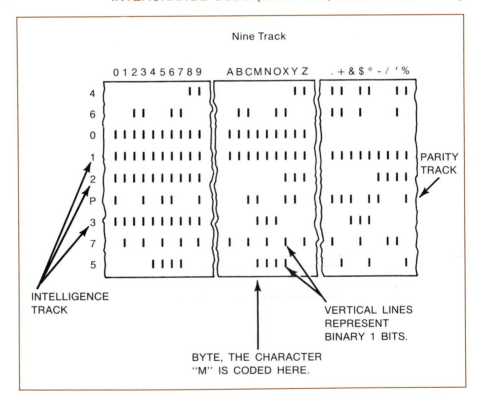

EBCDIC possesses one major advantage over other codes. It allows two decimal numbers to be packed into one byte, thereby increasing efficiency and storage capabilities. Since eight intelligence tracks are available, two BCD numbers (each using only four tracks) can be stored in one byte. The 9th track holds the check bit to maintain accuracy. This system is very efficient for transmitting and storing large amounts of numerical data.

Data Conversion

Data is converted into different codes during the processing cycle of input, manipulation by the CPU, output, and storage. The computer will automatically handle the conversion. Human operators need only feed data to computers as punched cards or coded on paper or magnetic tape. (See Figure 8.11.)

Input devices accept source data recorded in one of several representation codes. Card readers, for example, accept data punched in the 12-bit Hollerith code or EBCDIC. They convert these hole combinations to electronic pulses for input to the CPU. Data recorded on magnetic tape in ASCII or EBCDIC are converted to electronic pulses and entered directly to the CPU.

The CPU automatically converts input data into binary for manipulation. When processing is completed, the CPU automatically reconverts the data into ASCII or EBCDIC for outputting. The output device will convert it back to the proper form. For storing on tape, the electronic pulses will be converted to magnetic bits in ASCII or EBCDIC. Data is output by a line printer in a form understandable to humans.

FIGURE 8.11   DATA CONVERSION WITHIN THE COMPUTER

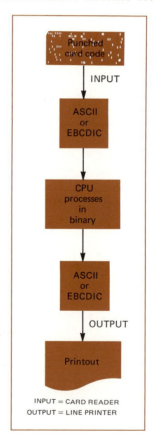

KEY TERMS   Base   BCDIC
             Place value   TWX Paper Tape Code
             Decimal notation   ASCII
             Binary notation   EBCDIC
             Hexadecimal notation   Parity check
             BCD   Check bit
             Baudot Code   Intelligence
             BCD Alphameric Code   Channel
                                                     Track

EXERCISES   1. What is meant by the term "base 10 system"?
             2. List three advantages and several disadvantages of binary representation.
             3. What is the decimal equivalent of the following binary numbers:

                         1101   0010   0110   0111

             4. What is the binary equivalent of the following decimal numbers:

                         16   8   3   32

             5. Add the following binary numbers. Perform the work in binary.

                         0010   1111   1010
                        +0110   +0010   +1110

             6. In what ways are the rules of binary addition similar to those for decimal addition?
             7. Convert the following hex values to decimal numbers:

                         7BC0   ABC1   111C4

             8. Convert the following decimal numbers to hex values:

                         1,356   17,000   299

             9. What is the function of the parity check? How does the parity system detect the loss of a bit?
            10. How do even and odd parity differ?
            11. What is the function of longitudinal parity?
            12. Refer to Figure 8.9. Write your name in the ASCII code combinations.
            13. Obtain a piece of punched paper tape from your instructor or data center. Compare it with the illustrations in this chapter. Label and translate 20 characters punched into it.
            14. Using the same tape as above, determine whether even or odd parity is used. Redraw the code, changing the parity.

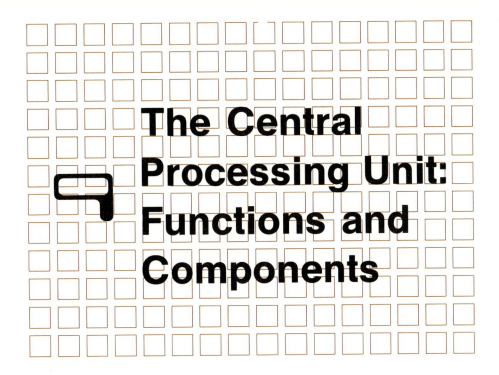

The Central Processing Unit: Functions and Components

The central processing unit (CPU) is the heart of the processing system. It is that portion of the computer which contains the control, main storage, and arithmetic units. It is designed to make arithmetic calculations and logical decisions. It is capable of storing a program and executing it, line-by-line, on data. It controls and schedules the overall operation of the computing system.

The CPU is linked to the I/O devices through I/O channels (discussed in Chapter 7). Data from tape readers, magnetic storage devices, card read punches, etc., flows to the CPU through these channels. It is processed in the CPU and then fed back through the channels for output on the I/O devices.

The CPU uses registers, primary storage areas, and secondary storage areas to provide storage and working space for all data during the processing of a program. This section is concerned with primary storage areas. Registers are explained in the next section, and secondary storage in the next chapter.

PRIMARY STORAGE

Primary storage is the basic means of storing data within the CPU itself. It holds a special program called the operating system (discussed in Chapter

193

15), which controls the computer. Primary storage acts as the main memory and holds problem programs, data files, and frequently used routines; it also provides a temporary work area for data produced by intermediate calculations and manipulation. Data ready for output is held in primary storage in the format required by the problem program.

Primary storage (often called core storage) is a reusable storage area. It is like a huge scratch pad, instantaneously available to the computer for saving directions, answers, and data, but easily erased by reading new data into the same area, on top of the old.

Advantages and Limitations

Data can be retrieved from primary storage in millionths of a second. Access is random (direct), and each item is located by its address.

Primary storage is limited by the physical composition of the CPU. This storage area must be shared by the control program of the CPU, the programming instructions, and the data for processing.

Small computers may provide only 12K bytes of core storage. That is, only 12,288 characters can be held in primary storage at one time. Larger computers may have from 64K to more than a million bytes of primary storage.

A large primary storage capacity allows many instructions and a large amount of data to be held for instantaneous use. This means that more complex programs can be processed faster. Smaller machines require a complex program to be broken into sections or modules, which are executed one at a time.

A large primary storage capacity is expensive because data is stored in physical hardware. Each byte of data in core storage must be held in a device, such as a ferrite core, flux ring, or plate wire.

Since data is held in fixed locations within the CPU, it cannot be physically removed, filed, or carried from the computer. Data can be transmitted to other computers, but information in core storage remains tied to the physical hardware.

Types

Ferrite core storage is a widely used, efficient, dependable means of storing data in the CPU. However, it is not the only method of primary storage in use. Other methods include flux rings, monolithic circuitry, plated wire, and thin film memories. (See Figure 9.1.) To represent a bit of data, specific areas or points on the memory devices are magnetized.

Ferrite Core Storage

ORGANIZATION.   Ferrite core storage is composed of thousands of cores, strung on wires to form a network. The cores are tiny doughnut-shaped objects pressed from iron ferrite. (See Figure 9.2(A).) Each core may be magnetized in either the clockwise or counterclockwise direction. Cores magnetized in the clockwise direction represent the "zero" state; in the counterclockwise direction, the "one" state. Once charged, the cores hold their direction of magnetism, or flux, until data is read out, or new data is read in.

FIGURE 9.1   PRIMARY STORAGE MEDIA

(A) MAGNETIC CORE MEMORY;

(B) MONOLITHIC MEMORY;

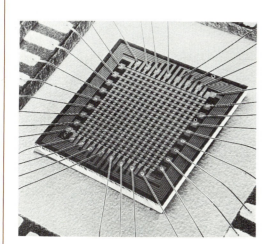

(C) THIN FILM MEMORY;

(D) THIN FILM MEMORY

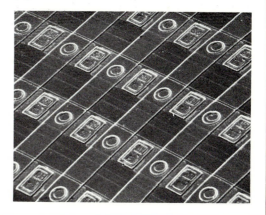

Each core is capable of holding one bit of data. The core networks are called planes. A flat surface with a core arrangement on it is a core plane. (See Figure 9.2(B).) The core planes are stacked in groups of eight or nine, depending upon the particular computer. If data is stored in the EBCDIC code (mentioned in the previous chapter), nine planes are necessary to allow eight bits of intelligence and one parity bit to be stored on a different plane. A column of bits representing one character is a byte.

The ASCII code system requires eight planes to allow for seven intelligence bits and one parity bit.

READING DATA IN. Each core is strung on a group of wires, called the X wire, Y wire, and sense wire as shown in Figure 9.2. To read in a bit of data, a specific core is magnetized by passing a small current of electricity through the X and Y wires. (See Figure 9.3.) Half of the current is sent

FIGURE 9.2   (A) FERRITE CORE; (B) CORE PLANE

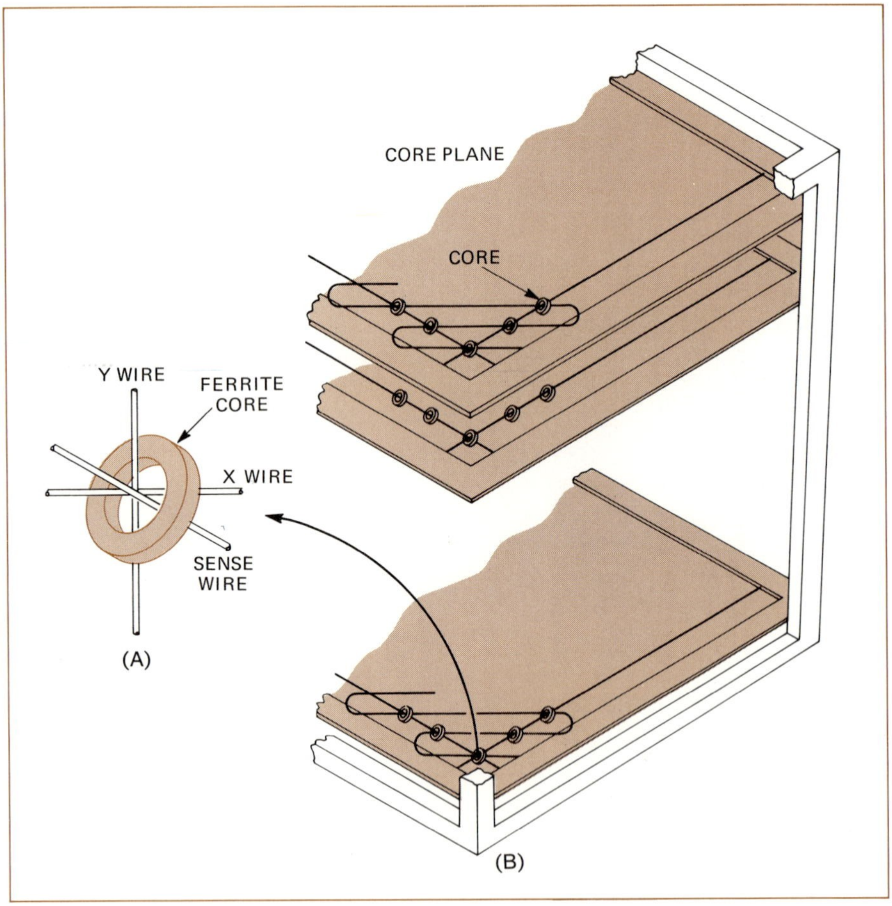

CORE PLANE

CORE

Y WIRE   FERRITE CORE

X WIRE

SENSE WIRE

(A)

(B)

FIGURE 9.3   CHARGING A CORE

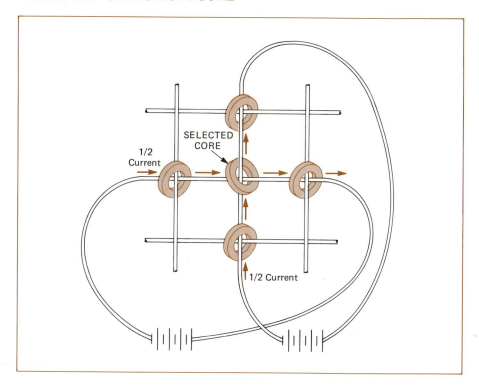

through the X wire; half through the Y wire. Only the core at the intersection of the two wires receives the full current and will be magnetized, or selected.

READING DATA OUT.   Data can be read out of core and copied into another area by sensing which cores have been magnetized. Basically, this is done by passing a voltage through the X and Y wires of each core, in succession, and monitoring the output on the sense wire. A charged core, receiving a full current through the X and Y wires, emits a weak electrical pulse, and the sense wire relays the pulses out of the core plane. Only one wire is required to sense all the cores on one plane. (See figure at left.)

Data flows from the cores in serial fashion, forming a pulse train. Each pulse represents one bit of data. A group of pulses represents a byte or character. These pulses are read into another work or storage area or sent to an output device.

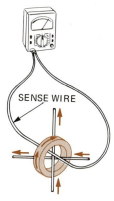

SENSE WIRE

Storage
Addresses

The core storage areas of the CPU are divided into smaller sections, called storage modules, shown in Figure 6.7. These modules, in turn, are broken down into small units composed of groups of cores. Each group of cores is called a storage location and has its own address. (See Figure 9.4.) Usually

FIGURE 9.4   STORAGE ADDRESSES

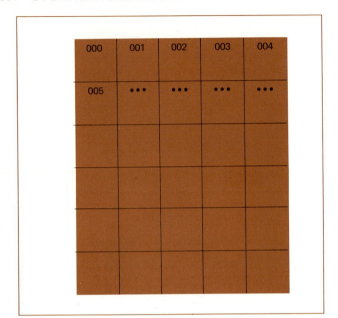

the first position or location in storage is assigned the address 000. The next one is 001, the next 002, and so on.

The numbers of bits (cores) in a storage location varies from one computer to another. All the bits stored in one location are treated as a unit and form a computer word. In some machines, each word has its own address. These machines are word addressable. Other machines are byte addressable. A word is addressed by the location of the first byte of the word.

A computer is built to store fixed- or variable-length words. Some computers can handle both. In a computer with fixed-length words, all words have the same number of bytes. In a machine using variable-length words, the words will vary in the number of bytes they contain. (See Figure 9.5.)

We address core storage in a manner similar to the way we address apartment buildings. The storage module can be compared to an apartment building where one street address refers to the whole building and all the apartments in it. Each apartment in the building is the same as a storage location (or word) with an individual number, A, B, C, and so on. In a fixed-length building, each apartment would have the same number of rooms. In a variable-length building, apartments would have different numbers of rooms.

In a computer with fixed-length words, every address refers to the same number of bytes. For example, assume a machine has a fixed word length of six bytes (and uses an eight-bit code). Data from location 120 is needed. The

FIGURE 9.5   WORD LENGTH

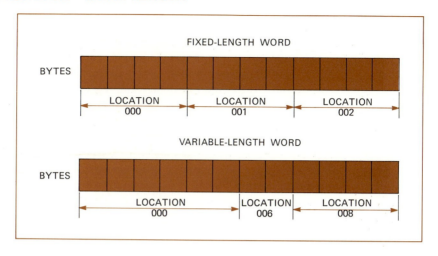

CPU will go to that location and read out the data from the next 48 cores (6 bytes × 8 bits = 48). The information stored in that location may be a two-digit number and fill only two of the available six bytes. The remaining four bytes will be unused storage space and may contain leading zeroes.

In a computer with variable word length, each byte has its own address. It would be very time consuming and tedious to address each letter in a name, or each digit in a number individually. It would be much more convenient to tell the computer that ten bytes in locations 205 to 214 belong together and form a word. To do this, it is necessary to signal the computer when the end of the word has been reached. One method is to use a word mark or control bit in the data representation code. It is turned on only in the last byte of each word.

A second method is to indicate in the programming instructions the number of bytes in each word. Some systems allow variable-length words to include as many as 256 bytes. Thus, one or two sentences, containing up to 256 characters, punctuation marks, and spaces, can be considered one word and can be easily referred to by one address and manipulated by one instruction.

Some computers can operate with both fixed-length and variable-length words, depending on the language used or the programmer's instructions. The CPU handles the details involved in aligning the word-length boundaries between the two systems.

DATA IN STORAGE.   A clear distinction exists between the data stored in a given location and the address itself. Let us return to the apartment building analogy. An apartment has an address and an occupant. They are not the same thing. The address refers to the location and does not change, but the occupant may change from time to time. Although an occupant can be located by his address, the address refers to his apartment and not to him.

In the same way, an address does not refer to data stored in a location, but to the location itself. (See Figure 9.6.) The data it holds will change, but the address will not. Each storage location is, in effect, a reusable container. Different data may be read in and out of one location several times during a program. To call data from storage, the programmer need not know the actual contents of the data, only the address at which it is stored. The circuitry will locate the value stored in the location and relay it for processing.

The ability to locate data from its address gives the CPU much of its power. The programmer can instruct the computer to perform a series of operations on the contents of an address. In this way, a series of operations can be repeated many times during a job, each time on a new piece of data read into a particular storage location. The programmer has only to instruct the computer to store the data in the proper location.

To illustrate, suppose a programmer directs the computer to read two numbers into locations 013 and 214. The numbers are to be added, and the answer is to be sent to location 041 and then printed out on the line printer. Then the computer is to return to the beginning of the program and repeat the cycle on two more numbers.

When executing the program, the CPU will first read the two numbers,

FIGURE 9.6   DATA IN STORAGE LOCATIONS

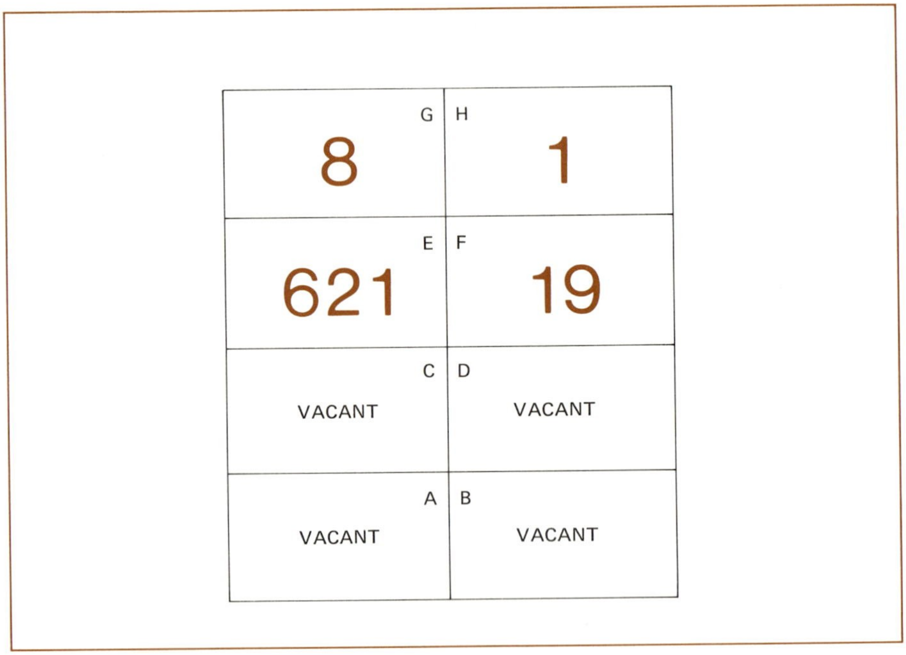

G	H
8	1
E	**F**
621	19
C	D
VACANT	VACANT
A	B
VACANT	VACANT

(say 109 and 216) into storage locations 013 and 214. Later the CPU will call them and feed them to the arithmetic unit for processing. Here they will be added and the result fed to location 041. Instructions then direct the computer to print out the contents of location 041 on the line printer. The number 325 will be printed out. Then the CPU will begin the next cycle, bring in two new numbers (say 382 and 418), and read them into locations 013 and 214. It will add, send the result (800) to location 041, and print it out. The cycle will be repeated until all numbers have been added.

REGISTERS

The CPU contains a group of storage areas called registers, which are similar in concept to core storage, but hold only a few bytes of data, or a limited number of words. (See Figure 9.7.) Registers serve different purposes. Some are used by the control function of the CPU, some by the arithmetic and logical unit, and others as temporary storage devices. Data can be read in and out of these registers in millionths of a second.

Registers are electrical circuits composed of transistors or magnetic cores. Being electronic devices, transistors are either on or off, either in an emitting or nonemitting state. An emitting transistor represents the value "1" stored in that position. A nonemitting transistor represents the value "0." Similarly, magnetic cores can represent "1's" or "0's."

General- and Special-Purpose Registers

The system of registers is an indispensable part of the CPU, and gives it its ability to "process" data. The electrical changes that take place in the transistors or cores of the registers allow the computer to actually count, store data, compare electrical pulses, and perform mathematics. There are two kinds of registers: general purpose and special purpose.

A general-purpose register can be used for many functions, in addition to those operations performed by the special-purpose registers. For example, general-purpose registers will index (act as a counter), act as an

FIGURE 9.7 CORE REGISTER

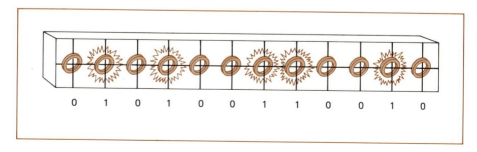

0 1 0 1 0 0 1 1 0 0 1 0

BREEDING TURKEYS BY COMPUTER

A computer at Williams Turkey Breeding Farms, Inc., in California is helping scientists breed turkeys that will produce poults with desirable characteristics, such as superior body conformation, fast weight gain, and high meat yield, that meet the specific requirements of the market in North and South America and Europe.

The company keeps computer records on every breeder bird—dating back five and six generations—and notes its characteristics. This allows experts to mate certain birds and predict the attributes of the offspring.

With the computer, Williams is able to check quality constantly to see that a particular flock is meeting pre-set standards of growth and egg production.

To assure economical egg production, the company maintains computerized records on each flock. When production begins to falter—usually after 20 to 26 weeks of laying—the turkeys are processed for the table.

The computer also keeps track of the eggs, by flock, from the day they are laid until they hatch. Thus researchers can determine if variations in feed and other factors affect the number and quality of the eggs.

SOURCE   IBM Data Processing Division, 3424 Wilshire Blvd., Los Angeles, California, Press Information Release on Williams Turkey Breeding Farms, P.O. Box 2, Oakdale, California 95361.

accumulator, and hold addresses or data for processing. In most systems, general-purpose registers are available to the programmer.

Special-purpose registers are reserved by the CPU for specific jobs. They include the address register, instruction register, storage register, and accumulator register.

INSTRUCTION REGISTER. One instruction at a time is pulled from primary storage by the CPU and placed in registers for execution. The instruction register holds the part of an instruction which indicates what process is to be performed.

ADDRESS REGISTER. The address register holds the part of an instruction which indicates where the data to be used is stored.

STORAGE REGISTER. A storage register acts as a temporary storage area for data awaiting processing. (Actual processing does not take place in storage registers—they are more like waiting rooms where data needed for the next step in an operation is kept ready.) While part of the CPU is operating on one piece of data, another part can locate the next piece from core and have it ready in a readily accessible storage register.

ACCUMULATOR REGISTER.   The accumulator register holds results of calculations. Accumulator registers hold binary bits of data, such as numbers, sums, quotients, and products. Each time a new value is added to a running total, for example, it is added to the accumulator register, updating the total. When the calculations have been completed, the results in the accumulator register can be read into storage or another register for further processing.

OTHER CPU COMPONENTS

Other functions of the CPU are to perform mathematical calculations and to make logical decisions. Many electronic components built into the CPU are used in the performance of these functions. They include the cycle clock, counters, decoders, and mathematical and logical circuitry.

© Datamation®

Cycle Clock   At the center of the CPU is a clock which sends out pulses at the rate of billions of cycles per second. These electrical pulses are sent to parts of the CPU to control its operations and timing. The pulse causes electrical circuits to open or close. Completed circuits create new paths for the pulse to follow and, in turn, these open other paths. All operations of the CPU are actually only a matter of different paths which the circuitry opens. Each change in the electrical condition within the CPU is in time with, and in response to, the pulses from this clock. Each step the computer takes to solve a problem is governed by this internal clock.

Counters   CPU's contain modules called counters, which have only one function: to count and remember the number of pulses sent to them. They are not mechanical devices, but groups of transistors and diodes arranged in a "flip-flop" circuit. (See Figure 9.8.) Flip-flop circuits increase by one each time they receive an electrical pulse.

FIGURE 9.8   FLIP-FLOP COUNTER

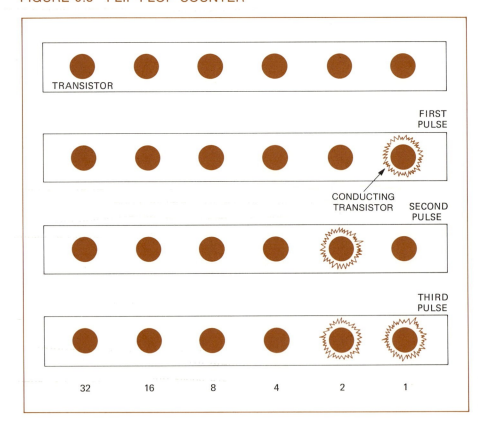

A transistor in a flip-flop circuit reverses its electrical state when a pulse hits it. If it is already conducting and is fed another pulse, it passes the current on to the next transistor and changes to a nonconducting state.

At the beginning of the counting cycle, all transistors are set to zero and are nonconducting. The first pulse turns on the first transistor (creating a binary one). The second pulse causes it to flip flop, turn on the next transistor, and turns off (creating a binary 2). The next pulse turns on the first transistor again (creating a binary 3), and so on.

Counters can work in a positive or negative direction. They are controlled by the CPU and used for specific functions during the processing of a job. For example, counters are used to keep track of the number of times a given series of steps is carried out. If the computer is to repeat a cycle, say 100 times, the counter will add one each time a cycle is completed. When the counter reaches 100, the computer will go on to the next instruction. Or if a number is to be multiplied by itself (raised to a power), for example, 10^6, a counter will increase each time the number is multiplied, until the limit 6 has been reached.

Counters also keep track of instructions. Instructions are assigned consecutive storage spaces in core. The instruction counter will be indexed to the address of the first instruction. This counter will increase each time the CPU processes an instruction, indicating the address of the next instruction to be processed.

Suppose a series of 30 instructions is held in core storage in positions 000 to 029, as shown in Figure 9.9. A counter is set to 000, the address of the first instruction. The CPU will call the contents of storage space 000 and perform the operations directed by the instruction. Meanwhile, the counter will increase and equal 001. When the CPU is ready, it checks the counter to learn the location of the next instruction. Then this instruction is called and executed, and the counter again increases by 1. This procedure will continue until all 30 instructions have been processed.

Decoder

A decoder is an electronic device in the CPU, which sets up an electrical pathway in response to a specific code.

Operation decoders convert an instruction into the electrical paths or circuits that will perform the proper operation. For example, suppose the computer is directed to perform addition. Say that in the computer language being used the word ADD is the code for addition. In binary, ADD might be expressed as 0101 1010. This string of binary bits is sent to a decoder. The decoder senses the bit pattern and prepares the circuitry that performs addition. It will allocate storage registers to hold the augend (number on top), the addend (number on bottom), and the sum.

Command decoders prepare the proper pathways for program instructions which have been input from the console. Other decoders convert expressions from a code to a more easily understood form. For example, decoders convert binary strings to their decimal equivalents.

Encoders are similar devices which convert an expression into a coded

FIGURE 9.9   ADDRESS COUNTER FOR INSTRUCTIONS

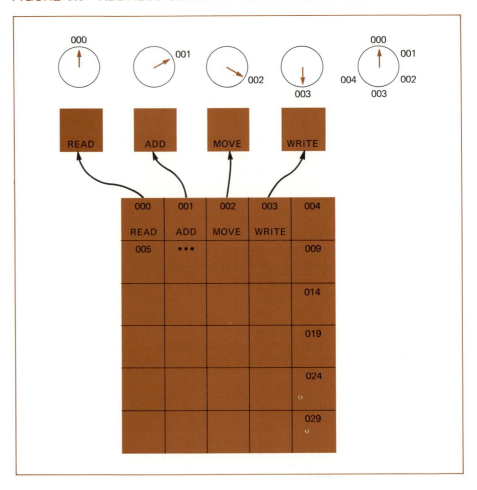

form. For example, they will change a decimal number into its binary value for use by the CPU.

Mathematical and Logical Circuitry   The actual mechanics involved in addition, subtraction, and logical decisions are performed by a group of specialized circuits within the CPU. These circuits use gates. Gates are transistors and diodes wired in special arrangements which open different pathways, depending on the pulses they receive.

Many kinds of gates are used in a CPU. They are wired in different arrangements and combinations. Gates are capable of adding and subtracting binary numbers, comparing values to determine whether a value is equal to, or greater than, another, etc. Gates are the heart of the computer's mathematical and logical ability. Some common CPU gates are AND gate, OR gate, and NOR gate.

To illustrate the use of gates, below is a brief description of the function of the AND gate, used in performing addition. This gate is a special transistor with two input wires and one output wire. If a pulse is sent to both of the input wires, the transistor conducts a signal to the output wire. If a pulse is received by only one of its input wires, it will not conduct a signal. An AND gate will trigger its output wire *only* if pulses are sent to both input wires simultaneously.

Some gates emit a pulse only when one input wire receives a pulse. Other gates continue to emit pulses until they are stopped by a pulse to an input wire.

To actually perform a mathematical operation, the numbers to be processed will be called out from storage and fed into registers. Electrical pathways are set up which feed the pulses representing these numbers to the proper gates. The output from the gates passes through other circuitry and into accumulator registers. From there, the pulses may go back to storage, be used for other processing, or perhaps sent to an output device.

Logical decisions are made in gates similar to the mathematical ones described above. Logical gates test the voltage from one value against another. They can indicate whether a given value is equal to, greater than, or less than the other value. This result can then be used by the CPU to branch control to one of several paths specified in a program.

INSTRUCTION AND EXECUTION CYCLES

The previous sections of this chapter discussed the individual parts of the CPU and their functions. All components are electrical devices which operate only when they receive a signal from another electrical component, or from the program. The end result of all this activity is to process the job. The CPU takes the series of pulses representing data from a payroll or sales orders, for example, moves them around, changes their order, and restructures the data into another form.

The computer cannot perform any of these activities on its own. It must be fed a list of the operations to be performed. These directions trigger the circuitry involved in processing the job. Some of these instructions are from the control program stored in the CPU.

Other instructions are prepared by the programmer to fit the needs of his particular job. These programming instructions are entered into storage units of the CPU and stored in consecutive storage locations.

Programming Instructions   Computer instructions have two basic parts: the operation code and the operands.

INSTRUCTION:

OPERATION CODE	OPERANDS

The operation code (op code) tells the control unit what function is to be performed and the computer will prepare the circuitry that performs that function. Typical operations are ADD, SUBTRACT, MOVE DATA, COMPARE, etc.

The operands indicate the location of the data to be operated on. Most instructions will use two operands called OPA and OPB. The data represented by OPA and OPB may be manipulated in different ways. OPB will be subtracted from OPA. OPA will be added to OPB. OPB will be stored in the location indicated by OPA, etc. Below is how an instruction with two operands will look.

INSTRUCTION:

OPCODE	OPA	OPB
SUB	BAL	PAY

In this case, OPCODE is the code for the operation that is to be performed. OPA is the location of the first piece of data; and OPB, the location of the second piece of data. When the computer executes the above instruction, it will perform the activity directed by OPCODE on the data indicated as OPA and OPB.

Machine Cycles The procedure for executing programming instructions involves two cycles, which are synchronized with the pulses coming from the cycle clock. These cycles are the instruction (I) cycle, which sets up circuitry to perform a required operation, and the execution (E) cycle, during which the operation is actually carried out.

Computers alternate between the two cycles millions of times per second, in time with the pulses from the cycle clock. The first cycle is always the instruction cycle, and it is followed by the execution cycle. The time spent on the instruction cycle is called I time; that spent on the execution cycle, E time.

During the instruction cycle, the computer locates the instruction in storage and places it in a storage register. The operation code is sent to the instruction register and the operand to the address register. The operation decoder converts the op code into the specific circuitry necessary to perform the job. During I time, the address counter increments, informing the computer of the location of the next instruction.

The function of the execution cycle is to manipulate the data as specified in the op code of the instruction. The data specified by the operand is pulled from storage and sent to the proper devices by the circuitry initiated by the op code. During the execution cycle, the computer may move data electronically from core to register, and vice versa. It adds numbers, moves data, subtracts values, etc. The results of these or other functions are placed in appropriate registers or storage. After execution is completed, the cycles are repeated for the next instruction. This continues until the last instruction in the program has been executed.

KEY TERMS

Core storage
Core plane
X wire
Y wire
Sense wire
Storage address
Computer word
Fixed-length word
Variable-length word
Word mark

Register
Cycle clock
Counter
Decoder
Gate
Instruction cycle
Execution cycle
Op code
Operand

EXERCISES

1. Draw a ferrite core and label each of the wires it is strung on.
2. Contrast the differences between the ways data is read into and out of core.
3. What are the differences between fixed- and variable-length words?
4. What functions does primary storage perform?
5. In what ways does register storage differ from core storage?
6. Briefly define the functions of the following:
   a. Address register
   b. Instruction register
   c. Storage register
   d. Accumulator register
7. What is the function of the cycle clock?
8. What are gates? How do they differ?
9. How is counting performed in the CPU?
10. Arrange a group of dominos or other objects into a flip-flop counter. Increase this counter by manipulating the dominos.
11. What are the differences between the instruction and execution cycles?
12. List five operations and assign them operation codes.
13. What is the purpose of having two operands in an instruction?
14. Draw core storage capable of holding 20 bytes of data. Label storage positions and assign addresses.
15. What are some common means of primary storage?

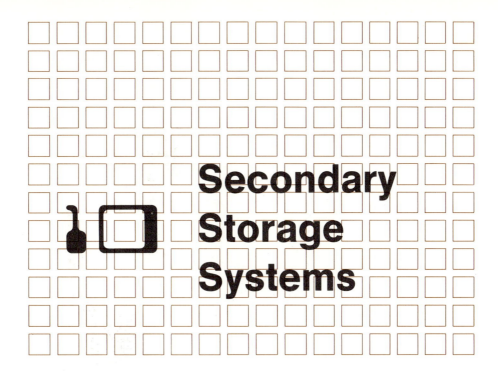

Secondary Storage Systems

As discussed in Chapter 9, primary storage is located within the CPU and is directly accessible to it. Data can be read in and out of core in only a few millionths of a second. Secondary storage devices are indirectly accessible to the CPU and provide it with additional, virtually unlimited storage facilities. Data that the CPU will need only occasionally (files, for example) is kept in secondary storage.

ACCESS TIME

The average time required to locate and retrieve a given piece of data from storage is known as the average access time. To illustrate, estimate how long it would take you to look up information in your class notes. Obviously, if your notes are with you in class and consist of only a few pages, it would not take as long as it would if they filled several notebooks and were at home. The time necessary to locate the required information could be called your access time. Thus, access time is a function of

① The location of the data
② The amount of data to be searched
③ The speed of hardware

Because primary storage is located within the CPU, it naturally has a shorter access time than secondary storage. Primary storage, too, is limited

211

in capacity and thus contains less data. These factors combine to make primary storage more readily accessible than secondary storage.

ACCESS METHODS

Two methods are used to access data in secondary storage: sequential access and random access.

Sequential access means that to locate a given piece of data each item in a file must be searched in sequence. Magnetic tape is the most commonly used form of sequential access storage. Data is stored on magnetic tape in the order in which it was recorded. To find a piece of data, the computer rewinds the reel of tape to the beginning and checks each item on the tape until it finds the specified data.

Random access storage devices can retrieve data from storage without searching in sequence. To do this, the storage media is divided into storage locations, and addresses are assigned to each location. Each data record being read into storage is assigned to one of these locations. Given the address, the computer can locate a specific piece of data without searching through every item in the file. Because the computer can go directly to the item in storage, random access is often referred to as direct access. Data stored on random access devices can, of course, be accessed sequentially as well. Magnetic disks and drums are common random access devices.

Understandably, sequential access devices are slower than random access.

SELECTION OF STORAGE MEDIA

The selection of the storage devices largely depends on the needs of the business firm. Firms that have millions of records to be filed will need large secondary storage systems. A firm must also consider whether files are in sequential or in random order, cost of storage systems, data access speeds, and core storage capabilities. Most computer installations use a combination of media to provide high-speed access for certain files and high-capacity storage for others.

Four principal methods of secondary storage have been developed and are widely used in data processing: magnetic tape, magnetic disk, magnetic drum, and data cell.

MAGNETIC TAPE STORAGE

Magnetic tape is a sequential access storage medium. One or more tape units may be placed on-line with the CPU to give the computer access to data stored on more than one reel of magnetic tape at a time.

**Code
System**
Two common code systems are used to record data on magnetic tape: the seven-channel BCD Alphameric code and the nine-channel EBCDIC code. The BCD Alphameric code requires seven tracks of data, six for intelligence and one for a parity check bit. In the EBCDIC code, nine tracks are used to record data, eight for intelligence and the ninth for a parity check bit.

**Physical
Description**
Magnetic tape is $\frac{1}{2}$-inch-wide plastic ribbon that has been coated with a thin layer of ferromagnetic material and wound on reels. (See Figure 10.1.) The two most common reel sizes are $10\frac{1}{2}$ inches in diameter, holding 2,400 feet of tape, and $8\frac{1}{2}$ inches in diameter, holding 1,200 feet.

FIGURE 10.1   (A) MAGNETIC TAPE; (B) REEL WITH FILE
PROTECTION RING

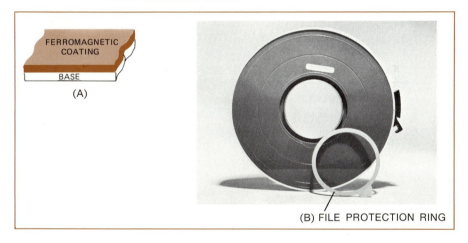

(B) FILE PROTECTION RING

Each reel of magnetic tape contains two indicator marks, which note the beginning of usable recording tape and the end of the reel. These marks are called

load-point mark: beginning of usable tape

end-of-reel mark: end of usable area on tape

The load-point mark is a small piece of reflective foil bonded to one edge of the tape. (See Figure 10.2.) Photocells in the drive mechanism sense the mark and automatically index the tape to this point.

The end-of-reel mark is a similar piece of reflective material bonded to the opposite edge of the tape, near the end of the reel. Photocells sense this mark and stop the movement of the tape through the transport. No data can be recorded beyond the end-of-reel mark.

The tape reel is equipped with a special plastic ring, called the file protection ring. (See Figure 10.1.) When the ring is in place on the reel, new data can be recorded or old data erased from the tape. When the ring is removed, no new data can be recorded over the existing bits of information.

FIGURE 10.2   TAPE MARKER

LOAD-POINT MARK

The removal of this ring serves as a protection against accidental destruction of important data, since it requires a deliberate act by the computer operator to replace it.

Recording Data

Data is recorded by magnetizing areas of the coating as the tape passes under a write head. The head converts electronic pulses (representing alphabetic and numeric characters) to magnetized spots on the moving tape. Data is read from the tape by a reverse procedure. The read head senses the magnetized spots on the tape, induces a current in a pickup coil, and converts the magnetic fields to electronic pulses. These pulses, representing coded data, are sent to the CPU for processing. The same head may be used for both writing and reading and is often referred to as a read/write head. (See Figure 10.3.)

TAPE RECORD. A tape record is a group of bytes relating to a single transaction. Tape records can be either fixed or variable in length. A record can be only one byte or as many as several thousand. Each record on the tape is separated by a 0.6-inch-wide space, called the inter-record gap (IRG),

FIGURE 10.3   RECORDING ON MAGNETIC TAPE

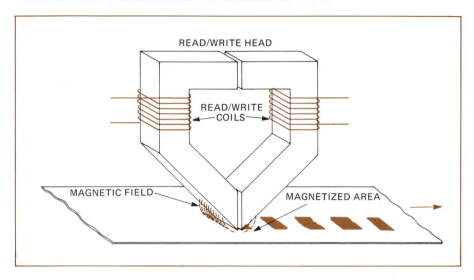

shown in Figure 10.4. When a computer reads a file, the tape drive comes to a stop after each record, starts again, moves to the next record, stops again, etc. Approximately 0.6 of an inch of tape will be reeled during the time required for the drive to go from a stopped position to the proper speed for reading or writing.

Inter-record gaps waste space on the tape, however, and fewer bytes of data can be stored on a reel. One method of avoiding this loss is to block or combine several records without IRG's, as shown in Figure 10.5. Each block is separated by an IRG, sometimes called an interblock gap (each record is separated by a group mark inserted during programming).

IBM 3420 Magnetic Tape Series   This machine, shown in Figure 10.6, is capable of reading and writing data on magnetic tape. The unit contains two reel spindles, a drive mechanism called the tape transport, and a read/write head.

The 3420 Tape Unit reads or writes on tape at densities of 800 or 1,600 bytes per inch. It uses even or odd parity, and will process tape in either seven- or nine-channel codes.

MAGNETIC DISK STORAGE

Magnetic disk storage machines are random access devices which are connected on-line to the CPU to provide additional secondary storage capacity.

Code System   Data is recorded as magnetized areas on the surface of the disk. The EBCDIC coding system is used.

FIGURE 10.4   INTER-RECORD GAP

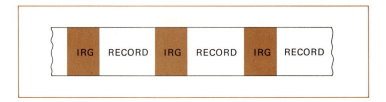

FIGURE 10.5   BLOCKING RECORDS

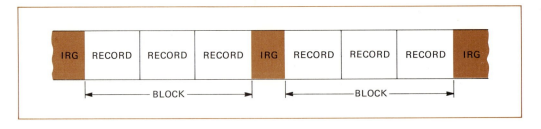

FIGURE 10.6   IBM 3420 MAGNETIC TAPE SERIES

Physical
Description

A magnetic disk is a round metal plate coated with a thin layer of ferromagnetic material. Each disk is approximately 14 inches in diameter and has from 200 to 500 concentric circles, called tracks, per surface. Data is recorded one byte at a time along each track. Depending on the system used, from 3,625 to 7,294 bytes of data can be recorded on each track. A disk pack is a collection of two or more disks (usually six) mounted on a common shaft. (See Figure 10.7.) A disk drive rotates the pack at 2,400 revolutions per minute. Each disk pack weighs about ten pounds and can be removed from the drive mechanism and stored in a filing cabinet.

FIGURE 10.7   DISK PACK

The vertical alignment formed by one track from each surface of a disk is called a cylinder. A sector is a pie-shaped section of a disk.

Recording
Data

Data is recorded on both the top and bottom surfaces of each disk (except for the top and bottom surfaces of the pack). A disk pack with six disks will have ten recording surfaces. A group of read/write heads attached to movable arms record data on the disk pack. (See Figure 10.8.) The arms move back and forth across the surfaces of the disks. Two read/write heads attached to one arm service the bottom of one disk and the top of another. On some models, the heads may move in unison with each accessing

FIGURE 10.8   DISK ACCESS MECHANISM

READ/WRITE HEAD

different tracks of the same cylinder. On other models, the arms work independently. To locate a given piece of data, the arms advance across the disks to the appropriate cylinder. A read head senses the magnetized areas on the revolving disk and converts them into electronic pulses.

DISK RECORDS.   Records stored on a disk can be either fixed or variable in length. Storage locations on a disk pack are identified by disk surface number and track number.

IBM 2311
Disk Storage

The IBM 2311 Disk Storage device shown in Figure 10.9, has ten read/write heads which move in unison. It has a spindle for mounting disk packs, a switch panel, and related circuitry. Each 2311 disk pack will store $7\frac{1}{4}$ million bytes of data. Average access time is 75 milliseconds. Normally, up to eight 2311's can be connected to a single control unit. Data is transferred from the disk to the CPU at the rate of 156,000 bytes per second.

MAGNETIC DRUM STORAGE

Magnetic drum is a random access device similar in principle to the magnetic disk. The magnetic drum usually has a smaller storage capacity than either

FIGURE 10.9   IBM 2311 DISK STORAGE UNIT

magnetic tape or disk, but a much faster access time. It is used like a scratch pad to record data that will be used repeatedly during a job, such as programs, operating systems, or mathematical functions.

Code
System

Encoded data is recorded on the drum in addressable tracks. The EBCDIC code is used to record data.

Physical
Description

A metal cylinder coated with a thin layer of ferromagnetic material is mounted on a drum storage drive. There are 200 tracks around the diameter of the drum, numbered 0 to 199. Each of these tracks, in turn, is made up of four subtracks, making a total of 800 tracks. Each of the main tracks will store up to 20,483 bytes of data and over four million bytes can be stored on a single drum. The drive rotates the drum under a group of magnetic read/write heads at the rate of 3,500 revolutions per minute. (See Figure 10.10.) Each track has its own permanently mounted read/write head.

Recording
Data

As the drum rotates, data is recorded on its surface by a read/write head. To retrieve data from the drum, a read head senses the magnetized areas on the

PHONY PHONE CALLER GETS A HANG UP

California leads the nation in fraudulent credit card telephone calls, accounting for one-half of the national total. Pacific Telephone & Telegraph Company is attacking the problem with a computer programmed to say "no" in a feminine voice.

The recorded voice has stopped the completion of 80,000 bogus credit card calls since it was put into operation last January.

When a credit card call is placed, the operator keypunches the card number into the computer. If the number checks out, the feminine voice will say "okay." If it's a phony, the voice says "no." It repeats the number and says "no" again. The entire process takes 22 seconds.

The caller caught in the act is given the choice of paying for the call or hanging up.

Note: For security reasons, the computer's location is kept secret.

SOURCE   "Phony Phone Caller Gets a Hang Up," News/Analysis, *Business Automation*, May 1972, Vol. 19, No. 5, p. 6.

FIGURE 10.10   DRUM STORAGE DEVICE

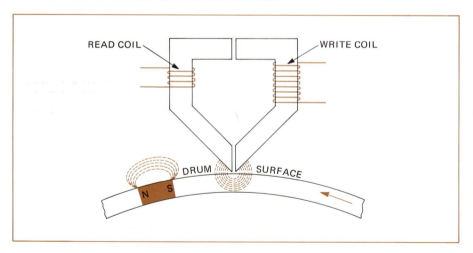

rotating drum and converts them to electronic pulses, which are fed to the CPU for processing.

DRUM RECORDS.   Storage locations are addressed by track numbers. Drum records may be fixed or variable in length. Records can be from 1 to 65,535 bytes in length.

IBM 2301   This unit, shown in Figure 10.11, has a drum drive system, which rotates the
Drum Storage drum at 3,500 revolutions per minute. A group of fixed-position read/write
             heads are located across each track. Data is transferred from the drum to the
             CPU at the rate of 303,800 bytes per second.

DATA CELL STORAGE

The data cell is a random access medium with a high storage capacity. Each
cell will store up to 40 million bytes of data. By coupling ten cells into a data
cell array, as many as 400 million bytes of data can be accessed by the CPU.

Code   Encoded data is recorded on a strip in addressable tracks. The EBCDIC
System   coding system is used.

Physical   The data cell drive is a cylinder that stores magnetic strips. The strips are
Description made of plastic and coated with a thin layer of ferromagnetic material. Ten of
            these strips form a subcell; 20 subcells make up one data cell. The cell drive
            can hold ten cells. (See Figure 10.12.)

"This is rich, Harry. Account
number 345-26-4155 wishes correspondence
with a human being."

© Datamation®

FIGURE 10.11   IBM 2301 DRUM STORAGE UNIT

Recording Data

To read or write data, the data cell drive rotates until the proper data cell is under a strip selection mechanism. This device pulls the strip out of the subcell and wraps it around a drum. The drum rotates the strip under a read/write head. After reading or writing, the strip is automatically replaced in the cell. Cells are replaceable and interchangeable.

FIGURE 10.12   DATA CELL DRIVE

DATA STRIP
(100 Tracks per Strip)

SUBCELL
10 Strips per Subcell

DRIVE
10 Cells per Drive

CELL
20 Subcells per Cell

IBM 2321
Data Cell
Drive

This device, shown in Figure 10.13, has ten cells. Each cell contains 20 subcells, each holding ten magnetic strips. Each magnetic strip has a hole at the top. The read/write mechanism uses this hole to pull the strip from the cell and replace it.

This system of strip access provides high-density storage capacity with

FIGURE 10.13   IBM 2321 DATA CELL DRIVE

relatively slow access time. Each drive can hold a total of 2,000 strips. A group of 2,000 strips can hold 40 million bytes of data.

ADVANTAGES AND LIMITATIONS OF SECONDARY STORAGE

Secondary storage is an efficient, compact means of storing large amounts of data. Large files can be maintained in a limited amount of physical space. Since magnetic surfaces are used to record data, cost per byte of storage is much less than core storage. A reel of magnetic tape, which weighs about four pounds, will hold an amount of data equivalent to what could be stored on a thousand pounds of punched cards. Magnetic disk storage is even more efficient. A ribbon of magnetic tape, about 2,400 feet long, costs less than

$20. The same amount of data recorded on punched cards would cost approximately $200.00.

Secondary storage devices, such as magnetic tape or disk packs, are easily carried, or filed. Disk packs for example, can be carried from one computer to another. Magnetic tape reels can be filed in racks, carried about, or sent through the mails. Tape reels can be given to computer centers not directly connected to the CPU; files are often delivered to other departments for additional processing, or made available to other firms or governmental agencies.

Average access times differ among secondary storage devices, but all are slower than core storage. Capacity also depends on the media and the particular model being used. Table 10.1 compares average access time, storage capacity, and access methods of several common media.

TABLE 10.1 COMPARISON OF ACCESS DEVICES

DEVICE	AVERAGE ACCESS TIME	CAPACITY IN BYTES	ACCESS METHOD
MAGNETIC TAPE	5 seconds	1600 per inch 40 mil. per reel	sequential
MAGNETIC DRUM	8.6 milliseconds	4 million per drum	random
MAGNETIC DISK	75 milliseconds	29.17 million per disk pack	random
DATA CELL DRIVE	350 milliseconds	400 million per cell	random

One can readily see that in random access devices there is a trade-off between storage capacity and access time. As more and more records are stored in a given system, the access time is increased.

FILE MAINTENANCE

File maintenance is a major responsibility of data processing. It is the operation of keeping files current and up to date. It involves posting debits, credits, removing inactive names, adding new names to files, updating payroll records, etc.

In unit record systems, file maintenance is performed by moving cards in and out of card files. In computerized systems, file maintenance procedures use secondary storage devices. Instead of keeping files on punched cards, master files are maintained on magnetic tape, disks, or drums. Files are

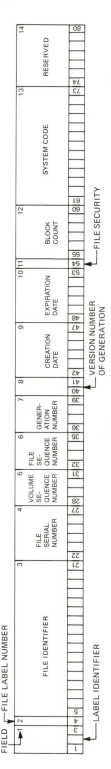

manipulated by merging and updating the contents of reels of tape, disk, drums, etc.

Many large firms maintain large files of accounts receivable, payroll, personnel, inventory, and sales data. These master files are kept on disk or tape devices. As new data is obtained, it is added to the master file to keep it current. The updated information on the master file is available at any time that it may be needed. Status reports may be printed out on a daily, weekly, or monthly basis. In other systems, the master file is queried by direct, on-line access, from a remote terminal.

In any file maintenance procedure, care must be taken to see that the correct files are being processed. Updating the wrong inventory file, or posting charges to the wrong list of customers, would cause many problems. A file identification system is especially important in secondary storage systems, where data is stored in a magnetic code that the human operator cannot read to verify identification.

Data processing techniques have been developed to accurately identify files and prevent errors. These techniques are based upon volume and file labels. These labels are similar to a book's table of contents. They contain information on the files stored on a reel of tape or a disk, and where they are located. Volume and file labels are not physical labels applied to the cell, disk or reel of tape, but are magnetized bits of information recorded on the media. Physical labels (readable by humans) may also, of course, be applied to the media.

Volume labels are the first item recorded on a disk or reel of tape. They list the name and location of all files contained in that unit. On magnetic tape, file labels are located at the beginning and end of each file. They identify the file and contain other information such as expiration date, file serial number, length of file. Labels assure the programmer that information is fed to the proper file and prevent an unexpired file from being accidentally erased. The figure in the left margin illustrates the layout of a tape file label.

KEY TERMS

Read/write head	Random access
Disk pack	File label
Magnetic disk	Volume label
Magnetic tape	IRG
Magnetic drum	Blocking
Data cell	Load-point mark
Access time	End-of-reel mark
Sequential access	

EXERCISES

1. Define primary and secondary storage.
2. Give three uses for primary storage and three for secondary storage.
3. What features do magnetic disk, tape, drum, and cell storage devices have in common?
4. Explain storage capacity and why it is important in secondary storage systems.
5. Define average access time. What factors affect it?
6. Ask a friend to look up five words in the dictionary at random. Using a stop watch, record his minimum and maximum access times. Calculate the average.
7. What are the advantages of random access storage and sequential access storage?
8. What is the purpose of labeling files?
9. Draw a length of magnetic tape and indicate the load-point mark, end-of-reel mark, and several records separated.
10. What kinds and types of secondary storage are available on the system in use at your data center?
11. Select one storage device used in your data center. Determine how it is used, what its average access time is, and how it is called in and out by the programmer.

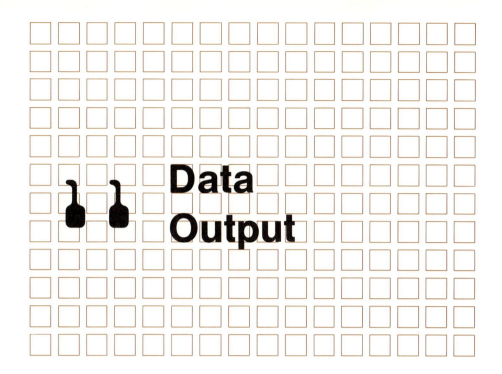

Data Output

Data output devices convert the electronic pulses emitted by the CPU into a form more convenient for man. These devices convert processed data into holes punched in paper tape or cards, into bits recorded on magnetic tape or disks, or into graphic representations. The most common forms of computer output are magnetic tapes, magnetic disks, paper tapes, punch cards, printed characters, characters on a video tube, photographic emulsions, graphs, and spoken words.

Some output devices convert the electronic pulses into a form suitable for storage or further processing, such as magnetic or paper tapes, magnetic drums, and data cells. (This output is not readable by man.) Earlier chapters have explained the principles involved in such output. Other devices, such as printers, convert processed data into a form directly readable by man.

PRINTERS

Impact Printers

Most typewriters use the type bar principle. Type hammers form the images by striking a ribbon against a sheet of paper. (On each hammer is a character in relief.) Type-bar output is slow and, therefore, not suitable for high-volume data processing.

Another method used to print characters is a type element or type ball,

229

FIGURE 11.1 TYPE ELEMENT

shown in Figure 11.1. A set of numbers and characters (called a font) is molded on each type element. To print a character, the element is indexed to the proper position and struck against the ribbon onto the sheet. Type element output is used on some console typewriters and small computers. The type element prints at a speed of 15 characters per second—too slow for high-volume computer output. However, the advantage of type element printers is that type sizes and styles can easily be changed by substituting elements.

The type wheel printer, shown in Figure 11.2, is a third method of generating characters. Each type wheel contains a full font of characters. To print a character, the wheel is rotated until the appropriate character is in position. An image is made by a hammer striking the sheet from behind or moving the type wheel forward against the page. One type wheel is used in each print position. Type wheel printers are faster than type element or type bar machines (they can print 200 to 300 lines per minute), but are also too slow for high-speed data output.

High-speed output is possible with the train printer principle, illustrated in

FIGURE 11.2 TYPE WHEEL PRINTER

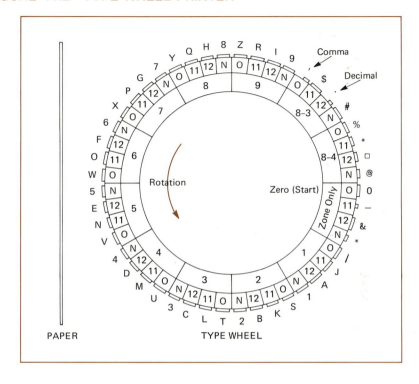

PAPER   TYPE WHEEL

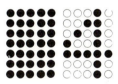

Figure 11.3. Type slugs are mounted on a moving train, or type chain. Gears move each slug past printing positions. A ribbon is placed between the page and the train. To print a character, a hammer behind the paper forces the sheet up against the moving type train. When the sheet is brought into contact with the moving train, a letter image is transferred to the paper. Train printers can produce 1,100 lines per minute. One or more full fonts of characters are available on each train.

Printed characters can also be generated with a wire matrix. (See the figure in the left margin.) Keypunch machines and some computer terminals use this principle. A group of 35 wires or rods is arranged in a 5 × 7 matrix pattern. Numbers and characters are formed by selectively striking the ends of the rods or wires. To print the digit "4," for example, the rods that form the image of the number are struck from behind and forced against the paper and the image is transferred. (A ribbon inserted between the rods and the page provides inking.)

Other Types
A comparatively new method of generating characters has been developed, which uses heat and heat-sensitive paper. Letter forms are generated by heating selected rods in a matrix. When the ends of the selected rods touch the heat-sensitive paper, the image is transferred. Though thermal imaging is relatively slow, it is practical for low-volume output.

FIGURE 11.3   TRAIN PRINTER MECHANISM

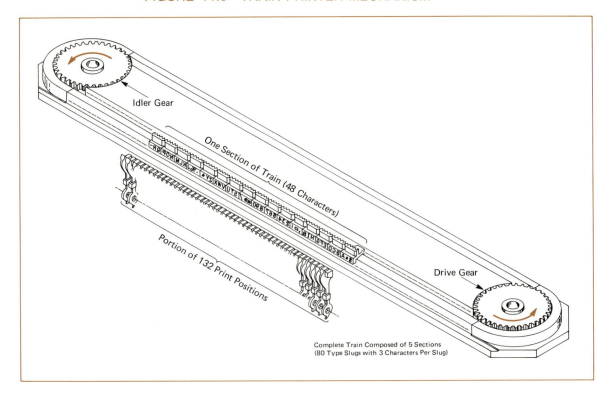

Idler Gear

One Section of Train (48 Characters)

Portion of 132 Print Positions

Drive Gear

Complete Train Composed of 5 Sections
(80 Type Slugs with 3 Characters Per Slug)

Electrostatic imaging is another method of outputting data. Images or letter forms on the face of a cathode ray tube are made permanent by copying them on a device similar to an ordinary photocopy machine. The concept is similar to making a Xerographic copy from a sheet of paper, except that the image is copied from a cathode ray tube.

Photographic techniques can also be used to create output images. (See Figure 11.4.) A beam of light is focused through a rotating disk containing a full font of characters. The image of a character is projected onto a piece of film or photographic paper. The print or negative is developed and fixed, similar to ordinary photographs. This form of output prints out high-quality, letter-perfect images and is often used in bookmaking.

Character Printing Sequence

Characters are printed in two ways: serial and parallel. In serial printing, one letter at a time is struck. For example, a line of 100 characters would be printed letter by letter, usually from left to right. The ordinary typewriter, type bar, and type element printers use this principle. Generally, serial printing is not used for high-volume computer output. It is, however, economical from a machine design standpoint and hence used for low-cost or low-volume output systems.

FIGURE 11.4   PHOTOGRAPHIC IMAGING

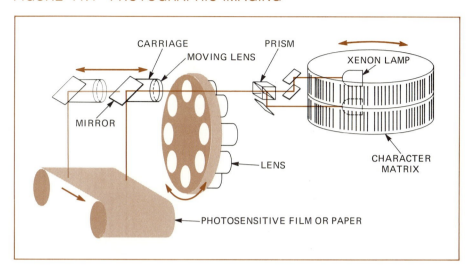

In parallel printing, all characters on a line are struck at the same instant. The type wheel printer uses this principle. To produce a line 100 characters wide, the output device will index 100 type wheels across the page to the proper images. At a signal, 100 hammers will strike the page, forcing it against all the type images at the same instant. Naturally, serial printing is much slower than parallel printing.

CATHODE RAY TUBE DEVICES

With all the forms discussed above, a permanent, hard copy record is generated. Occasionally, it is not necessary or even desirable to provide a permanent record of the output. The cathode ray tube (CRT) is frequently used to output a "soft copy" of data. (See Figure 11.5.) The principles involved are similar to those in forming images on an ordinary TV screen.

An electron beam is scanned back and forth across the face of a phosphor-coated tube at high speeds. The beam of electrons is modulated (turned on and off) as it swings back and forth. When the beam is on, it activates the phosphor coating on the inside of the tube and causes it to glow. The glowing spots on the tube create patterns—the letter images—visible from the outside. Curves, lines, and other figures can be generated in the same manner.

ON-LINE/OFF-LINE OUTPUT

In recent years there has been a proliferation of output media. The selection of a particular medium depends upon the needs of the user, facilities

FIGURE 11.5   CATHODE RAY TUBE

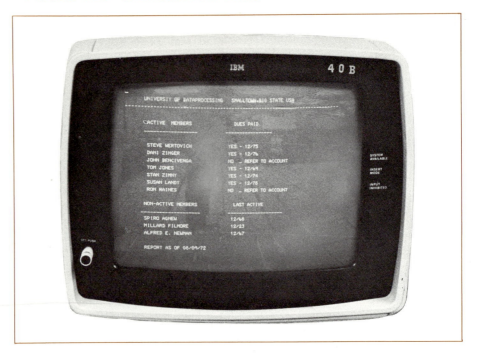

available in the computer center, cost, and quality factors. On-line output machines receive pulses directly from the CPU. Transmitted data is recorded on output records without being held in intermediate storage. Off-line machines receive data recorded on paper tape, magnetic tape, or other storage media and are not connected directly to the CPU. The tape is placed on the off-line machine to produce charts, graphs, pages for reproduction by the printing process, etc.

On-Line Output Machines

IBM 1403 PRINTER.   This widely used machine converts electronic pulses into printed characters on a page. (See Figure 11.6.) The IBM 1403 can print from 340 to 1,100 lines per minute, and each line can have as many as 132 print positions.

A pin-feed mechanism allows multiple-part forms, carbonless paper, or register forms to be accurately positioned for printing. The IBM 1403 feeds continuous accordion-folded forms from a paper magazine at the base of the machine to the paper carriage for printing. A carriage control tape punched with a special code and placed in the carriage control mechanism will cause the carriage to skip spaces between lines. (See Figure 11.7.) Standard spacing is ten characters per inch and six or eight lines per inch, but special spacing arrangements can be made. Thus, statements, invoices, and other documents can be prepared on the line printer. A print train is used to print

FIGURE 11.6   IBM 1403 PRINTER

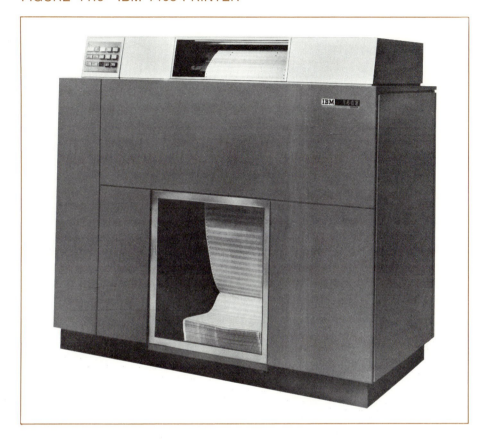

out characters. After being printed, the paper moves over a bale and down into the paper receiver, where the sheets are stacked for removal by the operator.

IBM 2520 CARD READ PUNCH.   The IBM 2520, shown in Figure 11.8, converts electronic pulses to holes in a punched card. The machine is equipped with a card-feed hopper, capable of holding 1,200 cards, and a transport mechanism, which moves the cards past a read station and a punch station to either of two card stackers. The IBM 2520 is connected to the CPU through a multiplexer or selector channel (discussed in Chapter 7) and can be used either buffered or in the byte-interleaved mode.

To punch cards, data received from the CPU in the EBCDIC or ANSCII code is checked for parity and then stored in a punch buffer. The buffer holds each byte of data until a full record is received. When the IBM 2520 is

FIGURE 11.7   IBM 1403 CARRIAGE CONTROL

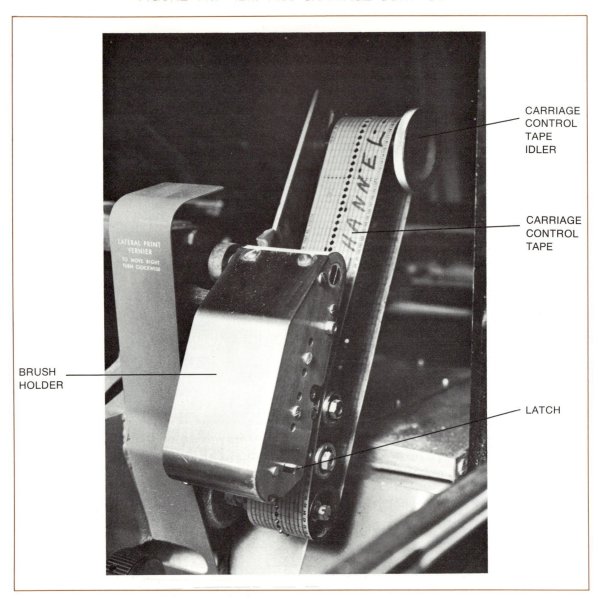

CARRIAGE
CONTROL
TAPE
IDLER

CARRIAGE
CONTROL
TAPE

LATCH

BRUSH
HOLDER

LATERAL PRINT
VERNIER
TO MOVE RIGHT
TURN CLOCKWISE

ready, the data is moved to the punch station where a group of punch dies convert the code into punched holes at a rate of 500 cards per minute.

IBM 3275 DISPLAY STATION.   The machine shown in Figure 11.9 resembles an ordinary television set with an attached keyboard. It converts electronic

FIGURE 11.8   IBM 2520 CARD READ PUNCH

FIGURE 11.9   IBM 3275 DISPLAY STATION

pulses into visual images and displays them on a cathode ray tube. The IBM 3275 can display either 480 or 1,920 characters at any one time.

Instructions, input data, corrections, etc. can be typed on the keyboard and inputted to the CPU. The corrected information will be displayed instantly on the screen.

The IBM 3275 is connected to the CPU by a control unit, which converts the pulses from the CPU into characters for display. Characters displayed on the face of the tube look like images on a television screen. Each character remains on the screen until replaced by new data from the CPU, or the unit is turned off. No hard copy is generated.

UNIVAC 1558 DISPLAY CONSOLE.   The UNIVAC 1558 Display Console resembles the IBM 3275 and performs a similar function. However, in addition to numbers and characters, it can also display lines, graphs, curves, and drawings. A unique feature called a *light pen* is used to change or replace data displayed on the screen. When touched to the screen, a light beam from the pen will modify the data as desired. (See Figure 11.10.)

The UNIVAC 1558 is coupled to the CPU by a controller. A small, self-contained computer, the controller generates characters from code received by its CPU and relays them to the cathode ray tube for display.

The machine has a 12″ × 12″ display screen with a 1,024 × 1,024 position grid. A point on a graph or chart can be placed at any of the intersections on the grid. A full screen of data can be displayed in 32 microseconds. Data remains on display until replaced by new output from the CPU, or the unit is turned off. No hard copy is generated.

HAZELTINE CORPORATION 2000 VIDEO DISPLAY TERMINAL.   Figure 11.11 shows a multipurpose machine. Like the above machines, it displays data on a video tube and can receive input via keyboard. In addition, a small line printer coupled to it enables it to produce hard copy of the data displayed on the screen.

The printer will type up to 30 characters per second on a $8\frac{1}{2}$-inch wide page. Data typed in on the keyboard can be printed out as well. The CRT will display up to 1,998 characters (27 lines with 74 characters per line).

UNIVERSITY COMPUTING COMPANY ON-LINE PLOTTER.   This machine converts data emitted from the CPU into graphic shapes, such as lines, curves, or figures. (See Figure 11.12.) The UCC plotter is equipped with a pen, movable carriage, drum, and chart paper holder. The pen moves across the page along the *y* or horizontal axis, and the drum drives the paper along the *x* or vertical axis.

Digital information received from the CPU causes either the drum to rotate or the pen to move across the carriage. This creates a visual line representing the output data. Line drawings, curves, analogs, and similar *x-y* axis output are prepared on the plotter.

FIGURE 11.10   UNIVAC 1558 DISPLAY CONSOLE

FIGURE 11.11   HAZELTINE CORPORATION
2000 VIDEO DISPLAY
TERMINAL

FIGURE 11.12   UNIVERSITY COMPUTING COMPANY ON-LINE PLOTTER

COMPUTERIZED DIETETICS

Central State Hospital, in Milledgeville, Georgia, is a city unto itself. Serving the population of some 8,300 are a fire department, security force, general hospital, chapels, and recreation facilities. Central State also has patient-operated stores, warehouses, a lumberyard, laundry, steam plant, and bus service.

A main kitchen, the size of two football fields, services (via truck) 68 dining rooms in 25 different buildings. The food service prepares and serves 31,000 meals a day (or in excess of 10 million a year). The annual food budget is approximately $3 million based upon $.25 a meal for raw food costs.

The key to food savings at Central State is computer-assisted menu planning (CAMP). Since CAMP was installed in 1969, menu items have been repeated less frequently and food costs have been cut by 5 percent.

Central State's CAMP system works with constraints such as nutrient value, separation ratio, dominant food attributes, and cost suboptimization. The hospital is capable of controlling eight nutrients. Once a food item has met the nutrient requirements, it is then checked to see when it was last served. For example, an item with a separation ratio of seven could be used once every seven days. Moreover, those items that have met and passed the previous requirements are evaluated by cost. Prices are updated a minimum of every 30 days.

"It takes two dieticians, the food service director, and myself only one hour to review the print out and produce a satisfactory 90-day menu," reports the food service administrator. "In the past, it took ten people two hours every week to plan one week's menu."

When the 90-day menu is prepared, the data processing department prepares a food usage report itemizing day-by-day food requirements. Purchasing is now made easier. Items are bought out of need not out of habit.

The food item costs are based upon forecast information from publications such as the *Wall Street Journal* and trade magazines. Changes in the menu due to item availability, cost, food donations, and government surplus are fairly easy to make with the menu-planning system. Dietitians code the nutrient value and separation ratio of the new foods and can then substitute them in the menu without upsetting the pre-planned balance. A nutritional analysis is run every 90 days to verify that each meal served met the nutrient specifications.

SOURCE Abstracted from "A Few Guests For Dinner—Like 8,000 Plus," *Data Processor,* Vol. XIII, No. 5, December 1970/January 1971, p. 9.

IBM 7772 AUDIO RESPONSE UNIT. The audio response unit, shown in Figure 11.13, converts data outputted by the CPU into an audible signal that sounds like a human voice. It outputs data in English, as sentences, numbers, words, or phrases. The IBM 7772 is physically located near the CPU. Users query the CPU and receive answers via ordinary telephone lines.

A caller dials the computer and enters a query by means of a touch-tone phone, push-button phone, or other instrument that allows numbers to be fed in by depressing buttons. The query can be a request for price information, inventory, credit rating, etc. The CPU will process the inquiry and retrieve data from a record or file as needed. Then the CPU directs the IBM 7772 to assemble a verbal reply to be outputted over the telephone. From a prerecorded vocabulary stored on a direct access storage device, the IBM 7772 assembles an audible message and then plays it into the telephone.

The IBM 7772 can be used, for example, in a brokerage house. A master file of over-the-counter stock prices can be put on-line and queried by buyers and sellers. Or, a master file of accounts, balances, and credit ratings could be queried by bank tellers. Or, in the hotel–motel industry, a master file of available rooms, facilities, and rates could be queried by travel or sales agents. Messages of varying length and vocabulary to suit a particular need can be stored on the IBM 7772.

Off-Line Output Machines ADDRESSOGRAPH-MULTIGRAPH 747 PHOTOTYPESETTER. This machine, shown in Figure 11.14, converts the code punched into the paper to typeset characters on photographic film or paper. It is similar in purpose to the line printer, but produces a high quality, letter-perfect image, suitable for reproduction.

© Field Enterprises, Inc., 1971

"I don't know where it's supposed to go . . . plug it in and let it work it out for itself!"

FIGURE 11.13   IBM 7772 AUDIO RESPONSE UNIT

The machine is equipped with a paper tape feeder, a photographic exposure system, changeable type disks, and film transport mechanism.

The A-M 747 is used to set type from computer-generated tape for newspapers, books, etc. The length of the printing line can be varied as needed and can be set justified (even right- and left-hand margins) at speeds up to 12 characters per second. Images are formed by passing a beam of light through letter forms on a revolving type disk. (The A-M 747 has interchangeable type disks, each of which holds three different type fonts. Each font consists of 112 characters.) The projected image is focused onto sensitized photographic paper or film. The exposed film is processed in a separate unit and the output can be reproduced by the printing process.

FIGURE 11.14   ADDRESSOGRAPH-MULTIGRAPH 747
PHOTOTYPESETTER

UNIVERSITY COMPUTING COMPANY MODEL M-2000. The Model M-2000 plotter, shown in Figure 11.15, draws lines, curves, and graphs on a page. It produces a visual output from data on magnetic tape, punched cards, or paper tape. For example, data output from the CPU is first recorded on magnetic tape. This tape is then fed to the Model M-2000 for conversion into a graphic plot.

The plotter will produce lines up to $29\frac{1}{2}$ inches wide at speeds up to seven inches per second. Very precise charts, lines, and figures can be prepared because the pen can be positioned in any one of 45,000 points in each square inch.

The Model M-2000 can be used to plot many different kinds of business and scientific data, such as stock market curves, utility price curves, trend lines, and supply and demand curves, and to construct figures, symbols, and bar graphs.

FIGURE 11.15   UNIVERSITY COMPUTING COMPANY
MODEL M-2000

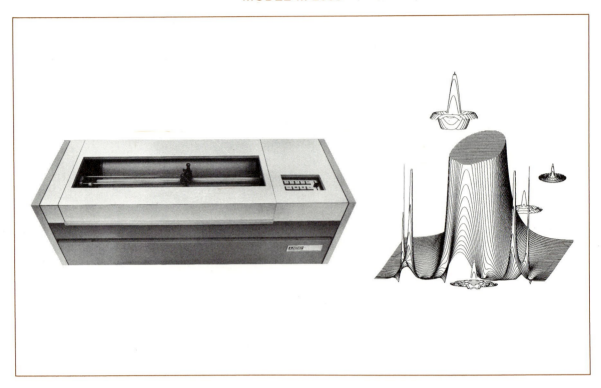

PROBLEMS IN DATA OUTPUT

Like input, data output is limited by a differing operating speed from that of the CPU. The CPU can perform thousands of calculations in the time it takes a line printer to type out one line. When the CPU has completed processing a block of data, it must have some place to put it. If the only output media is a slow line printer tied up with the previous job, trouble arises. The CPU must wait until the line printer is ready before it can output its data and begin processing the next job.

A system is said to be I/O bound when the input or output devices on the system prevent the CPU from processing the maximum number of jobs during a given time period. Several methods are used to ease this bottleneck.

Multiple Outputs   Several input devices can be connected on-line, simultaneously, to increase computer throughput. Additional output devices can be coupled in the same way. Selector and multiplexer channels can also be used to feed data to a number of line printers, card punches, etc. at the same time.

Channel addresses are assigned to each output unit on the system, just as they are to input devices. Using these addresses, the programmer can call specific units in and out of service during the program run. Card punches, line printers, tape punches, etc. may be indicated by referring to the assigned channel, control unit, and device number. (See page 156.)

FIGURE 11.16   SPOOLING

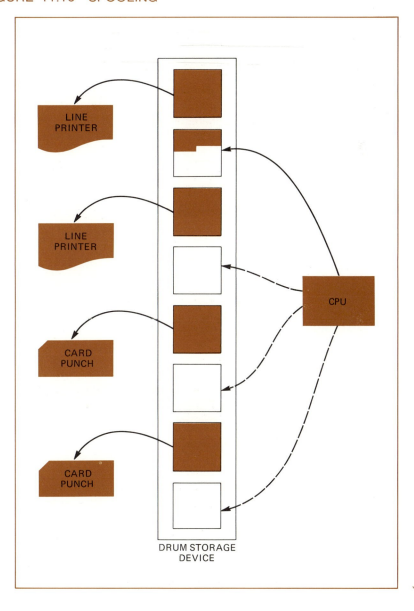

LINE PRINTER

LINE PRINTER

CARD PUNCH

CARD PUNCH

CPU

DRUM STORAGE DEVICE

Buffering   Buffering has special importance in data output. Buffering involves holding bytes of data or records in temporary storage until either the designated unit or the CPU is ready to process it.

If the output device has a buffer, the CPU can transfer processed data into the buffer and proceed with the next job. The output device can operate at its own speed and print out the data from the next job in line.

Spooling and off-line I/O operations are other ways to take better advantage of the CPU's speed.

Spooling   Spooling, illustrated in Figure 11.16, allows the CPU to process data at maximum speeds without waiting for slow output devices. In spooling, the CPU records the output on an intermediate storage device, such as a magnetic drum. The jobs are transferred to the output devices when these units are ready.

Assume, for example, that two line printers, two card punches, and a drum unit are used in a spooling operation on a computer system. A control program coordinates assignment of jobs to the output devices.

As data is fed at maximum speed from the CPU, it is stored on the drum and sent to slower devices for output. As a result, the CPU can output at

FIGURE 11.17   OFF-LINE I/O OPERATION

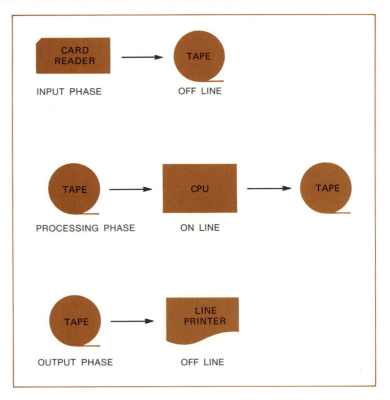

maximum speed, while several relatively slow output units operate simultaneously to process it. Spooling can also be used to buffer a job.

Off-Line I/O   Another means of breaking the I/O bottleneck is to provide off-line data input and output facilities. (See Figure 11.17.) Some computer installations do not feed data directly to the CPU from card readers, paper tape readers, etc., nor do they connect the line printers directly to the CPU. Instead, all data is inputted and outputted via high-speed tape units.

For example, input data from punched cards is first recorded on off-line magnetic tape units. These reels of tape are then placed on the computer for processing. Similarly, output data is recorded on magnetic tape by the CPU. Later these tape reels are placed on an off-line line printer to generate the final output.

Tapes used as an intermediate off-line step markedly increase throughput. A system of off-line I/O allows data to be sent to the CPU without delays due to mechanical problems. It is not uncommon for a CPU to remain idle while the operator removes a torn card from the card reader or loads paper into the line printer. In the time taken to remove a card from the card reader, the CPU could process another 1,000 cards or more. Tapes also give the data processing department increased flexibility. Card-to-tape and tape-to-printer units allow a job to be processed in discrete steps and at different times.

KEY TERMS

Line printer
Print train
Phototypesetter
Cathode ray tube
Plotter
Spooling
Off-line output
On-line output
Type bar

Type element
Type wheel
Wire matrix
Thermal imaging
Electrostatic imaging
Photographic imaging
Serial printing
Parallel printing

EXERCISES

1. List three applications suitable for video display terminals. List three applications for which they are not suited.
2. What are plotters and what kinds of information do they display?
3. How does the audio response unit respond to queries from a user?
4. Why is buffering critical for output devices?
5. What is the difference between an I/O bound system and a CPU-bound system?
6. What is spooling? Why is it useful?
7. How does off-line I/O differ from on-line I/O? What problems does it solve?
8. Compare the advantages and disadvantages of type bar, typewheel, and type element printers.
9. How does serial printing differ from parallel printing?
10. Visit your data center and determine if the bulk of the computer's I/O is on-line or off-line. Does the center take full advantage of the capability of its CPU?

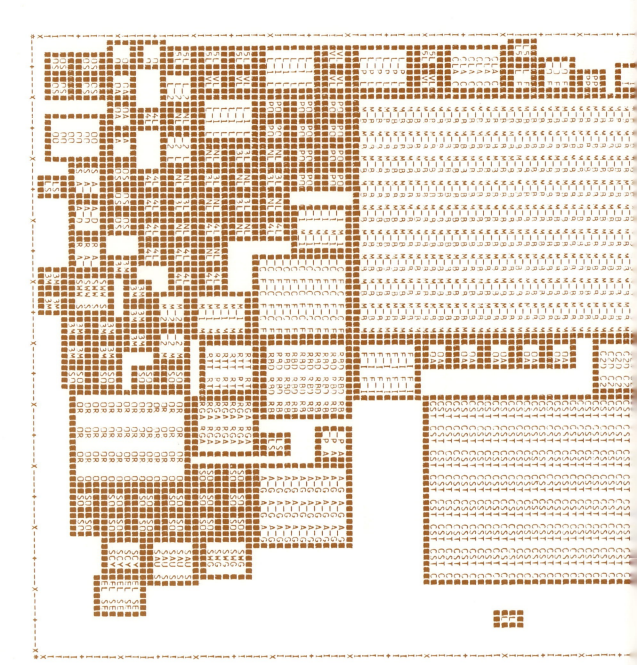

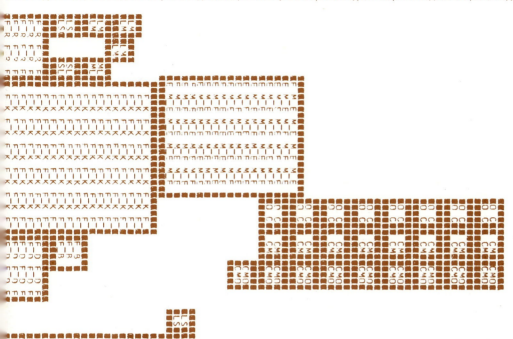

PART FOUR

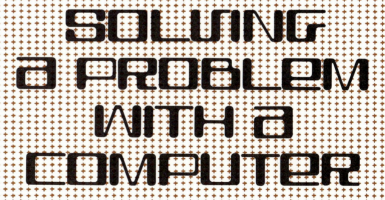

SOLVING
a PROBLEM
WITH a
COMPUTER

12 Flowcharts and Program Logic

The resources of the computer can be applied to a problem only when the method for solving the problem has been reduced to a series of discrete, logical instructions coded in a language the computer understands. A problem is prepared for the computer by programmers and systems analysts. The set of statements, or instructions, coded in a computer language is called a program.

Flowcharts are the graphic means used to illustrate the sequence of steps the computer will follow in executing a program. Program logic is the strategy used to solve the problem.

PRINCIPLES OF FLOWCHARTING

Definition   A flowchart is a diagram, prepared by the programmer, of the sequence of steps involved in solving a problem. It provides either a detailed view or an overview of the program and indicates the direction of program flow. A flowchart is like a blueprint in that it shows the general plan, architecture, and essential details of the proposed structure.

A flowchart illustrates the strategy and thread of logic followed in the program. It allows the programmer to compare different approaches and alternatives on paper and often shows interrelationships that are not immediately apparent. Figure 12.1 is a flowchart of a washing machine's

FIGURE 12.1 WASHING MACHINE CYCLES

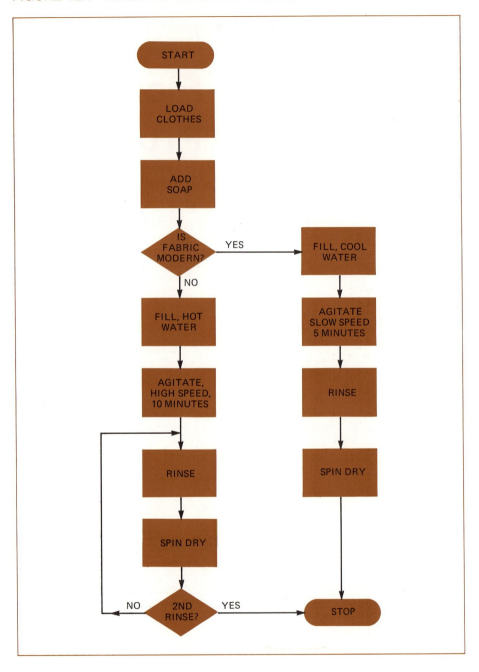

cycles. In a similar way, a sequence of data processing steps may be diagrammed.

The flowchart is an essential tool for the programmer. By forcing him to state the logic in clear terms and to state the essential details, a flowchart helps the programmer avoid fuzzy thinking and accidental omissions of intermediate steps. The flowchart is also a communication tool used to link the programmer, the user of the program, the systems analyst, and the computer operator.

Types and Functions

A flowchart may be drawn informally in longhand, lettered in pen and ink, or typed by machine on a sheet of paper. It can be written either horizontally or vertically and may take from one to as many as several dozen pages.

A flowchart serves as a map or guide for the programmer when he is writing a program. Each programmer uses the flowchart in a way that best suits the problem-solving activity he faces.

Flowcharts are divided into two basic types: the system flowchart and the program flowchart. The program flowchart is further divided into modular and detailed program flowcharts.

SYSTEM FLOWCHART. The system flowchart is designed to present an overview, or bird's-eye view, of the data flow through all parts of a data processing system. The system flowchart stresses people, activities, documents, and media. It shows the data-flow relationships of the various departments and work stations to the whole. It describes data sources, their form, and the stages through which they will be processed.

Figure 12.2 illustrates the channels of data flow and processing in a merchandising system. It includes activities such as generating source documents, keypunching, and computerized sorting and processing.

MODULAR PROGRAM FLOWCHART. The modular program flowchart is sometimes called a block diagram or macro flowchart. Each block in the flowchart represents a major step in the program logic.

The modular flowchart shows only the gross phases of the solution and does not obscure essentials with details. It provides the programmer with a broad-brush picture of the strategy and flow of data in a particular situation.

More refined and detailed flowcharts can be prepared from this flowchart for use in the actual writing of the program. Each block in the modular flowchart may be expanded and exploded into many programming steps. The module "CALCULATE PRICE" in Figure 12.3, for example, may contain dozens of steps and calculations.

DETAIL PROGRAM FLOWCHART. A detail program flowchart is sometimes called a micro or detail flowchart. It outlines each step, calculation, test, and comparison involved in the solution of the problem. It provides a microscopic view of each element in the system.

FIGURE 12.2　SIMPLE SYSTEM FLOWCHART

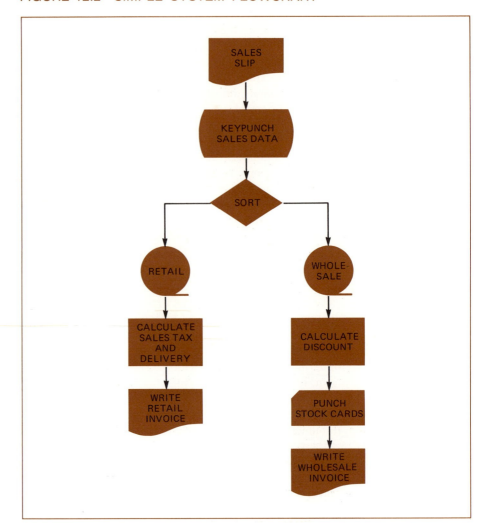

The detail program flowchart expands the blocks of the modular flowchart into programmable steps, used as a guide for writing the program. This flowchart helps the programmer make sure that all steps are included, that branches refer to the correct points in the program, etc.

In Figure 12.4, the programmer has drawn in each decision point, branch, and calculation and made provisions for handling exceptional situations, such as errors.

Common Flowchart Symbols　Each type of operation the computer is to perform can be indicated by the use of a different shape, called a symbol. About two dozen widely used symbols cover the most common programming situations. A template, Form

FIGURE 12.3   MODULAR PROGRAM FLOWCHART

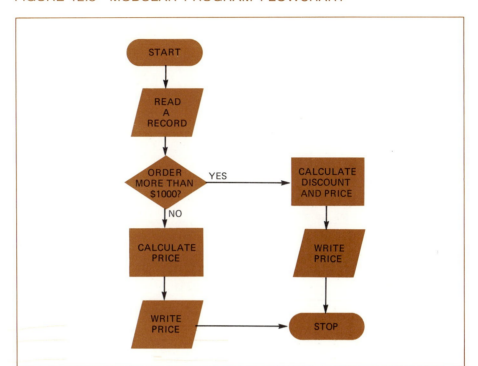

X-20-8020-1, available from IBM, is a convenient aid in drawing flowcharts. (See Figure 12.5.) (Templates in various sizes are also manufactured by Rapid Design, Inc. to conform to the ANSI X3.5 standard.) Most programmers prepare working and development flowcharts with a template, pencil, and scratch paper. Permanent flowcharts are usually drawn in ink, although a computer can be used to print them. The most common flowchart symbols are as follows.

TERMINAL.   The terminal symbol is an oval and the words START, STOP, or HALT are usually written in the center. START, the first symbol of the flowchart, marks the beginning of the logic train. STOP or HALT, the last symbol of the flowchart, marks the end of the logic train. This symbol is also used at other points in a program to show where different branches terminate or where the program is to stop due to an error condition. Used in this manner, the oval means a programming step, not a remote or display terminal.

INPUT/OUTPUT (GENERAL).   A parallelogram indicates where data is to be input or output during a program. It is a general form and is used for all input/output media, such as read or punch a card, write on a printer, or display on a video tube. A few words in the center of the symbol describe the input or output action and the data involved.

FIGURE 12.4 DETAIL PROGRAM FLOWCHART

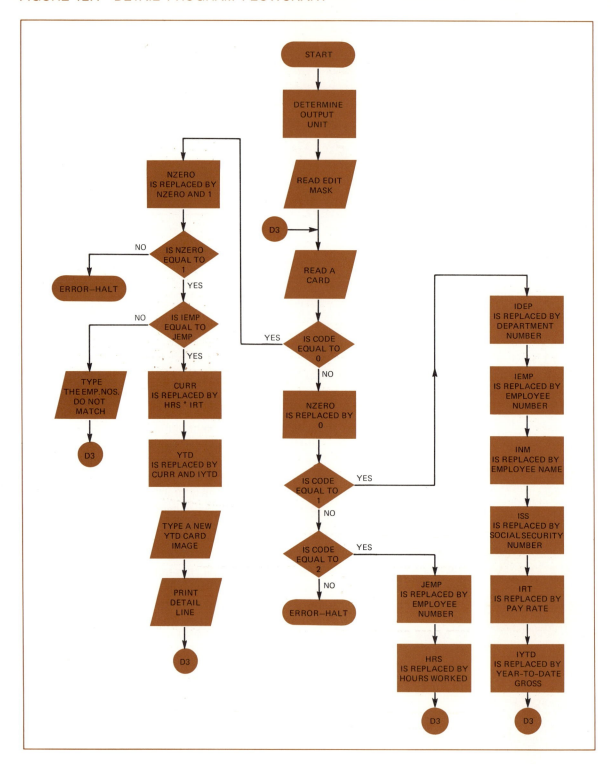

FIGURE 12.5   FLOWCHARTING TEMPLATE

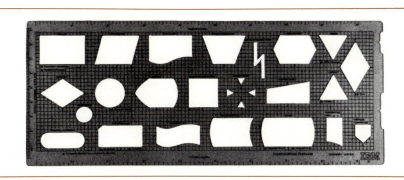

PROCESS. The process symbol, a rectangle, indicates an operation that is to be performed by the computer. It may be a mathematical calculation such as addition, subtraction, compute, or find square root. The specific action should be identified in the center of the box.

CONNECTOR. The connector symbol, a small circle, is used to tie parts of a flowchart together. It allows the programmer to draw portions of a chart elsewhere on the page. Keys such as GO TO 19 or GO TO READ CARD help the reader follow the continuity of the program. The symbol is useful when charts have many branches or run onto many pages.

DECISION. A diamond-shaped symbol indicates that a branch, or decision point, has been reached in the program. A few words within the symbol briefly describe the decision that must be made and the action the computer should take for each possible answer. For example, labels such as YES or NO, GO TO A, GO TO B, or GO TO C identify possible paths.

PUNCHED CARD. A special symbol, shaped like a card, indicates that data is to be read or punched on a card. It differs from the general input/output symbol in that it only represents punched cards.

DOCUMENT. The document symbol, which looks like part of a sheet of paper, shows that a hard-copy document is being read or generated. The term hard-copy document refers to a paper or sheet of print out. It should not be confused with microfiche or microfilm "documents." It is a specialized form of the general input/output symbol and is used where data is to be read from, or output on, a document, such as an invoice, check, or order form.

MAGNETIC TAPE. A circle with a horizontal line at the bottom is another specialized input/output symbol. It is used to represent data being read from or written on magnetic tape.

DIRECT-ACCESS STORAGE DEVICE. A portion of a round drum cylinder is a specialized input/output symbol. It is used to represent data stored on random access media such as disk, drum, or cell.

COMMUNICATION LINK. This jagged symbol, which looks like a bolt of lightning, indicates that data is being transmitted from one location to another via communication lines.

The symbols on a flowchart are connected by straight lines. Arrows along the straight lines show the direction of program flow. Figure 12.6 illustrates some symbols with a statement in each to facilitate following the logic.

FIGURE 12.6 COMMON SYMBOLS

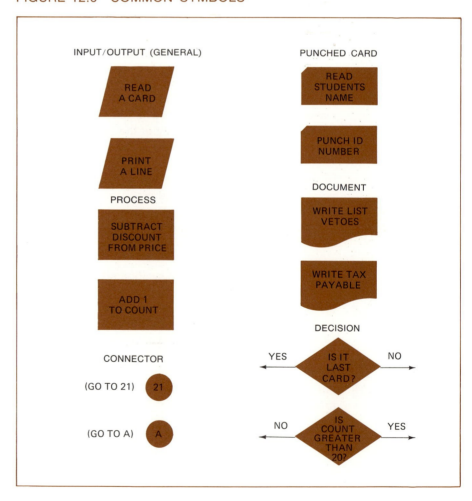

DECISION TABLES

For many programming activities, the programmer can write the program from the flowchart alone. But, if the program contains a multitude of actions and conditions, a decision table is very helpful. Decision tables are graphic means of showing the alternatives and branches in a program. They visually document all possible conditions and the actions to be taken in each case. The details of preparing complex decision tables are often the responsibility of the systems analyst or advanced programmer. The programmer relies on the flowchart and decision tables in his coding for assurance that all possible conditions and actions have been accounted for.

Decision tables resemble the familiar income tax schedule, shown in Figure 12.7, used in determining tax liability. The table accounts for all possible conditions (varying income, number of exemptions, etc.), and the actions (amount of tax due) suitable to each. Fundamental to this table is the IF/THEN concept. IF one has a given income and number of exemptions, THEN his tax will be a given amount. For each given set of conditions (income and exemptions), there is a given tax.

Decision tables for computer programs are also based on the IF/THEN relationship. IF the customer orders more than 1,000 units of an item, THEN a "low inventory" message must be sent to the stockroom. IF the employee worked more than 40 hours, THEN overtime must be added to his paycheck. Each entry is then translated into coded instructions in the program.

Programmers often prepare decision tables on a form similar to the one shown in Figure 12.8. A decision table is divided into four portions. (See Figure 12.9(A).) The *condition stub* (upper left portion) lists all possible conditions that may be encountered. The *condition entry* portion (upper right

FIGURE 12.7 INCOME TAX SCHEDULE

TABLE 1.—Returns claiming ONE exemption (and not itemizing deductions)

If adjusted gross Income is—		And you are—				If adjusted gross Income is—		And you are—				If adjusted gross Income is—		And you are—			
				Married filing separate return claiming						Married filing separate return claiming						Married filing separate return claiming	
At least	But less than	Single, not head of household	Head of household	Low income allowance	% Standard deduction	At least	But less than	Single, not head of household	Head of household	Low income allowance	% Standard deduction	At least	But less than	Single, not head of household	Head of household	Low income allowance	% Standard deduction
		Your tax is—						Your tax is—						Your tax is—			
$0	$775	$0	$0	$0	$0	$2,675	$2,700	$139	$135	$223	$253	$6,200	$6,250	$795	$755	$916	$866
775	800	0	0	0	1	2,700	2,725	143	138	227	256	6,250	6,300	806	765	927	877
800	825	0	0	0	4	2,725	2,750	147	142	231	260	6,300	6,350	816	774	938	888
825	850	0	0	0	8	2,750	2,775	151	146	236	264	6,350	6,400	827	784	949	899
850	875	0	0	0	11	2,775	2,800	155	150	240	268	6,400	6,450	837	793	960	
	900	0	0	0	14	2,800	2,825	159	154	244	271	6,450	6,500	848	803	971	
	925	0	0	0	17	2,825	2,850	163	158	248	275	6,500	6,550	858	812	9..	
	950	0	0	0	20	2,850	2,875	167	162	253	279	6,550	6,600	869	822		1,468
	975				23			171	166	257				879	831		1,480
2,075						5,050	5,100	576		676	641	8,900					1,493
2,100	2,190		54	132		5,100	5,150	586	561	685	649	8,950	9,000	1,3..	..9	1,574	1,518
2,125		58	58	136		5,150	5,200	595	570	696	657	9,000	9,050	1,392	1,299	1,586	1,530
2,150	2,175	61	61	139	178	5,200	5,250	605	579	707	665	9,050	9,100	1,403	1,308	1,599	1,543
2,175	2,200	65	65	143	181	5,250	5,300	614	588	718	674	9,100	9,150	1,413	1,318	1,611	1,555
2,200	2,225	68	68	147	185	5,300	5,350	624	597	729	682	9,150	9,200	1,424	1,328	1,624	1,568
2,225	2,250	72	72	151	188	5,350	5,400	633	606	740	690	9,200	9,250	1,434	1,337	1,637	1,580
2,250	2,275	76	75	155	192	5,400	5,450	643	615	751	700	9,250	9,300	1,445	1,347	1,651	1,593
2,275	2,300	79	79	159	195	5,450	5,500	652	624	762	709	9,300	9,350	1,455	1,356	1,665	1,605
2,300	2,325	83	82	163	199	5,500	5,550	662	633	773	719	9,350	9,400	1,466	1,366	1,679	1,618
2,325	2,350	87	86	167	202	5,550	5,600	671	642	784	729	9,400	9,450	1,476	1,375	1,693	1,F..
50	2,375	91	89	171	206	5,600	5,650	681	651	795	738	9,450	9,500	1,486	1,385	1,707	
	2,400	94	93	175	209	5,650	5,700	690	660	806	748	9,500	9,550	1,497	1,395	1,72..	
2,400	2,425	98	96	179	213	5,700	5,750	701	670	817	757	9,550	9,600	1,507	1,404		
2,425	2,450	102	100	183	216									1,518	1,414		
2,450	2,475	10.			220												

portion) includes various combinations of conditions that may be present. The *action stub* (lower left portion) lists all possible actions to be carried out in the program. The lower right portion, called the *action entry,* indicates the actions to be taken for a given set of conditions.

Condition entries are usually a Y (yes) to indicate a positive condition, or an N for the negative condition. Other symbols, such as $=$, $>$, $<$, could be used to indicate relationships. The action entries are usually indicated with an X and describe the action to be taken for each set of conditions. Each vertical column (containing Ys, Ns, and Xs) is called a *rule* or alternative. Each rule represents a given set of conditions and the actions that must be taken for that particular set.

To use a decision table, the programmer locates the rule that meets a given set of conditions and programs the computer to carry out the action entries checked within that rule.

For example, suppose a programmer wants to write a program that will prepare a holiday bonus mailing to employees. Bonus checks, holiday greetings, certificates for turkeys, and letters from management or from the personnel department are to be mailed to each employee, depending upon

FIGURE 12.8   DECISION TABLE FORM

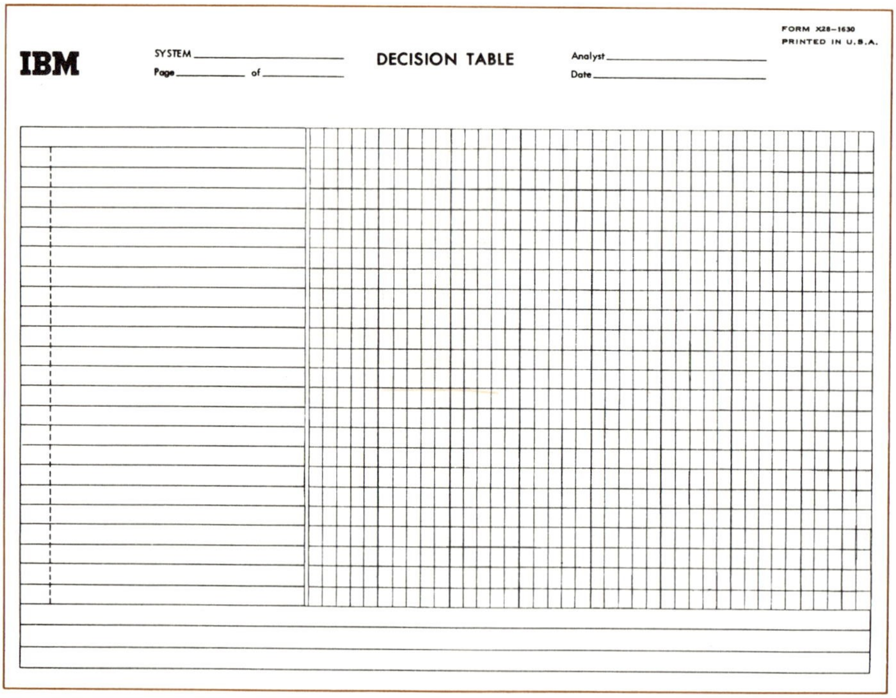

FIGURE 12.9   (A) PORTIONS OF DECISION TABLES
              (B) DECISION TABLE—HOLIDAY BONUS PROGRAM

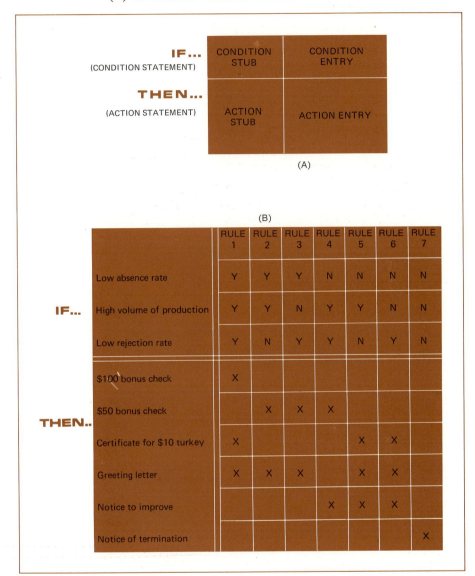

IF...
(CONDITION STATEMENT)

	CONDITION STUB	CONDITION ENTRY

THEN...
(ACTION STATEMENT)

	ACTION STUB	ACTION ENTRY

(A)

(B)

		RULE 1	RULE 2	RULE 3	RULE 4	RULE 5	RULE 6	RULE 7
IF...	Low absence rate	Y	Y	Y	N	N	N	N
	High volume of production	Y	Y	N	Y	Y	N	N
	Low rejection rate	Y	N	Y	Y	N	Y	N
THEN..	$100 bonus check	X						
	$50 bonus check		X	X	X			
	Certificate for $10 turkey	X				X	X	
	Greeting letter	X	X	X		X	X	
	Notice to improve				X	X	X	
	Notice of termination							X

certain conditions. These conditions are employee absenteeism, level of production, and rejection rate.

Before writing the program, the programmer prepares a decision table showing the IF/THEN relationships between all possible conditions and actions. (See Figure 12.9(B).) The table defines the intent and objectives of the program and ensures that all conditions and actions have been accounted for.

AN $18 MILLION HYPHEN

"Programming is like writing music," says one specialist. "There are very limited figures with which you can deal. You have to express the problem in sequences and combinations of these figures." Total precision in writing a program is vital, he adds, since the computer blindly executes the instructions given it. "You can't settle for 99.9 percent accuracy. You're either absolutely all right or all wrong."

Because of the vast number of detailed instructions involved, mistakes are hard to avoid. The more obvious errors can be detected during "debugging" or trial runs by a special "diagnostic" program in the computer's control system. The computer may be programmed to respond to a simple error by printing out "Illegal procedure," or "Parenthesis left off," or sometimes a more irreverent "You dope, you missed a comma." But as yet there is no way to program a computer to detect semantic errors that can dramatically alter the intent of the program.

The amount of damage that even a seemingly minute programming error can do was dramatically demonstrated by NASA some years ago. An Atlas-Agena rocket blasted off the launch pad, carrying what was to be the first U.S. spacecraft to fly by Venus. The rocket was about 90 miles above Earth when it started to wander erratically and had to be blown up from the control center on the ground. Later analysis showed that a mathematician had inadvertently left out a hyphen in writing the flight plan for the spacecraft; in this case the hyphen was the symbol for a whole formula. It must have been history's costliest hyphen—an $18,500,000 rocket was lost.

SOURCE Abstracted from "Help Wanted: 50,000 Programmers," Gene Bylinksy, *Fortune Magazine*, March 1967, p. 141.

PROGRAM LOGIC

Algorithms A strategy for solving a problem must be established before the actual programming efforts are begun. This strategy is the *algorithm*. An algorithm is a list of steps, or a set of rules, leading to the solution of a problem.

A problem can often be solved by more than one strategy or algorithm. For example, monthly statements can be prepared in several different ways. One way would be to process the whole group of statements in separate steps. First, debits and credits would be posted to all of the accounts. Next, the entire group of statements would be typed. Then the envelopes would be prepared, and, finally, the statements would be folded and inserted into the envelopes.

Another way to achieve the same result would be to prepare each statement separately. The debits and credits are posted to an account and

START

READ ALL RECORDS

SORT INTO THREE GROUPS

PROCESS 1ST GROUP OF STATEMENTS

PROCESS 2ND GROUP OF STATEMENTS

PROCESS 3RD GROUP OF STATEMENTS

STOP

the statement and envelope typed. The statement is then folded and inserted, ready for mailing. Then the statement for the next account prepared.

The end results would be the same, but the strategies used are different. The choice of algorithm is affected by factors such as personnel, available equipment, time considerations, and office layout. The algorithm that best suits all conditions will be selected.

As another example, consider the ways in which a credit and collection letter could be processed. Assume each account must pay $20 per month. Customers who pay less receive an appropriate collection letter, those who pay $20 receive an acknowledgement, and those who overpay receive a letter indicating a credit has been posted toward next month's payment.

One algorithm for solving the problem would involve sorting the accounts into three categories: those who paid less than $20, those who paid $20, and those who paid more than $20. Then each group of letters could be prepared as a batch. The top left figure flowcharts this algorithm.

An alternative strategy would be to check one customer payment at a time and prepare the appropriate letter. The bottom left figure illustrates this approach.

To use the computer to best advantage, factors that bear on the problem, such as computer storage capability, number of steps in the instructions, and access time, must be examined. The algorithm that best meets all the needs is selected. Once the algorithm is chosen, the actual programming details can be worked out.

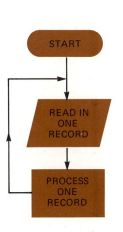

START

READ IN ONE RECORD

PROCESS ONE RECORD

"SHOULD'NT THAT BE AN EXCLUSIVE-OR?"

Illustrations of Program Logic

Programmers use several basic procedures in planning and writing programs. The choice of procedures depends on the complexity of the program. Some programs are simple and have only a few steps. Others are complex and branch into one of several tracks, test against known values, and loop through a set of calculations, comparisons, or operations many times.

Some of the most common procedures used by programmers are discussed below.

SINGLE-PASS EXECUTION.   The most elementary program moves through a set of statements in sequence, from beginning to end. Figure 12.10 illustrates a program that computes shipping charges. The program involves only one pass through the calculations.

First, a shipping rate schedule is read in and stored by the computer. Next, it reads the weight of the shipment and computes the shipping charges. Finally, it writes out the answer. The computer will move through the sequence from START to STOP only once. The program has no branches or loops and is executed the same way each time it is run. If a new set of values is to be read and computed, the program must be fed into the computer with the new set of data.

FIGURE 12.10 SINGLE PASS

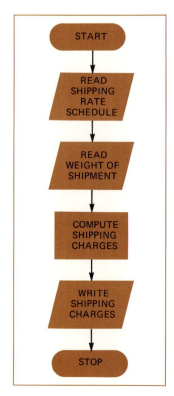

FIGURE 12.11   BRANCHING TO PARALLEL TRACKS

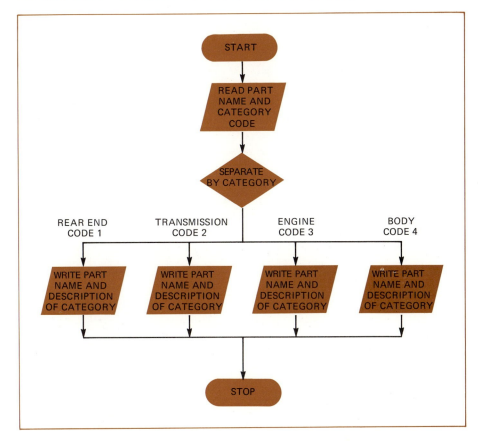

BRANCHING TO PARALLEL TRACKS. The computer can also read a value and select one of several courses depending on the value read. In Figure 12.11, the computer reads a part name and category number. Depending on the category, it will select one of four paths to follow. Each path directs the computer to write out the part name and description of the category in which it belongs.

Basically, this is a single-pass execution—the program will read only one record, perform the classification only once, and then direct the computer to terminate execution. The computer, however, has a choice of paths to follow. The selection of the particular path depends upon the category code read.

SIMPLE LOOP. Figure 12.12 is an example of a program that directs the computer to perform calculations several times. It computes the percentage of sales in relation to advertising expenses for each office of a large company.

FIGURE 12.12   SIMPLE LOOP

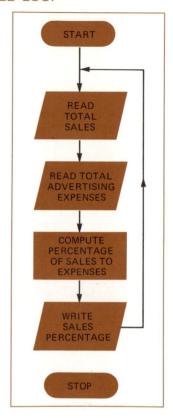

Upon completing the first pass through to the WRITE statement, the program will loop back to the beginning and read another record. It again computes the sales percentage, writes the answer, and loops back. As the program is now written, the machine will continue to perform the looping operation and calculations until it runs out of data records. In practice, a method of indicating that the end of the file has been reached would be written into the program.

A loop is a useful device for the programmer because it enables him to instruct the computer to perform an operation many times without having to write new instructions for each pass. The computer will automatically repeat a cycle until directed to stop. The weakness of the simple or unconditional loop is that the programmer has no control over, or knowledge of, the number of times it is executed.

LAST-RECORD LOOP.   Figure 12.13 shows another type of looping. The machine is to read and write a list of identification numbers from a file until it encounters the last record in the file. In this example, a signal punched card (differentiated by a code in a specific field) is inserted as the last record in the data set. This card is sometimes called a trailer card or end-of-file card.

FIGURE 12.13   LAST-RECORD LOOP

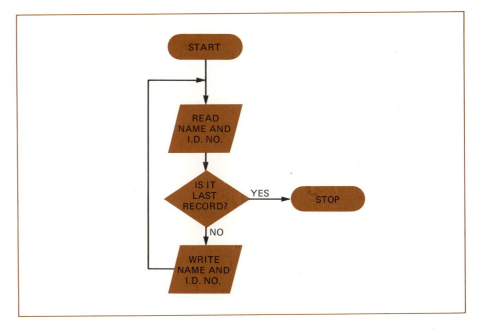

As the program is written the computer will read a record and test whether it is the last record. If not, it will write the name and I.D. number and go back to read another record. When it finally encounters the last record, the computer will direct control to STOP.

The trailer card is an accepted method of indicating to the computer that it has reached the end of the file. The programmer, however, has no way of knowing how many times the loop has been executed and can limit it only by the number of records in the file.

On reaching the last record, the computer does not have to stop. It can branch to another leg of the program and perform other calculations and steps. This concept is illustrated in Figure 12.14. The computer is instructed to read in salaries from a record, add the salary to a subtotal, and then write out a paycheck. When the last record is encountered, the computer does not immediately stop; it first writes out a value for the total salaries processed.

LOOP WITH COUNTER.   A programmer may find it necessary to limit the number of times a loop is to be executed. One way to do this is to write a counter into the program. The counter is incremented each time the computer passes that instruction. The program directs the computer to branch out of the loop when the counter reaches a predetermined value.

In Figure 12.15, the programmer uses a counter to print out a roster. He instructs the computer to read the name of a student and add one to the counter. The counter is tested to see if it equals 50. When it equals 50, the

FIGURE 12.14   LAST-RECORD LOOP

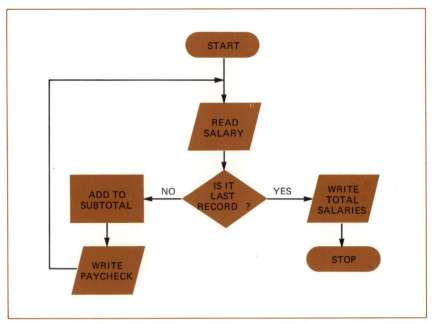

computer is instructed to write out the list of 50 students assigned to the class.

The programmer sets the initial value of the counter. Normally counters start at zero, but they can be initialized at any number. Counters may be set to increase by 1 during each loop, or by 5, or by 7, or by any number. Counters can also be initialized to a value calculated within the program. Counters may run in a positive direction, that is, adding one each time, or in a negative direction, that is, subtracting one each pass.

Counters can simplify the work of the programmer or reduce programming effort. A great variety of algorithms can be developed with counters. For example, they can be used to keep track of the number of data records read in. This count can be printed out later, or used in mathematical calculations, such as finding averages or means. And since counters may be set up anywhere in a program, they can be used as indices, to keep track of calculations, to count, or to limit the number of times a step is executed.

LOOP WITH COUNTER AND TEST FOR LAST RECORD.   Another common algorithm is a loop with a counter and a test for last record. This loop is limited by the test for last record (end of file). The counter is incremented each time the loop is executed and indicates the number of cycles performed. That is, if a loop reads in records from a file, the value of the counter will tell the number of records read.

FIGURE 12.15 LOOP WITH COUNTER

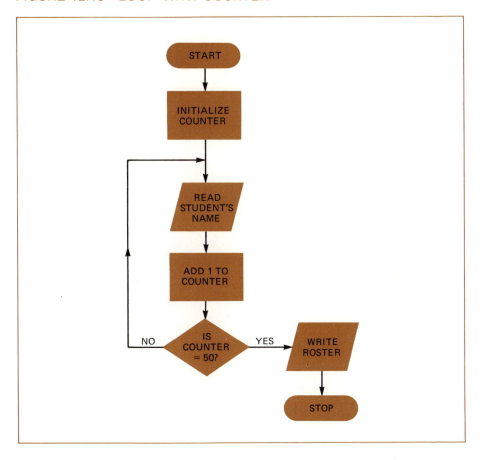

In Figure 12.16, the computer reads in a value called quality control and tests for last record. If it is not the last record, it adds one to a counter and performs some calculations. Upon reaching the last record, the computer writes out the count of records and prints out a report on the calculations.

LIMITED LOOP. A programmer often does not know the number of times a loop must be executed, but needs to set the maximum. He may have a limited amount of computer storage space available or may want to group data for statistical procedures.

One way to limit a loop is with a two-part test. One part sets the maximum times the loop may be repeated, and the other tests for last record. In this way, the computer will break out of the loop either when the last record has been encountered, or when the loop has been executed the predetermined number of times.

In Figure 12.17, the computer is to read the names of a group of

FIGURE 12.16   LOOP WITH COUNTER
AND TEST FOR LAST RECORD

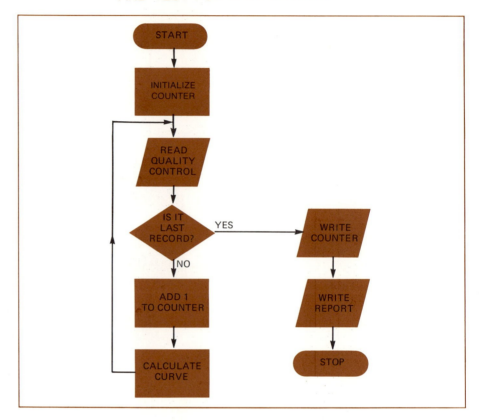

executives and print out a list. The computer will read and list up to 100 names. If the computer encounters a trailer or end-of-file card before reading the hundredth name, it will break out of the loop and go to the next procedure in the program. If, on the other hand, there are more than 100 records in the file, it will read the first 100 names, break out of the loop, and go on to the next procedure, ignoring the rest of the names. If the programmer needs to know how many times the loop was executed (names read and printed out), a counter could be included.

SOME ELEMENTARY FLOWCHARTS

The programmer frequently combines the elementary programming logic steps illustrated in the previous section into larger working units. Some typical business data processing problems and their flowcharts will be described in the remainder of this chapter.

FIGURE 12.17 LIMITED LOOP

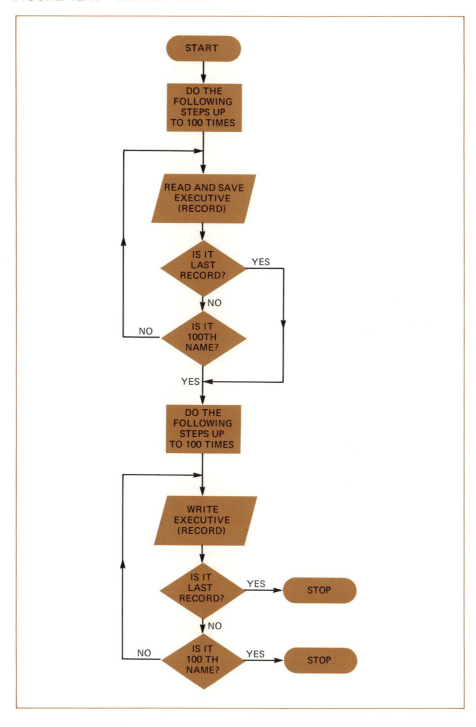

FIGURE 12.18   FRANCHISE REPORT

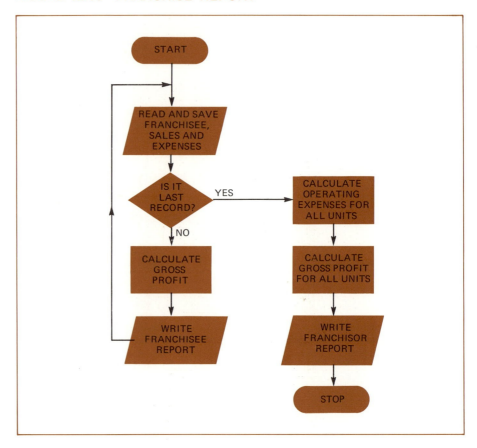

To better illustrate the examples, detailed and modular flowcharting concepts are used on the same chart. For example, a module such as "WRITE REPORT" would actually be composed of a dozen or more programming steps such as "WRITE HEADING," "WRITE TITLES," and "WRITE TEXT MESSAGE." "IS IT LAST RECORD," on the other hand, might represent only one programming step.

Franchise Report   Figure 12.18 illustrates the use of a loop to print out a series of operating reports for a group of franchisees and a report for the franchisor.

The computer reads a record containing gross expenses, receipts, and other cost data from a franchisee. The computer calculates the operating expenses and gross profit and prepares a report summarizing these data for that franchisee. This completes one loop. The computer then cycles back to read a record from another franchisee, perform the calculations, and prepare another report. The computer continues to cycle through the loop until the

FIGURE 12.19 BILLING AND COLLECTION PROGRAM

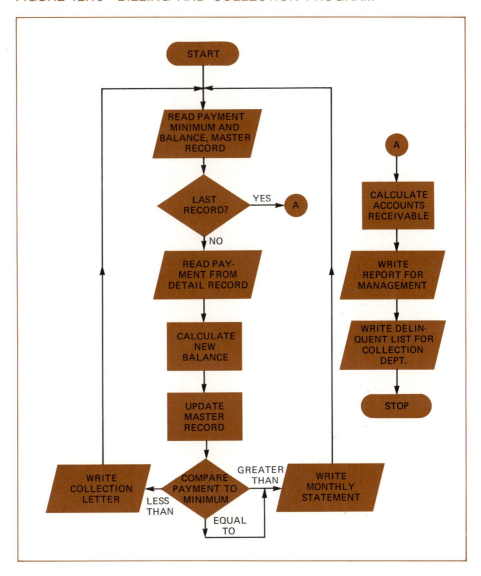

last record in the file has been reached, at which point the computer branches to a management routine. The management routine is designed to prepare summary data for the franchisor. In this routine, operating expenses and gross profits for all units are calculated. Then a management report is printed out.

This problem illustrates a typical programming situation in which individual records are processed, and a summary report is prepared on reaching the last record in the file.

Billing and
Collection Program

In Figure 12.19 an accounts receivable file is maintained, and two reports, in addition to collection letters and monthly statements, are prepared.

The computer reads a record from a master file, which contains the current balance and minimum payment due for each account. Then it reads a record from the detail file, which contains monthly payments made. The program calculates the new balance for each account and updates the master file. It then decides whether the monthly payment received is greater than or equal to the minimum amount due for that account. If it is, it prepares a monthly statement for the account and loops back to read another account record. If the payment received is less than the minimum amount due, the computer prints out a collection letter to inform the account of the overlooked payment. The computer then loops back to read another account record.

After each master record is read, an end-of-file test is made. When the last record has been processed, the computer branches to a management report routine. This routine calculates total accounts receivable and prints out a report of the status of all accounts. Then the computer prepares for the collection department a special report containing the names, addresses, and phone numbers of all overdue accounts.

KEY TERMS

Flowchart	Loop
Program flowchart	Last record loop
System flowchart	End-of-file record
Hard copy document	Counter
Algorithm	Modular program flowchart
Single-pass execution	Detail program flowchart
Branching	Trailer card

EXERCISES

1. Why do programmers flowchart a problem?
2. What is the difference between a system flowchart and a program flowchart?
3. What is an algorithm? Select a problem and give several solutions to it.
4. Using the algorithms and solutions developed in Exercise 3, prepare flowcharts for each.
5. What is the difference between a single-pass execution and a simple loop?
6. List three problems that might be solved by using an algorithm that involves branching to parallel tracks.
7. What are loops? List four situations in which loops may be used.
8. Define a last-record loop. What is its function? Describe how it is used in a program.

9. Extend the flowchart in Figure 12.10 to change it from a single-pass execution to a limited loop.

10. Use another method to limit the loop in Exercise 9.

11. Flowchart programs to perform the following functions:
   a. Single-pass execution, which reads in balance, deposits, and withdrawals from a punched card, and computes and prints out the new balance.
   b. Read a part name and code from a record and branch to one of five parallel tracks.

12. Flowchart programs to perform the following functions:
   a. Perform a simple loop that reads in a list of names from a record and writes the list on the line printer.
   b. Read a record containing the number in stock and cost per unit. Multiply to find total cost and print it out. Then loop back to read another record. Include a "test for last record."

13. Flowchart programs to perform the following functions:
   a. Compute simple interest due on each account in a file.
   b. Read in the number of parts left in stock. If under 100, write a "short supply" message. If 100–500, write "adequate supply" message. If more than 500, write an "over supply" message.

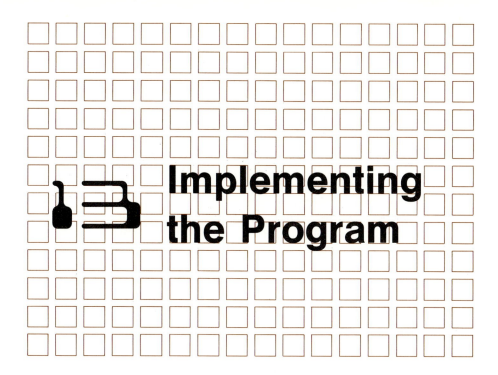

13 Implementing the Program

Once the program logic, or algorithm, for a job has been developed and flowcharted, the programmer must implement the program, or prepare it for processing on the computer. Implementation involves writing the program or coding the set of instructions in a computer language, keypunching or keyboarding both the instructions and data set, and, finally, submitting them to the computer for processing. After the problem has been processed, the results are checked for accuracy.

THE STAND-ALONE PROGRAM

In the stand-alone program, all instructions, data, and details for solving the problem are submitted to the computer as a unit. The programmer designs and writes a set of instructions to solve a specific problem. It may be a generalized program, or one suited to immediate, limited needs.

Usually, the cost of writing the program is borne by the firm that will use it to solve an internal data-processing problem, but stand-alone programs can also be written by computer manufacturers for distribution.

The distinguishing element of the stand-alone program is that it is written as an independent, self-sufficient package. The program is processed by the computer under the control of the CPU, without any intervention by the programmer.

277

Advantages
The stand-alone program is best suited for repetitive problem-solving activities, although it is often very valuable for solving a one-time, complex problem, that involves repetitive steps. Once the program has been written and tested, it may be used over and over to process different sets of data.

Because the program is written to solve a particular problem, the form of the input and output data and the method used to solve the problem can be designed for a specific user's needs. Such programs are written to do a specific firm's accounts receivable, billing, collection letters, inventory, etc.

Disadvantages
A major disadvantage of the stand-alone program is that the user must expend considerable programming time and effort. Since the problem is specific, a unique set of instructions must be written to solve it. Another disadvantage is that results are not always instantaneous. Output is usually not generated until the entire job has compiled and begun executing. Scheduling arrangements in the data center will also have an effect, since most data centers group stand-alone programs and run them in a batch.

IMPLEMENTING THE STAND-ALONE PROGRAM

Figure 13.1 illustrates the steps involved in implementing the stand-alone program. Generally the evolution from problem to program includes problem analysis, algorithm and flowcharting, coding, keypunching or keyboarding, running and debugging, and documentation. These phases may vary from one computer installation to another and with the needs of a given firm. Some installations require keypunching, whereas others allow the program to be entered via a terminal. Some firms require extensive documentation, others may not. In any case, all steps must be considered.

Problem Analysis
In this phase, the problem to be solved or the job to be performed by the computer is carefully analyzed. The problem is defined in terms of end results. The elements of the problem must be identified and reduced to quantitative terms—all variables must be converted into measurable numeric or alphabetic quantities.

For example, qualitative terms such as "poor credit," "Christmas bonus," "good employee," and "best accounts," must be converted into terms such as "delinquent more than 45 days," "$50," "absent less than five times," "purchases over $10,000." The expected outcomes are expressed in terms of these quantitative variables.

One of the elements often considered in problem analysis is the feasibility of solving the problem on the computer. Such things as costs, error rate, and time factor must be considered. If it appears that the computer solution is practical, then the programmer will proceed with the next phase.

Algorithm and Flowcharting
This step involves consideration of alternative algorithms or strategies and the selection of the most suitable one.

FIGURE 13.1 IMPLEMENTING THE PROGRAM

1. PROGRAM ANALYSIS. The problem is studied, defined. Input and output specifications are written. A method of computer solution is developed.

4. KEYPUNCHING. The keypunch operator converts each line on the coding sheet to a separate tab card. A keypunch machine punches holes in tab cards and prints the English equivalent at the top.

2. FLOWCHARTING. The programmer reduces the problem to discrete steps. Charts are prepared which graphically illustrate the flow of data.

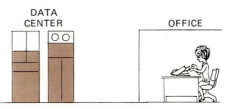

DATA CENTER   OFFICE

5. RUNNING AND DEBUGGING. The program is taken to a computer to compile and execute. If it doesn't, bugs must be removed so it will run. Consultation with others may uncover causes of trouble.

3. CODING. Each step of problem is reduced to an instruction or group of instructions printed in a language such as FORTRAN. Coding sheets and language manuals aid the programmer.

6. DOCUMENTATION. A write-up is prepared on the program, explaining program logic. Flowcharts, instructions and details are included to help others use the program or for later modification.

After the algorithm has been selected, it is graphically represented by the flowchart. By reducing the solution of the problem to discrete steps, the flowchart helps the programmer see the problem in its entirety. (Program logic and flowcharting techniques were discussed in the previous chapter.)

Coding
After a problem has been flowcharted, it must be converted into a set of instructions understandable to the computer. Coding is the process of converting the steps in the algorithm to a set of instructions written in a programming language.

The computer cannot be instructed by simply writing a set of commands such as

PLEASE FIGURE OUT WAGES PAID AND CASH RECEIVED FROM LAST MONTH'S BOOKS. ADD THEM TOGETHER AND GIVE THEM TO THE CONTROLLER.

In the future a compiler may accept instructions given in a free conversation form, but at present programming instructions must follow a precise format and set of conventions for each language. The instructions must direct the computer through each step in the algorithm and define each calculation in detail. They must give the computer such information as the size and type of numbers to be read in and out, their location on the records, and the exact form and layout of the output desired.

Programming instructions given to the computer must conform to the rules of spelling, structure, order, etc. for a particular language. Below are examples of excerpts from programs coded in COBOL and FORTRAN.

COBOL:
```
1070 READ-DATA.
1080      READ WAGE-FILE INTO WAGE AT END GO TO END-OF-JOB.
1090      READ CASH-FILE INTO CASH AT END GO TO END-OF-JOB.
1100      ADD WAGE, CASH, GIVING TOTAL.
1110 WRITE-DATA.
1120      MOVE TOTAL TO OUTPUT-AREA.
1130      WRITE OUTPUT-AREA AFTER ADVANCING 2 LINES.
```

FORTRAN:
```
READ (1,10) WAGE, CASH
TOTAL = WAGE + CASH
WRITE (3,20) TOTAL
```

The codes in these examples are very efficient and compact. Some interactive computer languages (discussed in Chapter 18) permit more freedom than the above examples. However, even in these languages the programmer must adhere to specific conventions.

The coded instructions will be translated into machine language by a special program, called a *compiler*. Each compiler translates instructions for only one language, but a computer may have more than one compiler available.

CODING FORMS.   Programming statements are coded on a standard form, ruled off in columns and lines. Each column on the coding sheet corresponds to a column on a card, and each line to an individual card.

FIGURE 13.2   DIFFERENT CODING FORMS

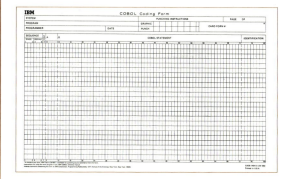

COBOL

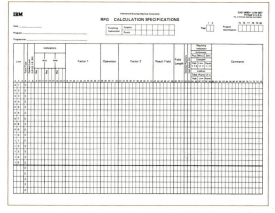

RPG

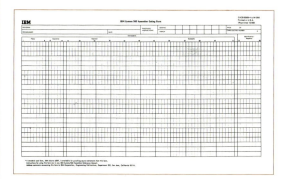

ASSEMBLER

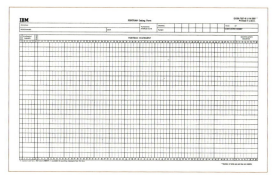

FORTRAN

Each coding form is designed to conform to the conventions of one of the programming languages. Figure 13.2 illustrates several of the forms in use. All the forms have the same function: they provide uniform pages on which to write computer instructions.

Keypunching

After coding, a keypunch operator converts the coded, handwritten instructions into machine-readable form. Each line on the coding sheet is punched into a separate card on a keypunch machine. A set of cards, called a source program (or, simply, a program), is generated. The data on which the program is to operate may also be punched into another set of cards, called the data deck.

At present, cards are frequently used to input data and source programs to the computer in the stand-alone program mode. Some computer installations also use key-to-tape, or key-to-disk equipment. This mode of input is fast and eliminates handling large numbers of cards. (Key-to-tape and disk equipment was discussed in Chapter 7.)

After the program and data decks have been keypunched, they are assembled with job control cards into a job stream, ready for input to the computer. (See Figure 13.3.) Job control cards tell the computer such things as a new job is being presented or a job is ending, and the language in which it is coded.

Running and Debugging

A program being processed by a computer must first be compiled. Compilation involves the conversion of each instruction in the program into machine language for processing by the CPU. Each programming statement must be free from coding or keyboarding errors and must conform to rules of syntax and structure before it will be compiled. When all statements are correct and are translated, the job is said to have compiled.

If, as often happens, the initial run of the program is unsuccessful, it is said to blow up, (that is, fail to compile or execute as planned). Few programs with more than a dozen instructions compile and execute the first time through a computer. The fault lies not with the computer but with bugs in the program. Bugs are logical or clerical errors that prevent the computer from properly compiling or executing the program. The programmer must change his program to correct errors in logic, coding, syntax, etc. This process is called debugging.

TYPES OF BUGS.   There are two major types of bugs in a program: compilation errors and execution errors. If either are present, the program will not run properly or will give inaccurate results.

Compilation Errors.   Compilation errors are discovered by the compiler and include

- Spelling errors
- Syntax errors
- Improperly sequenced statements
- Improperly labeled statements
- Conflict in names
- Illegal names or statements
- Invalid statements
- Missing punctuation

FIGURE 13.3 JOB STREAM

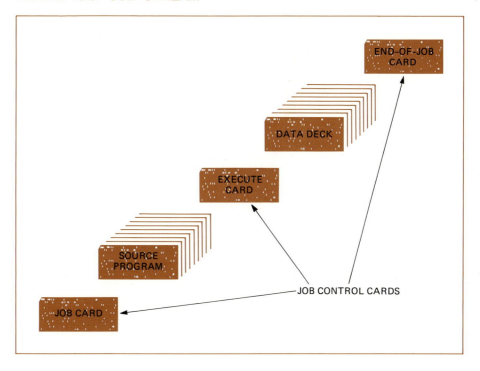

Execution Errors. Execution errors are discovered by the computer's operating system during the process of execution and include

- Numbers too large for storage area
- Incorrectly written input statements
- Mispunched characters in the data set

DIAGNOSTIC MESSAGES. When a compiler discovers errors in a program, it will communicate this information to the programmer by generating diagnostic messages, which are printed on the line printer with the program listing. Some error messages are informational, others require immediate or direct action by the operator or programmer.

Figure 13.4 illustrates some typical error messages. The errors have been flagged by the compiler as the program was listed. As an instruction is read, the compiler checks to see that it conforms to the language rules, syntax, etc. Those that do not conform have been flagged or marked in different ways. Some computers place a dollar sign ($) below the point of error; others use a carat or similar symbol. Execution errors are printed out at the end of the listing.

DEBUGGING PROCEDURES. The debugging phase of the programming effort requires patience and insight and can be the most frustrating part of

FIGURE 13.4   DIAGNOSTIC MESSAGES

```
                    C       CALCULATES RELIGIOUS DEMOGRAPHY
      0001              10 DO 50 I=1,5
      0002              20 READ(1,30) MANU LING, KHARMAH
                                            $              $
            01)    ILF003I NAME LENGTH           02)    ILF003I NAME LENGTH
      0003              30 FORMAT(I4,I4,I4
                                                                      $

            01)    ILF013I SYNTAX
      0004                 40 JADE=MANU+LING
                              $
            01)    ILF013I SYNTAX
      0005                 CONTINUE
      0006              30 WRITE(3,70)JADE
                           $
            01)    ILF006I DUPLICATELABEL
      0007                 FORMAT(' ',I5)
                               $
            01)    ILF002I LABEL
      0008              90 STOP
      0009              100 END
                            $
            01)    ILF043I ILLEGAL LABEL WRN.



                                ILF021I       UNCLOSED DO LOOPS
      50


                                ILF022I       UNDEFINED LABEL
      50                         70
```

programming. One small clerical or logical error may result in many trips to the computer center to run the program, check the results, make keypunch changes, and then resubmit the job.

A programmer looks for and corrects compilation errors in keypunching, coding, syntax, etc. If all these errors are corrected and the job compiles but still does not run, the programmer considers execution and logical errors. For example, the columns of the record being read by a computer must contain data, or the results may be erroneous. Because of a wrong input description a computer may read in 359 as 59 or 3,590. Errors in logic may prevent a job from running properly. A loop may begin the cycle at the wrong statement, or an error in branching may cause the computer to skip an important step.

A programmer attempts to find and eliminate these bugs by carefully checking a print out of the set of computer instructions and by reexamining his logic. He will trace a piece of test data through the program manually, checking at each step to see the results of the computer run. He may have the program print out the intermediate results after performing each operation.

When all errors are removed and the job compiles and executes properly, it is considered a running program ready for documenting.

One disadvantage of the stand-alone program is that errors and incorrect statements are not detected until the entire program has been keypunched and submitted to the computer for running. This is avoided in the interactive program, discussed in the next chapter.

Documentation   Completing documentation is the last step in the implementation of a program. Final documentation is explanatory material, flowcharts, instructions to the computer operator, sample test data, and other information relating to the details of a program, written and filed as a permanent record.

PURPOSES.   Documentation explains the program algorithm to others. It is a tangible record of logic, details, and input and output specifications—all easily forgotten items. Programmers find documentation useful when writing new programs. Well-documented programs are a source of notes, routines, algorithms, etc.

Documentation is essential if programs are to be modified or revised. It is much easier to retrace logic and follow through calculations with the help of documentation. Also, there is less chance of creating a logical error if the logic is clearly outlined on paper.

Documentation is important in production runs. The computer operator needs specifications to set up the machine properly, load the correct I/O units, and handle errors and problem situations.

Documentation varies according to the needs of individual firms and the purpose of the program. Sometimes a program listing is sufficient. At other times, a complete case history of the program is necessary.

CONTENTS OF THE DOCUMENTATION FILE.   There are no rules about what must be placed in a documentation file. It should be complete enough to enable changes and modifications to be made without difficulty. The following items are often placed in the file:

Abstract.   A one- or two-paragraph summary of the purpose of a program and its major features and options. It may include a bird's-eye view of the algorithm and general procedures followed. The abstract may also include

- Name of programmer
- Date program was written
- Brief description of program
- Summary of input and output requirements
- Minimum system requirements
- List of options available in program

The sample abstract in Figure 13.5 includes sufficient information to explain the basic program, yet avoids unnecessary detail.

Descriptive Narrative.   A written description of the program. It defines the problem and explains the algorithm, methodology, and logic followed in the program. All mathematical calculations and formulas should be shown. Any options are listed, with an explanation of how they are called out or used.

FIGURE 13.5   ABSTRACT

Program Name: _____Credit Authorization_____

Programmer: _____Max Sanders_____

Date: _____May 8_____

DESCRIPTION:

        This program processes purchasing orders. It reads in the account name, credit limit, name of purchasing agent, merchandise code, date account opened and account number. The program computes the purchase discount at the stated percentage, prints out a list of purchases by merchandise code and checks the amount of purchase against the credit limit. Accounts which exceed the limit are flagged with a message to contact the purchasing agent by name. Then the program reads in and processes the next account.

OPTIONS:

        The program has subroutines which generate several reports, including listing purchases by merchandise code, by type of accounts, and by salesman. The program can also list accounts which have not purchased items during the preceeding 12 months.

MINIMUM EQUIPMENT CONFIGURATION: Control Data 6400, with three disks.

LANGUAGE: COBOL

A good narrative should be clearly written and avoid undefined terms.

Graphic Narration.   Adequate graphic and visual devices to illustrate a program and its relationship to the system. Program flowcharts, system flowcharts, block diagrams, and coding sheets are used.

Program Listing.   An accurate program listing. The listing serves as the master record against which copies and revisions of the program are checked.

     A listing should include comment statements, which are special statements, available in most languages, that will not be compiled or executed. Comment statements should title the program and the major sections and precede all major branches.

Layout of Input and Output Records.   A complete set of specimen input and output records. Input records should be pasted down on a sheet of paper and each field labeled. (See Figure 13.6.) If an alphabetic or numeric code is

FIGURE 13.6   INPUT/OUTPUT RECORD DOCUMENTATION

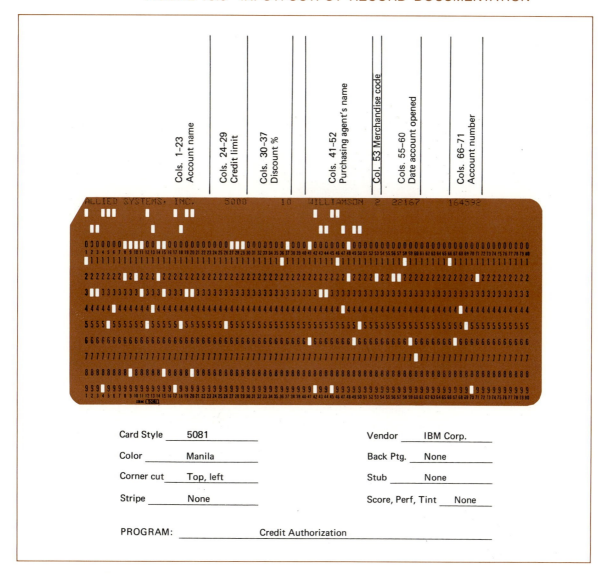

Card Style ____5081____   Vendor ____IBM Corp.____

Color _____Manila_____   Back Ptg. ____None____

Corner cut____Top, left____   Stub _____None_____

Stripe _____None_____   Score, Perf, Tint ____None____

PROGRAM: _____Credit Authorization_____

used to group data, it should be indicated and explained in the
documentation. Additional information about record style and format may be
included at the bottom of the page. Writing the program is simplified if record
documentation is designed early so that it can be used as reference
throughout the debugging cycle.

If several data records, such as master and detail records, are used, they
should all be shown and described in detail. A visual job stream will be
helpful here to show the sequence of the input. (See Figure 13.7).

FIGURE 13.7   VISUAL JOB STREAM

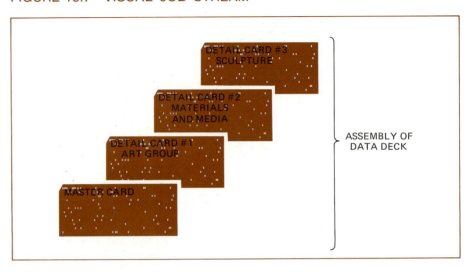

FIGURE 13.8   FORM FOR DOCUMENTING OUTPUT

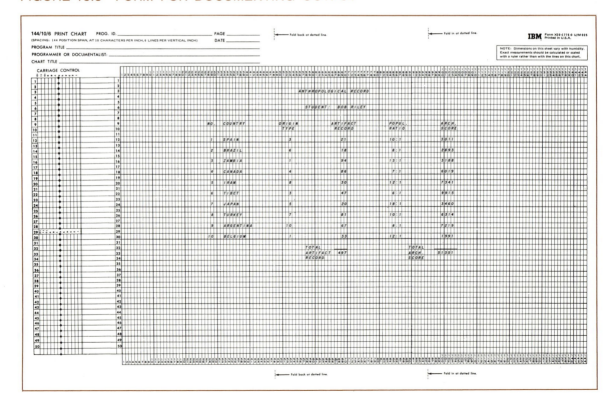

Specifications for output records should be shown and described. The fields for each piece of data on the records should be indicated. If output is to be printed, a sample should be included, and the size of the form and type of paper it is printed on noted.

A form similar to IBM X20-1776-0 is often used to document output records. (See Figure 13.8.) The layout of this form corresponds to the output of the line printer. All columns and spaces are labeled and identified. This form is a graphic record of the output layout.

Test Data for Checking. Test data sets are valuable testing and debugging aids. They should include data that forces the computer to execute all branches and possibilities in the program. Carefully checked print outs should be included as known standards for checking future runs.

Lapse Time. Summary of the time required for compilation and execution of a program. This statement helps the operator later discover any malfunctions in the run.

Run Manual. Documents necessary to actually run the job on the computer. The following information is usually included

- Carriage control tape
- Job stream setup, including all job cards
- Sequence of data cards
- Layout of input and output records
- Error messages

A run log or continuing record, showing changes or modifications made in the program during the run, is sometimes kept.

SAMPLE PROBLEM

We now follow a simple example of a common data processing situation through implementation.

Problem Analysis

A business firm wants a program that would indicate when there were fewer than 1,000 units of a given part in stock. The program then must calculate the total number of units in stock for each part and print a message telling the ordering department to order more. Some units are kept in the sales department, and some are stored in the warehouse. The number of units available in each department is recorded on a separate card by that department. The two files are in matching sequence by part number.

Algorithm and Flowcharting

The programmer studies the problem and defines the steps the computer must take to solve it. He decides that the best algorithm would be for the computer to read in the card from the sales department file, and then the one from the warehouse for each type of part and add these two quantities to get the current inventory. Then test the inventory. If it is less than 1,000, write a message indicating that more parts must be ordered. If the inventory is 1,000 or greater, print a notice that sufficient parts are on hand.

Figure 13.9 illustrates a modular program and a detail program flowchart, which diagram this example. They show how the programmer has converted the logic in his program into modular steps. These, in turn, are expanded to detailed steps the computer can follow to solve the problem.

Coding the Problem   The program must be coded in a language the computer can understand, for example, COBOL. Assume the data is available on the data records in the following format.

Records from the Sales Department:

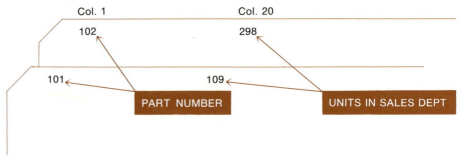

Records from the Warehouse Department:

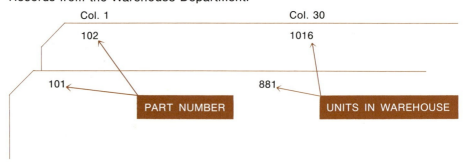

The first step is to break the problem down into workable smaller units. Some programmers develop a list from the flowchart:

- Start program
- Read a data card from the Sales Department file
- Test for end-of-file
- Read a data card from the Warehouse file
- Test for end-of-file
- Add UNITS-IN-SALES-DEPT to UNITS-IN-WAREHOUSE
- Compare INVENTORY to 1,000

FIGURE 13.9 FLOWCHARTING THE PROBLEM

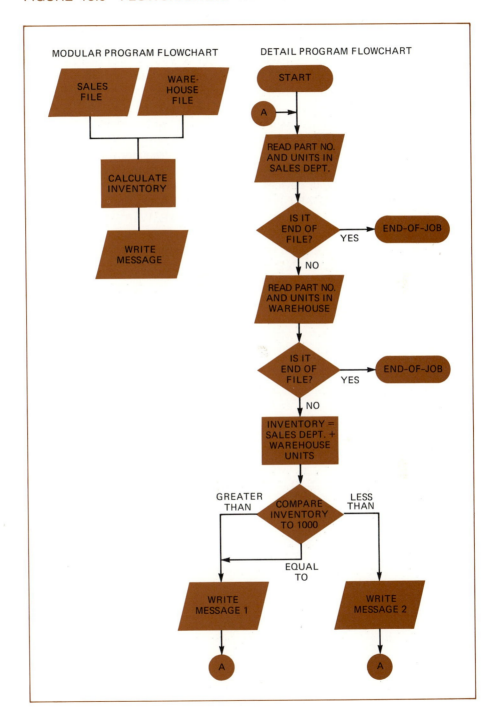

- Write out the message "REPLENISH STOCK OF PART-NUMBER xxx ORDER MORE UNITS IMMEDIATELY," if INVENTORY is less than 1,000
- Go back and read another data card from the Sales Department file
- Write out the message "THERE IS AN ADEQUATE SUPPLY OF PART-NUMBER xxx," if INVENTORY is equal to or greater than 1,000
- Go back and read another data card from the Sales Department file
- END-OF-JOB, close program

The next step is to actually write the instructions. Figure 13.10 shows some of the coded statements on the COBOL coding form. Figure 13.11 shows the instructions the programmer has given the computer.

The first two statements direct the computer to prepare the input and output devices that will be needed.

START-PROGRAM.
   OPEN INPUT SALES-FILE, WAREHOUSE-FILE, OUTPUT
      PRINT-FILE.

Next the programmer instructs the computer to read a card from the SALES-FILE with this code:

FIGURE 13.10   SAMPLE COBOL CODING

```
IBM                                         COBOL Coding Form
SYSTEM                                      PUNCHING INSTRUCTIONS        PAGE    OF
PROGRAM    CØBØL CØDING EXAMPLE             GRAPHIC                                          *
PROGRAMMER                    DATE          PUNCH               CARD FORM #

5020  START-PRØGRAM.
5030      OPEN INPUT SALES-FILE,WAREHØUSE-FILE,ØUTPUT PRINT-FILE.
5040  READ-DATA.
5050      READ SALES-FILE INTØ HØLD-INPUT, AT END GØ TØ END-ØF-JØB.
5060      MØVE UNITS-IN-SALES-DEPT TØ WØRKAREA-1.
5070      READ WAREHØUSE-FILE INTØ HØLD-INPUT, AT END GØ TØ END-ØF-JØB.
5080      MØVE UNITS-IN-WAREHØUSE TØ WØRKAREA-2.
5090  CALCULATIØNS.
5100      ADD WØRKAREA-1, WØRKAREA-2, GIVING INVENTØRY.
5110      IF INVENTØRY IS EQUAL TØ 1000, GØ TØ WRITE-MESSAGE-1.
5120      IF INVENTØRY IS GREATER THAN 1000, GØ TØ WRITE-MESSAGE-1.
5130      IF INVENTØRY IS LESS THAN 1000, GØ TØ WRITE-MESSAGE-2.
5140  WRITE-MESSAGE-1.
5150      MØVE PART-NUMBER TØ MESSG1.
5160      MØVE MESSAGE-1 TØ PRINT-LINE.
5170      WRITE PRINT-LINE AFTER ADVANCING 2 LINES.
5180      GØ TØ READ-DATA.
5190  WRITE-MESSAGE-2.
5200      MØVE PART-NUMBER TØ MESSG2.
5210      MØVE MESSAGE-2 TØ PRINT-LINE.
5220      WRITE PRINT-LINE AFTER ADVANCING 2 LINES.
5230      GØ TØ READ-DATA.
5240  END-ØF-JØB.
5250      CLØSE SALES-FILE, WAREHØUSE-FILE, PRINT-FILE.
```

*A standard card form, IBM Electro C61897, is available for punching source statements from this form.
Instructions for using this form are given in any IBM COBOL reference manual.
Address comments concerning this form to IBM Corporation, Programming Publications, 1271 Avenue of the Americas, New York, New York 10020.

GX28-1464-5 U/M 050
Printed in U.S.A.

READ-DATA.

    READ SALES-FILE INTO HOLD-INPUT, AT END GO TO
    END-OF-JOB.

The computer will move all 80 columns of the input record into a temporary storage area called HOLD-INPUT. It will check the card to see if it is a specially coded end-of-file card. If it is, the computer will branch down to the routine called END-OF-JOB. If it is not, the computer goes on to the next instruction.

    Since the program logic calls for only two values, UNITS-IN-SALES-DEPT and UNITS-IN-WAREHOUSE, to be added, the programmer will direct the computer to separate these quantities from the rest of the data on the record and move them into temporary working areas for manipulation.

    MOVE UNITS-IN-SALES-DEPT TO WORKAREA-1.

This instruction tells the computer to move the quantity named UNITS-IN-SALES-DEPT to the temporary storage area named WORKAREA-1.

    READ WAREHOUSE-FILE INTO HOLD-INPUT, AT END GO TO
    END-OF-JOB.

This statement tells the computer to read a record from the WAREHOUSE-FILE and move all 80 columns into HOLD-INPUT. This new

FIGURE 13.11 COBOL PROGRAM LISTING

```
LINE NO. SEQ. NO.            SOURCE STATEMENT

     1       5020 START-PROGRAM.
     2       5030     OPEN INPUT SALES-FILE, WAREHOUSE-FILE, OUTPUT PRINT-FILE.
     3       5040 READ-DATA.
     4       5050     READ SALES-FILE INTO HOLD-INPUT, AT END GO TO END-OF-JOB.
     5       5060     MOVE UNITS-IN-SALES-DEPT TO WORKAREA-1.
     6       5070     READ WAREHOUSE-FILE INTO HOLD-INPUT, AT END GO TO END-OF-JOB.
     7       5080     MOVE UNITS-IN-WAREHOUSE TO WORKAREA-2.
     8       5090 CALCULATIONS.
     9       5100     ADD WORKAREA-1, WORKAREA-2, GIVING INVENTORY.
    10       5110     IF INVENTORY IS EQUAL TO 1000, GO TO WRITE-MESSAGE-1.
    11       5120     IF INVENTORY IS GREATER THAN 1000, GO TO WRITE-MESSAGE-1.
    12       5130     IF INVENTORY IS LESS THAN 1000, GO TO WRITE-MESSAGE-2.
    13       5140 WRITE-MESSAGE-1.
    14       5150     MOVE PART-NUMBER TO MESSG1.
    15       5160     MOVE MESSAGE-1 TO PRINT-LINE.
    16       5170     WRITE PRINT-LINE AFTER ADVANCING 2 LINES.
    17       5180     GO TO READ-DATA.
    18       5190 WRITE-MESSAGE-2.
    19       5200     MOVE PART-NUMBER TO MESSG2.
    20       5210     MOVE MESSAGE-2 TO PRINT-LINE.
    21       5220     WRITE PRINT-LINE AFTER ADVANCING 2 LINES.
    22       5230     GO TO READ-DATA.
    23       5240 END-OF-JOB.
    24       5250     CLOSE SALES-FILE, WAREHOUSE-FILE, PRINT-FILE.
    25       5260     STOP RUN.
```

NOBODY'S PERFECT

Joseph Begley saved 2,000 cigaret coupons and mailed them to a British cigaret company in exchange for a watch. When the watch had not arrived he wrote and asked why.

Back came three watches. Begley wanted only one so he mailed back the other two.

The next day 10 parcels arrived from the cigaret firm. The following day 18 parcels arrived. The day after that the local post office telephoned and said 10 more parcels were waiting for Begley.

All of them were trade-in gifts given by the cigaret company in exchange for coupons Begley never had. Among the gifts were three tape recorders, a doll, a golf bag, two electric blankets, a cot, saucepans, a pressure cooker, and long-playing records.

Begley sat down and wrote a long, pleading letter to the firm, asking it to stop. In the return mail came a reply saying, "It was a computer error." The company gave Begley 10,000 coupons in compensation for his troubles. With these Begley ordered tools and a bedspread. He received a plant stand and two stepladders.

SOURCE "The Computer Erred, Erred, Erred, Erred," Dateline: Eveashan, Eng. (UPI), *Los Angeles Times*, March 18, 1972.

data will replace the information read in and stored there from the last card. The card is tested to see if it is the last card in the file. If it is, the computer will branch down to the END-OF-JOB routine. If it is not, the computer goes on to the next instruction.

MOVE UNITS-IN-WAREHOUSE TO WORKAREA-2.

The computer is instructed to separate the quantity needed for manipulation from the rest of the data on the record. It will be moved into temporary storage area named WORKAREA-2.

Now the programmer is ready to calculate the total current INVENTORY. He instructs the computer to add the quantities stored in WORKAREA-1 and WORKAREA-2 and place the answer in the storage area named INVENTORY.

CALCULATIONS.

ADD WORKAREA-1, WORKAREA-2, GIVING INVENTORY.

To test INVENTORY to see whether it is greater or less than 1,000, the programmer uses this code:

IF INVENTORY IS EQUAL TO 1000, GO TO WRITE-MESSAGE-1.

IF INVENTORY IS GREATER THAN 1000, GO TO WRITE-MESSAGE-1.

IF INVENTORY IS LESS THAN 1000, GO TO WRITE-MESSAGE-2.

The computer will perform the test as directed and branch to the appropriate paragraph.

The instructions that write the messages are

WRITE-MESSAGE-1.

    MOVE PART-NUMBER TO MESSG1.

    MOVE MESSAGE-1 TO PRINT-LINE.

The computer will move the PART-NUMBER stored in HOLD-INPUT into the reserved field in the MESSAGE-1 area. Then it will move MESSAGE-1 to the PRINT-LINE area.

    WRITE PRINT-LINE AFTER ADVANCING 2 LINES.

This tells the computer to double-space and print the data stored in the PRINT-LINE area on the line printer.

    GO TO READ-DATA.

With this statement, the programmer directs the computer to begin another loop and read in the next record from the SALES-FILE.

    If INVENTORY is less than 1,000, the computer will branch to the second message.

WRITE-MESSAGE-2.

    MOVE PART-NUMBER TO MESSG2.

    MOVE MESSAGE-2 TO PRINT-LINE.

    WRITE PRINT-LINE AFTER ADVANCING 2 LINES.

    GO TO READ-DATA.

"I THINK WHAT WE NEED NOW IS SOMEONE CALLED A COMPUTER PROGRAMMER."

© Datamation®

It will move the PART-NUMBER from the HOLD-INPUT area to the field reserved for it in the MESSAGE-2 area. Then it will move the entire group to the line printer for output. Again the machine is instructed to double-space before printing MESSAGE-2 on the line printer. Then the computer will loop back to read another record from the SALES-FILE.

When the computer reads in the end-of-file card from the SALES-FILE, or WAREHOUSE-FILE, it will branch to the END-OF-JOB routine.

    END-OF-JOB.
        CLOSE SALES-FILE, WAREHOUSE-FILE, PRINT-FILE.
        STOP RUN.

Here the programmer tells the computer that there will be no more records to write or read. STOP RUN informs it that it has reached the last statement in the program.

At this point, the computer compiles the COBOL statements and executes the instructions on the data files. Figure 13.12 is an example of the output that would be generated by this program.

FIGURE 13.12   OUTPUT FROM COBOL PROGRAMMING EXAMPLE

```
REPLENISH STOCK OF PART-NUMBER 101 ORDER MORE UNITS IMMEDIATELY

THERE IS AN ADEQUATE SUPPLY OF PART-NUMBER 102
```

This example was a simplified program used for illustration. It was assumed that each file contained matching cards in the same sequence. In practice, several more steps would probably be included, to verify matching of part numbers, to reinitialize numerical areas before each loop, and even to have the computer print out the reorder forms. The coding shown is only part of the entire program. Chapter 16 gives a more detailed discussion of the structure of the COBOL language.

Keypunching

After the programmer has written his set of coded instructions, each line on the coding sheet is converted into a separate punched card. Data for the Warehouse and Sales files and the required job control information are punched into cards. Finally, all cards are gathered together and assembled into a single deck called a job.

Running and Debugging

Depending upon the type of installation, the job is either run by the programmer himself, or submitted for run. One or more passes through the computer may be required to check the program for accuracy and to eliminate bugs or errors. Most programmers compare computer-generated results against known results calculated manually.

Documentation   Documentation is the last step in program preparation. The programmer
gathers together in a file, the program listing, a copy of the sample
data set, narrative description of the program and flowchart.

KEY TERMS   Stand-alone program   Compilation errors
Job control cards   Execution errors
Coding form   Diagnostic messages
Debugging   Documentation

EXERCISES   1. List and describe the six major steps in implementing the stand-alone
program.
2. Define coding. What is its purpose and how is it done?
3. List three instructions that are too general to be coded. List three
commands that are specific enough to be coded.
4. Select a simple business problem, such as calculate interest, or figure a
bank balance. Break the problem down into a series of discrete steps.
5. Flowchart the problem outlined in Exercise 4.
6. Compare several coding forms for different languages. How do they
differ?
7. What is the relationship between the lines on a coding form and the
punched source deck.
8. What is the purpose of running and debugging a program?
9. List three types of compilation errors.
10. How do compilation errors differ from execution errors?
11. What are diagnostic messages, and how are they indicated by various
compilers?
12. How do programmers debug a program?
13. What is the function of documentation?
14. List some items normally found in the documentation file.

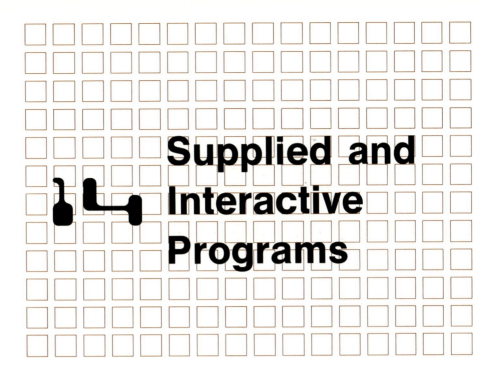

Supplied and Interactive Programs

In the two previous chapters we discussed flowcharting, structuring, and implementing the stand-alone program. We developed a unique solution to a specific problem and then implemented it on the computer.

We now discuss two other methods of solving problems: supplied and interactive programs. The user need not always write an original program to solve a specific problem. Programs are often already available, either in the computer's system library (tapes, disks) or from manufacturers, proprietary software firms, or time-sharing companies.

THE SUPPLIED PROGRAM

A supplied program is a program written by someone other than the user. It may be provided by a computer manufacturer, a private or public institution, or by a firm that specializes in writing programs for sale (proprietary software house). Such programs may be made available at no charge, at a flat fee, or on a monthly lease or rental arrangement.

Supplied programs are available to process many different business, scientific, and statistical problems. These programs may be delivered as a set of punched cards ready to be run on the user's computer, as a program recorded on magnetic or paper tape, or on a disk pack. Some supplied programs are available only as a program listing, and the user must keypunch a program deck or record it on tape or disk.

Sources of
Supplied Programs

MANUFACTURER-SUPPLIED PROGRAMS. A primary source of supplied programs is the computer manufacturer. Firms such as Burroughs, General Electric, and IBM provide customers with ready-made programs. Available programs are listed in a catalogue, which is supplied without charge to users and includes descriptive information and an abstract for each program. For a partial listing of supplied programs, see Table 14.1.

The manufacturer provides documentation, more details, and a copy of a specific program upon request. The documentation file may contain a copy of the program flowchart, program listing, descriptive material on the algorithm, and application notes. These programs are sometimes called "off the shelf," because they are readily available.

Manufacturer-supplied programs are generalized in nature and designed for common business applications. The following IBM-supplied programs are typical of the range available:

- Finance: Investing, borrowing, stocks, bonds, taxes and auditing
- Cost accounting: Labor, work in progress
- Payroll and benefits: Payroll, employee benefits, profit sharing, retirement, credit union
- Personnel: Recruiting, hiring, training, wages, salary
- Manufacturing: Scheduling, loading, job reporting, bill of materials
- Inventory: Stocking, inventory, equipment and tool inventory
- Purchasing: Preparation of purchase orders, accounts payable, purchase analysis
- Marketing: Sales forecasting, bid analysis, territory analysis

User-Supplied
Programs

Another group of supplied programs is provided by computer users themselves. These programs are made available by users, without charge, to the manufacturer, who, in turn, passes them along at no charge.

Users may supply programs similar to those provided by the manufacturer. However, user-supplied programs are often more limited in application, since they are written by private firms to meet specific local needs.

Schools and universities often make their programs available to other institutions. Although these programs may have required thousands of hours of programming time and many dollars in preparation, they are usually offered at little or no charge. The Biomedical Programs researched and developed by UCLA include dozens of routines for the health sciences. Many of these are statistical and analytical programs that can also be used to solve business problems. The entire group of programs is available on magnetic tape with a printed manual that outlines and documents the programs.

Proprietary
Programs

Many programs have been written by private firms, consultants, and banks and insurance companies and are available to other users at a charge. Proprietary software firms specialize in developing, writing, and marketing programs for profit. These firms offer general programs for a flat fee or a monthly lease or rental arrangement.

TABLE 14.1   INDEX PAGE

MARK II   BUSINESS AND FINANCE[a]

ACCOUNTING

BIGGL$***   Expanded version of PLBAL$ which handles up to 550 chart-of-accounts records.

JEDIT$***   Edits journal entry files prior to their input to PBAL$ or BIGGL$ for detecting invalid account codes or out-of-balance conditions. Also prints total income or loss resulting from journal entries for income tax determination.

PLBAL$***   Maintains the general ledger for a business and produces specified trial balances, detailed general ledger listings, total and departmental income statements, balance sheets, and schedules for selected accounts.

AUDITING

APSAM$***   Appraises the results of an audit by calculating the confidence limits on the cost questioned, using difference and ratio methods.

RANUM$***   Generates random numbers within specified range.

RASEQ$***   Generates sets of random numbers.

SAMSI$***   Calculates the size of an audit sample necessary to satisfy specified confidence limits on cost questioned.

BUSINESS MODELING

GENPS$***   Performs operating simulation of any system—mechanical or human. Provides a variety of statistical measures of system operation.

FINANCIAL ANALYSIS

ANNUIT***   Calculates payment or withdrawal annuity variables and prints annuity tables.

DEPREC   Calculates depreciation schedules.

FINAN$***   Prepares seven types of financial analyses and can handle ten historical and ten projected years.

LESEE$***   Determines net advantage of leasing with respect to borrowing funds and to buying the asset, with annual cash flows and sensitivity analysis.

LESIM$***   Calculates the risk of investing in an asset and then leasing.

LESØR$***   Calculates rate of return from investing in an asset and then leasing the asset to another party, with annual cash flows and sensitivity analysis.

[a] General Electric Company, Information Service Department, 7735 Old Georgetown Road, Bethesda, Md. 20014.
Program Library Index, "Mark II Applications Programs," p. 3.

The number and types of firms providing this service have grown in the past decade. Businesses often find that programs supplied by software firms are better written and cost less than programs written by users themselves, because software firms often employ specialized, highly qualified programmers.

The following proprietary programs will give some idea of the scope and type available:

File maintenance: Maintains large files such as payroll, personnel, inventory, and sales. Routines include searches, merges, file updating, and removing inactive names or records.

Payroll and taxes: Handles tax preparation for a range of business personnel. Calculates withholding taxes and prepares government and internal reports. Also calculates earnings, deductions, and tax liability, and prints paychecks.

Accounts receivable: Handles a firm's accounts receivable and order processing, customer payments, aged balances, and current inventory and stock level and generates up-to-date reports, invoices, and statements.

Finance company accounting: Processes all data, calculations, and operations. Calculates collections, fees, loans, and balances, records payments, prepares ledger and summary statements, and prints mailing labels.

Data plotting: Plots a variety of business, educational, and scientific data. Data may be computed or read in from cards and printed on the line printer as a plot.

Commercial banking: Handles a variety of commercial banking and savings and loan tasks. Processes mortgage payments, and certificates of deposits, provides management reports, and prepares the general ledger.

Implementing the Supplied Program

The potential user of a supplied program first obtains an abstract. If the program appears to solve the problem at hand, additional documentation, such as flowcharts and sample input and output records, is ordered. He then considers these data with other factors. For example, will the program run on the available computer? What modifications will be necessary? Would it be more economical to write an entirely new program?

If it is suitable, the program is recorded on cards, tape, or disk. The program is obtained from the vendor. It is then run on the computer, modifications are entered, and sample test data is run and checked.

Advantages of the Supplied Program

Some business firms find it cheaper to buy or lease a program from a proprietary firm than to pay for the programming effort and debugging time required to develop the program. In addition, off-the-shelf programs provided at no charge by computer manufacturers are attractive to users.

Since the supplied program is already written and tested, the user has only to check it out and prepare the modifications. Sometimes supplied programs include extra services, which a firm finds useful, but would not pay to develop specifically. And, in some cases, the supplier provides maintenance, revisions, and modification services as part of the rental agreement. For example, modifications resulting from changes in the tax rate or calculations or new laws affecting the program might be supplied as part of the maintenance agreement.

Disadvantages of the Supplied Program

A disadvantage of the supplied program is that it may be too generalized for a given firm's needs. The conversion costs or reprogramming effort required to bring it in line with needs may be as great as those for writing an original program. If the demand for a supplied program falls below a certain point the manufacturer may withdraw it from circulation and the user would lose supporting services, such as revisions, updating, and maintenance, which had been included.

THE INTERACTIVE PROGRAM

An interactive program is a program written either by a user or by a manufacturer that permits the user to enter data, branch, or change the course of the program flow during execution. It differs from the stand-alone program in that it is designed to stop and wait for the programmer's directions. Many firms have interactive programs available on their computer systems. Time-sharing companies also provide interactive programs.

A user interacts with the program via a remote terminal keyboard connected to the CPU by telephone lines. Figure 14.1 shows a remote terminal. A remote terminal allows the user to interact with the program in a conversational way, to enter commands and data during processing, and to receive data as an immediate response.

FIGURE 14.1 INTERACTIVE TERMINAL

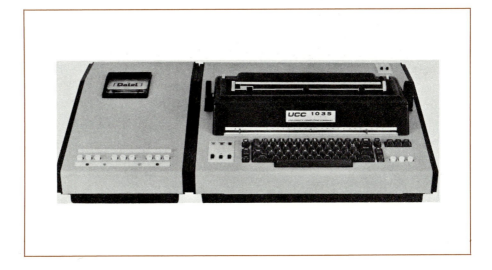

Interactive programs have many branches and options. The branches are determined at key points during the processing, as the user selects options and feeds in parameters and variables. Interactive programs allow a user the flexibility of selecting procedures based on the results of a previous step.

With an interactive program, a user with little programming experience can solve complex problems on the computer. The program asks the questions and provides the algorithms and logic; the user supplies the data and decides which algorithm to use.

Illustration of Interactive Programming

To illustrate one form of interactive programming, let us suppose a loan consultant has a customer applying for a $25,900 home loan at 7% interest. The customer asks the difference in monthly payments between a 20- and 30-year mortgage and the amount of equity that would have accumulated at the end of 10 years for each mortgage alternative.

The consultant has reviewed several interactive programs and selected a program that will perform the analysis he needs. He is seated before an interactive terminal connected via telephone lines to a computer. Let us follow the activity.[1] (The remarks typed by the computer are flush with the left margin, and the programmer's comments are indented and printed in color. A brief discussion of each message is in the column at the right.)

OLD   NAME—MORTGE***
READY.
          RUN

First, we call up the program. Then we type RUN, carriage return.

MORTGE   12:25   MON.   08–18–72

RATE = 1; LIFE = 2; AMOUNT BORROWED = 3; PAYMENT AMOUNT = 4

ENTER THE NUMBER YOU WANT TO FIND [1,2,3 OR 4]?
          4

We request the program to compute the payment amount.

NUMBER OF PAYMENTS PER YEAR?
          12

You can designate any number of payments in a year. Since we want monthly payments, we type 12.

NOMINAL ANNUAL RATE USING DECIMAL NOTATION?
          .07

This is the nominal annual rate in decimal form.

LIFE OF THE MORTGAGE: YEARS, MONTHS?
          20,0

The life of the mortgage in this case is 20 years, 0 months.

[1] The illustration is from Call-A-Computer, General Library, "Interest, Mortgage, and Annuity Programs," pp. 5–6.

AMOUNT TO BE BORROWED?
25900

This is the total amount to be borrowed.

FOR HOW MANY CALENDAR YEARS DO YOU WANT THE MORTGAGE TABLE PRINTED OUT?
10

We want to show the equity for 10 years, so we type 10.

MONTH [JAN = 1; ETC.] AND YEAR IN WHICH THE MORTGAGE LOAN WILL BE MADE?
9,72

Since the mortgage becomes effective in September, 1972, we enter 9,72. The program assumes that the first payment is made after the mortgage becomes effective.

TYPE A ONE [1] IF YOU WANT ONLY AN ANNUAL SUMMARY OF THE MORTGAGE TABLE; TYPE A ZERO [0] FOR A MONTHLY TABLE?
1

The annual summary will suffice since we want to know the amount of equity, so we type 1. By typing 0, we would get a monthly (periodic) listing by year of interest, principal repayment and outstanding principal.

*** MORTGAGE TERMS ***

NOMINAL ANNUAL RATE = 7 PERCENT
LIFE OF MORTGAGE = 20 YEARS, 0 MONTHS
AMOUNT BORROWED = $25900.00
PAYMENT AMOUNT = $200.80

This gives us a chance to check our data. It also indicates the payment amount.

*** MORTGAGE TABLE ***

YEAR	INTEREST	PRINCIPAL REPAYMENT	ENDING PRINCIPAL OUTSTANDING
72	452.378	150.029	25749.971
73	1782.635	626.994	25122.976
74	1737.310	672.320	24450.656
75	1688.708	720.922	23729.734
76	1636.592	773.037	22956.697
77	1580.709	828.920	22127.776
78	1520.787	888.843	21238.933
79	1456.532	953.098	20285.835
80	1387.633	1021.997	19263.838
81	1313.752	1095.877	18167.961
82	1234.531	1175.098	16992.862

Equity is the difference between loan amount and principal outstanding.

The consultant will then call up the same program and repeat the process, inserting data for a 30-year mortgage. The two print outs can then be compared and the customer can choose the mortgage alternative best suited to his needs.

Stand-alone programs can also be processed over remote terminals, but not in the interactive mode. The stand-alone program and data sets are entered via paper tape or keyboard and the computer takes over. It processes the job and prints the results on the remote terminal. There is no interaction between the program and the user, and the course of the program cannot be changed during execution.

The Interactive Terminal

An interactive terminal is an on-line, real-time terminal designed to input and output data from a keyboard. As you recall, on-line means the terminal is directly connected to the computer. This connection allows the user to change the course of execution of the program, to add in data, or to handle queries from the CPU at the time and place most convenient to him. Real time means that the CPU processes the data, or queries immediately, at the instant the keyboarding takes place.

The interactive terminal is remotely connected to the CPU over telephone lines and need not be in the same building or even the same city as the computer. It can be located where it has the greatest value to most users; many firms have more than one terminal available in different offices or departments.

Implementing the Interactive Program

The procedures used to solve a problem with an interactive program are less formal than with the stand-alone or the supplied program. In the latter instances, the programmer must plan all his steps in advance, keypunch or keyboard his program and data, and then turn it over to the computer. With an interactive program, the user examines his data and decides the type of manipulations he wants to perform on them. He requests the computer to do them but may change options as he proceeds.

Implementation of the interactive program usually requires several steps:

PROBLEM ANALYSIS.   The user must have a clear idea of his input data and the procedures he wants. His problem must be stated in quantitative terms suitable for solution by the computer. (In this regard, implementation is the same as in the stand-alone program.)

PROGRAM SELECTION.   The user reviews the programs available on his interactive terminal. He selects a program and studies its documentation to determine its suitability for the problem at hand. Will it print out the results in the form and style required? Is the logic and algorithm followed in the program acceptable? What are the input and output specifications? What options are available?

GO ON-LINE.   During this phase of manipulation, the user keyboards data and the program is executed. Using a very simple code, similar to English, the user directs the computer to call out the particular program from storage and make it available for execution. The program takes over, usually responding by giving a list of the options or routines it includes.

The user must determine the options needed to process his problem and then enter their names. The computer will ask questions and give instructions. At appropriate points in the execution, the computer will indicate that data should be entered and then will continue to process the information. Errors made when entering data are corrected by immediately retyping the new data. Results of the processing will be printed by the keyboard of the terminal.

DOCUMENTATION.   An interactive programming session is self-documenting. The print out generated contains a record of the dialogue between the computer and the user. It shows the computer's questions, the user's responses, the options used, and the data entered. Results of the processing are displayed on the print out and are thus available for further checking.

Most firms or data centers offering interactive programs usually provide comprehensive user manuals, which include not only documentation of the program, algorithm, and input/output specifications, but also directions for calling out and executing the program, and a summary of available options. The interactive mode is often used to solve one-time only problems, and hence less documentation is required than on the repetitive production runs usually handled by the stand-alone program.

Some Available
Interactive
Programs

The following list of programs, available from the General Electric Time Sharing Services, illustrates the varieties of programs available in this mode.[2]

Auditing: Appraises the results of an audit, and calculates confidence limits with different ratios. Calculates the size of an audit sample necessary to satisfy certain cost questions.

Accounting: Handles journals and chart of accounts, maintains general ledgers, prepares departmental income statements, balance sheets, and schedules for selected accounts.

Business modeling: Sets up a working model of any system. Provides statistical measures of system operation.

Bond analysis: Calculates potential gains on presently held securities and compares potential return on investment for each bond to determine average of trade. Calculates price that should be paid for bonds to realize a specified yield.

Cash flow analysis: Calculates the discounted rate of return and the present worth of cash flow over life of investment.

Inventory control: Simulates an inventory system, forecasts customer demand and time needed to build and maintain inventory. Calculates optimum inventory level.

Loans and interest: Calculates payment or withdrawal annuity variables,

[2] General Electric Information Systems, Program Library Index #800000 4-70, p. 3.

ANALYSIS OF WORLDWIDE POLITICAL BEHAVIOR

An inventive political scientist at the University of Southern California believes computer analysis can help experts anticipate future trouble spots in the complex realm of international political behavior.

Dr. Charles A. McClelland has compiled a historical file of relations between countries. He can illustrate this interplay with computer-generated graphs showing the ups and downs of political life between any of 169 nations around the world—more than 25,000 pairs of countries in all.

The federally funded project is built on thousands of facts culled from the *Los Angeles Times, London Times,* and *The New York Times.* Each item from the three source newspapers dealing with international affairs is clipped, and a coded version goes onto a punched card and is stored in the computer.

The coding system is simple, quick, and understandable. "First we assigned each nation a permanent code number," he said. "Then we established 63 categories of international political activity, from the mildest sort of action to outright war."

For example, 013 represents a nation's admission of guilt, an apology to another nation or verbal retreat. Next are such things as comments, praise, promises, and finally, on the positive side, agreements and proposals. After that the mood changes. The next category is rejection—of a treaty offer, for instance. Then come such increasingly offensive actions as charges, denunciations, complaints, protests, cancellations of treaties or aid, expulsion of envoys, and, finally, military force.

"At any time, then, we can get back from the computer a complete listing of all the goings on between any two countries. And when we direct the computer to plot out the results in graph form, we can see both the number of transactions between these countries and the seriousness of those actions."

The USC professor feels automated systems such as his offer a new perspective on the world situation.

"It seems apparent that patterns of international conduct can be boiled down and sorted out by computer," he said. "For instance, we can expect to discover that a certain nation always makes threats before it strikes, always says things in the same kind of language. Once such a pattern is established, we could be better able to figure out in advance what's likely to happen in a particular world trouble spot—or pinpoint such a trouble spot before the situation gets totally out of hand."

SOURCE Abstracted from "Computer Helps California Professor Analyze Worldwide Political Behavior," Press Information Release on University of Southern California, IBM Data Processing Division, Los Angeles.

and prints out annuity tables. Calculates nominal and effective annual interest rates for installment loans.

Management decisions: Makes yearly projections from average percentage change. Evaluates and compares alternative methods of plant and production expansion by the Monte Carlo simulation method.

Marketing and economic forecasting: Correlates as many as ten time series of data. Finds best-fit curve.

Production analysis: Projects work effort based on average work unit. Calculates output based on average learning curve theory.

Advantages of Interactive Programming

A major advantage of the interactive program is its real-time feature. Data is processed instantaneously and results made available immediately. Since the terminal can be placed wherever a telephone is located, it brings the power of the computer to the points in the business enterprise where and when it is most needed.

Interactive programming is basically simple, since the computer provides all of the programming effort. No time need be spent in coding, flowcharting, or debugging programs.

Since sophisticated, documented programs are available, a user with little or no programming experience or mathematical skills can perform mathematical and financial analysis procedures.

Interactive programming is practical for one-time only problems as well as production work. If a program is available for a procedure, no time need be lost writing a program for a single problem or solving it manually.

"FOR GOD'S SAKE, MAN, CAN'T YOU FIND SOMETHING BETTER TO WORRY ABOUT THAN THE EFFECT ON OUR REAL TIME SYSTEM?"

TABLE 14.2 PROGRAMMING MODE COMPARISON

	STAND-ALONE PROGRAM	SUPPLIED PROGRAM	INTERACTIVE PROGRAM
ALGORITHM	Selection of algorithm by user or vendor	Algorithm supplied by vendor; reviewed by user	Variety of algorithms available to user
CODING	By programmer on coding sheets	By vendor	Not required.
KEYPUNCHING	Program keypunched by user or vendor; data keypunched by user	Program keypunched by vendor; data punched by user	Responses and data entered directly from terminal
RUN AND DEBUG	Careful check after run of data and program by user	Done by vendor, revised by user; modifications prepared and tested by user	Program debugged by vendor
DOCUMENTATION	Complete file written by user or vendor	Supplied by vendor; modifications written by user	Only as needed by user
PROGRAMMING COST	Borne by user or vendor	Borne by vendor; modifications at user's expense	Borne by vendor
APPLICATION	To solve specific, local problem	Generalized routines for application by many users	Generalized routines with specific algorithm selected by user

Disadvantages of the Interactive Program

Costs may be higher for the interactive program than for the stand-alone program. CPU time must be made available for all users on the system in a time-sharing arrangement. Communication lines, which must either be rented or purchased outright, must be provided to each on-line terminal.

The limitations of some terminals preclude their use for production runs. Since most terminals are designed to accept keyboard or paper tape input, large data files cannot be easily or economically entered. Some firms do store data files at the data center. An operator then loads them on-line when they are queried from a remote terminal—a procedure that requires time and negates some of the advantages of the interactive program.

   Transmission line failure can cause troubles with on-line systems. The interruption of telephone service or electric power at any one terminal will lock out that terminal. Data cannot be processed until the service is restored.

   Table 14.2 contrasts the stand-alone, supplied, and interactive program modes. The comparisons are based upon general considerations and thus may not be true for all data processing installations.

KEY TERMS

Supplied program   Proprietary program
Manufacturer-supplied program   Interactive program
User-supplied program   Real time

EXERCISES

1. Who develops the logic, flowcharts, and algorithm for the supplied program?
2. Describe several supplied programs and explain how they may be used in a business firm.
3. What are the advantages and disadvantages of the supplied program?
4. What are proprietary suppliers? Give several examples of the type of programs they provide.
5. How does a firm select and implement a supplied program?
6. What is an interactive program? How does it differ from the stand-alone program?
7. Give several examples of available interactive programs.
8. What are the advantages of the interactive program?
9. What are the limitations on interactive programs?
10. What kinds of problems are best suited for on-line, real-time programming?
11. How does a user implement an interactive program?
12. Contact a time-sharing firm in your area and determine the kinds of interactive programs available from them.
13. How much skill and training are required to effectively use an interactive program?

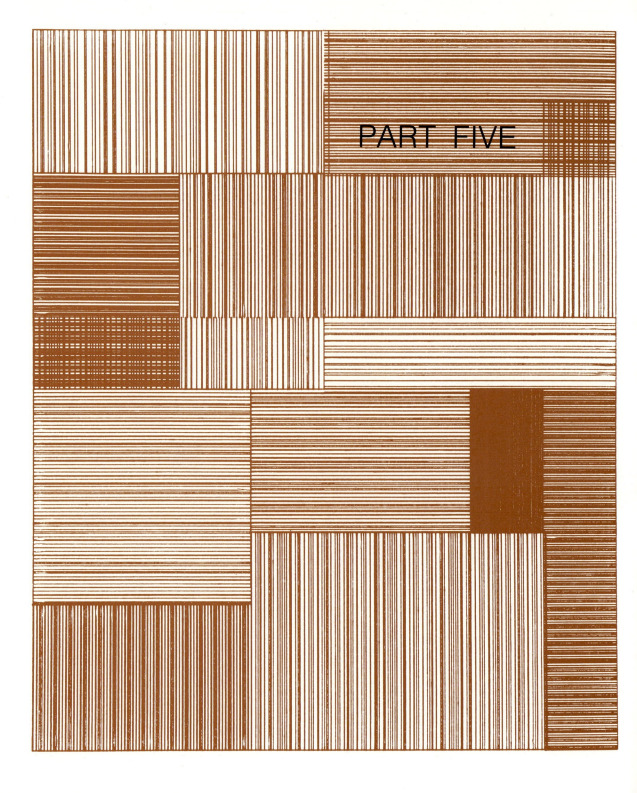

PART FIVE

COMPUTER
SOFTWARE

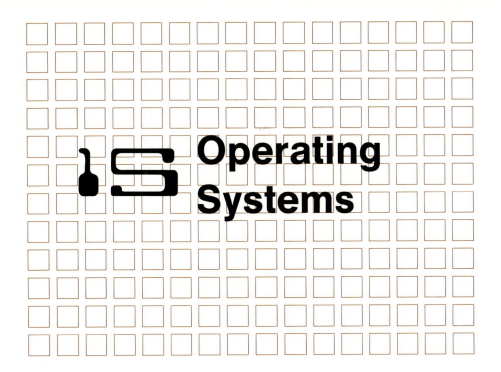

15 Operating Systems

Early in the evolution of computer systems it became obvious that the human operator was a limiting factor in the development of technology. As computer hardware increased in complexity and jobs could be processed more rapidly, human operators could no longer keep up with the system. Minutes, or even hours, were often lost, while an operator loaded cards, put paper in the line printer, removed jobs from the machine, logged in runs, and diagnosed errors and problems.

Computer designers realized that the computer could best schedule its own work and diagnose its own troubles. Programs were written to direct the computer through the steps involved in scheduling jobs, accounting for time used, assigning input and output devices and switching them on- and off-line at the proper times. These programs, called monitor or supervisor programs, were supplied by the computer manufacturer. They enabled the operator to concentrate on physically loading and unloading the jobs from the input and output devices. The computer, controlled by an internal program, processed each job in the most efficient way. Error conditions were immediately brought to the attention of the operator. Freed of the scheduling responsibility, he could apply his time to diagnosing and eliminating the error conditions.

As computer hardware developed, more complicated programs, called operating systems, were written to handle even more tasks. Manufacturers call these systems master control programs, executive control systems, or comprehensive operating supervisors. Operating systems differ from problem (source) programs in that they are written by the computer manufacturer. Problem (source) programs are written by the user to solve a direct, local, data-processing problem.

PRINCIPLES OF OPERATING SYSTEMS

An operating system is a complex group of programs and routines that enables a computer to schedule work in the most efficient way. Operating systems supervise the overall operation of the computer, control the flow of jobs in and out of the system, switch input/output machines in and out, and call programs from storage. They include language translators (or compilers), which convert coded programs into machine language. Table 15.1 is a partial list of routines (modules) that make up an operating system. Operating systems are usually written by the computer manufacturer for each series of computers he makes.

Types of Operating Systems The sets of instructions that make up the operating systems are held in secondary storage on disk, tape, or drum. The unit that holds the operating system is usually referred to as the resident storage device. The particular unit used as resident storage device is reserved exclusively for this purpose.

Manufacturers have given different names to their operating systems depending on the medium on which it is stored. IBM refers to several operating systems as follows:

TAPE OPERATING SYSTEMS (TOS). An operating system that is stored on tape. When a given routine is needed, it is located on the tape and transferred to core storage by the system. A number of routines may be called from the tape in the execution of a single program.

DISK OPERATING SYSTEMS (DOS). Operating systems may also be stored on a disk pack. As various routines are needed, they are called into active storage from the disk.

BASIC OPERATING SYSTEMS (BOS). The Basic Operating System is another method of controlling the computer. The system is stored on disks, but differs from the DOS in that the operator communicates with the computer in number codes rather than in English terms. This system is more limited in its functions and is used on smaller computers.

OPERATING SYSTEMS (OS). With the Operating System (OS), used on most large computers, the controlling program is often stored on a random-access magnetic drum. This system allows the computer to process many jobs simultaneously. Core storage and input/output devices are assigned with more flexibility than in the previously mentioned systems.

TABLE 15.1 OPERATING SYSTEM MODULES[a]

PREFIX	IBM-PROGRAM NUMBER	COMPONENT
IHD	360N-CB-452	COBOL Library Subroutines
IJB	360N-CL-453	System Control and Basic IOCS (disk supervisor)
IJC		I/O Card
IJD		I/O Printer
IJE		I/O Paper Tape
IJF		I/O Magnetic Tape
IJG	360N-IO-476	Consecutive Disk IOCS
IJH		Indexed Sequential Direct Access
IJI		Direct Access Method
IJJ		Device Independent Access Method
IJK	360N-PL-464	PL/I Library Subroutines
IJM	360N-IO-478	OCR Devices
IJN	360N-UT-472	Vocabulary File Utility (7772)
IJO	360N-SM-450	Disk Sort/Merge
IJP	360N-SM-400	Tape Sort/Merge
IJQ	360N-AS-465	Assembler
IJR	360N-RG-460	RPG
IJS	360N-CB-452	COBOL Complier
IJT	360N-FO-451	Basic FORTRAN Compiler
IJU	360N-IO-477	MICR Devices
IJV	360N-PT-459	Autotest
IJX	360N-PL-464	PL/I Compiler
IJY	360N-AS-466	Assembler F
IJZ	360N-DN-481	On-Line Test Executive Program
IKL	360N-CV-489	COBOL LCP

[a] IBM Systems Reference Library, "IBM System/360, DOS: System Generation & Maintenance," C24-5033-8, p. 306.

System Generation

System generation, sometimes called system initiation, is the procedure of designing, organizing, and setting up an operating system to meet the needs of a specific firm. Programs, utilities, and routines are selected and recorded on the system's resident storage device (tape, drum, or disk). System generation is usually done when a new computer system is installed by a firm. The resources of the operating system are custom tailored to the particular demands of the user.

Functions of the Operating System

Operating systems can be divided into two major types of programs: control programs and service programs. Here are some examples of these two groups.

CONTROL PROGRAMS

1. *Schedule Input and Output Operations.* The CPU can normally process more data per second than a single input and output device can feed in or receive. Thus, many input/output devices must be switched in and out at the proper time.
2. *Communicate with the Operator or Programmer.* The operating system directs the computer to type messages on the console typewriter regarding the status of the computer system, such as I/O devices that need attention, errors in job flow, or abnormal conditions.
3. *Handle Interruptions.* Interruptions caused by errors or input/output problems are processed in an orderly way to reduce time lost from the regular job flow. If an error is detected, the computer does not stop and wait for the operator. It prints a message and goes on to the next job without delay.
4. *Log Jobs.* The program keeps a list of jobs run and clocks them in and out. It records and prints out the elapsed compilation and execution time.
5. *Monitor Status.* The operating program monitors the status of the computer system and performs error and parity checks.
6. *Combine Phases of a Job into a Complete Run.* Parts of a job that is too large to run as a unit can be processed in smaller blocks.
7. *Handle Multiprogramming.* The program will switch between several jobs and allocate time or assign priority. It maintains checkpoints so that jobs can be resumed at the proper place.

SERVICE PROGRAMS

1. *Load Programs and Language Translators* (*Compilers*). These programs are read from the system's inactive storage areas to active core storage by the operating system.
2. *Maintain the System Library.* Computer systems are capable of storing frequently used routines and programs for use by programmers. These routines are usually held in secondary storage, called the system library. The operating system catalogues and retrieves the routines for the programmer.

Using the Operating System to Control the Computer's Activities

As an illustration of how a computer controls its own activities, suppose a source program punched in cards is submitted to the computer for run. However, it contains a programming error serious enough to prevent the computer from completing the run.

Without an operating system, the job input, processing, error interruption, and output, would have been handled as follows: the program would be fed to the computer by a human operator. He would manually switch in the card reader, place the cards in the hopper, turn on the device, and start the CPU. He would also prepare the output device (line printer, for example). He would log in the time and job name on the log sheet. Only then could the computer proceed to process the job.

The computer would begin compilation, but the error would prevent it from executing the job. The operator would have to determine the cause of the failure. Is it a machine failure, a programming error, a paper jam, or a mispunched data card?

Suppose the operator were busy loading cards into a card reader. The computer would remain idle until he became aware of the stoppage, found and corrected the trouble, and restarted the machine.

When an operating system handles the scheduling, the same situation would be handled as follows: the operator loads the cards into the card reader and then starts the processing cycle by pressing a button. The machine switches the card reader on-line and begins processing the job. When the machine encounters an error in the program, it diagnoses the difficulty as, for example, a programmer error. It immediately prints a message to the operator and runs the cards for that job out of the card reader. Then without delay it begins to input the next run.

EXAMPLE OF AN OPERATING SYSTEM

Although operating systems vary from manufacturer to manufacturer, there are several features common to all. The following describes the organization of an IBM system. (Although the basic concepts are the same, other manufacturers may use different terminology.) The IBM operating system is composed of control programs and processing programs.

Control Programs

In the IBM system control programs consist of three types of routines or subprograms:

❶ Supervisor Program
❷ Job Control Program
❸ Input/Output Control Program

SUPERVISOR PROGRAM.   The supervisor program is designed to control the overall scheduling of the computer operations. The supervisor pulls required routines from the resident storage device (disk, tape, or drum) and loads them into core. The supervisor schedules input and output operations and allocates channels to I/O devices. It types messages to the computer operator, indicating error conditions, I/O devices that need attention, etc.

JOB CONTROL PROGRAM.   Another important program in the control group is the job control program, designed to facilitate batch processing. In batch processing, the computer operator assembles many individual jobs into a group, called a job stream, for processing on the computer. (See Figure 15.1.) The job stream is fed to the card reader or other input device, and the machine processes each job in turn, without operator intervention. The computer operator is thus free to perform other tasks.

FIGURE 15.1   JCL CARDS IN JOB STREAM

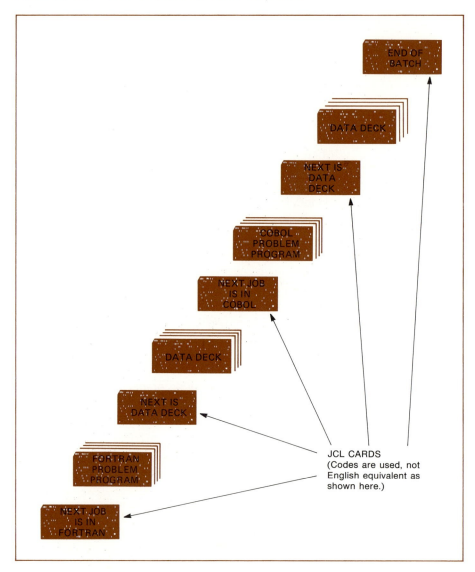

Within the job stream are a number of job control cards. Some of these cards indicate the beginning and the end of each job in the group. Others, included in each individual job, give the computer the programmer's instructions for his job. The job control program translates the code on the job control cards into machine language instructions to the CPU.

INPUT/OUTPUT CONTROL PROGRAM. I/O devices cannot be scheduled for the CPU in an indiscriminate manner. Careful and efficient allocation of card readers, line printers, card punches, tape units, etc. is essential if the CPU is to run at maximum processing speed and without interruption.

In most computers, the Input/Output Control System (IOCS) performs these functions rapidly and efficiently. The IOCS continually monitors the I/O devices. If the line printer is out of paper, or the card reader is jammed, it will signal the operator by typing a message on the console typewriter (or displaying it on a video screen). It will substitute other devices if they are available so that processing will not be interrupted.

The IOCS prepares input and output devices for use. For example, it will load reels of magnetic tape, check identification labels, and index the reels to the required point. The IOCS opens the circuitry that permits data to flow between the I/O devices and the CPU. It checks parity of data being transmitted and manages the job of buffering as the data moves in and out of the CPU.

Processing Programs

The processing programs work with the control programs to enable the computer to receive a problem written in a programming language, process it, and proceed to the next job in an orderly fashion. IBM classifies their processing programs as

1. Language Translators
2. Service Programs

LANGUAGE TRANSLATORS.   Language translators, often called compilers, were discussed in Chapter 6. Since computers can only operate on instructions coded in machine language, and most programs are written in languages resembling English or mathematical representation, a system of

FIGURE 15.2   LANGUAGE TRANSLATOR

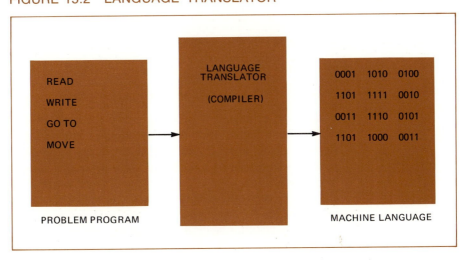

| PROBLEM PROGRAM | LANGUAGE TRANSLATOR (COMPILER) | MACHINE LANGUAGE |

COMPUTER ON THE BEAT

When the Kansas City policeman radioed headquarters to request a license check of a suspicious car, he received an answer within seven seconds. He was told the car was clean. There were no outstanding warrants against it. So the policeman continued on his rounds, and the motorist drove off, unaware that a check had been made.

"A year ago that check would have taken about 35 minutes," said the Assistant Chief of Police, "because nine different files have to be scanned for this kind of inquiry. Now, all of them have been coordinated under one system and we get answers in three to seven seconds."

The network operates in real time, and the files reflect up-to-the-minute information on the city's 57 patrol beats. Data is fed in 24 hours a day from 35 locations throughout the metropolitan area, including precincts, sheriffs' offices, municipal courts, prosecuting attorneys, juvenile courts, and parole officers.

By typing a simple instruction (on a terminal) plus an address, the police chief can determine the number of persons with criminal records living in an apartment house in the city. He can thus prepare his men for possible trouble before they enter the building.

Aside from increased efficiency for the police, it has definite advantages for civilians. "It protects the citizen's right to pass freely. Before the computer, we had to stop a motorist for questioning. Now if a quick check shows the car is clean, no stop is made."

On the other hand, if the driver is wanted, or the vehicle is listed as stolen, that is considered probable cause for an arrest, and the officer can proceed under Supreme Court rules. The system also protects the offender's right to privacy. Program locks built into the system safeguard all records from access by unauthorized persons or agencies. Some 4,000 of the 48,000 persons listed in the file have been flagged as armed, dangerous, mental cases, or persons known habitually to resist arrest and assault policemen. Such data is classified and available only to authorized personnel.

SOURCE   Abstracted from "A Different Beat," *Data Processor*, February 1970, p. 18.

translation is needed. A program called a compiler, or language translator, illustrated in Figure 15.2, does this job. A compiler translates instructions for only one language, or version of a language, into machine language. The machine language equivalents of the instructions are then fed to the CPU for processing.

Small computers may have only one or two compilers available, for example, for the Assembler and FORTRAN languages. Large systems may have compilers for several languages, such as FORTRAN, COBOL, PL/I, RPG, BASIC, ALGOL, and SNOBOL. With the larger system, the programmer has the option of writing his program in the language that best suits his specific needs. In all cases, the specific compiler is called out by a job control card in the job stream.

SERVICE PROGRAMS. Service programs are subprograms that perform frequently used routines and functions for the programmer. They make a great variety of procedures available to the programmer and thus save him much programming time and effort. These programs are called out by job control cards.

BERRY'S WORLD

© 1971 by NEA, Inc.

"It looks as though we might have some trouble with this one. It wants a longer lunch period and shorter hours!"

The computer's ability to store and call out these service programs give it much of its power and capability. Some common service programs are as follows:

1. *Librarian.*   The librarian is a service program that maintains the system library. It allocates the proper storage area in the computer system for a program, or part of a program, that a programmer wishes to save. It keeps track of where the program has been stored, for future use. This process is called cataloging a program. A system library is usually kept on disk or tape.

    The system library contains programs from many sources. Some are frequently accessed programs or modules catalogued by users. Other programs are catalogued in the system library by the manufacturer. These programs have wide applications in the routine processing performed by many users.

2. *Sort/Merge Programs.*   Other useful service programs are the sort and merge routines. Much of the data processing task is the preparation and maintenance of files, which must often be merged, updated, or sorted. Routines to perform these common tasks are stored in the operating system and are called out by job control cards. Usually these programs are general in nature and have multiple functions.

3. *Utilities.*   Similar in nature to the merge/sort programs are the utility programs. The utility programs perform such tasks as transferring data from cards to tape, from tape to the line printer, and reblocking data. They are called out by the appropriate job control cards.

    For example, suppose a programmer has a program that processes data recorded on magnetic tape. But the data is only available on punched cards. He could transfer the data in the file with off-line equipment and then have the computer process the job. Or, he could use job control cards to call out the card-to-tape utility program available in the operating system. The computer would then transfer and process the data during the same run.

PROCESSING THE JOB

When a job stream is fed to the computer for processing, the operating system logs in the name of the job from the first job control card and the time on the line printer or the console typewriter. It then reads and follows the instructions on the succeeding job control cards.

The operating system will load the proper language translator (compiler), read and compile the problem program, and prepare an object deck or module. An object module is the machine language translation of the coded programming statements. It is stored as electronic bits in a secondary storage device. An object deck is a set of cards punched with the machine language instructions. (See Figure 15.3.) Then the computer executes the program on the data deck.

FIGURE 15.3 OBJECT MODULE AND OBJECT DECK

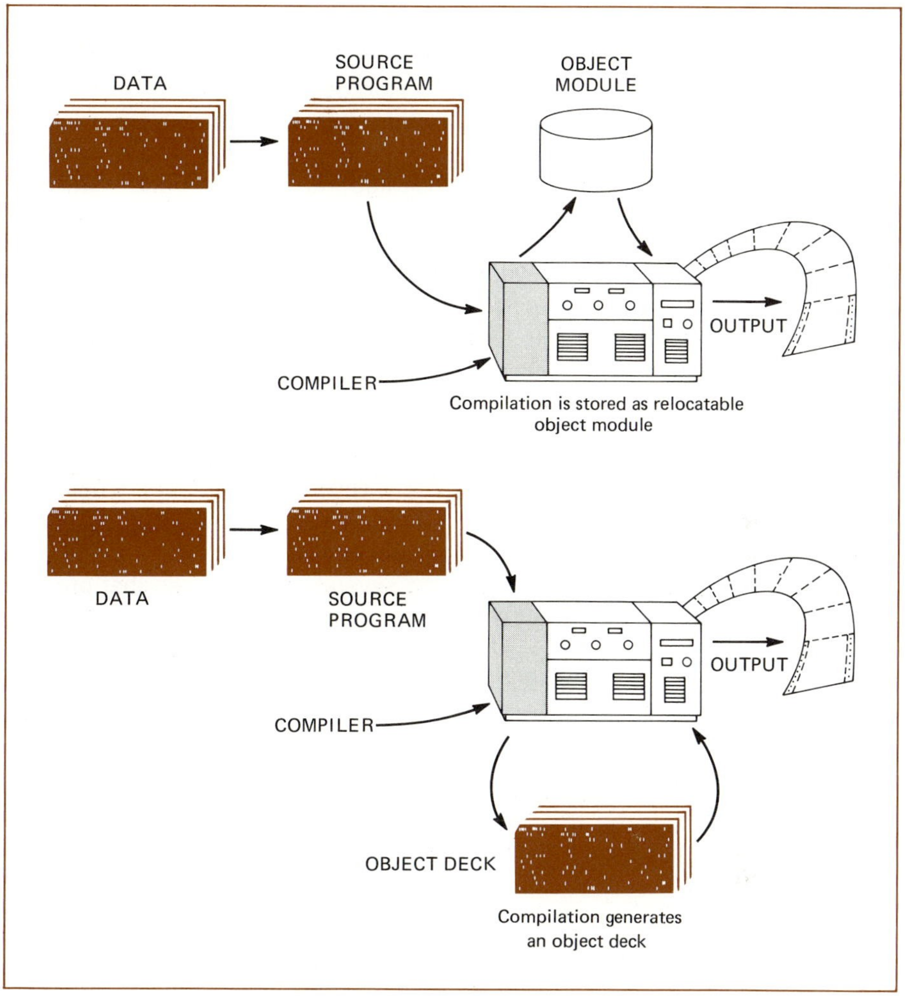

Upon encountering the job control card that signals the end of the job, the computer records the elapsed time and logs out the job. Then it moves to the next job in the batch.

Job Control Cards Job control cards are referred to by various names, depending on the system in which they are used. Burroughs, for example, refers to "program control cards" and "program parameter cards." IBM refers to these instructions as "job control language" (JCL) and the cards on which they are punched as JCL cards. General Electric calls them "control cards."

The job control program recognizes most job control cards in the job stream by a special symbol, or symbols, punched in the first one or two columns of a card. Some systems use a "?," others a "$" or the letters

"CC." The JCL cards for the IBM 360 (DOS) system, for example, use a slash in the first column.

When the computer recognizes a job control card, the Job Control Program translates it and calls the appropriate routine of the operating system into working storage.

Although variations exist, most systems require the same types of job control cards to compile and run a job. The most common cards used in the IBM system are illustrated in Figure 15.4 and include

1. JOB CARD.   This card identifies a new job. Most job cards include an identifying name and the JCL code symbols that identify a new job to the system. The system will log in the name of the job and the time on the console typewriter and the output media of the program.

2. OPTION LINK.   Directs the computer to save the object modules it produces.

3. COMPILER CARD.   This card instructs the computer to call a specific compiler from storage and transfers control of the system to that compiler. Only those compilers available to the system can be called. Most machines are equipped with several compilers, so that programs may be written in different languages.

   Problem Program.   The problem (source) program is next in line. Some systems require that it conclude with an (/*) END OF FILE JCL card.

4. EXEC LNKEDT.   Instruction to combine one or more object modules, ready for processing.

5. EXECUTE CARD.   This card tells the computer to begin execution of the program. The style of the execute card varies, but its purpose is to indicate to the system that it has compiled the programming instructions and execution should begin. A program may, or may not, have a data deck.

   Data Deck.   The data deck follows the execute card. Some systems require that it conclude with an (/*) END OF FILE JCL card.

6. END OF JOB (EOJ).   This card tells the computer the end of the job has been reached. It shifts control from the program under execution back to the operating system. Upon encountering the (/&) END OF JOB card, the computer logs out the job on the console typewriter. The system is then ready to begin the next job in the batch.

In the example in Figure 15.4, the programmer instructed the computer to compile and execute the job on a data deck. This was done with an appropriate set of JCL cards in the job stream. JCL cards may also be set up to perform a variety of compile and run combinations.

FIGURE 15.4   COMMON JCL CARDS

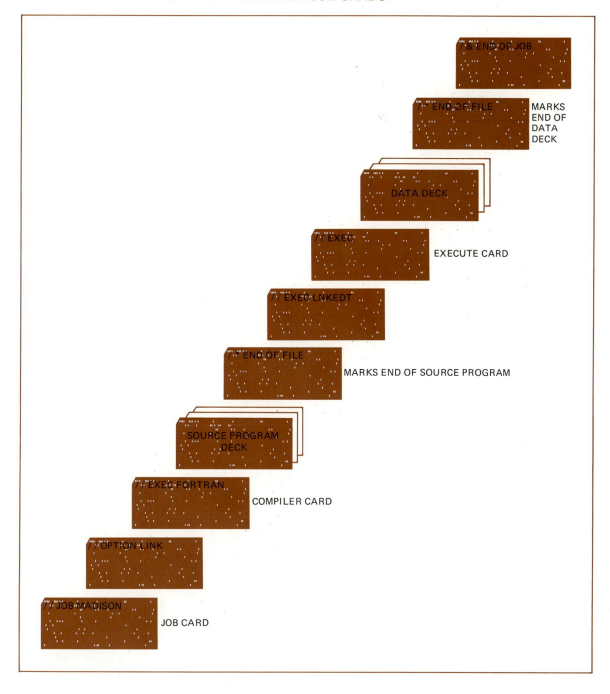

FIGURE 15.5   JOB CONTROL COMBINATIONS

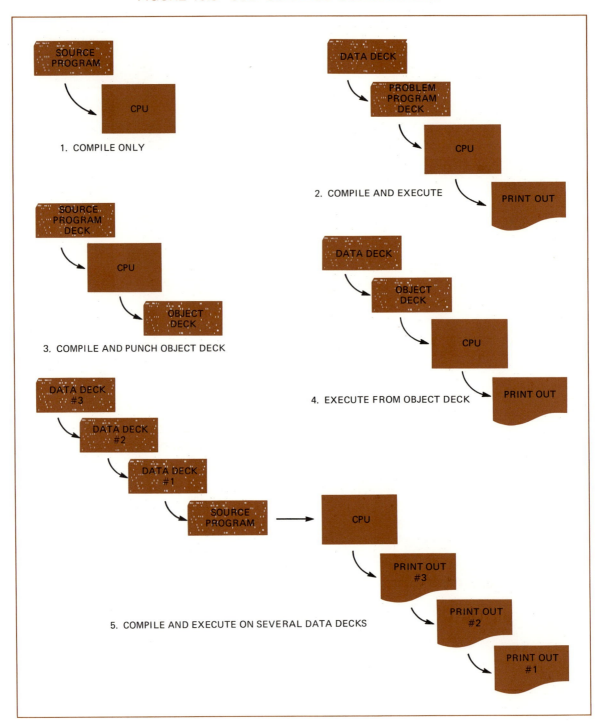

Options   Figure 15.5 illustrates some of the options available to the programmer using the IBM system. He can set up the job to compile and execute on one data deck or on many data decks. At times he may only want to determine if the problem program will compile. In this way he can see if it has been correctly written to agree with the rules of the language.

The programmer can also use JCL cards to instruct the computer to compile his program and punch an object deck of the machine instructions. (An object deck submitted to the computer does not require compilation. This can save considerable CPU time in repetitive runs.)

The options available on a computer system vary. The most common ones on an IBM system are

1. LIST SOURCE PROGRAM.   The computer will list the source program on the output device. Each instruction in the program is listed on the line printer in the order that it is read. This option is important during the debugging phase or when working with a new program.

2. DUMP MAIN STORAGE.   The computer will dump the contents of its main storage in the event of abnormal program termination. A dump is a listing in the HEX code of the contents of each position in storage. It is used in debugging to indicate the point at which a program failed.

3. LOG.   This card tells the computer to list the job name and all JCL statements on the console typewriter.

KEY TERMS

Supervisor program	Batch processing
Operating system (OS)	Job stream
Basic Operating System (BOS)	Compiler
System generation	Object deck
Control program	Object module
Processing programs	List source program
Tape Operating System (TOS)	Dump main storage
Disk Operating System (DOS)	Log
Job Control Program	Librarian
Input/Output Control Program	System library
Resident storage device	Merge/sort programs

EXERCISES

1. What are the limitations of using human operators to schedule work for computer systems?
2. Define an operating system.
3. Summarize the functions of the operating system.
4. Compare the four major types of operating systems.

5. What is the function of system generation? What are the determining factors in generating a new system?
6. What are the differences in function between control programs and processing programs?
7. Briefly summarize the functions of the major job control cards.
8. What are some options that may be called out by job control cards?
9. List five common language translators available on modern computer systems.
10. What are the functions of service programs? How do they save time and programming effort?
11. Obtain a copy of the system log (output from the console typewriter) from the operator in your data center. List the type of information it contains.
12. What language translators or compilers are available on the system in your data center?
13. What service and utility programs are available on your system?
14. What job control cards are used on your system? If a keypunch is available, punch a set of job control cards to run and execute a simple program.

COBOL Programming Language

16

To give directions to the computer, a programmer must be able to communicate with the system. Machine languages can be understood directly by the computer, but they are difficult for man to learn and to use. Therefore, many programming languages have been developed to facilitate man-machine communication. Computer languages, such as COBOL, FORTRAN, and PL/I, are structured to meet the processing needs of the users, not the computer's limitations, and must depend on compilers to translate them into machine language. These languages are called problem-oriented languages, or POL's.

The selection of a specific language for a given programming effort depends upon the needs of the firm, skill of personnel, hardware available, and the nature of the problem to be solved.

In this chapter, we discuss a major POL known as COBOL (COmmon Business Oriented Language), which is used extensively in business and industrial programming.

COBOL is unique because it is supported entirely by its users; that is, large firms, governmental agencies, and other users contribute time and money toward the improvement, development, and modification of the language.

Other languages, such as FORTRAN, have no formal sponsor supporting the planning and implementation of improvements. Each computer manufacturer or user is left to his own resources to modify the language. Modification is essential if the language is to remain in use and extend its utility.

The initial draft of COBOL was presented in 1960 by the Conference on Data System Languages (CODASYL). This group was formed by many large users, computer manufacturers, and the U.S. Department of Defense to develop a universal language of a business nature. One goal was to develop the language in such a way that COBOL programs could be run on different models and makes of computers. Major interest in the language was generated when the federal government required that all large computers purchased by them be equipped for COBOL. The CODASYL group now meets regularly in committee to evaluate changes, alterations, additions, and improvements to the language.

Advantages of COBOL

One of COBOL's major advantages is its close resemblance to English. Since COBOL was intended to reflect common business usage, it incorporates such terms as

ADD   SUBTRACT   MOVE TO   WRITE   PERFORM   PAY-RECORD

Complicated mathematical notation and symbols and binary code have been avoided in favor of common English terms. As a result, programs written in COBOL can be followed by nonprogrammers with little or no training. For example, one does not have to be a computer expert or a mathematician to understand an instruction like

IF PRICE IS GREATER THAN COST, PERFORM LOSS-ROUTINE.

or

ADD STOCK, SHIPMENT, GIVING GOODS.

Because the coding is easy to understand, programs written in COBOL generally require little or no documentation to explain each step in the program. COBOL program documentation does, of course, include flowcharts, descriptive narratives, and input/output specifications.

COBOL has good literal capability. Literal capability is the language's ability to manipulate words, sentences, or paragraphs of textual material. This is an important asset in business data processing, since names, addresses, lists, descriptive material, sentences, etc. are very frequently used.

COBOL is machine independent; that is, a program written in the language can run on different makes or models of computers, with little or no revision. Thus, a business firm can change its computer equipment, farm out jobs to other machines, or send programs to other users with considerable assurance that the program will run satisfactorily. (Some programming languages are machine dependent. Programs written in these languages can only be run on a given make or model of computer. To run them on other machines would require that all or part of a program be rewritten.)

COBOL is the major language used in business data processing, and COBOL compilers are available on most large computers used in business.

Limitations of COBOL

Although COBOL has many advantages, it does have limitations. Compilers for the full range of statements require a large amount of primary storage. These compilers fill many thousands of bytes of core storage and, hence, cannot be used in small machines. Thus, the utility of COBOL is limited to firms with access to medium and large systems.

COBOL is also verbose. It is not a tightly written language. Programs written in COBOL require dozens of statements, each one like a complete sentence constructed from English language words and names. This structure makes COBOL easy to follow, but results in a long, wordy program.

For example, a COBOL program to process an employee payroll might require 400 instructions. The same program written in a more terse language such as FORTRAN, might require only 30 or 40 instructions. However, it should be noted that the more compact the language used and the greater its reliance on symbols and codes, the more difficult it is for the nonprogrammer to follow.

Since COBOL suffers from some mathematical limitations, it is not the preferred language of the scientific or mathematical programmer. It is generally more difficult to perform complex mathematical operations in COBOL than in many other languages.

The COBOL programmer must follow certain rules, conventions, and limitations of form and structure. An error such as a misspelled word or a misplaced period may cause an entire program to fail. However, most POL's have similar limitations.

STRUCTURE OF COBOL

Standard Character Set

All written languages are composed of a group of symbols. These symbols, called letters or characters, are combined into meaningful words to make sentences and phrases.

Programming languages also have standard character sets. Table 16.1 illustrates the set used in COBOL. All programs written in COBOL must be developed from the characters shown here. The program will not compile if any others are used.

Sentence Structure

COBOL, like English, has rules of sentence structure, spelling, and syntax. The basic unit of the COBOL language is the sentence. Sentences are composed of words, which consist of characters from the standard set.

Many COBOL sentences are imperative; that is, they direct the computer to perform a given task. Others are conditional; they direct the computer to follow one of several courses depending upon the value of a quantity in storage, or the result of a calculation.

Sentences are grouped to form paragraphs. Each paragraph is assigned a unique name by the programmer. Paragraphs usually contain one or more sentences referring to the same operation. The statements that calculate payroll deductions may make one paragraph; all the instructions needed to

TABLE 16.1   COBOL STANDARD CHARACTER SET

ALPHABETIC CHARACTERS	NUMERIC CHARACTERS
A	0
B	1
C	2
D	3
E	4
F	5
G	6
H	7
I	8
J	9
K	
L	
M	SPECIAL CHARACTERS
N	
O	(blank) $
P	+
Q	− ;
R	/ >
S	= <
T	.
U	)
V	*
W	'
X	(
Y	' (apostrophe)
Z	

print out an overdue notice to a delinquent customer may be another. The programmer can refer to all the steps in a paragraph by the paragraph name.

Paragraphs are further grouped into sections. Sections may be compared to chapters in a book, each concerned with a different aspect of a subject. Finally, all sections are grouped into divisions. Each division performs a different function, but all are interrelated parts of the same program. Figure 16.1 illustrates the structure of COBOL programs.

Types of Words   A programmer follows many rules and conventions when he composes a sentence in COBOL. The words that make up the sentences are not chosen arbitrarily. Three types of words, reserved words, names, and optional words, are used in COBOL, and each type has its own function.

RESERVED WORDS.   The COBOL language has a group of special reserved words listed in Table 16.2. These words are the commands that direct the

FIGURE 16.1   COBOL PROGRAM STRUCTURE

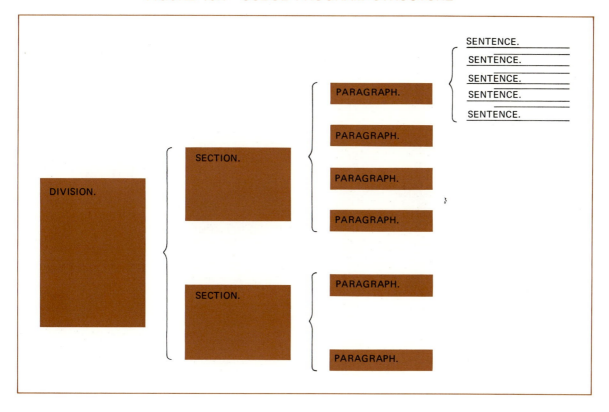

computer to perform various tasks. The COBOL compiler will convert them into step-by-step, machine-language instructions, which tell the CPU how to perform a specified activity.

The reserved words have a particular meaning in the language and their use is restricted by several conventions. They may be used only in the way the language allows and spelling must be exact. For example, the reserved word ADD in a COBOL sentence always tells the computer to set up the circuitry to perform addition. A programmer could not use such words as ADDED, PLUS, or AND to perform this calculation.

NAMES.   Names are also used in composing sentences. Names are words selected by the programmer to represent quantities or data calculated or stored in the computer. Names represent the quantities that will be manipulated by the reserved words. In this way, a programmer can refer to and manipulate a quantity even though its value changes during a program.

A programmer assigns names to fields in a data record, to the totals, intermediate totals, paragraphs, and temporary storage areas. Words chosen to be names must conform to certain rules of the language: they may not be

TABLE 16.2 COBOL RESERVED WORDS

ACCEPT	DEPENDING	I-0	PROCESSING	TALLY
ACCESS	(DESCENDING)	I-0-CONTROL	PROGRAM-ID	TALLYING
ACTUAL	(DETAIL)	IS	PROTECTION	(TERMINATE)
ADD	DIRECT			THAN
ADVANCING	DIRECT-ACCESS	JUSTIFIED	QUOTE	THEN
AFTER	DISPLAY		QUOTES	THRU
ALL	DISPLAY-ST	KEY		TIMES
ALPHABETIC	DIVIDE		RANDOM	TO
ALTER	DIVISION	LABEL	(RD)	TRACE
ALTERNATE		LABELS	READ	TRACK-AREA
AND	ELSE	(LAST)	READY	TRACKS
APPLY	END	LEADING	RECORD	TRANSFORM
ARE	ENDING	LEFT	RECORDING	(TRY)
AREA	ENTER	LESS	RECORDS	(TYPE)
AREAS	ENTRY	LIBRARY	REDEFINES	
(ASCENDING)	ENVIRONMENT	(LIMIT)	REEL	UNIT
ASSIGN	EQUAL	(LIMITS)	(RELATIVE)	UNIT-RECORD
AT	ERROR	(LINE-COUNTER)	(RELEASE)	(UNITS)
AT END	EVERY	(LINE)	REMARKS	UNTIL
AUTHOR	EXAMINE	LINES	REPLACING	UPON
	EXHIBIT	LINKAGE	(REPORT)	USAGE
(BEFORE)	EXIT	LOCK	(REPORTING)	USE
BEGINNING		LOW-VALUE	(REPORTS)	USING
BLANK	FD	LOW-VALUES	RERUN	UTILITY
BLOCK	FILE		RESERVE	
BY	(FILE-LIMIT)	MODE	RESET	VALUE
	FILES	MORE-LABELS	RESTRICTED	VARYING
CALL	FILE-CONTROL	MOVE	RETURN	
(CF)	FILE-ID	MULTIPLY	REVERSED	WHEN
(CH)	FILLER		REWIND	WITH
CHANGED	(FINAL)	NAMED	REWRITE	WITHOUT
CHARACTER	FIRST	NEGATIVE	(RF)	WORKING-STORAGE
CHECKING	(FOOTING)	NEXT	(RH)	WRITE
(CLOCK-UNITS)	FOR	NO	RIGHT	WRITE-ONLY
CLOSE	FORM-OVERFLOW	NOT	ROUNDED	
COBOL	FROM	NOTE	RUN	ZERO
(CODE)		NUMERIC		ZEROES
(COLUMN)	(GENERATE)		(SA)	ZEROS
(COMMA)	GIVING	OBJECT-COMPUTER	SAME	
COMPUTATIONAL	GO	OCCURS	(SD)	
COMPUTATIONAL-1	GREATER	OF	SEARCH	
COMPUTATIONAL-2	(GROUP)	OMITTED	SECTION	
COMPUTATIONAL-3		ON	SECURITY	
COMPUTE	(HEADING)	OPEN	SELECT	
CONFIGURATION	HIGH-VALUE	OR	SENTENCE	
CONSOLE	HIGH-VALUES	ORGANIZATION	SEQUENTIAL	
CONTAINS	(HOLD)	OTHERWISE	SIZE	
(CONTROL)		OUTPUT	(SORT)	
(CONTROLS)	IBM-360	(OVERFLOW)	(SOURCE)	
COPY	(ID)		SOURCE-COMPUTER	
(CORRESPONDING)	IDENTIFICATION	(PAGE)	SPACE	
COUNT	IF	(PAGE-COUNTER)	SPACES	
CREATING	IN	PERFORM	(SPECIAL-NAMES)	
(CYCLES)	INCLUDE	(PF)	STANDARD	
	INDEXED	(PH)	STOP	
DATA	(INDICATE)	PICTURE	SUBTRACT	
DATE-COMPILED	(INITIATE)	(PLUS)	(SUM)	
DATE-WRITTEN	INPUT	POSITIVE	SYMBOLIC	
(DE)	INPUT-OUTPUT	(PRINT-SWITCH)	(SYSIN)	
(DECIMAL POINT)	INSTALLATION	PROCEDURE	(SYSOUT)	
DECLARATIVES	INTO	PROCEED	SYSPUNCH	
	INVALID	(PROCESS)		

more than 30 characters long; they must begin with an alphabetic letter; a reserved word cannot be chosen as a name.

OPTIONAL WORDS. Finally, optional words are used in composing sentences. These words have no effect on the program flow, but are used in COBOL sentences to improve readability. Some optional words are

IS   THAN   ARE

In COBOL some punctuation marks, such as a comma (,) and semicolon (;), are also optional. Values that will not change may be written directly into the program. For example, if the sales tax, interest rate, or markup is a constant value, the programmer may choose to use it as a number and write it directly into the instructions.

Combinations of these three types of words in sentence form direct the computer to perform various tasks. For example, IF CHARGE-BALANCE IS EQUAL TO 1000, GO TO OVER-LIMIT-NOTICE. In this case, the programmer directs the computer to compare a quantity to 1,000 and branch to a routine if they are equal. He forms his instruction using the reserved words IF, EQUAL TO and GO TO, assigned names CHARGE-BALANCE and OVER-LIMIT-NOTICE, optional word IS, and constant value 1,000.

Coding Forms and Conventions

A standard coding form, shown in Figure 16.2, is used by COBOL programmers in writing programs. Coded instructions are written longhand on the forms. Then a keypunch operator punches each line on the coding sheet into a separate card. This set of cards is the problem program deck.

COBOL PROGRAM SHEET LAYOUT. The standard form contains space at the top of the page for the programmer's name, program name, and other related data. This data is not part of the program deck. The form has 80 columns across the page and 25 lines for instructions.

CONVENTIONS. The COBOL compiler is designed to expect certain kinds of data in selected columns on the punched card, as shown in Figure 16.2. Columns 1 to 6 are reserved for sequence numbers—numbers assigned to each instruction, in sequence, to help keep cards in the program in order. These numbers are not used in the actual manipulations within the program.

Column 7 is called the continuation column and is only used to continue a non-numeric literal statement from one line to another. Columns 8 to 72 are reserved for programming statements. Column 8 is called Margin A, and Column 12, Margin B. They are used like headings in an outline to show paragraphs and different levels of statements. Columns 73 to 80 are used to identify each card in the deck with a label or program number. They are not read by the COBOL compiler.

COBOL PROGRAM DIVISIONS

A COBOL program has four divisions, each with its own function. These divisions allow "routine housekeeping tasks" to be separated from the steps

FIGURE 16.2 COBOL CODING SHEET

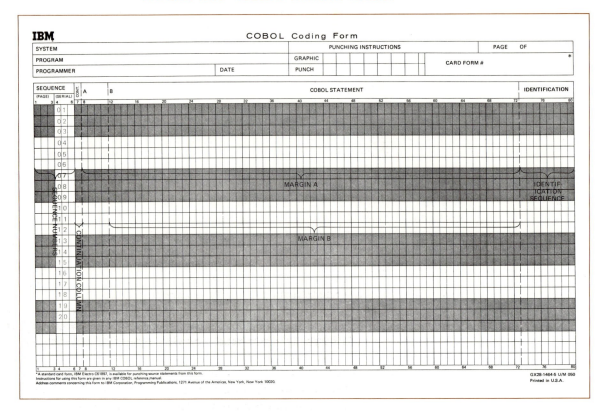

involved in carrying out the logic of the problem. The programmer can assign input and output devices, set up storage spaces, and assign names without being concerned with the details of the algorithm. Changes in one division can be made without disrupting another division. Table 16.3 lists the four major divisions in the COBOL program and their functions.

TABLE 16.3 COBOL PROGRAMMING DIVISIONS

DIVISION NAME	FUNCTION
Identification	Identify programmer, program, and company.
Environment	Assign files to input and output devices. Specify computer.
Data	Assign names to quantities and fields, allocate storage spaces, and define format of data records.
Procedure	Define actions and steps computer is to follow in solving problem.

Identification Division

The first division in the COBOL program provides the computer with routine identification data, such as the name of the program, name of the author, the installation, and the date written. Figure 16.3 illustrates the Identification Division of a program.

The Identification Division is strictly informational and contains no instructions on procedures. It is not involved with the logic or program algorithm content.

FIGURE 16.3   IDENTIFICATION DIVISION

```
110 IDENTIFICATION DIVISION.
120 PROGRAM-ID. 'CLIDER'.
130 AUTHOR. JOHN STEIN.
140 INSTALLATION. RETAIL-HOUSE.
150 DATE-WRITTEN. 9-20.
160 REMARKS. THIS PROGRAM READS DATA FROM COL. 1-60 ON CARD.  PRINTS
161     IT OUT RE-FORMATTED.  THIS EXAMPLE IS A NAME AND TELEPHONE
162     DIRECTORY.  THE NAMES ARE PUNCHED IN COL. 1-20, ADDRESSES
163     21-50, PHONE NUMBER, 51-60.  PRINTED SPACED OUT OVER 132
164     CHARACTER LINE .  30 LINES TO A PAGE.
```

Environment Division

The next division of the program describes the make and model of computer that the program should be run on, and designates the type of input and output media the computer is to use. It specifies whether the input devices are to be card readers, or magnetic tape units, etc., and whether the output devices are to be line printers, card punches, or magnetic tape units.

The Environment Division is the only machine-dependent division in a COBOL program. It is tied to the specific installation upon which the job will be run. Since systems have different models of I/O devices available, the programmer must make sure that those he designates are available on the system he is using. If the job is to be run on another system, the I/O designations in this division must be changed. However, this normally involves only a few cards. Figure 16.4 illustrates the Environment Division of a program.

Data Division

The Data Division tells the computer the kind and format of the data being read in and out and the kinds of temporary storage that will be needed. Figure 16.5 illustrates part of the Data Division. The Data Division is divided into two sections: File and Working-Storage. In the File Section, the programmer details the layout of the data records for each file. He assigns names to each field and indicates the kind of data, such as alphabetic or numeric, it holds.

In the Working-Storage Section the programmer describes and allocates all temporary and intermediate storage areas needed during processing. He

FIGURE 16.4 ENVIRONMENT DIVISION

```
200 ENVIRONMENT DIVISION.
210 CONFIGURATION SECTION.
220 SOURCE-COMPUTER. IBM-360.
230 OBJECT-COMPUTER. IBM-360.
240 INPUT-OUTPUT SECTION.
250 FILE-CONTROL.
260     SELECT CARD-FILE ASSIGN TO 'SYS001' UNIT-RECORD 2540R.
270     SELECT PRINT-FILE ASSIGN TO 'SYS002' UNIT-RECORD 1403.
```

FIGURE 16.5 DATA DIVISION

```
300 DATA DIVISION.
310 FILE SECTION.
320 FD  CARD-FILE
330     RECORD CONTAINS 80 CHARACTERS
340     BLOCK CONTAINS 1 RECORDS
350     LABEL RECORDS ARE OMITTED
360     RECORDING MODE IS F
370     DATA RECORDS ARE INPUT-CARD.
380 01  INPUT-CARD.
381     03  NAME-1-20X          PICTURE X(20).
382     03  ADDRESS-21-50X      PICTURE X(30).
    .
    .
    .
500 WORKING-STORAGE SECTION.
510 01  SAVE-AREA.
520     03  LINE-COUNT          PICTURE 999.
530 01  DETAIL-LINE.
540     03  CARRIAGE-CONTROL    PICTURE X      VALUE SPACES.
550     03  FILLER              PICTURE X(10) VALUE SPACES.
560     03  NAME                PICTURE X(20).
570     03  FILLER              PICTURE X(10) VALUE SPACES.
580     03  ADDRESS             PICTURE X(30).
590     03  FILLER              PICTURE X(10) VALUE SPACES.
600     03  TELEPHONE-NUMBER.
610         05  FILLER          PICTURE X      VALUE IS '('.
620         05  AREA-CODE       PICTURE XXX.
```

may also include and name values that will be needed for processing, but are not read in from a data file.

For example, suppose a programmer is going to compute interest. In the File Section of the Data Division, he tells the computer that the data to be read in (principal) will be found in columns 21 to 30 of the card. He gives the interest rate in the Working-Storage Section and also sets up and names a temporary storage area for the result. Later in the program, the computer will be directed to print out the results.

Data descriptions should tell the computer how many columns alphabetic and numeric values have, and the position of the decimal point if it is a decimal number. Output record descriptions are included, indicating what spacing should be observed if results are to be written on the line printer, or what the record format should be if the output will be on magnetic tape. All this information must be provided before the programmer can give specific instructions on how to calculate the answer.

Procedure Division

In the Procedure Division, the programmer specifies the steps the computer is to follow in executing the program. Figure 16.6 illustrates part of the Procedure Division of a program.

In this section, the powerful COBOL verbs are used to implement the logic and program algorithm chosen to solve the problem. The programmer opens files, moves data, performs mathematical calculations, branches, writes data, closes files, etc. All data are referred to by their assigned names, and instructions are grouped into paragraphs, each with a unique name. The programmer can direct the computer to repeat a group of instructions by referring to its paragraph name.

FIGURE 16.6 PROCEDURE DIVISION

```
1000  PROCEDURE DIVISION.
1010  INITIALIZE.
1020      OPEN INPUT CARD-FILE.
1030      OPEN OUTPUT PRINT-FILE.
1040  WRITE-HEADING.
1050      MOVE HEADING-LINE TO PRINT-LINE.
1060      WRITE PRINT-LINE AFTER ADVANCING 0 LINES.
1070      MOVE SPACES TO PRINT-LINE.
1080      WRITE PRINT-LINE AFTER ADVANCING 1 LINES.
1090      MOVE ZEROES TO LINE-COUNT.
1100  READ-CARD.
1110      READ CARD-FILE AT END GO TO EOJ.
1120      MOVE NAME-1-20X TO NAME.
```

SAMPLE COBOL STATEMENTS

The COBOL language contains many powerful reserved words, which allow the programmer to direct the computer through many sophisticated mathematical and logical operations. The following statements are given as examples of COBOL programming techniques and the use of reserved words and data names. They are only a few of the many statements which could be used.

READ Data   One of the most fundamental words in COBOL programming is READ. It directs the computer to read data from a file and place it in storage. Once the data is read in, it is available for further processing or output.

EXAMPLE:

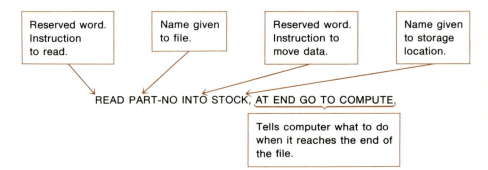

Explanation: In this statement, the programmer instructs the computer to read a record from a file (PART-NO) and place the data in a storage location named STOCK. When it reaches the end of the file, the computer will branch to a portion of the program called COMPUTE. Previous divisions in the program have given all pertinent descriptions. The specific input media (such as a card reader) was specified in the Environment Division. In the Data Division, the programmer described the data on the input record and set up a storage location named STOCK.

WRITE Data   The WRITE statement is a basic instruction for outputting data in COBOL programming. It instructs the computer to output data previously read in or calculated during the program.

EXAMPLE:

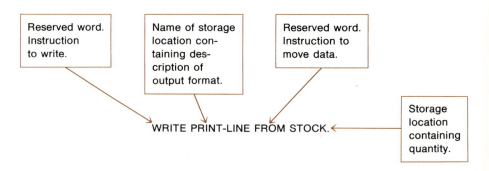

Explanation: In this example, the programmer tells the computer to write a previously read in or calculated quantity on the line printer. WRITE and FROM are reserved words directing the action. PRINT-LINE is the name for a

reformatted location, and STOCK is the assigned name of the storage
location containing the required data.

The Data Division gave the computer all instructions for the graphic layout
of the output record. The hardware used (line printer in this case) was
specified in the Environment Division. The description of the storage location
STOCK was given in the Data Division.

Branching An important ability of the computer is its capacity to test a numeric or
non-numeric quantity and make a logical decision to branch to one of several
paths. The COBOL language contains several kinds of branch statements.
One form uses the reserved word IF in an instruction. In this case, the
computer compares two values and branches control of the program to a
specified paragraph depending on the results of the comparison.

EXAMPLE:

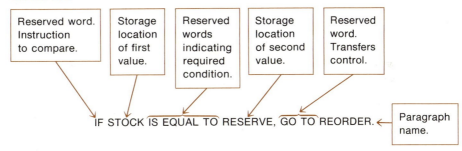

IF STOCK IS EQUAL TO RESERVE, GO TO REORDER.

| Reserved word. Instruction to compare. | Storage location of first value. | Reserved words indicating required condition. | Storage location of second value. | Reserved word. Transfers control. | Paragraph name. |

Explanation: In this instance, the programmer tests and compares the value
of STOCK. If the value of STOCK is equal to the value of RESERVE, the
computer is to branch to the paragraph labeled REORDER. If the condition
for the branch is not met (the value of STOCK is not equal to RESERVE),
control will flow to the next statement in the program.

PERFORM The programmer can instruct the computer to loop through a given sequence
of calculations or operations a specific number of times. One way to do this
is with a PERFORM instruction. Here the programmer specifies the number of
times he wants the loop performed. The computer executes the series of steps
repeatedly until a counter in the CPU reaches the preset limit. The computer
then returns to the statement in the program after the PERFORM instruction.

EXAMPLE:

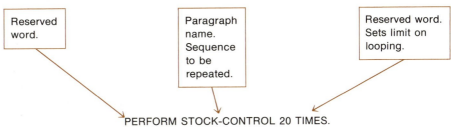

PERFORM STOCK-CONTROL 20 TIMES.

| Reserved word. | Paragraph name. Sequence to be repeated. | Reserved word. Sets limit on looping. |

COMPUTERS AND TRANSPORTATION

In the past decade our technological achievements have astounded the world. Yet . . . we are still plagued with a problem that has developed from man's simplest invention—the wheel. Mass transportation, whether it be transporting ourselves or our products, has become a critical problem in the U. S. today. Why? How can the problem be solved?

More and more municipalities are realizing that computerized traffic control systems can pay off in smaller cities as well as larger ones. In fact, the computerized system in use in Toronto, Ontario has cut vehicle stops and delays by 10 to 50%. Besides the obvious advantage in traffic flow, the system also detects defective signals and pinpoints the nature of trouble. It can change each light's timing to handle any bottleneck in any given area and keeps a car-count and other valuable information needed to evaluate the effects of different signal patterns on traffic flow. The system proves especially helpful in controlling traffic in special areas outside ballparks, theaters, drive-in movies, and other areas where sporadic traffic problems arise.

Probably the most valuable asset of the computer in traffic control is its simulation powers both present and future. A network can be simulated on a computer to see how it will react under varying traffic conditions. This type of application is one of the most sophisticated available today. Using a simulated network, a traffic engineer can find out how the existing traffic flow affects the existing network, how predicted traffic will affect the existing network, how existing traffic will affect future roads, and, finally how future traffic will flow on future highways.

In other words, the computer can show the engineer exactly how the network will react to any given situation. This, of course, gives the engineer a virtual crystal ball to avoid the obvious pitfall of roads and networks becoming obsolete before their completion.

SOURCE "Computers and Transportation," by Edward K. O'Connor, *Computer Usage*, Vol. 1, No. 1, Winter Issue, 1965.

Explanation: Upon encountering the above instruction, the computer will return to the paragraph named STOCK-CONTROL and execute the steps in the sequence 20 times. It will then proceed to the statement following the PERFORM statement and continue processing.

Addition The computer is capable of performing a variety of mathematical procedures. The COBOL programmer instructs the computer to perform mathematics by including specific reserved words in the instructions. Some reserved mathematical words are ADD, SUBTRACT, and MULTIPLY. The computer will perform the required operation on the data in storage and place the results in the assigned space.

EXAMPLE:

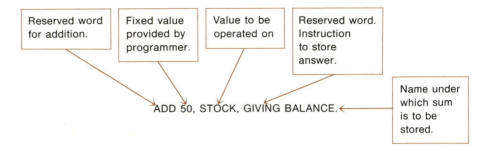

| Reserved word for addition. | Fixed value provided by programmer. | Value to be operated on | Reserved word. Instruction to store answer. |

ADD 50, STOCK, GIVING BALANCE.

Name under which sum is to be stored.

"Sound an alert . . . It's contacted other computers and they've formed a union!!"

Explanation: In this case, the programmer wants to add 50 to the value of STOCK. The sum is to be placed in storage under the name BALANCE. Upon encountering the instruction, the computer will perform the required mathematical operation (add 50 to the current value of STOCK) and place the sum in the assigned space, BALANCE. Both STOCK and BALANCE have been described and named in the Data Division.

Arithmetic Expressions

The computer can be programmed to perform a variety of mathematical steps in a single sentence. This is done by inserting one or more reserved words in the instruction.

EXAMPLE:

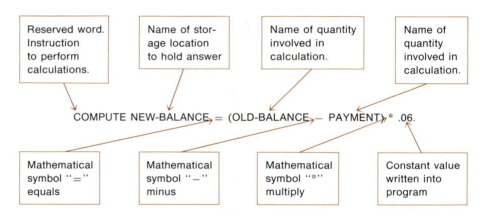

Explanation: This instruction performs several mathematical steps in a single sentence. The programmer directs the computer to calculate a value called NEW-BALANCE. It is found by subtracting PAYMENT from OLD-BALANCE and multiplying the remainder by .06. The parentheses tell the computer to perform the subtraction before the multiplication. The product will be placed in storage under the name NEW-BALANCE. The Data Division contains the descriptions of the quantities and storage areas needed.

SAMPLE PROGRAM

Figure 16.7 is the flowchart for a COBOL program. This program is designed to read in data from one record and manipulate these figures to print out a salary table. The input data is shown in Figure 16.8.

Function of the Program

The program will read in data from a record called the CONTROL-CARD. The data includes hourly starting salary, maximum and minimum monthly salaries, (named MAX-MON-SAL and MIN-MON-SAL) and an incrementing factor called INCREMENT and DELTA-FACTOR.

FIGURE 16.7 FLOWCHART FOR SALARY TABLE

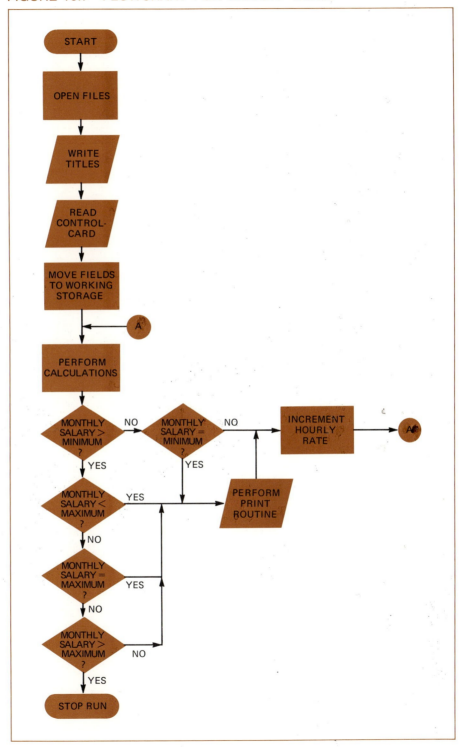

FIGURE 16.8   INPUT DATA LISTING FOR COBOL SALARY TABLE PROGRAM

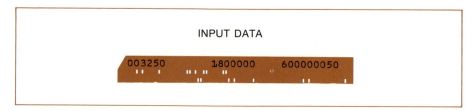

INPUT DATA

The program is shown in Figure 16.9 and the output in Figure 16.10. The steps followed in the algorithm are

1 The files are opened and title lines written.

2 The CONTROL-CARD is read and the fields moved into SAVE-AREA.

3 Calculations are performed.

4 Then the computer tests to see that the MONTHLY-SALARY is above the minimum level required, and below the maximum level set by the programmer.

5 All amounts between these limits are printed out.

6 Amounts below the minimum branch the computer back to increment the monthly salary and repeat calculations.

7 An amount above sends the computer to the end of job routine.

FIGURE 16.9 COBOL PROGRAM LISTING—SALARY TABLE

```
 1     1010 IDENTIFICATION DIVISION.
 2     1020 PROGRAM-ID. 'SALTAB'.
 3     1030 AUTHOR. BETTY CHAN.
 4     1040 INSTALLATION. STATE JC.
 5     1050 DATE-WRITTEN. 3-27.
 6     1060 REMARKS.  THIS PROGRAM WRITES A SALARY TABLE. IT CALCULATES DAILY
 7     1070     WEEKLY, MONTHLY AND ANNUAL SALARIES, STARTING FROM A GIVEN
 8     1080     AMOUNT, ADDING AN INCREMENT EACH CYCLE.  IT LISTS AMOUNT BE-
 9     1090     TWEEN THE SPECIFIED MINIMUM AND MAXIMUM MONTHLY SALARY.  IT
10     1095     OPERATES FROM ONE CONTROL CARD.
11     2010 ENVIRONMENT DIVISION.
12     2020 CONFIGURATION SECTION.
13     2030 SOURCE-COMPUTER. IBM-360.
14     2040 OBJECT-COMPUTER. IBM-360.
15     2050 INPUT-OUTPUT SECTION.
16     2060 FILE-CONTROL.
17     2070     SELECT CARD-FILE ASSIGN TO 'SYS001' UNIT-RECORD 2540R.
18     2080     SELECT PRINT-FILE ASSIGN TO 'SYS002' UNIT-RECORD 1403.
19     3010 DATA DIVISION.
20     3020 FILE SECTION.
21     3030 FD  CARD-FILE
22     3040     RECORD CONTAINS 80 CHARACTERS
23     3050     BLOCK CONTAINS 1 RECORDS
```

```
24    3060      LABEL RECORDS ARE OMITTED
25    3070      RECORDING MODE IS F
26    3080      DATA RECORDS ARE CONTROL-CARD.
27    3090 01   CONTROL-CARD.
28    3100      03   START-HOURLY-RATE    PICTURE 999V999.
29    3110      03   FILLER               PICTURE X(4).
30    3120      03   MAX-MON-SAL          PICTURE 9(7)V999.
31    3130      03   MIN-MON-SAL          PICTURE 9(7)V999.
32    3140      03   INCREMENT            PICTURE V999.
33    3150      03   FILLER               PICTURE X(47).
34    3200 FD   PRINT-FILE
35    3210      RECORD CONTAINS 133 CHARACTERS
36    3220      BLOCK CONTAINS 1 RECORDS
37    3230      LABEL RECORDS ARE OMITTED
38    3240      RECORDING MODE IS F
39    3250      DATA RECORDS ARE PRINT-LINE.
40    3260 01   PRINT-LINE               PICTURE X(133).
41    4000 WORKING-STORAGE SECTION.
42    4010 01   SAVE-AREA.
43    4020      03   HOURLY-RATE          PICTURE 999V999 COMPUTATIONAL-3.
44    4030      03   DAILY-RATE           PICTURE 9(4)V999 COMPUTATIONAL-3.
45    4040      03   WEEKLY-RATE          PICTURE 9(5)V999 COMPUTATIONAL-3.
46    4050      03   MONTHLY-RATE         PICTURE 9(7)V999 COMPUTATIONAL-3.
47    4060      03   ANNUAL-RATE          PICTURE 9(9)V999 COMPUTATIONAL-3.
48    4070      03   LINE-COUNT           PICTURE 999.
49    4080      03   DELTA-FACTOR         PICTURE V999 COMPUTATIONAL-3.
50    4140 01   SALARY-HEADING.
51    4150      03   CARRIAGE-CONTROL     PICTURE X VALUE IS '1'.
52    4160      03   FILLER               PICTURE X(5) VALUE SPACES.
53    4170      03   AST-1                PICTURE X(37) VALUE  '* * * * * * *
54    4180-               '* * * * * * * * * * *'.
55    4190      03   AST-2                PICTURE X(13) VALUE ' S A L A R Y '.
56    4200      03   AST-3                PICTURE X(37) VALUE  '* * * * * * * *
57    4210-               '* * * * * * * * * *'.
58    4220      03   FILLER               PICTURE X(40) VALUE SPACES.
59    4230 01   TIME-PERIOD-HEADING.
60    4240      03   FILLER               PICTURE X(6) VALUE SPACES.
61    4250      03   HR-6-16X             PICTURE X(11) VALUE 'HOURLY RATE'.
62    4260      03   FILLER               PICTURE X(20) VALUE SPACES.
63    4270      03   DAILY-37-41X         PICTURE X(5) VALUE 'DAILY'.
64    4280      03   FILLER               PICTURE X(10) VALUE SPACES.
65    4290      03   WEEKLY-52-57X        PICTURE X(6) VALUE 'WEEKLY'.
66    4300      03   FILLER               PICTURE X(10) VALUE SPACES.
67    4310      03   MONTHLY-68-74X       PICTURE X(7) VALUE 'MONTHLY'.
68    4320      03   FILLER               PICTURE X(10) VALUE SPACES.
69    4330      03   ANNUALLY-85-92X      PICTURE X(8) VALUE 'ANNUALLY'.
70    4340      03   FILLER               PICTURE X(40) VALUE SPACES.
71    4450 01   DATA-LINE.
72    4460      03   FILLER               PICTURE X(6) VALUE SPACES.
73    4470      03   HOURLY               PICTURE $$$9.999.
74    4480      03   FILLER               PICTURE X(19) VALUE SPACES.
75    4490      03   DAILY                PICTURE $$,$$9.999.
76    4500      03   FILLER               PICTURE X(5) VALUE SPACES.
77    4510      03   WEEKLY               PICTURE $$$,$$9.999.
78    4520      03   FILLER               PICTURE X(4) VALUE SPACES.
79    4530      03   MONTHLY              PICTURE $$,$$$,$$9.999.
80    4540      03   FILLER               PICTURE X    VALUE SPACES.
81    4550      03   ANNUALLY             PICTURE $$$$,$$$,$$9.999.
82    4560      03   FILLER               PICTURE X(39) VALUE SPACES.
83    5010 PROCEDURE DIVISION.
84    5020 INITIALIZE.
85    5030      OPEN INPUT CARD-FILE.
86    5040      OPEN OUTPUT PRINT-FILE.
87    5050 HEADING-ROUTINE.
88    5060      MOVE SALARY-HEADING TO PRINT-LINE.
89    5070      WRITE PRINT-LINE AFTER ADVANCING 0 LINES.
90    5080      MOVE TIME-PERIOD-HEADING TO PRINT-LINE.
91    5090      WRITE PRINT-LINE AFTER ADVANCING 1 LINES.
```

```
 92    5100      MOVE SPACES TO PRINT-LINE.
 93    5110      WRITE PRINT-LINE AFTER ADVANCING 1 LINES.
 94    5120      MOVE ZEROES TO LINE-COUNT.
 95    5130 READ-CONTROL-CARD.
 96    5140      READ CARD-FILE AT END GO TO EOJ.
 97    5150      MOVE START-HOURLY-RATE TO HOURLY-RATE.
 98    5160      MOVE INCREMENT TO DELTA-FACTOR.
 99    5170 CALCULATIONS.
100    5680      MULTIPLY HOURLY-RATE BY 8 GIVING DAILY-RATE, ROUNDED.
101    5190      MULTIPLY HOURLY-RATE BY 40 GIVING WEEKLY-RATE, ROUNDED.
102    5200      MULTIPLY WEEKLY-RATE BY 52 GIVING ANNUAL-RATE, ROUNDED.
103    5210      DIVIDE 12 INTO ANNUAL-RATE GIVING MONTHLY-RATE, ROUNDED.
104    5220 CHECK-MONTHLY-RATE.
105    5230      IF MONTHLY-RATE IS LESS THAN MIN-MON-SAL ADD DELTA-FACTOR TO
106    5240           HOURLY-RATE      GO TO CALCULATIONS.
107    5250      IF MONTHLY-RATE IS EQUAL TO MIN-MON-SAL GO TO PRINT-DATA.
108    5260      IF MONTHLY-RATE IS LESS THAN MAX-MON-SAL GO TO PRINT-DATA.
109    5270      IF MONTHLY-RATE IS EQUAL TO MAX-MON-SAL GO TO PRINT-DATA.
110    5280      IF MONTHLY-RATE IS GREATER THAN MAX-MON-SAL GO TO EOJ.
111    5300 PRINT-DATA.
112    5310      MOVE MONTHLY-RATE TO MONTHLY.
113    5320      MOVE HOURLY-RATE TO HOURLY.
114    5330      MOVE DAILY-RATE TO DAILY.
115    5340      MOVE WEEKLY-RATE TO WEEKLY.
116    5350      MOVE ANNUAL-RATE TO ANNUALLY.
117    5360      MOVE DATA-LINE TO PRINT-LINE.
118    5370      WRITE PRINT-LINE AFTER ADVANCING 1 LINES.
119    5380      ADD 1 TO LINE-COUNT.
120    5390      IF LINE-COUNT IS GREATER THAN 29 PERFORM HEADING-ROUTINE.
121    5400      ADD DELTA-FACTOR TO HOURLY-RATE.
122    5410      GO TO CALCULATIONS.
123    5500 EOJ.
124    5510      DISPLAY 'NORMAL EOJ' UPON CONSOLE.
125    5520 CLOSE-FILES.
126    5530      CLOSE PRINT-FILE.
127    5540      CLOSE CARD-FILE.
128    5550      STOP RUN.
```

Program Analysis   The following discussion traces the program by paragraphs. The numbers listed at the left margin are keyed to the line numbers of the program, illustrated in Figure 16.9.

LINE NUMBER	EXPLANATION
1–18	These are the Identification and Environment Divisions. They identify the program, the computer used, and the input/output devices required.
19–20	Begin Data Division and File Section.
21–33	Describe input CARD-FILE and fields on record. Record is named CONTROL-CARD.
34–40	Describe output PRINT-FILE. Record is named PRINT-LINE.
41	Working-Storage Section.
42–49	Describe, name, and initialize several storage areas used in the

program to hold intermediate values. COMPUTATIONAL-3 tells the computer they will be used in mathematical calculations.

50–70 Set up and describe two lines of titles, SALARY-HEADING and TIME-PERIOD-HEADING.

71–82 Set up DATA-LINE, working area which re-formats calculated values and inserts required punctuation where necessary.

83–86 Begin Procedure Division and open files.

87–94 HEADING-ROUTINE paragraph writes titles and initializes LINE-COUNT.

95–98 READ-CONTROL-CARD reads in data record, tests for end-of-file and moves data to fields in SAVE-AREA.

99–103 Perform calculations needed for salary table.

104–110 Test for minimum and maximum limits of table.

111–122 Move data from SAVE-AREA to the PRINT-LINE for outputting. Increases and tests LINE-COUNT to see if it is greater than 29. Adds DELTA-FACTOR to HOURLY-RATE and loops back to CALCULATIONS to repeat another cycle.

123–128 End of job routine instructs computer to close files and end program.

FIGURE 16.10 OUTPUT FROM SALARY TABLE PROGRAM

```
* * * * * * * * * * * * * * * * * * * * S A L A R Y * * * * * * * * * * * * * * * * * * * *
HOURLY RATE              DAILY              WEEKLY              MONTHLY              ANNUALLY

  $3.500               $28.000            $140.000             $606.667            $7,280.000
  $3.550               $28.400            $142.000             $615.333            $7,384.000
  $3.600               $28.800            $144.000             $624.000            $7,488.000
  $3.650               $29.200            $146.000             $632.667            $7,592.000
  $3.700               $29.600            $148.000             $641.333            $7,696.000
  $3.750               $30.000            $150.000             $650.000            $7,800.000
  $3.800               $30.400            $152.000             $658.667            $7,904.000
  $3.850               $30.800            $154.000             $667.333            $8,008.000
  $3.900               $31.200            $156.000             $676.000            $8,112.000
  $3.950               $31.600            $158.000             $684.667            $8,216.000
  $4.000               $32.000            $160.000             $693.333            $8,320.000
  $4.050               $32.400            $162.000             $702.000            $8,424.000
  $4.100               $32.800            $164.000             $710.667            $8,528.000
  $4.150               $33.200            $166.000             $719.333            $8,632.000
  $4.200               $33.600            $168.000             $728.000            $8,736.000
  $4.250               $34.000            $170.000             $736.667            $8,840.000
  $4.300               $34.400            $172.000             $745.333            $8,944.000
  $4.350               $34.800            $174.000             $754.000            $9,048.000
  $4.400               $35.200            $176.000             $762.667            $9,152.000
  $4.450               $35.600            $178.000             $771.333            $9,256.000
  $4.500               $36.000            $180.000             $780.000            $9,360.000
  $4.550               $36.400            $182.000             $788.667            $9,464.000
  $4.600               $36.800            $184.000             $797.333            $9,568.000
  $4.650               $37.200            $186.000             $806.000            $9,672.000
  $4.700               $37.600            $188.000             $814.667            $9,776.000
  $4.750               $38.000            $190.000             $823.333            $9,880.000
  $4.800               $38.400            $192.000             $832.000            $9,984.000
  $4.850               $38.800            $194.000             $840.667           $10,088.000
  $4.900               $39.200            $196.000             $849.333           $10,192.000
  $4.950               $39.600            $198.000             $858.000           $10,296.000
```

KEY TERMS

Problem-oriented language (POL)
COBOL
Literal capability
Machine dependent
Standard character set
Machine independent
Reserved word
Optional word

Assigned name
Identification Division
Environment Division
Data Division
Procedure Division
Working-Storage Section
File Section

EXERCISES

1. Give six advantages of COBOL.
2. Give several disadvantages of COBOL.
3. How is a COBOL program structured?
4. What are reserved words? Give three examples.
5. How do assigned names differ from reserved words?
6. Label the reserved columns on a blank COBOL coding sheet.
7. What is the function of the Identification Division?
8. What is the function of the Environment Division? How does running a program on different computers affect this division?
9. What is the function of the Data Division?
10. What is the function of the Procedure Division?
11. What advantage does COBOL offer by separating the Procedure Division from the hardware designation?
12. List the reserved words you would use to write a program that reads a list of numbers, adds them, and writes out the answer.

FORTRAN Programming Language

Developed in the late 1950s by a group from IBM, FORTRAN (FORmula TRANslating System) was intended to be a language scientists and mathematicians could use to program their technical problems.

Thousands of hours were invested in writing a compiler that would accept statements in algebraic form and convert them into machine language instructions. During the next two decades, several improved and enlarged versions were written, expanding FORTRAN's utility into many other areas, among them business.

Unlike COBOL, FORTRAN is not supported by a group of users. Instead, each manufacturer and user modifies, improves, and changes the language to suit his own needs.

To eliminate some of the confusion and differences that might arise when a language develops in an unorganized, unplanned way, an effort has been made at standardization. The American National Standards Institute (ANSI) publishes several approved versions of FORTRAN that establish guidelines for computer manufacturers and compiler writers. As new versions and improvements of FORTRAN are written, ANSI studies them for inclusion in their uniform standards. Each manufacturer, however, tends to broaden or expand the available statements in the language for use on his computer. Since the examples and programs in this chapter are illustrative of the IBM version of FORTRAN, a few of the programming features used are not found in the ANSI versions.

353

FORTRAN's primary advantage is its excellent mathematical capability. The language closely resembles algebraic equations, which are familiar to most individuals working in scientific or mathematical areas. In FORTRAN, a programmer can read in and store alphabetic and numeric data, manipulate data, perform complex mathematical and logical operations, and write out the results.

FORTRAN is also a very compact language. Usually only a few statements are necessary to direct the computer to solve a complex problem. COBOL requires many more statements to open files, move, process, and output data.

Because some versions of FORTRAN require a compiler that uses only approximately 4K bytes of storage, FORTRAN compilers are available on small as well as large computers. Most computer manufacturers write FORTRAN compilers for each new machine put on the market, thus assuring the programmer that his job will run on almost any modern computer.

Improvements in the FORTRAN language have increased its literal capability, and it is no longer limited to mathematical applications. It can manipulate words, sentences, and whole paragraphs of textual material. However, FORTRAN still does not have the ease of literal or alphabetic manipulation that COBOL has.

FORTRAN also eliminates many routine housekeeping details required in COBOL programming. For example, in FORTRAN, storage areas are set up more easily and with less detailed description than required in the COBOL Data Division. Fields in a data record are more compactly and conveniently described. Open- and close-file routines are handled by the compiler, freeing the programmer from these details.

And finally, FORTRAN was the pattern followed in the development of the BASIC (Beginners All-Purpose Symbolic Instruction Code) language. BASIC is a widely used language for computer terminals. A programmer who knows the fundamentals of FORTRAN can write programs in BASIC with little difficulty.

FORTRAN bears closer resemblance to mathematical notation than to ordinary business English, because it relies on codes and symbols. It is more difficult for a nonprogrammer to understand or trace program logic in FORTRAN than in COBOL. FORTRAN programs must be fully documented to explain the logic used in the program and the input/output specifications.

As in COBOL, basic rules of punctuation, syntax, spelling, etc. must be followed in FORTRAN programming. The loss of one comma or a misplaced parenthesis in a FORTRAN program can prevent an otherwise acceptable program from executing.

STRUCTURE OF FORTRAN

FORTRAN has a standard character set shown in Table 17.1. This set consists of the alphabet, numbers 0–9, and a group of special characters.

TABLE 17.1   FORTRAN STANDARD CHARACTER SET

ALPHABETIC CHARACTERS	NUMERIC CHARACTERS
A	0
B	1
C	2
D	3
E	4
F	5
G	6
H	7
I	8
J	9
K	
L	
M	
N	SPECIAL CHARACTERS
O	
P	(blank)
Q	+
R	−
S	/
T	=
U	.
V	)
W	*
X	,
Y	(
Z	' (apostrophe)
$	&

Since the FORTRAN compiler recognizes only these characters, all programming statements must be written from this group.

Statement Structure   In FORTRAN, the basic unit of the language is the statement, not the sentence as in COBOL. The statement is a group of symbols, words, and punctuation formed into an expression. Each expression tells the computer to perform one or more operations.

The statement is composed of names assigned by the programmer, symbols called arithmetic operators (+, −, *, /, for example), and reserved words, which direct the computer to perform operations, move data, do calculations, etc.

FORTRAN statements resemble algebraic equations. They do not look like English text matter, do not conclude with periods, and are not formed into paragraphs, as in COBOL.

In the previous chapter we saw that a COBOL statement took the form of
ADD STOCK, SHIPMENT, GIVING GOODS.
The same instruction in FORTRAN would look like this:
GOODS = STOCK + SHIP
There are several differences between these two examples. The COBOL
example is a sentence that ends with a period and uses ordinary English
words instead of abbreviations. The instruction to perform a mathematical
operation is indicated by the word ADD instead of by an arithmetic operator.
In the second example, the statement is written as an equation. STOCK is to
be added to SHIP and the sum placed in the location named GOODS.
Abbreviations are frequently used in FORTRAN and more reliance is placed
on symbols and codes.
Several other examples will illustrate differences:

COBOL:

MOVE EMPLOYEE-NAME TO PAYCHECK-NAME.

FORTRAN:

PAYNME = EMPNME

COBOL:

IF ITEM IS LESS THAN MINIMUM GO TO ORDER.

FORTRAN:

IF (ITEM − MIN) 50, 100, 100
(50 is the statement number of ORDER)

Types of Words

The FORTRAN language contains two types of words, reserved words and
names.

RESERVED WORDS. The reserved words shown in Table 17.2 have a
particular meaning to the computer and can be used only to perform that
specific task. They are incorporated into programming statements along with
the names of the quantities on which they are to operate.

NAMES. Names are assigned to represent quantities in storage or data fields
on a record. Assigned names conform to certain FORTRAN rules. They may
not be more than six characters long and, in some cases, must begin with
certain letters of the alphabet. A reserved word cannot be used as a name.
Optional words, as used in COBOL, are not used in FORTRAN.

Coding Forms and Conventions

A standard coding form is used by FORTRAN programmers to write
programs. (See Figure 17.1.) After coding, instructions are usually
keypunched into cards. This set of keypunched instructions becomes the
source program which is input, with the data deck, to the computer for
processing.

TABLE 17.2   FORTRAN RESERVED WORDS

BACKSPACE	FIND
CALL EXIT	FORMAT
CALL LINK	FUNCTION
CALL LOAD	GO TO
CALL	IF
CALL PDUMP	INTEGER
CALL SSWTCH	INTEGER FUNCTION
COMMON	PAUSE
CONTINUE	READ
DATA	REAL
DEFINE FILE	REAL FUNCTION
DIMENSION	RETURN
DO	REWIND
END	STOP
END FILE	SUBROUTINE
EQUIVALENCE	WRITE
EXTERNAL	

FIGURE 17.1   FORTRAN CODING FORM

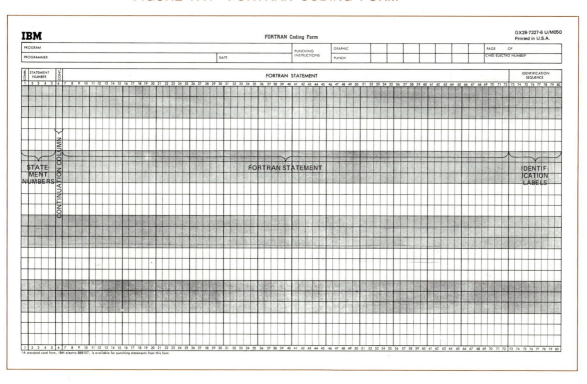

FORTRAN PROGRAM SHEET LAYOUT. At the top of the standard form is a space for entering the programmer's name and other related data. Each page is divided into 80 columns and has approximately 24 lines for writing instructions. Each column corresponds to a column of a punched card and holds one character.

CONVENTIONS. The FORTRAN compiler is designed to expect certain kinds of data in selected columns of the punched card. Columns 1 to 5 are reserved for statement numbers. The programmer directs control to different statements during branching and looping by referring to statement numbers.

     Column 6 is the continuation column. A character is recorded in this column if an instruction is too long to fit on one punched card. Columns 7 to 72 are reserved for programming statements. The actual coding directions to read data, write data, FORMAT statements, etc. are recorded here. Columns 73–80 are not read by the compiler and are used to record labels, program names, or numbers for identification for each card in the deck.

FORTRAN ELEMENTS

A FORTRAN program has no special sections or divisions. FORTRAN statements are placed in the program in the order in which they are to be carried out. The computer executes each instruction, one at a time, branching where directed, until the last statement in the program has been reached.

     A programmer constructs FORTRAN statements by combining mathematical operators, reserved words, names, etc. He must give certain information to the compiler with these instructions. He must describe the format of the I/O data. He must indicate whether numbers are whole numbers, decimals, exponentiations, etc.

Types of Statements   The FORTRAN language consists of several different types of programming statements.

     Four of the most important types are

1. CONTROL STATEMENTS. These statements control the sequence of operations that the computer is to follow. They instruct the machine to branch to a given statement, to repeat a sequence a given number of times, to terminate execution, etc. For example,

$$\text{GO TO 50}$$

This statement instructs the computer to execute statement 50 next. It causes the computer to branch to another statement instead of executing the next instruction in line.

2. ARITHMETIC STATEMENTS.   These statements cause the computer to perform such mathematical operations as addition, subtraction, exponentiation, and square root. For example,

TOTAL = CASH + DEPOS − REFUND

This statement directs an arithmetic procedure. The computer will add the value of CASH to DEPOS, subtract the value of REFUND, and place the answer in a slot named TOTAL.

3. INPUT/OUTPUT STATEMENTS. These statements cause the computer to read in, or write out, data. They call in and out card readers, card punches, line printers, magnetic tape units, etc. They schedule the flow of data in and out of the CPU. For example,

WRITE (3,10) CASH

This statement directs the computer to write the value of CASH on the line printer. The number 3 within the parentheses is a code indicating the line printer. The number 10 tells the computer to refer to statement 10 for details on how the line is to be printed. (See FORMAT statement below.)

4. FORMAT STATEMENTS. These statements give the computer information on the kind of data to be input and output and the fields where they are located on a record. FORMAT statements tell the computer whether whole or decimal numbers are involved, how many digits they have, and how many places past the decimal point.
They also give the computer instructions on the graphic layout of the output. For example, they indicate when lines should be skipped by the line printer and in what columns data should be printed out.

A FORMAT statement is associated with one or more input/output statements. The related I/O statements instruct the computer to read or write data, the name of the quantities, what I/O units to use, and which FORMAT statement to refer to for details on how the line is to be printed. For example,

10 FORMAT ('1', F5.2)

This FORMAT statement is the one referred to in the previous example. It states that data is to be written out at the top of a new page (indicated by the '1'),* that it is a decimal number (indicated by the code F), and that it fills five columns with two places past the decimal (indicated by 5.2).

FORTRAN Terminology   Several mathematical and general terms are used in specific ways in FORTRAN. Many refer to the data being processed by a program, and others

* In IBM version of FORTRAN.

to elements of the program itself. Following are some of the main terms with which a FORTRAN programmer should be familiar:

A constant is a fixed quantity whose value does not change during execution of a program. It may be represented by an assigned name, or by the actual number itself.

For example, a programmer may want to multiply pay rate by 40 when figuring paychecks. The constant in this program would be 40, since it represents the number of hours each employee works and will be the same for all paychecks prepared.

The programmer may use the number "40" in his programming statement:

$$PAY = RATE * 40$$

Or he may assign a name to the constant 40:

$$TIME = 40$$

and use the name in his statement:

$$PAY = RATE * TIME$$

Constants are used in mathematical procedures involving other numbers and constants, but the numeric value they represent does not vary during a program.

A variable is a quantity whose value will change during a program run. A variable may be alphanumeric characters or a numeric value. It may be read in or out of the computer, or be the result of calculations performed. Since its value changes, the programmer uses an assigned name to refer to it.

In the example above, the programmer uses the name RATE to refer to the hourly wage for each employee. RATE is a variable since its value will not be the same for all employees.

PAY represents a variable that will be calculated by multiplying a constant (TIME) by a variable (RATE).

Numeric variables may be read into a program, printed out, calculated within a program or used in mathematical procedures to calculate other variables or constants.

Variables can also be alphanumeric characters.

$$30 \ READ \ (3,40) \ EMP$$

In this example, EMP is a variable representing an alphanumeric quantity (name) that will be different for each employee. The first paycheck may be prepared for AMOS, the second for DIAZ, etc.

Alphanumeric variables are read into a program from data records and can be listed as part of the output. They usually represent names of parts or people, code identification numbers, labels, etc.

An integer is a whole number. It is a numerical quantity that does not contain a decimal point. Some examples of integers are

> 1   414   54,675   0002

no decimal

A real number is a decimal number. It is also called a floating-point number. Some examples of real numbers are

> .1   41.4   54,675.00   .0002

has a decimal

A literal constant is a string of characters the computer considers as a single group. They can be manipulated, moved in storage, or printed out. They are called "literals" because they are composed of alphanumeric and special characters, and "constant" because they do not change during the run of a program. Literal constants are often used to label output and to identify data.

Examples of literal constants are:

> 80 WRITE (3,90)
> 90 FORMAT (' TAXABLE INCOME')

> 50 WRITE (3,60)
> 60 FORMAT (' COMMISSION RATE IS 25 PERCENT')

In each case above, the literal constant is a string of numbers, letters, or characters that the programmer has written into the program. They will always appear in the print out exactly as in the quotes. Literal constants are often used in FORTRAN programming to label output and quantities, and to identify data.

Language Features

ARRAYS. FORTRAN is particularly rich in its ability to read in, store, and manipulate large collections of related data. Only a minimum of programming effort is required to direct the computer to set up consecutive storage spaces sufficient to hold several thousand variables and assign a unique name to each location. This storage arrangement is called an array. The process of reading data into an array is called arraying data.

The programmer tells the computer the size and name of the array he will need. The computer will reserve the storage spaces and assign a name to each location, depending on its position within the array. For example, the first location in an array named MARY might be called MARY(1), the second MARY(2), and the third MARY(3), etc. The number used to indicate the position of a storage location within an array, is called a *subscript*. The first subscript may be any number. The computer will automatically assign consecutive numbers as the remaining subscripts.

Subscripts may be used by the programmer for identification. For example,

ARRAY—GROSS NATIONAL PRODUCT

GNP(1965)
GNP(1966)
GNP(1967)
GNP(1968)
GNP(1969)
GNP(1970)

The programmer can have the computer print out the Gross National Product for 1969 by directing it to write the contents stored in GNP(1969), or he can add GNP(1969) to some other quantity, or compare it to another year.

The ability to array and assign subscripts is a powerful tool for the programmer. It enables him to read in and store tables of all kinds, lists of numbers, quantities, names, records, etc. He can refer to, process, or change any item in the array by using its subscript.

SUBROUTINES AND FUNCTIONS. Another important aspect of FORTRAN is the availability of built-in functions and subroutines. A function is a mathematical subprogram that can be called into use by a problem program to perform a specific mathematical task. A subroutine is a service subprogram that can be called in by a problem program to perform a variety of operations.

FORTRAN contains many built-in functions. Some examples are listed in Table 17.3. To illustrate, suppose the FORTRAN programmer wants to find the square root of a number, say 10. He can write a program directing the computer to perform each step involved in finding a square root. But it would be much easier to use the square root function (SQRT) available in the compiler, like this

ROOT = SQRT(10)

SQRT Function

When the computer encounters this statement, it will extract the square root of 10 and place the answer in storage under the name ROOT, ready for read out or further processing.

Subroutines may be written by the programmer or the manufacturer and stored in the computer subprogram library. Some subroutines perform housekeeping duties involved in processing a program, such as terminating execution. Others perform alphabetic and numeric sorts, calculate interest payments or payroll deductions, etc. In fact, any frequently used, repetitive procedure can be handled by a subroutine.

To use a subroutine, the programmer inserts a CALL SUBROUTINE statement in his problem program at the proper point. The compiler will locate the subroutine he has named and transfer temporary control to it. When the procedure it performs is completed, the subroutine returns control, and the answer, to the calling program and processing continues.

TABLE 17.3 FORTRAN LANGUAGE FUNCTIONS

Exponential
Natural logarithm
Common logarithm
Arcsine
Arccosine
Arctangent
Trigonometric cosine
Trigonometric tangent
Trigonometric cotangent
Square root
Error function
Complemented error function
Gamma
Log-gamma
Modular arithmetic
Absolute value
Truncation
Largest value

SAMPLE FORTRAN STATEMENTS

Many powerful and complex programming statements can be written using the arithmetic operators, reserved words, and assigned names. The following statements illustrate some of the varied operations that can be performed in FORTRAN.

List Comment Statement

This statement tells the computer to read in a comment and write it out on the line printer, as the program is listed. It is used to title a part of a program or to include explanatory material. The statement will be listed, but not compiled.

EXAMPLE:

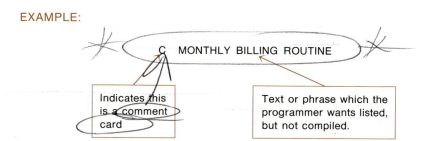

Explanation: The programmer wants to include the title MONTHLY BILLING ROUTINE in the program listing. The comment statement is punched in a card and inserted in the program deck. The statement appears at the beginning of the listing, but is not compiled or entered into the working storage of the computer. The "C" in column 1 of the statement tells the computer that this is a comment statement. One or more comment statements can be used at almost any point in the program.

Read a Whole Number   This statement tells the computer to read a whole number and store it in memory ready for further processing.

EXAMPLE:

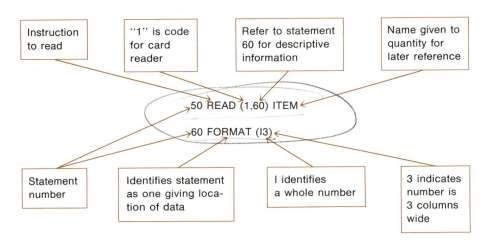

| Instruction to read | "1" is code for card reader | Refer to statement 60 for descriptive information | Name given to quantity for later reference |

50 READ (1,60) ITEM
60 FORMAT (I3)

| Statement number | Identifies statement as one giving location of data | I identifies a whole number | 3 indicates number is 3 columns wide |

Input Data:

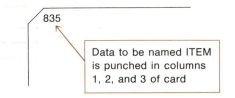

835

Data to be named ITEM is punched in columns 1, 2, and 3 of card

Explanation: The programmer assigns the name of the quantity for later reference. The details of the FORMAT statement are dictated by the whole number being read in. To read 835, which is a three-column-wide whole number, I3 is used. To read the whole number 3,947, I4 would be used in the FORMAT statement. Had the number contained six digits, such as 845,903, I6 would have been used. In each case, the letter I indicates that the number to be read is a whole number. The number following the I specifies how many columns wide the number to be read is. I must always be used when reading whole numbers.

The 1 in the READ statement is the code number for the card reader. (Code numbers for I/O devices will vary from one installation to another.)

The 60 tells the computer that FORMAT statement 60 describes where the number will be found on the card.

Write a Whole Number   This statement tells the computer to write a whole number. The number has been read into storage earlier or calculated by the computer from other data.

EXAMPLE:

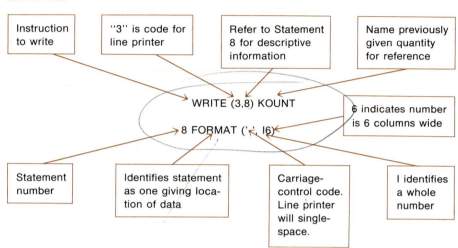

| Instruction to write | "3" is code for line printer | Refer to Statement 8 for descriptive information | Name previously given quantity for reference |

WRITE (3,8) KOUNT

8 FORMAT (' , I6)

6 indicates number is 6 columns wide

| Statement number | Identifies statement as one giving location of data | Carriage-control code. Line printer will single-space. | I identifies a whole number |

Output Data:

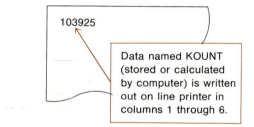

103925

Data named KOUNT (stored or calculated by computer) is written out on line printer in columns 1 through 6.

Explanation: The name KOUNT has been assigned earlier by the programmer. The quantity it represents either was read in earlier in the program and given the name KOUNT or is the result of a calculation performed by the computer and named KOUNT.

    The details of the FORMAT statement are dictated by the number being output. To write 103,925, a six-column-wide whole number, I6 was used.

    The 3 in the WRITE statement is the code number for the line printer. The 8 tells the computer that FORMAT statement 8 describes where the data is to be written on the line printer.

Branch—IF Statement   This statement causes the computer to take one of several paths depending on the value of a quantity in storage. Branching is limited to only three paths and is based upon the relationship of the value in storage to zero. This statement enables the programmer to branch back to the beginning, to a point within the program, or to the end of the program.

EXAMPLE:

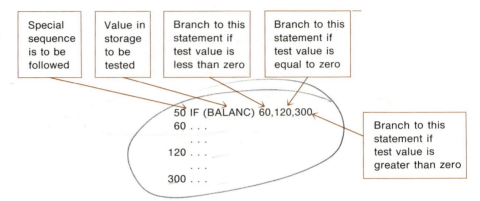

Special sequence is to be followed	Value in storage to be tested	Branch to this statement if test value is less than zero	Branch to this statement if test value is equal to zero

```
50 IF (BALANC) 60,120,300
60 . . .
     . . .
120 . . .
     . . .
300 . . .
```

Branch to this statement if test value is greater than zero

Explanation: A branch is to be made in the program at statement 50. Control is to branch to statement 60, 120, or 300, depending on the value of BALANC. If the value of BALANC is less than zero, the computer will automatically branch to the statement number in the first position (60). If the value of BALANC is equal to zero, it will branch to the statement number in the second position (120). If the value of BALANC is greater than zero, it will branch to the statement number in the third position (300).

Repeat a Cycle— DO Loop Instruction

Unless otherwise instructed, the computer will execute a statement only once and will follow the instructions in the program consecutively. It is often necessary to repeat a cycle several times. A DO loop statement can be used to instruct the computer to execute a series of statements a predetermined number of times. The maximum times the cycle is executed can be written into the program, or calculated during the time of execution.

EXAMPLE:

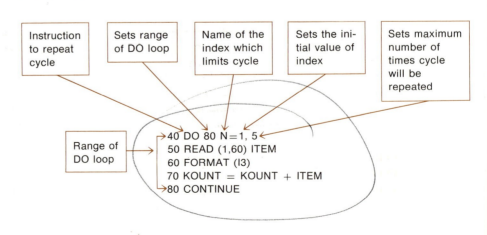

Instruction to repeat cycle	Sets range of DO loop	Name of the index which limits cycle	Sets the initial value of index	Sets maximum number of times cycle will be repeated

Range of DO loop

```
40 DO 80 N=1, 5
50 READ (1,60) ITEM
60 FORMAT (I3)
70 KOUNT = KOUNT + ITEM
80 CONTINUE
```

Explanation: In this example, a DO loop is used to cause the computer to repeat a READ statement and mathematical calculation five times. The DO instruction consists of the word DO followed by the last statement number in the cycle being repeated, and an index. The index keeps track of the loops and indicates the maximum number of repetitions.

The index contains a name (N in this example), followed by its initial value (1) and its limit (5). Each time a loop is performed, the index is incremented by one. When the limit is reached (5), control goes to the next statement following the CONTINUE.

Addition This statement tells the computer to add two or more decimal numbers, or two or more whole numbers. (Many compilers cannot add whole and decimal numbers together. Either the whole number must be converted to a decimal and then added, or vice versa.) The computer will perform the indicated calculation and store the answer under an assigned name. This answer may be written out or used for further processing.

EXAMPLE:

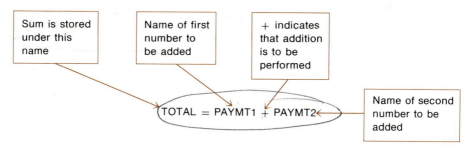

Data in Storage:

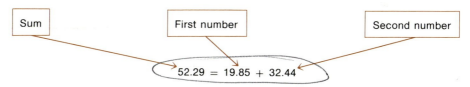

Explanation: Two numbers are to be added. The first (19.85) has been previously read in or calculated and is stored under the name PAYMT1. The second (32.44) has been assigned the name PAYMT2. The computer will add the numbers on the right-hand side of the expression and place the answer in the location named TOTAL. The values of PAYMT1 and PAYMT2 may change throughout the program. The values that will be summed are always those in storage at the time the computer reaches the instruction.

Complex Arithmetic Statements This statement directs the computer to perform more than one arithmetic operation in the same instruction. Calculations using addition, subtraction, multiplication, division, and/or other functions can be indicated in one instruction. The computer will perform all arithmetic procedures indicated and store the answer under the assigned name. This answer may be written out or used for further calculations.

EXAMPLE:

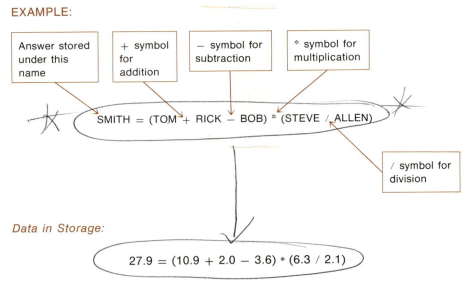

Data in Storage:

$$27.9 = (10.9 + 2.0 - 3.6) * (6.3 / 2.1)$$

Explanation: The computer performs mathematical calculations according to a definite order or hierarchy

1. Exponentiation
2. Multiplication and division
3. Subtraction and addition

Unless directed to the contrary, it will move from left to right in performing the hierarchy. Calculations enclosed within parentheses will always be performed before those not enclosed.

The statement in this example includes subtraction, addition, multiplication, and division. The computer will evaluate the terms on the right side of the expression, following the hierarchy, and place the answer on the left under the name SMITH. The parentheses will be cleared first, left to right. The calculation, involving addition and subtraction, enclosed within parentheses, will be performed first. Then the other parentheses, involving division, will be cleared. Finally, the two intermediate results will be multiplied.

SAMPLE PROGRAM

Function of the Program   A simple FORTRAN program is given to illustrate how the various statements in the language are assembled.

FIGURE 17.2   FORTRAN SAMPLE PROGRAM

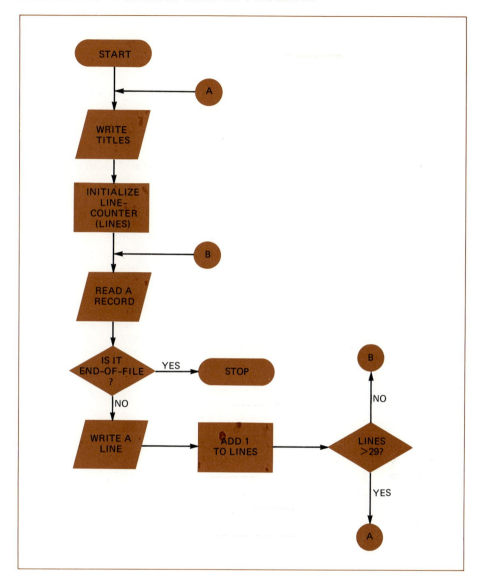

The program is designed to read data from cards and print out a name and address list on the line printer. The steps in the program are graphically shown in the flowchart in Figure 17.2. The steps the program algorithm follows are

❶ The titles are written and the line counter (LINES) is initialized to zero.
❷ A data record is read and tested for end of file. If it is, the computer branches to the STOP instruction and the program terminates.

JOHN VON NEUMANN AND THE ALL-PURPOSE COMPUTER

In the 25 years since John von Neumann designed the first fully modern electronic computer, tens of thousands of the controversial machines have dramatically altered the shape of today's society. John von Neumann, a warm outgoing mathematical genius, already stands as one of the giants of twentieth century scientific thought.

Von Neumann was a true mathematical genius. As a six-year old in his native Budapest he could divide two eight-digit numbers in his head. At 24 he had developed "game theory," a mathematical method of studying competitive and cooperative interactions. Three years later he wrote a treatise on quantum mechanics that was to be a cornerstone of this branch of atomic physics. During World War II he was involved in the Manhattan Project, which produced the atomic bomb. In 1955, von Neumann was named to the Atomic Energy Commission. He died in 1957 at the age of 53.

Von Neumann's contribution converted the electronic computer from a special-purpose machine to a flexible, all-purpose device. Previous computers relied on slow mechanical methods [using plugboards] of storing the program, the set of instructions that direct the computer's operations. Von Neumann developed a concept that did away with the plugboard method. He designed a machine in which the program could be written in numbers and stored in the memory exactly as if it were numbers to be manipulated in the computation.

The internally stored program made possible a general-purpose computer that could, almost instantaneously, electronically reorganize its internal circuits to meet special needs simply by feeding in a set of numbers.

This design, which included a new organization of the computer subassemblies—once referred to as the "von Neumann architecture" or the "von Neumann machine"—remains the basic pattern on which nearly all digital computers are made.

SOURCE   Abstracted from "Man and Computer: Uneasy Allies of 25 Years," by Boyce Rensberger, *The New York Times*, June 27, 1972, p. 43.

❸ If the data record is not the end of file, it is written on the line printer.

❹ Since only 30 lines on a page are desired, a line counter is included to keep track of the lines printed. The counter, LINES, is incremented by one each time a line is output.

❺ The counter is tested to see if it is greater than 29. If it is, the computer branches to start a new page. If not, the computer loops back to read another record.

Program Analysis   The discussion on page 372 traces the program in a step-by-step fashion. The numbers listed at the left margin are the statement numbers shown in Figure 17.3. The input data for this program is shown in Figure 17.4(A); the output is shown in Figure 17.4(B). (Input data was punched into cards.)

FIGURE 17.3   LISTING OF FORTRAN SAMPLE PROGRAM

```
C       CLIENT DIRECTORY
   10 IN=1
   20 IOT=3
C       WRITE HEADINGS AND INITIALIZE LINE COUNT
   30 WRITE(IOT,40)
   40 FORMAT('1',T19,'NAME',T52,'ADDRESS',T83,'TELEPHONE'/)
   45 LINES=0
C       READ IN NAME, ADDRESS AND TELEPHONE OF CLIENT
   50 READ(IN,60,END=110)NAME1,NAME2,NAME3,NAME4,NAME5,ADD1,ADD2,
      2ADD3,ADD4,ADD5,ADD6,ADD7,ADD8,NAREA,NPRFX,NUMBR
   60 FORMAT(5A4,7A4,A2,I3,I3,I4)
C       WRITE OUT NAME, ADDRESS AND TELEPHONE OF CLIENT
   70 WRITE(IOT,80)NAME1,NAME2,NAME3,NAME4,NAME5,ADD1,ADD2,ADD3,
      2ADD4,ADD5,ADD6,ADD7,ADD8,NAREA,NPRFX,NUMBR
   80 FORMAT(' ',T11,5A4,T41,7A4,A2,T81,'(',I3,') ',I3,'-',I4)
   90 LINES=LINES+1
  100 IF(29-LINES)30,50,50
  110 STOP
      END
```

"En garde, Mr. Benson!"

FIGURE 17.4(A)   INPUT DATA FOR FORTRAN SAMPLE PROGRAM

```
ALLEN, MAXIME        1681 THIRD ST., LOS ANGELES    4123328211
BARRON, CLEVELAND    18322 HERRINGTON, LOS ANGELES 4111694283
DIAN, MANUEL         9252 W. 9TH AVE., LOS ANGELES 4125463275
GARCIA, SUSAN        12112 LELAND, LOS ANGELES      4131725358
GOLDBERG, SAM        6821 MAGNOLIA, LOS ANGELES     4115725364
KIM, SANDRA LEE      2811 RIVERTON, LOS ANGELES     4125108462
ONO, MIDORI          6661 NINA ST., LOS ANGELES     4134701908
POLSKI, JACK         2193 CENTRAL, LOS ANGELES      4131042860
```

FIGURE 17.4(B)   OUTPUT FROM FORTRAN SAMPLE PROGRAM

```
       NAME                        ADDRESS                    TELEPHONE

ALLEN, MAXIME           1681 THIRD ST., LOS ANGELES        (412) 332-8211
BARRON, CLEVELAND       18322 HERRINGTON, LOS ANGELES      (411) 169-4283
DIAN, MANUEL            9252 W. 9TH AVE., LOS ANGELES      (412) 546-3275
GARCIA, SUSAN           12112 LELAND, LOS ANGELES          (413) 172-5358
GOLDBERG, SAM           6821 MAGNOLIA, LOS ANGELES         (411) 572-5364
KIM, SANDRA LEE         2811 RIVERTON, LOS ANGELES         (412) 510-8462
ONO, MIDORI             6661 NINA ST., LOS ANGELES         (413) 470-1908
POLSKI, JACK            2193 CENTRAL, LOS ANGELES          (413) 104-2860
```

STATEMENT NUMBER	EXPLANATION
10, 20	Assign the I/O device code numbers to the names the programmer has chosen. Only the names are used throughout the program. In this way, if the program is to be run in an installation with different code numbers, only these statements must be changed.
30, 40	Instruct the computer to skip to a new page, write the titles, and skip an extra line.
45	Initializes the line-counter LINES to zero.
50, 60	Instruct the computer to read in the NAME, ADDRESS, and PHONE NUMBER from data card and test for end of file. If it is, control branches to statement 110, STOP. If it is not, control transfers to the next statement. (Since the FORTRAN compiler will store only four alphanumeric characters under one name, each four-character group has been given a unique name.)

70, 80	Instruct the computer to write out the NAME, ADDRESS, and PHONE NUMBER following a different format.
90	Increments LINES by one.
100	Tests to see if LINES is greater than 29. This is done by subtracting LINES from 29. If the answer is zero or greater than zero, LINES is not more than 29, and the computer branches to statement 50 to read in another record. If the answer is less than zero, LINES is now greater than 29 (30 lines have been printed out) and the computer branches to statement 30, which starts a new page.
110	STOP and END instructions terminate execution.

KEY TERMS

FORTRAN
Standard character set
Control statements
Arithmetic statements
Input/Output statements
FORMAT statements
Reserved words
Assigned names
Constant
Variable

Integer
Real number
Literal constant
Array
Subscript
Subroutine
Function
Comment statement
DO loop
Index

EXERCISES

1. How did the development of FORTRAN differ from that of COBOL?
2. List five advantages and two limitations of FORTRAN.
3. How does the structure of FORTRAN statement differ from that of COBOL?
4. What is the function of control statements?
5. What is the function of input/output statements?
6. What is the function of FORMAT statements?
7. Label the reserved columns on a FORTRAN coding sheet.
8. Define the term constant and list three examples.
9. Define the term variable and list three examples.
10. How do literal constants differ from other constants?
11. What is an array and what function does it serve in programming?
12. What are functions and subroutines? How are they used in FORTRAN?
13. Write a simple FORTRAN program that includes a DO loop and one or more mathematical calculations.

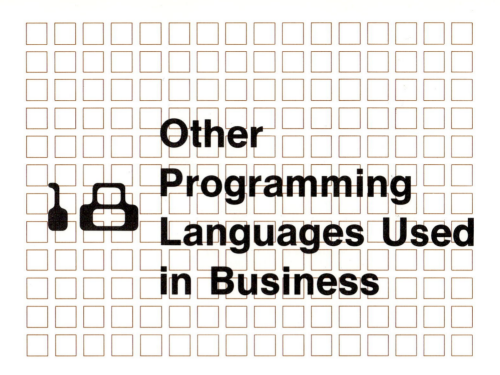

Other Programming Languages Used in Business

Many computer languages were developed for batch processing applications. They are suitable for processing large files of data, repetitive jobs, and for scheduling jobs to maximize the efficiency of the computer. They enable a programmer to write a program as an independent unit, which can be processed at any time, without his control, direction, or intervention. Both COBOL and FORTRAN are examples of batch processing languages.

As computer usage increased, new methods of programming and accessing the computer developed. For some of these methods, batch processing languages were no longer adequate as the bonds between user and machine.

New languages, called interactive languages, were developed. They are suited to real-time, remote processing, via typewriter-like terminals. Most require less programming effort than batch processing languages.

Thus, we may classify the common computer languages as interactive or batch languages. Table 18.1 lists examples of each group.

BATCH PROCESSING LANGUAGES

In this section, we briefly discuss three common batch processing languages. (COBOL and FORTRAN were discussed in previous chapters.)

TABLE 18.1   LANGUAGE TYPES

Batch Processing Languages
      COBOL (COmmon Business Oriented Language)
      FORTRAN (FORmula TRANslating System)
      RPG (Report Program Generator)
      Assembler Language
      PL/I (Programming Language I)[a]
Interactive Languages (Terminal Languages)
      APL (A Programming Language)
      BASIC (Beginners All-Purpose Symbolic Instruction Code)[b]
      ATS (Administrative Terminal System)

[a] Suitable as a batch processing language and an interactive language.
[b] BASIC is not to be confused with Basic FORTRAN.

PL/I (Programming Language I)

PL/I was developed by IBM as a multipurpose language. It is a business and scientific language, suitable for batch processing and terminal usage. Designed to include the best features of FORTRAN and COBOL, PL/I is similar to both, but many new features and capabilities have been incorporated. PL/I is used to program a variety of business, educational, social science, scientific, and other problems.

ADVANTAGES. A principal advantage of PL/I is its free style. Unlike other languages, it has no restrictions regarding columns, paragraphs, and statement numbers. PL/I is modular. A novice programmer can use the language after learning only a small part of it. As he gains skill, he can extend his programming capabilities by learning additional features. (In many other languages, the programmer needs a fairly thorough understanding of the entire language before he can use any part of it.)

PL/I has built-in features, called *default options,* that will correct common mistakes made by programmers. Upon detecting a minor programming error or omission, the PL/I compiler will assume it knows what the programmer's intentions were, make a correction, and continue with the program. This makes programming easier and prevents minor errors or bugs from blowing up an otherwise acceptable program.

LIMITATIONS. PL/I compilers require a sizable amount of core storage and cannot be used on small computers. PL/I is a proprietary language: written at the expense of IBM, it is controlled by them. As a result, use of PL/I is limited to IBM computers.

GENERAL CHARACTERISTICS. PL/I is a free-form language, that is, it has few coding conventions. Programming statements are entered as a string of words, numbers, and symbols. Source statements are separated by semicolons. Statements are not confined to individual lines on coding sheets, do not have margin restrictions, and are not blocked into paragraphs.

PL/I has a standard character set, which includes the alphabet, numbers, and a group of special characters. Many of the special characters are code symbols, called operators, that cause the computer to perform various functions.

Special operators have specific meaning for the computer. They include the mathematical symbols, $+$, $-$, $*$, and $/$. Additional symbols allow the programmer to make logical and mathematical comparisons. He can, for example, compare two numbers in storage and determine if they are equal, or if one is less than or greater than another. He can connect strings of characters or cause the computer to branch depending on the value of a quantity.

Identifiers are names assigned to quantities in storage or to strings of characters. They can label a single quantity, alphabetic or numeric arrays, entire data files, groups of statements, or even conditions.

Identifiers are combined with operators and reserved PL/I words (called key words) to form statements. With them, the programmer can manipulate data, move quantities, perform calculations, and store or output results. The statements that make up a PL/I program are written on coding sheets as shown in Figure 18.1. These statements may be keypunched and assembled into a source program for batch processing. Or they may be keyboarded and transmitted to the CPU via a remote terminal. Figure 18.2 illustrates a sample program coded in PL/I.

RPG (Report Program Generator)

RPG is more a system of preparing reports than a true language. It is widely used on small computers to prepare business reports, accounts receivables, inventory listings, statements, etc.

ADVANTAGES.   RPG is one of the easier languages to learn. It has few formal language rules, syntax, or reserved words. It requires a minimum of programming effort and skill to prepare business reports and other documents. The basic pattern of execution is fixed, and the programmer merely determines what will take place within each step. RPG is designed to facilitate the processing, updating, and maintenance of large data files. It requires a smaller compiler than most POL's and is usable on small computers.

FIGURE 18.1   PL/I CODING FORM

```
BILLING: PROCEDURE;
     NEXTCARD: READ DATA (MORNO, OBAL, PAYM, RATE);
               CHARGE = OBAL*RATE/12;
               PRINPAID = PAYM-CHARGE;
               BALANCE = OBAL-PRINPAID;
          WRITE DATA (MORNO, OBAL, CHARGE, PRINPAID,
                      BALANCE);
     GO TO NEXTCARD;
END BILLING;
```

FIGURE 18.2 SAMPLE PROGRAM

```
PRINT: PROC OPTIONS(MAIN);

        DCL IN FILE RECORD SEQUENTIAL INPUT,

                DATA CHAR(100),

                LAB(3) LABEL INIT(A,B,C);

        DO I=1 TO 3;

            ON ENDFILE(IN) GO TO OUT;

            GO TO LAB(I);

            A: OPEN FILE(IN) TITLE('T1');

                GO TO READ;

            B: OPEN FILE(IN) TITLE('T2');

                GO TO READ;

            C: OPEN FILE(IN) TITLE('T3');

            READ: READ FILE(IN)  INTO (DATA);

                    PUT FILE(SYSPRINT) SKIP LIST(DATA);

                    GO TO READ;

            OUT: CLOSE FILE(IN);

                END;

        END PRINT;
```

LIMITATIONS. RPG is best used for report preparation, since it has restricted mathematical capability. It will perform addition, subtraction, multiplication, and division, but, compared to FORTRAN or COBOL, its facility for looping, branching, and making decisions is limited.

RPG is not a standardized language. It is machine dependent, and each computer has its own version. A program written in RPG for one computer may need extensive modification before it will run on another.

GENERAL CHARACTERISTICS. RPG is designed to facilitate file processing. It is concerned with file description, file manipulation, and outputting results.

The language consists of names, codes, numbers, and letters entered in specific columns of coding forms. The specifications sheets used in coding RPG programs, shown in Figure 18.3, are

- file description specifications
- file extension specifications
- line counter specifications
- input specifications
- calculation specifications
- output format specifications

FIGURE 18.3 RPG CODING FORMS

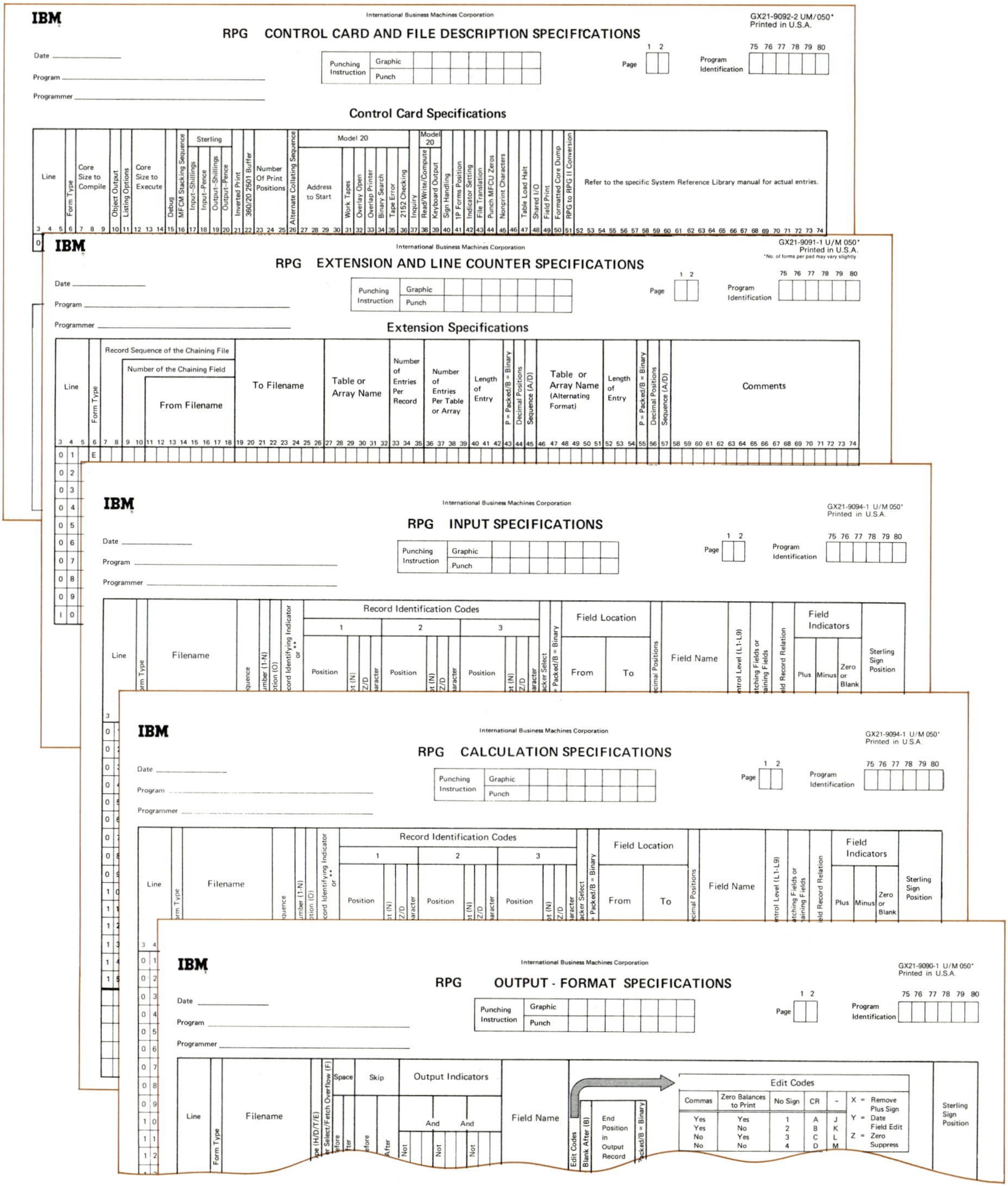

IBM

International Business Machines Corporation

GX21-9092-2 UM/050*
Printed in U.S.A.

RPG   CONTROL CARD AND FILE DESCRIPTION SPECIFICATIONS

Date _____

Program _____

Programmer _____

Punching Instruction — Graphic / Punch

Page 1 2

Program Identification   75 76 77 78 79 80

Control Card Specifications

Refer to the specific System Reference Library manual for actual entries.

IBM

International Business Machines Corporation

GX21-9091-1 U/M 050*
Printed in U.S.A.
*No. of forms per pad may vary slightly

RPG   EXTENSION AND LINE COUNTER SPECIFICATIONS

Date _____

Program _____

Programmer _____

Punching Instruction — Graphic / Punch

Page 1 2

Program Identification   75 76 77 78 79 80

Extension Specifications

IBM

International Business Machines Corporation

GX21-9094-1 U/M 050*
Printed in U.S.A.

RPG   INPUT SPECIFICATIONS

Date _____

Program _____

Programmer _____

Punching Instruction — Graphic / Punch

Page 1 2

Program Identification   75 76 77 78 79 80

IBM

International Business Machines Corporation

GX21-9094-1 U.S.A.
Printed in U.S.A.

RPG   CALCULATION SPECIFICATIONS

Punching Instruction — Graphic / Punch

Page 1 2

Program Identification   75 76 77 78 79 80

IBM

International Business Machines Corporation

GX21-9090-1 U/M 050*
Printed in U.S.A.

RPG   OUTPUT - FORMAT SPECIFICATIONS

Date _____

Program _____

Programmer _____

Punching Instruction — Graphic / Punch

Page 1 2

Program Identification   75 76 77 78 79 80

Edit Codes

Commas	Zero Balances to Print	No Sign	CR	−	X = Remove Plus Sign
Yes	Yes	1	A	J	Y = Date
Yes	No	2	B	K	Field Edit
No	Yes	3	C	L	Z = Zero
No	No	4	D	M	Suppress

The specifications forms are used to define files and fields to be read by the computer, the fields to be operated upon, and any mathematical computations to be performed. They also specify how the data is to be output, column heads to be listed, and the graphic layout to be followed.

The information on these sheets is keypunched onto cards to form the source deck. The source deck is combined with control cards and input to the computer for compilation. Then the data set to be processed is entered and the job run. Figure 18.4 shows a sample RPG program ready for keypunching.

Assembler Language

Assembler Language is a machine-dependent, coding language that is more closely related to machine language than the others discussed in these chapters. It is an efficient language from the standpoint of the machine because it can make the most compact use of the computer's core storage capacity. It is used to program long, repetitive, production-type jobs.

ADVANTAGES. Programs written in Assembler Language are designed to fully utilize a computer's core storage and register capacities during all procedures and phases of a program. This can save processing time on a long production run.

Use of Assembler Language facilitates modular programming. Programs are often written as subroutines, or modules. Modules can be combined to solve different problems. Assembler Language is available on most computers and requires less core storage than most POL's.

LIMITATIONS. The efficiency of Assembler Language on the computer is at the cost of the programmer's time and effort. It is much more difficult to write an Assembler Language program than a similar program in one of the higher level languages. Each minute step in processing and manipulation of data must be detailed, byte by byte. Storage areas must be figured and specified.

To use Assembler Language, the programmer must have a thorough understanding of the computer's architecture, register system, and mnemonic codes. He must be familiar with HEX, binary coding, packed decimal, ASCII, and EBCDIC coding systems and be able to convert from one to the other.

Assembler Language is machine dependent. A program written in Assembler Language for one computer will not necessarily run on a machine of a different model or make.

GENERAL CHARACTERISTICS. Assembler Language is a symbolic language based upon mnemonic codes, assigned names, and storage addresses. Each operation, such as add, move data, or compare, is assigned a mnemonic code. Assembler Language statements are formed by indicating the mnemonic codes and the assigned names or locations of the operands. This tells the computer what operation is to be performed and the quantities or locations involved. The Assembler Language programmer uses HEX, binary, packed decimal, ASCII, and EBCDIC codes to increase the program efficiency

FIGURE 18.4 RPG SAMPLE PROGRAM

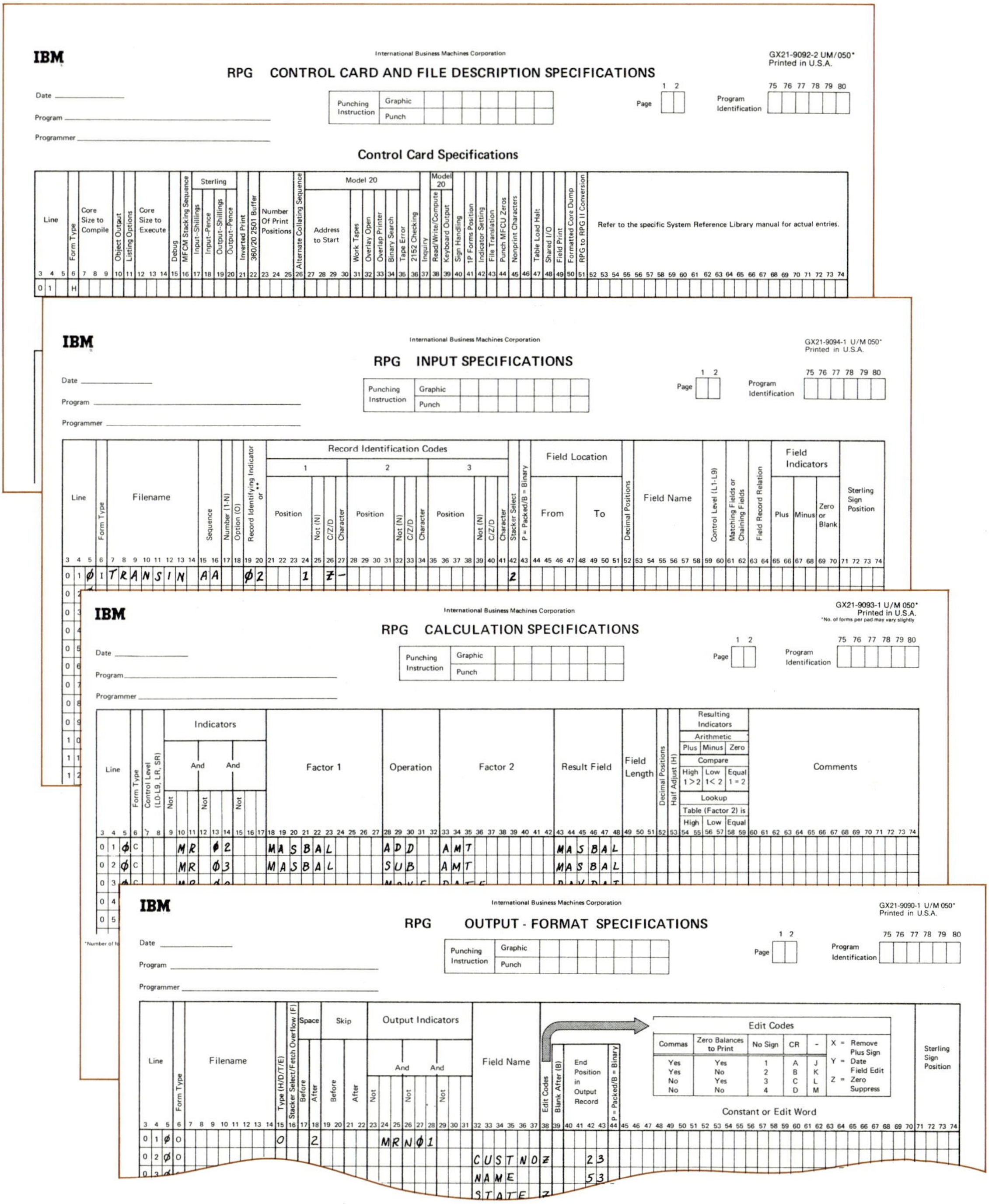

IBM

International Business Machines Corporation

RPG   CONTROL CARD AND FILE DESCRIPTION SPECIFICATIONS

GX21-9092-2 UM/050*
Printed in U.S.A.

Date _____

Program _____

Programmer _____

Punching Instruction — Graphic / Punch

Page [1 2]   Program Identification [75 76 77 78 79 80]

Control Card Specifications

Refer to the specific System Reference Library manual for actual entries.

Line	Form Type	...
0 1	H	

IBM

International Business Machines Corporation

RPG   INPUT SPECIFICATIONS

GX21-9094-1 U/M 050*
Printed in U.S.A.

Date _____

Program _____

Programmer _____

Punching Instruction — Graphic / Punch

Page [1 2]   Program Identification [75 76 77 78 79 80]

Line	Form Type	Filename	Sequence	Number (1 N) Option (O)	Record Identifying Indicator or **	Record Identification Codes			Field Location		Field Name	...
0 1	Ø I	TRANSIN	AA	Ø2	1	Z -				2		

IBM

International Business Machines Corporation

RPG   CALCULATION SPECIFICATIONS

GX21-9093-1 U/M 050*
Printed in U.S.A.
*No. of forms per pad may vary slightly

Date _____

Program _____

Programmer _____

Punching Instruction — Graphic / Punch

Page [1 2]   Program Identification [75 76 77 78 79 80]

Line	Form Type	Control Level (L0-L9, LR, SR)	Indicators And / And	Factor 1	Operation	Factor 2	Result Field	Field Length	...	Comments
0 1	Ø C		MR Ø2	MASBAL	ADD	AMT	MASBAL			
0 2	Ø C		MR Ø3	MASBAL	SUB	AMT	MASBAL			

IBM

International Business Machines Corporation

RPG   OUTPUT - FORMAT SPECIFICATIONS

GX21-9090-1 U/M 050*
Printed in U.S.A.

Date _____

Program _____

Programmer _____

Punching Instruction — Graphic / Punch

Page [1 2]   Program Identification [75 76 77 78 79 80]

Edit Codes	Commas	Zero Balances to Print	No Sign	CR	X = Remove Plus Sign
	Yes	Yes	1	A J	Y = Date
	Yes	No	2	B K	Field Edit
	No	Yes	3	C L	Z = Zero Suppress
	No	No	4	D M	

Constant or Edit Word

Line	Form Type	Filename	Type (H/D/T/E)	Space / Skip	Output Indicators And / And	Field Name	Edit Codes	End Position in Output Record	...
0 1	Ø O		O	2	MRNØ1				
0 2	Ø O					CUSTNOZ		23	
0 3						NAME		53	
						STATE			

The basic character set used in Assembler Language depends upon the particular computer. Generally, it includes the full alphabet, numbers, and a dozen or so special characters.

Each operation or procedure the computer performs, such as ADD, MOVE DATA, or MULTIPLY, is initiated by a machine language code. The HEX translations of these machine language codes are called operation codes or, simply, "op codes." Each op code has also been assigned a mnemonic code to identify the operation it performs. The op codes and their mnemonic names used on the IBM System/360 are shown in Table 18.2. For example, addition of values in storage slots is specified by the op code A; addition of values in registers is specified by AR; compare algebraic values is specified by the code C. The assembler translates these codes into the machine language equivalent for execution.

Most Assembler Language statements are translated line for line into machine language, and each minute step involved in processing and manipulating data must be described to the computer in detail. Only a few of the Assembler Language statements are designed to generate a group of machine language instructions to direct the computer through a routine. This type of statement is called a *macro instruction*.

The basic Assembler Language instruction is coded as follows:

NAME	OPERATION	OPERAND A	OPERAND B	REMARKS

The programmer may assign a name to the line of instructions. This name can be referred to later in the program to direct or transfer control during looping and branching. In the operation part of the instruction, the programmer writes his op code mnemonic to indicate the procedures he wants performed. Operands are the assigned names or addresses of data that is to be located or moved. Operand A is the address of the first quantity or storage location to be used in the instruction and Operand B is the address of the second quantity or storage location involved. (Not all instructions use a second operand.) The programmer may use the rest of the columns for documentation and explanation. Some sample statements are

Name	Operation	Operands A and B	Remarks
ADDSTK	A	3,STOCK	STOCK added to value in Reg. 3
	MVC	INV(6),SALE	Move value in Loc. SALE to INV.
	LA	6,PYROLL	Load address of PYROLL into Reg. 6
OVRAMT	C	10,LIMIT	Compare LIMIT to value in Reg. 10

The use of registers is basic to Assembler Language programming. Registers are temporary storage devices within the CPU that hold data while it is being processed. (Computers may have 16 or more registers for the programmer's use.) Registers serve as counters and indexes; they hold data involved in mathematical calculations or comparisons, etc. Programming

TABLE 18.2 ASSEMBLER LANGUAGE OP CODES[a]

NAME	MNEMONIC	NAME	MNEMONIC
Add	AR	Shift Right Double	
Add	A	Logical	SRDL
AND	N	Store	ST
AND	NI	Store Character	STC
Branch and Link	BALR	Store Halfword	STH
Branch and Link	BAL	Store Multiple	STM
Branch on Condition	BCR	Subtract	SR
Branch on Condition	BC	Subtract	S
Branch on Count	BCTR	Supervisor Call	SVC
Branch on Count	BCT	Test Under Mask	TM
Branch on Index High	BXH	Translate	TR
Branch on Index Low		Translate and Test	TRT
or Equal	BXLE	Unpack	UNPK
Compare	CR		
Compare	C	**Floating-Point Feature Instructions**	
Compare Halfword	CH		
Compare Logical	CLC	Add Normalized	
Convert to Binary	CVB	(Short)	AE
Convert to Decimal	CVD	Compare (Short)	CE
Divide	DR	Divide (Short)	DER
Divide	D	Halve (Short)	HER
Exclusive OR	X	Load Complement	
Exclusive OR	XI	(Short)	LCER
Execute	EX	Load (Short)	LE
Insert Character	IC	Multiply (Short)	MER
Load	LR	Multiply (Short)	ME
Load	L	Store (Short)	STE
Load Address	LA	Subtract Normalized	
Load and Test	LTR	(Short)	SER
Load Halfword	LH	Subtract Normalized	
Load Multiple	LM	(Short)	SE
Load Positive	LPR		
Load PSW	LPSW	**Decimal Feature Instructions**	
Move	MVI		
Move	MVC	Add Decimal	AP
Move Numerics	MVN	Compare Decimal	CP
Move with Offset	MVO	Divide Decimal	DP
Multiply	M	Edit	ED
OR	OR	Edit and Mark	EDMK
OR	OI	Multiply Decimal	MP
Pack	PACK	Subtract Decimal	SP
Set Program Mask	SPM	Zero and Add	ZAP
Set System Mask	SSM		
Shift Left Single	SLA	**Protection Feature Instructions**	
Shift Right Single	SRA	Insert Storage Key	ISK
		Set Storage Key	SSK

[a] *A Programmer's Introduction to the IBM System/360 Architecture, Instructions and Assembler Language*, student text. C20-1646-4, Appendix A, p. 218.

FIGURE 18.5   ASSEMBLER LANGUAGE CODING FORM

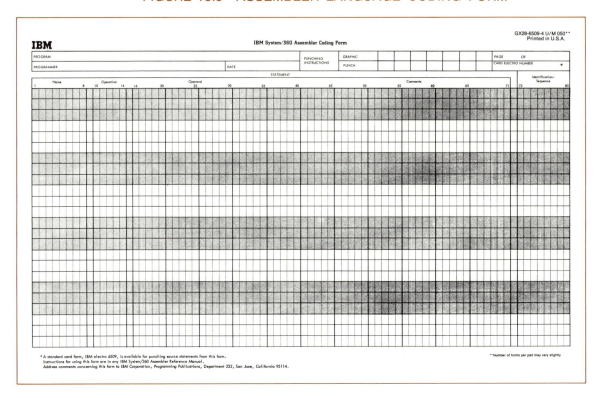

instructions direct the computer to move data between general storage and registers, to manipulate quantities stored in registers, or to load storage addresses of quantities into a register, etc.

The form shown in Figure 18.5 is used in coding Assembler Language instructions. The form has provisions for identifying the programmer and other data at the top. Columns 1 to 8 are used for the name of the instructions. Columns 10 to 14 are usually used for the op code; columns 16 to 71 for operands and comments. Column 72 is the continuation column, and columns 73 to 80 are for identification labels. Figure 18.6 is a computer listing of part of a sample program coded in Assembler Language.

INTERACTIVE LANGUAGES

Several interactive languages have been developed to enable the programmer to converse directly with the computer. They are mainly used to solve one-time only problems, where the user needs instantaneous results. They are handled from remote real-time, on-line terminals and usually involve a limited amount of data input and output.

FIGURE 18.6 ASSEMBLER LANGUAGE SAMPLE PROGRAM

LOC	OBJECT CODE	ADDR1	ADDR2	STMT	SOURCE STATEMENT		
000000				1 SORTPGM	START 0		
000000	05A0			2	BALR 10,0		
000002				3	USING *,10		
				4	OPEN CDFILE,PTFILE		
				5+* 360N-CL-453	OPEN CHANGE LEVEL 3-3		3-3
000002	0700			6+	CNOP 0,4		
000004				7+	DC 0F'0'		
000004	4110 A2D6		002D8	8+	LA 1,=C'$$BOPEN '		
000008	4500 A012		00014	9+IJJ00001 BAL	0,*+4+4*(3-1)		
00000C	00000310			10+	DC A(CDFILE)		
000010	00000348			11+	DC A(PTFILE)		
000014	0A02			12+	SVC 2		
000016	5830 A2CE		002D0	13	L 3,TABSTRT	ADD. OF TABLE INTO REG3	
00001A	1B22			14	SR 2,2		
00001C	5A30 A2E6		002E8	15 LOOPA	A 3,=F'80'	ADD 80 TO TABLE LOC FOR NEXT SLOT	
000020	5920 A2EA		002EC	16	C 2,=F'1000'	COMPARE COUNT TO MAXIMUM	
000024	4780 A044		00046	17	BE SORTA	IF 1000 GOTO SORTA	
000028	5A20 A2EE		002F0	18	A 2,=F'1'	ADD 1 TO COUNT	
				19	GET CDFILE,CDWORK		
				20+* 360N-CL-453	GET CHANGE LEVEL 3-0		
00002C	5810 A2F2		002F4	21+	L 1,=A(CDFILE) GET DTF TABLE ADDRESS		
000030	5800 A2F6		002F8	22+	L 0,=A(CDWORK) GET WORK AREA ADDRESS		
000034	58F1 0010		00010	23+	L 15,16(1) GET LOGIC MODULE ADDRESS		
000038	45EF 0008		00008	24+	BAL 14,8(15) BRANCH TO GET ROUTINE		
00003C	D24F 3000 A0EE	00000	000F0	25	MVC 0(80,3),CDWORK	MOVE 80 BYTES TO LOC AT REG3	
000042	47F0 A01A		0001C	26	B LOOPA	READ ANOTHER CARD	
000046	1852			27 SORTA	LR 5,2	SAVE COUNT IN REG5	
000048	1842			28	LR 4,2	SAVE COUNT IN REG4	
00004A	5830 A2CE		002D0	29 SORTB	L 3,TABSTRT	GO BACK TO BEGINNING OF TABLE	
00004E	1824			30	LR 2,4	RESET COUNTER	
000050	5A30 A2E6		002E8	31 SORTC	A 3,=F'80'	BEGIN COMPARISON, ADD 80 BYTES TAB.	
000054	4620 A07A		0007C	32	BCT 2,SORTD	COUNTS COMPARISONS	
000058	D504 3000 3050	00000	00050	33	CLC 0(5,3),80(3)	COMPARE 5 BYTES OF 2 LINES OF TABLE	
00005E	4720 A064		00066	34	BH SWITCH		
000062	47F0 A04E		00050	35	B SORTC	MAKE ANOTHER COMPARISON	
000066	D74F 3000 3050	00000	00050	36 SWITCH	XC 0(80,3),80(3)	TRANSPOSE 80 BYTES	
00006C	D74F 3050 3000	00050	00000	37	XC 80(80,3),0(3)		

Interactive languages are translated by a special compiler, sometimes called a processor. The processor converts instructions received from a terminal into executable machine instructions. A feature of the interactive language processor is its ability to process many programs simultaneously, enabling several programmers to use the system at the same time. The processor can receive data from each of many terminals, process it, and respond with the answers to the proper terminals. Each user on the system appears to be on-line with the computer by himself.

Because of the instantaneous response received and the lack of formal coding, the interactive languages are often called conversational languages. Three of the most common are APL, BASIC, and ATS.

APL
(A Programming
Language)

APL was developed by IBM specifically as a conversational language. A user with only a minimum amount of programming skill can perform many tasks. For example, he can type in two rather large numbers, separated by a plus sign ($+$) and the computer will sum the two numbers and print out the answer on the next line. Or he can subtract, multiply, divide, find the square root, or perform many other mathematical calculations by listing only the values and the operator that specifies the procedure.

ADVANTAGES. APL is one of the most powerful interactive languages yet developed. It is modular in structure, offering simple, easy-to-use features for

COMPUTERS HELP CURE STUTTERING

Traditionally, stuttering has been blamed largely on deep-seated emotional problems, and treatment has usually been directed toward uncovering some psychic trauma. But research by Dr. Ronald L. Webster, chairman of the Hollins psychology department, convinced him that if anxiety had anything to do with stuttering, it was the result of the disorder rather than the cause.

Stuttering, Webster believes, is a behavioral problem based on faulty learning of how to make sounds, and perhaps also on physical defects in the auditory mechanisms controlling speech. Speech, he explains, is regulated by feedback mechanisms. The muscle movements involved in speaking, according to this concept, are detected by sensors in the ear and in the muscles themselves and then relayed to the brain to guide further speech movements. Webster has shown that a normal speaker can be made to stutter by interfering with feedback.

Webster has found that stutterers tend to make sounds incorrectly, especially at the onset of a new sound. They are apt to begin a sound too abruptly and too loudly and make transitions from one sound to another with excessive speed. His fluency-shaping program is designed to retrain stutterers in the making of speech sounds.

The program is intensive, requiring four to seven hours of drill each day. But it quickly gets results—the average patient completes the course in two or three weeks.

Recently, Webster has enlisted the aid of a computer as a co-therapist. The device is programmed to recognize normal sound formations. As the patient speaks into a microphone, the computer compares his sounds to the reference sounds in its memory bank. When the patient achieves a good approximation, a printout tells him so—it rewards success with a simple "OK," and greets failure with silence.

The computer has several advantages over a human therapist. It is more consistent than a human listener in making decisions about minute variations in sound; and because he is not distracted by the presence of another person, the patient can often progress more rapidly when drilled by the computer.

Eventually Webster hopes to program the computer to diagnose speech deficiencies in individuals and print out prescriptions based on the sounds that seem to need the most practice. More intriguing is the possibility of establishing "dial-a-therapy" networks in which stutterers could correct speech patterns by telephone contact with a computer miles from home.

SOURCE   Abstracted from "New Help For Stuttering," *Newsweek*, June 5, 1972, p. 59.

the novice programmer and complex, sophisticated features for the experienced programmer.

APL handles most of the routine housekeeping tasks for the programmer. Data input and output is easily handled with no need for detailed field descriptions, etc. The programmer can assign names to values stored, perform calculations, store arrays of numbers, names, lists, etc., and manipulate data.

APL has a wide variety of sophisticated mathematical and processing tools available for the programmer. These are called out by striking the appropriate symbol on the terminal keyboard.

A feature of APL is its line-by-line execution. Each instruction is executed immediately and the results printed out on the next line. Unacceptable statements are detected immediately. There are no format restrictions on data input and output. The processor accepts decimal numbers, whole numbers, exponent values, and other data as they come in from the terminals. Results are printed out with the required decimal points and exponents supplied by the processor.

A very important advantage of APL is the convenience and efficiency it offers the user. An on-line, real-time terminal is as easy to use as an adding machine. No formal programming is required on some problems, and no time lost on visits to the data center.

LIMITATIONS.   APL programs can only be run on larger computers, since the processors require a sizable core storage capacity. APL processors use greater core storage than compilers for FORTRAN. APL programs can only be entered via special terminals.

TERMINALS.   An APL terminal and keyboard are shown in Figure 18.7. This terminal is connected to the computer through a unit called a phone coupler. The phone coupler converts the keystrokes to audible sounds, which are transmitted over the telephone line to the APL processor. To use the APL terminal, the user dials the telephone number of the computer and places the phone handset in the coupler. This connects the terminal to the computer

'...SCALPEL, FORCEPS, PROGRAMMING MANUAL'

FIGURE 18.7 APL KEYBOARD AND TERMINAL

and allows the user to enter data, process information, and receive results on the terminal.

GENERAL CHARACTERISTICS. APL is a free-form language with very little formal structure. It is composed of symbols called operators, assigned names, and reserved words. Figure 18.8 is a sample APL program showing its general form.

Much of the power of APL is due to its operators. These 50 or more operators are code symbols such as ρ, ι, Γ, $\lozenge$, and $\spadesuit$. With them, the programmer can make many arithmetic or logical comparisons, perform functions, find square roots, maximum or minimum values, replace quantities, branch transfer control, etc.

The APL language can process data in an execution or a definition mode. In the execution mode, the APL language is much like a desk calculator. Data is entered, operations specified, and results are available instantly.

FIGURE 18.8   APL SAMPLE PROGRAM

```
        ∇ STUCOH
[1]     H←G←0
[2]     D←0
[3]     C←0
[4]     'ENTER NUMBER OF STUDENTS IN CLASS'
[5]     A←□
[6]     'ENTER NUMBER OF HOURS PER WEEK CLASS MEETS'
[7]     B←□
[8]     'ENTER NUMBER OF OFFICE HOURS PER WEEK'
[9]     C←□
[10]    D←A×B
[11]    E←C+B
[12]    'YOUR STUDENT CONTACT HOURS ARE ';D
[13]    G←G+D
[14]    'YOUR ASSIGNED HOURS ARE ';E
[15]    H←H+E
[16]    'DO YOU WANT TO ENTER ANOTHER WORKLOAD? 0=NO, 1 = YES'
[17]    F←□
[18]    →2×⍳F=1
[19]    'THE FACULTY CONTACT HOURS ARE ';G
[20]    'THE FACULTY ASSIGNED HOURS ARE ';H
        ∇

        STUCOH
ENTER NUMBER OF STUDENTS IN CLASS
□:
        50
ENTER NUMBER OF HOURS PER WEEK CLASS MEETS
□:
        3
ENTER NUMBER OF OFFICE HOURS PER WEEK
□:
        4
YOUR STUDENT CONTACT HOURS ARE 150
YOUR ASSIGNED HOURS ARE 7
DO YOU WANT TO ENTER ANOTHER WORKLOAD? 0=NO, 1 = YES
□:
        1
ENTER NUMBER OF STUDENTS IN CLASS
□:
        75
ENTER NUMBER OF HOURS PER WEEK CLASS MEETS
□:
        5
ENTER NUMBER OF OFFICE HOURS PER WEEK
□:
        5
YOUR STUDENT CONTACT HOURS ARE 375
YOUR ASSIGNED HOURS ARE 10
DO YOU WANT TO ENTER ANOTHER WORKLOAD? 0=NO, 1 = YES
□:
        0
THE FACULTY CONTACT HOURS ARE 525
THE FACULTY ASSIGNED HOURS ARE 17
        ∇STUCOH[□]∇
```

In a definition mode, a list of instructions is entered. Compilation and execution does not occur until after the list is entered and the programmer instructs the computer to begin.

SPECIAL FEATURES

Editing. Like most interactive languages, APL has an editing feature to permit corrections and revisions of programming statements and data to be made from the terminal. As the APL programmer enters statements, they are stored in the CPU's memory. They can be changed or replaced by typing in the number of the line and the new information. The computer will automatically make the replacement of the corrected data. This feature permits file updating, selective replacement of values, corrections, etc.

For example, the programmer assigns a value of 50 to the letter A this way:

$$A \leftarrow 50$$

If he types the letter A on the keyboard, the computer will respond with

$$50$$

Later, if he types in A←100, the computer will make the substitution and A will now equal 100 in the computer's memory.

Arrays. An important capability of APL is its ability to handle and process groups of numbers, called arrays. For example, a string of numbers can be typed on the terminal and assigned a name.

$$B \leftarrow 2 \ 4 \ 6 \ 8$$

If the programmer later types the letter B, the computer will respond by printing out:

$$2 \ 4 \ 6 \ 8$$

If the programmer types in the following statement:

$$2 \times B$$

The computer will multiply each item in the array by 2 and print out the results as follows:

$$4 \ 8 \ 12 \ 16$$

BASIC (Beginners All-Purpose Symbolic Instruction Code)

The BASIC language, developed at Dartmouth College, New Hampshire, closely resembles FORTRAN. It is designed for easy data input and output and offers editing features.

On most computer systems, a BASIC program is compiled and executed after the entire program has been input.

ADVANTAGES.   BASIC is a simple terminal language, which does not require detailed format descriptions of data input and output. BASIC programming does not require a special terminal or keyboard. Programming is done from a remote terminal, such as that shown in Figure 18.9, connected via ordinary telephone lines to the computer. The terminal is equipped with a paper tape reader and punch, and both program and data can be input and output on tape. The use of low-cost Teletype terminals brings the power of the computer to many medium and small firms who otherwise could not afford this service. They buy time from a large computer center or time-sharing firm and process their problems, coded in BASIC, from the Teletype terminal located in their office.

LIMITATIONS.   Because it is a terminal language, BASIC is inefficient for handling large quantities of input and output data. All data is entered via tape or keyboard and printed out on the Teletype terminal. This is relatively slow and not suited to processing of large files of data. However, large amounts of data may be stored on disk packs at the data center and accessed from the terminal.

FIGURE 18.9   BASIC TERMINAL

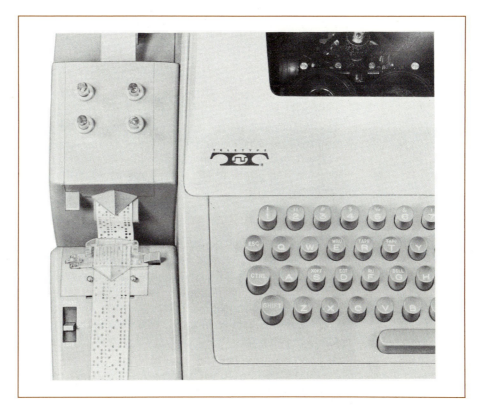

GENERAL CHARACTERISTICS. BASIC bears a strong resemblance to FORTRAN and possesses much of its power. It is less restrictive in its demands on the programmer, however. A set of instructions, similar to a stand-alone FORTRAN program, is coded and entered line by line from the terminal. The data is also entered from the keyboard. The programmer initiates processing by typing in the word RUN. The results are fed back to the teletype terminal from the computer as soon as execution is completed. Figure 18.10 shows a sample BASIC program.

The BASIC character set consists of the alphabet, numbers, and a group of special characters.

Each statement in the BASIC language is numbered and typed on a separate line. Program statements are assembled from names, operators, or data placed in storage. A group of reserved words, such as READ, PRINT, GO TO, IF, etc., causes the computer to perform different tasks.

Revisions or changes in a BASIC program are easily made. The programmer types in the statement number of the line to be corrected and then the revised data. The compiler will substitute the new line in the proper position. New data also can be inserted in the program listing by this method.

ATS (Administrative Terminal System)

ATS is an interactive language designed for preparing reports, bulletins, manuscripts, and other text documents. It is particularly valuable when extensive text editing is required. Text editing, involving revisions, corrections, alterations and changes in copy, usually requires a great deal of retyping. Each time a revised draft is prepared, most or all of the document must be retyped.

When ATS is used, this procedure is simplified. The copy is typed in only once and the computer remembers the keystrokes. Revisions, corrections, changes, and alterations are typed in and these keystrokes saved. Lines, words, phrases, or sentences can be substituted or rearranged. The computer inserts all revisions into the stored text, and, at the programmer's request, prints out an updated draft. The programmer can instruct the computer to print out the same copy using a different format, line width, or page depth.

ADVANTAGES. ATS is an efficient method of preparing textual material that must be extensively edited. It saves retyping and allows for reformatting. The ATS compiler will center lines, provide automatic page numbering, or insert heads or footings. The ATS system can store data typed in from a remote keyboard in one format, and print it out in another. Both line width and page depth can be changed. In addition, lines can be printed out right justified (right margins evenly aligned). ATS requires learning only a few basic instructions and commands.

LIMITATIONS. ATS is a specialized language with a limited application: text editing. The language does not provide branching, looping, or very extensive mathematical manipulation.

FIGURE 18.10   BASIC SAMPLE PROGRAM

```
10 REM CALCULATE STUDENT CONTACT HOURS
20 LET D = 0
25 LET C = 0
30 PRINT "ENTER NUMBER OF STUDENTS IN CLASS"
40 INPUT A
50 PRINT "ENTER HOURS PER WEEK CLASS MEETS"
60 INPUT B
70 PRINT "ENTER NUMBER OF OFFICE HOURS PER WEEK"
80 INPUT C
90 LET D = A*B
100 LET E = C+B
110 PRINT "YOUR STUDENT CONTACT HOURS ARE ";D
115 LET G = G+D
120 PRINT "YOUR ASSIGNED HOURS ARE ";E
125 LET H = H+E
130 PRINT "DO YOU WANT TO ENTER ANOTHER WORKLOAD? 0=NO,1=YES"
140 INPUT F
150 IF F = 1 THEN 20
160 PRINT "THE FACULTY CONTACT HOURS ARE ";G
170 PRINT "THE FACULTY ASSIGNED HOURS ARE ";H
180 END


RUN

ENTER NUMBER OF STUDENTS IN CLASS
?50
ENTER HOURS PER WEEK CLASS MEETS
?3
ENTER NUMBER OF OFFICE HOURS PER WEEK
?4
YOUR STUDENT CONTACT HOURS ARE   150
YOUR ASSIGNED HOURS ARE   7
DO YOU WANT TO ENTER ANOTHER WORKLOAD? 0=NO,1=YES
?1
ENTER NUMBER OF STUDENTS IN CLASS
?45
ENTER HOURS PER WEEK CLASS MEETS
?3
ENTER NUMBER OF OFFICE HOURS PER WEEK
?5
YOUR STUDENT CONTACT HOURS ARE   135
YOUR ASSIGNED HOURS ARE   8
DO YOU WANT TO ENTER ANOTHER WORKLOAD? 0=NO,1=YES
?1
ENTER NUMBER OF STUDENTS IN CLASS
?70
ENTER HOURS PER WEEK CLASS MEETS
?3
ENTER NUMBER OF OFFICE HOURS PER WEEK
?6
YOUR STUDENT CONTACT HOURS ARE   210
YOUR ASSIGNED HOURS ARE   9
DO YOU WANT TO ENTER ANOTHER WORKLOAD? 0=NO,1=YES
?0
THE FACULTY CONTACT HOURS ARE   495
THE FACULTY ASSIGNED HOURS ARE   24
```

GENERAL CHARACTERISTICS. Information to be processed in the ATS language is typed in from a terminal keyboard without regard to line width or spacing.

FIGURE 18.11(A)   MARKED-UP DRAFT OF TEXT STORED IN ATS PROCESSOR

Simplicity of operation is *the* a keystone of the ATS/360 System. It does not require the user to undergo extensive training. ~~Neither does it require a special machine operator.~~ After a brief orientation, anyone who can type can use the system.

One reason for this short learning *period* is that ~~the user~~ *you* uses a familiar typewriter keyboard to give information and instructions to the computer. In fact, when you are not using the typewriter as a terminal, you can put it to work to produce fine quality business correspondence. &Another reason the system is easy to learn is that ATS/360 operating procedures are *straight forward* ~~uncomplicated.~~ They were designed with the secretary in mind, and you will find them very easy. For example, to correct an error, you simply backspace and retype.

Everyone in your office ~~can really put the~~ power of the system to work.

Insert: ← THE ATS SYSTEM *makes your job easier!*

insert above Except for a key which alerts the computer, this keyboard is the same as a SELECTRIC typewriter.

The text is entered as a stream of characters. Errors are corrected by backspacing and striking over. This corrects the character in the computer's memory. Words, phrases, or sentences may be replaced, rearranged, or deleted. New copy can be added as required.

After all text editing is completed, the user tells the computer the format to use in printing out the draft. The finished draft can contain page headings, footings, page numbers, etc., and can be right justified. It will be evenly spaced and neatly typed.

Figure 18.11(A) illustrates a piece of copy that has been keyboarded and stored in the ATS processor. It has been marked with corrections and alterations, which are to be made in the final draft. Figure 18.11(B) illustrates the reformatted print out as it appears at the ATS terminal, with all changes and alterations made.

Table 18.3 provides a comparison of all the programming languages discussed thus far.

FIGURE 18.11(B)   FINAL DRAFT PRINTED OUT BY ATS PROCESSOR

```
     Simplicity of operation is the keystone of the
ATS/360 System.  It does not require the user to
undergo extensive training.  After a brief orientation,
anyone who can type can use the system.

     One reason for this short learning period is
that you use a familiar typewriter keyboard to give
information and instructions to the computer.  Except
for a key which alerts the computer, this keyboard
is the same as a SELECTRIC typewriter.  In fact, when
you are not using the typewriter as a terminal, you
can put it to work to produce fine quality business
correspondence.

     Another reason the system is easy to learn is
that ATS/360 operating procedures are straightforward.
They were designed with the secretary in mind, and you
will find them very easy.  For example, to correct
an error, you simply backspace and retype.

     The ATS System makes your job easier!
```

TABLE 18.3 PROGRAMMING LANGUAGE COMPARISON

	COBOL	FORTRAN	RPG	ASSEMBLER	PL/I	APL	BASIC	ATS
Easy to learn	X		X				X	X
Programmer oriented		X			X	X	X	
Good math capabilities	X	X		X		X	X	
Good alpha-capabilities	X				X	X		X
Resembles English	X				X			X
Self-documenting	X				X			
Available on many machines	X	X	X	X				
Standardized	X	X						
Manufacturer controlled				X	X	X		X
Efficient on computers				X				
Large core capacity required	X				X	X		
Interactive capability					X	X	X	X
Default options					X			
Machine dependent			X	X				

KEY TERMS   Interactive languages   Processor
            Batch processing languages   APL
            PL/I   Execution mode
            Operators   Definition mode
            Identifiers   Default options
            RPG   Editing
            Assembler Language   BASIC
            Mnemonics   ATS
            Op code   Macro instruction
            Operand

EXERCISES   1. Define batch processing languages and give several examples.
            2. Define interactive languages and give several examples.
            3. What are the major advantages and limitations of PL/I?
            4. How does the PL/I program in Figure 18.2 differ from the FORTRAN
               program in Figure 17.3?
            5. For what kind of job is RPG best suited? What are its limitations?
            6. What are the advantages and limitations of Assembler Language
               programming? How does the Assembler Language program in Figure 18.6
               differ from the PL/I program in Figure 18.2?
            7. What are the major advantages and limitations of APL?
            8. What is the difference between the execution mode and the definition
               mode in APL?
            9. What are operators in APL and how are they used?
           10. Why is BASIC a widely used terminal language? What kind of terminal is
               usually used for the language?
           11. What is meant by text editing? How does ATS facilitate it?
           12. If there is a computer terminal at your school, determine what kind it is
               and what languages can be programmed on it.
           13. If an APL or BASIC terminal is available, enter the program from either
               Figure 18.8 or Figure 18.10, and execute it.

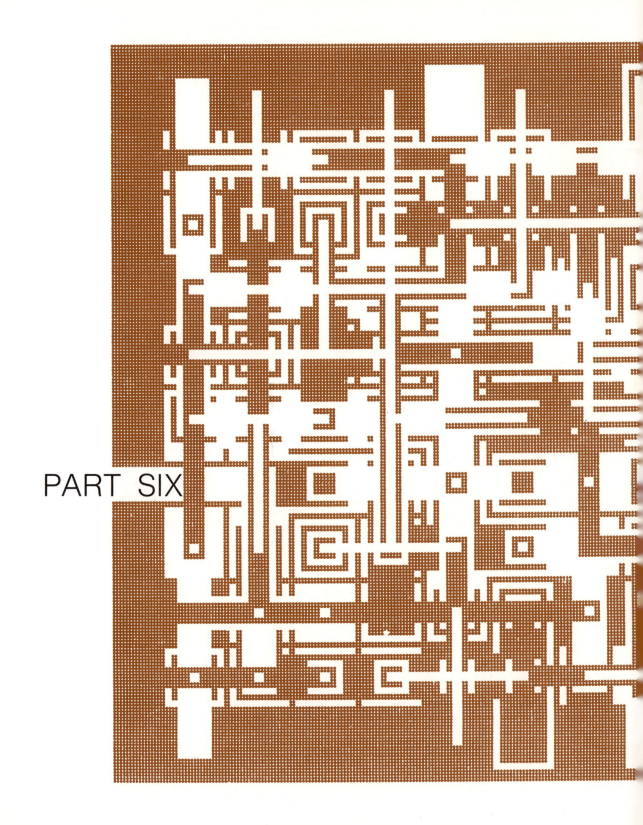

PART SIX

BUSINESS SYSTEMS

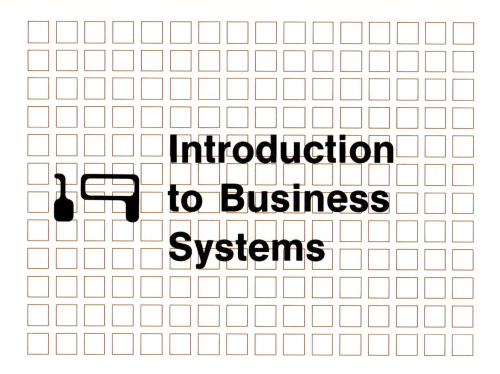

Introduction to Business Systems

Decision making is a fundamental process and function of a business enterprise. The life and success of the modern firm depends on the right decision, quickly arrived at. Vital to the decision-making process is the availability of complete, accurate, relevant data. As our society becomes more complex, so do the factors affecting the decision-making process. The traditional methods of solving problems are often inadequate today. They are being replaced by techniques that rely on information processing, electronic data processing, and the science of business systems analysis.

WHAT ARE BUSINESS SYSTEMS?

Systems are collections of objects, procedures, or techniques that function as an organized whole. They are groups of men, machines, or methods necessary to accomplish specific functions. Business systems are the organizational structures within a firm that enable it to achieve its goals. Business systems include policies, methods, personnel, data processing software and hardware, and communications procedures.

Systems are composed of subsystems. These smaller units have individual functions, but act in accord with the goals of the larger system. The advantage of the system is that the total is greater than the sum of the parts. Figure 19.1 shows a simplified business system of a firm. Administration in a

FIGURE 19.1   SIMPLIFIED BUSINESS SYSTEM

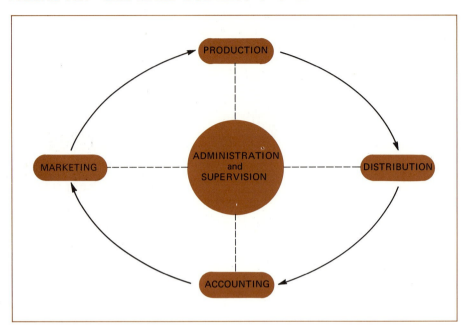

business system usually consists of a Board of Directors and management. An essential function of the Board of Directors is to select long- and short-range goals or objectives. These goals may be to reach a given dollar volume in sales, realize a given return on investment, earn a specific percentage of profit, or build a new plant.

The establishment of objectives requires a careful analysis of business conditions, the market, customer needs, buying patterns, production capacity, staff, finances, etc. The accurate assessment of each of these elements requires the acquisition, processing, and reporting of data in the form most useful to management.

Once the Board of Directors has selected certain objectives, it is management's job to direct the subsystems of the firm toward these goals. To effectively measure the amount and direction of progress, even more data is needed. Information, such as numbers of hours worked, products shipped, cash flow, receivables due, percentage of plant utilized, and money owed, must be analyzed.

Data in Business Systems   Since management needs information from all parts of the firm, one of the major assets of a firm can be its facilities for recording, manipulating, and reporting data.

The value of business data is relative. Some data is important only at certain times and places in the business cycle. For example, information about an account's purchasing patterns may be needed when a firm is bidding for business. After the contract has been signed or lost, such information may have little value.

To be of greatest value to a firm, data should be

1 Available when it is needed
2 Available where it is needed
3 At the right level of accuracy
4 The kind and quality necessary
5 Gathered, processed, and reported at a reasonable cost

Need for Business Systems

Large business firms cannot afford to solve clerical or data flow problems in an unorganized, unsystematic way. Processing costs are high; mistakes are expensive; time is limited.

A planned and organized strategy for processing paperwork and clerical matters is needed by firms to

1 Gain maximum cost savings in processing and handling data
2 Gain maximum time savings in outputting results
3 Establish an orderly procedure for growth
4 Develop a uniform method of operation and thus avoid foreseeable problems by establishing policies
5 Avoid costly errors
6 Improve the quality of business decisions
7 Improve organization responsiveness to customers' needs
8 Improve allocation of physical resources
9 Produce the best product at the lowest cost
10 Eliminate duplication of effort

Evolution of Business Systems

Around 1900, when firms were small and material and labor costs were low, data processing needs were minimal. Few firms used systematic business methods to plan their activities and carry out their goals. When a problem came up, it was solved on the spot, resulting in a patchwork of policies and procedures.

The solution chosen was often the easiest one to implement. Careful analysis of problems and attention to strategy were ignored in favor of finding easy answers, quickly. This approach is sometimes called "brush fire" problem solving. Even today some firms use these measures.

As firms grew and the capital investment and costs of labor and materials increased, management turned to more scientific, orderly, and structured means of solving problems. At first, one or two employees were assigned the task of applying scientific methods to solving business problems. They soon became known as business systems engineers or business systems analysts.

Eventually, many firms established a separate unit called the business systems department. This department was responsible for applying scientific methods to clerical and data flow problems in a company.

SCOPE OF MODERN BUSINESS SYSTEMS DEPARTMENTS

Since World War II, the job of the business systems department has grown in importance. The team of business systems engineers, analysts, and data processing specialists has become an indispensable part of many business firms. Figure 19.2 illustrates the organization of an average systems department. The members of the department are brought into many areas and departments of the firm in the performance of their work. They make critical studies and recommendations affecting many operations, procedures, and methods throughout the firm.

Responsibilities of the Business Systems Department

The business systems department is responsible for

❶ Systems planning and design
❷ Systems implementation
❸ Office layout
❹ Establishment of procedures and policies
❺ Design of forms
❻ Work measurement
❼ Information retrieval and file design
❽ Selection of personnel
❾ Software preparation
❿ Communications
⓫ Hardware selection

SYSTEM PLANNING AND DESIGN.   A major responsibility of the business systems department is the planning and design of new systems to facilitate the flow of data. The business systems analyst uses scientific methods and techniques to review existing procedures. He proposes changes and improvements to overcome weaknesses in existing systems.

In studying a system, the analyst reviews its forms, procedures, policies, and methods. He analyzes the personnel, machines, space requirements, and office layout to determine whether a better system can be developed.

He frequently asks six questions in investigating each element in his study:

❶ Why is it done?
❷ Who does it?
❸ When is it done?
❹ Where is it done?
❺ What is done?
❻ How is it done?

FIGURE 19.2   BUSINESS SYSTEMS DEPARTMENT
ORGANIZATION

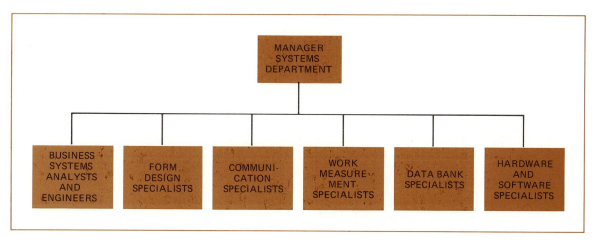

The business systems analyst conducts many types of surveys to evaluate the system under consideration. The feasibility study (discussed in Chapter 20), for example, is used to determine whether a new system will be practical from an economic standpoint. Data flow and word processing studies point out bottlenecks, weaknesses, or problem areas. Time and motion studies further define problems and even indicate solutions.

SYSTEM IMPLEMENTATION.   Once a new system has been designed, the business systems department must implement it properly. System implementation requires careful planning to see that the transition is made without waste, errors, or excessive costs. Employee morale must be considered. The business systems analyst must solicit the cooperation of both employees and management. Personnel must be shown the advantages of the new system and how it will affect each individual.

A new system may be implemented in several ways. It can begin ''all at once,'' or ''step by step.'' Sometimes a new system is implemented in a parallel manner. The new system is put into operation alongside the old. When the new system is running smoothly, the old system is dropped. The business systems analyst must observe the new system in operation and see that there is no backsliding into the old, inefficient method.

Implementation sometimes requires designing new forms, writing computer programs, writing procedure, policy, and instruction manuals, acquiring new equipment, rearranging offices, etc.

OFFICE LAYOUT.   Another major responsibility of the business systems department is office layout. The analyst must recommend the most efficient office layout to facilitate data flow. (See Figure 19.3.) He is concerned with

FIGURE 19.3   OFFICE LAYOUT

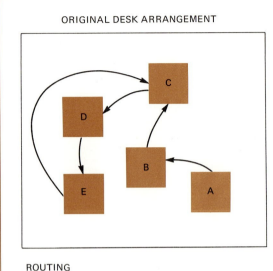

ORIGINAL DESK ARRANGEMENT

CHANGES RECOMMENDED BY ANALYST

ROUTING
SCHEDULE: A→B→C→D→E→C

ROUTING
SCHEDULE: A→B→C→D→E→C

shortening processing time and reducing labor and equipment costs. The analyst may also be responsible for the purchase of any new office equipment required by a system. He must then arrange for the efficient use of equipment.

ESTABLISHMENT OF PROCEDURES AND POLICIES.   A new system must be documented to help employees learn how to use it efficiently. The business systems analyst often uses manuals for this purpose. These manuals are a source of uniform statements on methods and policies. They specify which forms to use, when to use them, how to handle exceptions, and where forms are to be routed.

    Well-written policy manuals help both the employee and the organization. They not only provide the employee with a clear statement of company policy and methods but also assure that each branch or division in the company will acquire, report, and process data in the most efficient way.

DESIGN OF FORMS.   Data forms are essential to almost all business systems. In some cases, hundreds of different forms are used within a firm. The success of a new system often depends on whether adequate forms and source documents have been developed.

    The business systems analyst must specify contents, layout, distribution, and routing of the forms. He is also responsible for designing source documents and reports.

Forms design includes analysis of the physical characteristics of the form as well as its content. Consideration must be given to size, paper, type size, number of carbons, printing process, and cost. The analyst must also determine the quantity to be ordered, the system of inventory to be used, and the methods of packing and dispensing the forms. He must periodically review forms to see that they are adequate, necessary, and up to date.

WORK MEASUREMENT. To test the effectiveness of a new system, or to measure the productivity of an existing system, a method of measuring work must be found. The business systems analyst develops the tools that can assess the output of both personnel and equipment. Some tools used in work measurement are

1. Time Study. The time study consists of observing and timing employees as they perform their duties.

2. Work Sampling. In work sampling, a measure is made of the kinds and types of calculations performed, the number and types of forms handled, etc. in order to approximate the content of each job.

Work measurement enables the analyst to compare the output of employees before and after implementing a new system. It allows him to measure the quantity as well as the quality of clerical work.

INFORMATION RETRIEVAL AND FILE DESIGN. The job of the analyst also includes the design of data files for information storage and retrieval systems. Modern business depends heavily upon data files to store records of transactions in the firm. The analyst should design files that are accurate, complete, compact, and easily corrected and updated.

SELECTION OF PERSONNEL. The business systems analyst may also write job descriptions and orders. Job descriptions outline the duties and functions of each job. Job orders specify the number of employees needed for each job classification. A sample job description and order is shown in Figure 19.4.

In writing a job description, the analyst must indicate the level of skill and training required in performing the job. This information then guides the personnel department in hiring new employees.

The duties of the business systems analyst may include planning programs for job orientation, or in-service training. He may have to arrange classroom training or instruction from vendors and prepare, revise, and order training manuals, teaching aids, slide films and other media, necessary to implement new systems.

SOFTWARE PREPARATION. If a system uses a computer or involves electronic data processing, programs must be written, debugged, tested, and maintained. Often, the analyst must specify the function and purpose of a proposed program, flowchart the preferred algorithm, and indicate the input/output requirements. These specifications are then given to a programmer or other systems analyst who actually writes the program. When

FIGURE 19.4   JOB DESCRIPTION AND ORDER

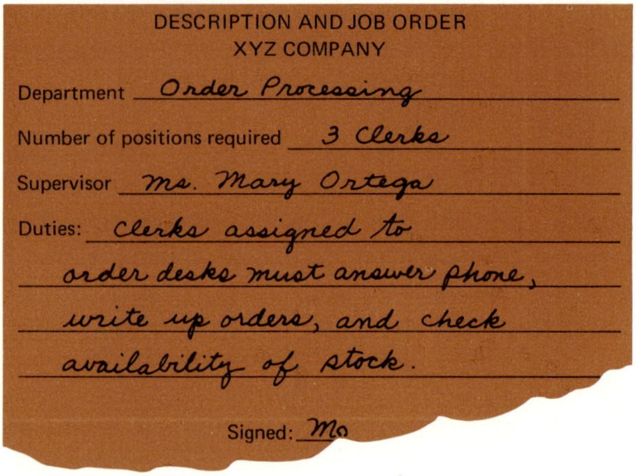

DESCRIPTION AND JOB ORDER
XYZ COMPANY

Department *Order Processing*

Number of positions required *3 Clerks*

Supervisor *Ms. Mary Ortega*

Duties: *Clerks assigned to order desks must answer phone, write up orders, and check availability of stock.*

Signed: *Mo*

the program is running satisfactorily, documentation must be prepared explaining the program logic, how data must be input, program options, etc.

COMMUNICATIONS.   The business systems analyst must consider the communications requirements of a new or existing system. If computer terminals are needed, he determines the type, number, and location. He provides instructions so that personnel may use them properly and effectively.

Some firms have access to computers located in different parts of the country and tied into a network by telephone lines (called a tie line service). It is the job of the systems analyst to plan this communications network. He must study communications needs, data flow, files, etc., and order the most efficient phone service.

HARDWARE SELECTION.   Specifying the type and make of computer and the peripheral equipment needed in the system is also a duty of the business systems analyst. He must review available equipment and judge the cost and capabilities of new equipment.

PROBLEM-SOLVING TECHNIQUES

The business systems department is actively involved in solving company data processing problems. As new tools and techniques have come into use, the methods of solving data flow problems have changed.

Before 1900 techniques such as the guess, the hunch, chance, intuition, habit, routine, or rule of thumb were used to solve clerical and data flow problems. Although some of these methods are still used, they are inaccurate and result in inconsistent or contradictory policies. Modern management personnel should not and cannot rely on these ineffectual methods.

The Scientific Method

About 1900 John Dewey described and documented a series of steps for solving scientific problems. Following these steps greatly increased the chances of a particular solution being precise, accurate, and dependable. This technique, called the scientific method, forms the basis of most logic followed in modern business systems analysis.

The scientific method demands a rigorous, logical approach or strategy. It involves a careful definition of the problem, a thorough analysis of alternatives, an orderly implementation of the best alternative, and, finally, a critical evaluation of outcomes. The figure on the left lists the steps taken in the scientific method.

The scientific method is characterized by

1. RECOGNIZE AND DIAGNOSE THE PROBLEM

2. DEFINE THE PROBLEM

3. ANALYZE AND PLAN POSSIBLE SOLUTIONS

4. SELECT AND IMPLEMENT A SOLUTION

5. EVALUATE THE SYSTEM

1. Rigorous attention to detail
2. Development and application of precise measuring tools
3. Consideration of alternatives
4. Use of statistical methods
5. Structured methods of implementation
6. Use of feedback, that is, use of system output to control system input

The scientific method leads not to the fastest, easiest solution, but to the most effective solution, indicated by measuring the output.

1. RECOGNITION AND DIAGNOSIS OF THE PROBLEM. Before a problem can be solved, it must be recognized. Problems may be brought to the attention of management by employees, customers, or outside consultants, or by systematic observation by management. Then the nature of the problem must be diagnosed. The systems analyst must determine and clearly state the details of the situation. The problem may be, for example, scheduling a new procedure, determining the most efficient way to prepare monthly statements, finding out why a procedure produces inaccurate or inadequate output, or discovering why the cost of a product is higher than projections indicated.

2. DEFINE THE PROBLEM. The second step in the scientific method is the definition of the problem in measurable terms. In this phase, the business systems engineer states the problem in a quantitative way. If output is low, by how much? If costs are too high, by how much? If data is inadequate, in what way? Reducing the problem to elements that can be measured creates a basis for comparing the output.

3. SYSTEM PLANNING AND ANALYSIS. The third phase of the activity involves investigating plans to solve the problem. Here the business systems analyst studies different approaches. What will happen if another system is tried? How many dollars will be saved? In what ways will data be more accurate, more prompt, or more economical to prepare? The business

THE IRS COMPUTER AND
THE ONE-PENNY BILL

When Mr. and Mrs. Charles F. Kinney paid their $34.61 income tax, they never expected a reply from the Internal Revenue Service—and they certainly never expected a letter politely requesting that they pay one cent more in taxes.

The Kinneys never thought of not paying their surprise one-cent bill—even though they were spending at least eight cents to mail the IRS a penny. So they paid the bill—in cash.

A spokesman for IRS admitted that his organization did the dunning, "It was a computerized error," he said, "and in this computerized age, there's not much we can do. But someone had to send the bill; and that person should have caught the error. We're sorry it happened."

The IRS spokesman was unable to estimate how much it cost to collect that penny. But it is clear that the IRS lost money on the operation. An expert in the computer field estimated that the IRS paid up to 24 cents, with computer time, operator pay, material cost, and mailing cost, to send the one-cent bill.

And because the Kinneys paid that one cent in cash, the IRS was required to go to the further expense of sending them a receipt. No one would estimate the cost of that.

SOURCE Abstracted from "IRS Blushes When Computer Rushes to Get Kinney's Penny," by Kristin Earl Drake, *Los Angeles Times,* July 21, 1972, Part 3, p. 15.

systems engineer uses an *if–then* strategy. *If* this method is used, *then* this will result. *If* that strategy is used, *then* that will result. All practical alternatives are considered and analyzed.

4. SELECTION AND IMPLEMENTATION.   In this step, the business systems engineer decides which plan provides the most logical, economical, and sound solution and proposes its implementation to management. Management then decides whether to accept the plan.

In the implementation stage, equipment is studied and purchased, employees are reassigned or new ones hired, policies and practices are defined in detail, manuals are written, forms are designed and printed, and programs are flowcharted and written.

5. EVALUATION.   The final step in the problem-solving process is the measurement of the outcomes of the new system. Were the expected results obtained? Did costs go down? by how much? Is data more accurate? in what way? If the benefits did not materialize, why not? How can the system be improved?

The output of the new procedure is evaluated. The business systems analyst modifies the original solution or selects another alternative for implementation. It is implemented and the output is evaluated again. This procedure is followed until the most efficient arrangement of staff, equipment, office layout, and data processing methods is found.

One of the most significant advances in management practices has been the coupling of the scientific method to the power of the computer. The computer's ability to manipulate data at high speed with a high level of accuracy enables the business systems analyst to prepare many of the reports, projections, schedules, and simulations necessary to management decision making.

Simulation and Modeling

An important systems analysis procedure is the modeling and simulation technique made possible by the computer. Simulation is the use of a computer to duplicate a system and then study what would happen if a certain situation occurred. With simulation different conditions, variations, and alternatives can be tested accurately without the expense and problems that would be encountered in actual marketing or production situations. (See Figure 19.5.)

BUILDING THE MODEL. The first step in simulation is to develop a model. The model is a representation of the situation being tested. Relevant data is gathered, and relationships and cause and effect conditions in the firm are studied by reviewing records and testing. These relationships are restated in quantitative terms to create the model.

"O.K., SHE'S CHECKING OUT FINE."

© Datamation®

FIGURE 19.5   SIMULATION

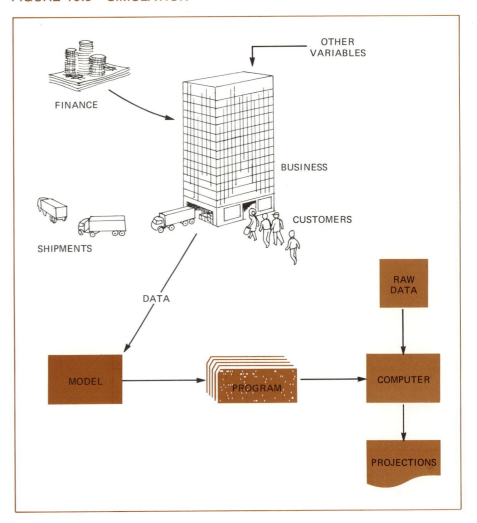

For instance, here is the relationship between a retail store's soda pop sales and the temperature.

TEMPERATURE	CASES SOLD
under 60°	1
60°	2
70°	4
80°	8
90°	12
100°	20
over 100°	14

With this information, the store management can make sales predictions and plan advertising and displays, size of orders to suppliers, how much stock to keep on hand, etc.

In effect, we have a mathematical model of a real situation. In this example, however, only two variables are involved. Usually models are complex and include many interdependent relationships and variables. Some even include such random occurrences as water supply or power failures.

Models can be developed of entire firms, such as trucking lines, hospitals, manufacturing companies, retailers, a single department within a company, or even of a product or service. The data that makes up the model is programmed and prepared for computer input via punched cards, tape, etc.

TESTING THE MODEL.   After the model has been set up, it is tested with known data. The test data is punched into cards, and the program and data are processed. The results of the test simulation are studied to determine the accuracy of the mathematical model. If the model is correctly developed, the predictions generated will represent how costs or conditions actually behaved. If the model does not deliver predictable results, it is modified or abandoned and a new model begun.

RUNNING THE MODEL.   The accurate model is now ready to simulate what would happen if some variables were changed. What would happen if prices were increased? Or another production plant were opened? What would happen if the supply of a certain ingredient were cut off? These data are restated as quantitative values, prepared as input, and fed to the computer with the programmed model. The output should be an accurate prediction of the conditions that will result. The figure on the left summarizes the steps involved in simulation.

ADVANTAGES.   Simulation permits many trial runs to be made with varying conditions. It is less costly to overload a model of a frozen food plant to learn where the system will break down, than to actually overload a real plant.

Errors in judgment made with actual customer's goods or services could be disastrous. But errors in judgment in a simulation cause no damage and often point up areas requiring further investigation. However, the results of the model are no better than the quality of the data entered. People tend to assume that the computer output is by its nature always accurate and objective. In reality, output reflects only the nature of the input data and the accuracy of the model.

Linear Programming (LP)   Linear programming is another quantitative decision-making tool made possible by the computer. Linear programming was developed during the Second World War to find the fastest, most efficient combination of men and machines to produce war materiel.

LP is a mathematical model program that will test a combination of elements and determine the most economical or best mix. (See Figure 19.6.)

1. CONSTRUCT MODEL

2. TEST MODEL

3. REVISE MODEL

4. RUN MODEL

5. OUTPUT

FIGURE 19.6   LINEAR PROGRAMMING

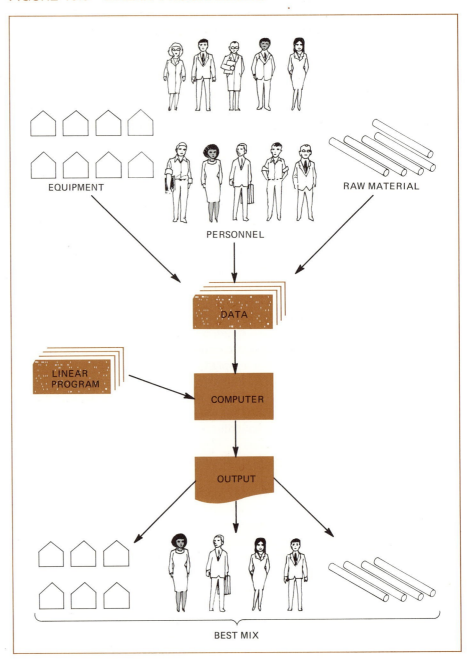

In LP, two statements are entered: one giving the optimum conditions desired and another listing the available resources. The program tests various combination of elements and determines the one that best meets the criteria given.

For example, suppose an airline wishes to find the minimum staff needed to move the maximum number of passengers. The problem is a complex one, because of the many employees involved in an airline's operations: pilots, baggage handlers, clerks, ground crews, stewardesses, managers, etc. Will hiring more pilots improve service? Will more clerks at the check-in desk help?

All the salaries and output of employees are stated as quantitative data and fed with a linear program to the computer. The computer will test all possible combinations of employees to determine the one that will allow the airline to handle a given passenger load at minimum salary expense. The results will be printed out as a list of the optimum or best mix of pilots, handlers, clerks, etc.

Performing the same tests in actual situations would be very expensive for the airline. And there would be no guarantee that the optimum arrangement would be discovered.

Program Evaluation and Review Technique (PERT)

PERT is a technique used to find the most efficient scheduling of time and resources when producing a complex product or project.

Firms involved in the manufacture of complicated equipment or the

FIGURE 19.7 SCHEDULE FROM A PERT PROGRAM

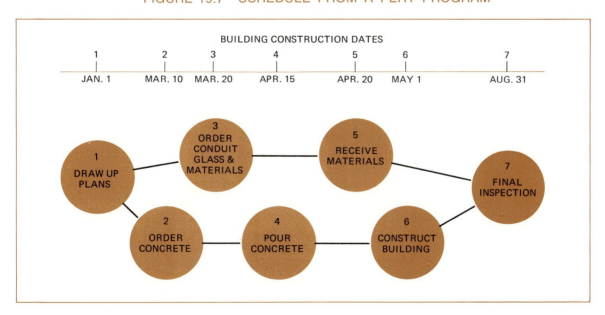

construction of large office buildings constantly face a difficult series of decisions. When should various equipment, supplies, and machines be placed on a job? What steps should be taken first? What elements are critical to the production of the goods and must be kept on schedule to avoid disrupting the other stages? How can the resources of the firm be best used to meet the costs and time deadlines of the project?

A PERT program will output a set of schedules answering these questions as shown in Figure 19.7. With this information, a manufacturer or builder can better control the time, costs, and deployment of his resources.

KEY TERMS

Business systems
Business systems analyst
Brush fire approach
Scientific method
Linear programming
PERT

Job description
Job order
Tie lines
Simulation
Model

EXERCISES

1. Define business systems.
2. Give four examples of business data with a particular time utility. Name four with a particular place value.
3. Contrast the early methods of solving business problems with those of the computer age.
4. Give several examples in which the guess, hunch, or chance method is used to solve business problems.
5. List the major steps in the scientific method of business systems analysis.
6. Select a simple data flow problem, such as inventory in a small retail store, and trace its solution through the five steps in the analytical approach.
7. What are the major responsibilities of the modern business systems department?
8. Select a data flow problem such as registration and enrollment in your college. Using the six questions often asked by business systems analysts, investigate an improved system.
9. Write a set of policies and procedures for handling returned merchandise in a small retail store.
10. Select a data flow task such as writing up a sales slip in a shoe store. Have several students go through the steps in filling out the forms. Perform a time study and work sampling on the operation.
11. Write a description of a job that involves the handling or processing of data, such as the job of sales clerk or shipping clerk.

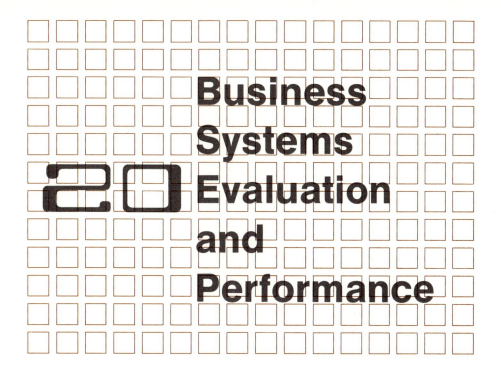

Business Systems 20 Evaluation and Performance

In the early days of data processing, the most costly piece of equipment was probably a typewriter, calculator, or desk-top accounting machine. Early systems designers could easily investigate available equipment by calling on a few vendors and checking prices. The decision to buy was often made right on the spot. If a mistake was made, it was easily remedied: the machine was exchanged for another or a new one was purchased. The dollar loss to the firm was nominal.

The decision to implement a modern business system is not a casual one. Alteration of the physical plant, installation of expensive air conditioning equipment, installation of special floors, and the purchase or lease of costly, highly specialized, complex equipment may be involved. The equipment may also require maintenance by trained equipment specialists. Errors in judgment in systems design can cost a firm hundreds of thousands of dollars.

Other factors such as the amount and complexity of data to be processed and the modern business firm's dependence upon it complicate the problem. A new system must be implemented without disrupting the flow of data. Should it be implemented all at once or step by step? Or should it operate alongside the old method for a period of time?

These decisions are difficult to make, and once made, often cannot be recalled. If the right decision is made, the firm benefits from an improved data flow. If the wrong decision is made, more money, time, and resources may be needed for correction.

417

In evaluating and comparing business systems, the business systems analyst weighs many factors. A principal consideration, of course, is cost—any new system must first be justified economically. The analyst must evaluate

❶ Customer and personnel relations

❷ Labor cost

❸ Human factors

❹ Dependability

❺ Precision level of results

❻ Capacity

❼ Maintenance costs

❽ Downtime for maintenance and servicing

❾ Training cost

❿ Equipment lease or purchase costs

⓫ Profit and return on investment

⓬ Intangible benefits

The feasibility study has become an important technique for evaluating the performance and success potential of a new system. Initially, feasibility studies were used to determine whether a firm should convert from manual or unit record systems to computerized methods. Today, the feasibility study is used to determine whether a computerized system should be updated or replaced. This study does not, however, guarantee results. At times, costly feasibility studies will provide few meaningful results.

WHAT IS THE FEASIBILITY STUDY?

A feasibility study is a careful assessment of the benefits expected from a new business system in terms of equipment, personnel, customers, and the physical plant. It aids management in determining whether implementing a new system is practical and economically feasible.

A feasibility study often moves through three phases

❶ Preliminary study

❷ Investigative study

❸ Final report and recommendations

If the preliminary study does not show promising results, no additional funds or efforts are expended on the next phase, and the approach is abandoned. If the results of the preliminary study are positive, the next phase is begun.

The preliminary and investigative studies build toward the final report and recommendations. Management will decide the fate of a new system on the basis of the recommendations in the final report.

Preliminary Study   The object of the preliminary study is to answer the question, "Does a new system appear to be sufficiently practical and economical to warrant further study and investigation?" The preliminary study looks at the fundamental needs of a business and reviews broad plans for change. It defines the problem, states ultimate objectives, and offers some tentative plans for solution.

During this phase, the business systems analyst discusses data processing needs with various department heads. He consults employees, managers, division heads, customers, vendors, and others involved in the data cycle.

SELECTION OF PERSONNEL RESPONSIBLE FOR STUDY.   An important part of the preliminary study is the selection of personnel who will conduct the feasibility study and a definition of their responsibilities. With the task force approach, management forms a committee of knowledgeable employees from various departments. After the committee has completed the study and made recommendations to management, it disbands.

A second approach is to appoint an ongoing committee of individuals from operating units, data processing and business systems departments, and managers. This committee is assigned the task of completing the preliminary study and the investigative phase and making recommendations to management. They have the continuing responsibility of implementing recommendations and monitoring the need for future modifications or changes.

Another approach is to place one individual in charge. He is given the title project director and the necessary funds and authority to carry out the feasibility study. He may have the additional responsibility of implementing changes and recommendations.

DEFINITION OF GOALS.   One of the first tasks of the preliminary study is to provide a clear definition of the goals of the new system. The outcomes desired from a new system are stated in measurable terms. How many dollars will be saved? What specific problems will be eliminated by the new system? How much faster, more accurate, and precise will the results be? What existing machines can be eliminated?

Often vendors are aware of other studies or have information of value. These companies can provide information which help the firm set goals and avoid pitfalls experienced by others.

The preliminary phase of the study is essential, since a new system cannot be built until its goals are defined. There would be no way of judging whether it was a success without a measure for comparison.

Investigative Study   The investigative phase of the feasibility study is the most detailed and complex. The elements involved in designing, implementing, and measuring the success of a new system are examined and evaluated.

FIGURE 20.1   INTERVIEWS DURING INVESTIGATIVE STUDY

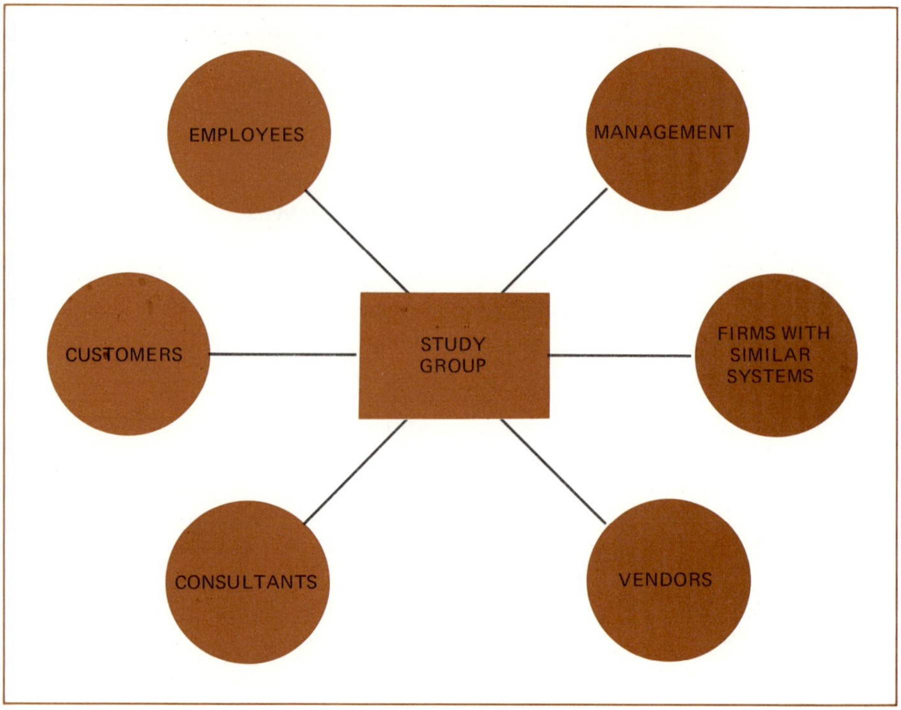

During this phase, a number of people, from both inside and outside the firm, are called upon for help and cooperation. (See Figure 20.1.) Outside consultants may be hired. Department and branch managers may be interviewed to determine their data needs. Specific pieces of equipment are evaluated in terms of their usefulness in solving the problem under consideration.

A great deal of time is spent working with vendors during the investigative phase. Equipment specifications are studied, machines tested, pilot jobs run on vendors' machines, etc.

As soon as specifications and requirements have been defined, proposals are written and sent to vendors for bids. The vendor reviews the proposal and prepares price quotations. Sometimes a quotation may outline the methods of solving a problem, suggest specific pieces of equipment, and offer advice for planning and designing a new installation. Many vendors employ a skilled staff of systems engineers, equipment planners, and layout people, whose services are available to clients.

STUDY TECHNIQUES.   A variety of techniques are used in the investigative study. The business systems analyst may observe a machine in operation or personnel at work. He may conduct work sampling studies to determine the kind of data being processed or time and motion studies on the methods used to gather data.

Logs, run books, histories, and records may be reviewed for an indication of the quantity of data processed by the firm. Special detailed records may be kept for a short period of time to learn more about the nature of a given data processing problem. For example, all the jobs run on a computer during a period of several months may be logged in a special record and studied in detail. This log will reveal the average length of run, language compiler most often used, use of disks, tapes, and core storage, as well as the demands made on card readers, line printers.

AREAS CONSIDERED.   The investigative phase of the feasibility study deals with several major areas:

1. Cost
2. Hardware
3. Software
4. Personnel
5. Time

Cost.   The study team must thoroughly examine all aspects of the new system to determine whether it is worth the expenditure and also to discover the cheapest and most efficient way to implement the system. Some of the questions asked are

- Should new equipment be leased or purchased?
- What will maintenance costs be?
- Which company will provide maintenance service at the lowest cost?
- What one-time costs must be borne?
- What recurrent costs are involved?
- What will be the cost of changing or expanding the new system at a later date?
- What training and implementation costs are involved?
- What will physical plant alterations cost?
- What will air conditioning, power, new floors, exits cost?

Hardware.   Any system that requires the purchase of new equipment will entail some study regarding performance, speed, and capacity of key pieces of equipment. The feasibility study asks

- What brand of computer is best?
- What size of CPU and core storage are best?
- What peripheral equipment should be purchased?
- Should tape drives, disk drives, or drum storage be selected?

- Can selected equipment be expanded to meet growth needs?
- Should equipment be centralized or decentralized?
- Should one large computer or several small ones be purchased?
- Who will be in charge of the new equipment?

Software.   The programming and software costs of a new system must also be studied. The time and effort required to program a given computer, consultation time, and availability of software libraries must all be considered. These questions are asked:

- What new programs will have to be written?
- Should programs be written or purchased on the outside?
- How long will it take to write, test, and debug new programs?
- What skill will the staff need to write the new software?
- What software is available from vendors at no cost?
- Can existing programs be converted to the new system?
- Can the new programs be run on machines that may be purchased later?

Personnel.   The implementation of a new system affects the people employed by a firm as well as the organization as a whole. The investigative phase studies this area too.

- Will new people be needed?
- How many employees will have to be relocated?
- Will retraining be necessary?
- How will salaries be affected?
- Are there people now employed by the firm with the new skills that will be needed?
- What will the effect be on employee moral?
- How many people will be laid off?

Time Factor.   A new system must be feasible from a time as well as an economic standpoint. The study group asks several important questions

- What would be the best period in the business cycle to install the new system?
- How long will the installation take?
- Should the old system be operated alongside the new? For how long?
- How long should consultants be employed to monitor the new system?
- Who should supervise the changeover?

Final Report   The last step in the feasibility study is the preparation of the final report and recommendations. This report records the results of the entire study.

A major part of the final report is the economic justification of the new system. The final report includes a statement showing the computed cost savings projected for the new system. It contrasts the new system with the old. It shows benefits expected in hours saved, reduction in personnel needed, and economies that will accrue in equipment lease costs. Figure 20.2 outlines a final report.

BENEFITS OF THE NEW SYSTEM. A statement lists the benefits of the new system in precise terms. The benefits are expressed in terms of dollars, hours, ratios, etc. Any improvements in error factors, fewer breakdowns, lower maintenance costs, profit, return on investment are quoted. Often costs go up, but sufficient offsetting benefits may justify a new system.

DETAILED STATEMENT OF EQUIPMENT NEEDED. A list of the equipment to be purchased or leased is included. This statement gives the vendor name, make, model number, and cost for each piece of equipment. The size of the CPU and model numbers of input and output devices are given.

FIGURE 20.2 FINAL REPORT OF STUDY TEAM

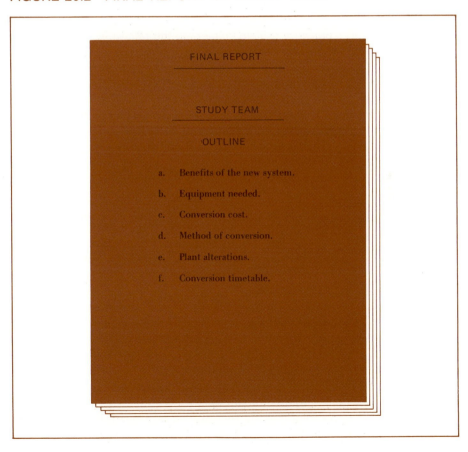

FINAL REPORT

STUDY TEAM

OUTLINE

a. Benefits of the new system.

b. Equipment needed.

c. Conversion cost.

d. Method of conversion.

e. Plant alterations.

f. Conversion timetable.

CONVERSION COSTS.   The procedures needed to convert to the new system are stated. The method of conversion (all at once, step by step, or parallel plan) is outlined. Changes required in the physical plant such as architectural revisions and air conditioning needs are detailed. Often, a timetable for implementation for each department is given.

Sometimes alternate plans are offered and the selection of a specific plan is left up to management. For example, if two methods are feasible, they might be summarized with an assessment of the merits and limitations of each. It is then up to management to select a plan.

Occasionally, the final report contains a quantitative measure of the cost of *not* implementing a new system. The statement may include a detailed estimate of the number of orders lost, cost of errors, and higher operating expenses that will be sustained if the company does not switch to the new system.

BUSINESS SYSTEM SELECTION

One of the major questions treated in the feasibility study is the selection of a business system suitable to the relative size and demands of the task. Complex data processing jobs require large processing equipment and a complicated data flow system. Smaller tasks make fewer demands and can often be done on less expensive, less complicated systems.

Criteria   A primary criteria in selecting a system is that it meet the needs of the firm. Needs vary greatly and so do system and hardware capabilities. What may be suitable for one firm, may not be adequate for another.

Some companies are file oriented; others are calculation oriented. File-oriented firms require a system to process and perform simple calculations on large files that contain thousands of records. Calculation-oriented firms may have only a few records to be processed, but require computers to perform long, complex, arithmetic and CPU-oriented procedures. Some firms are batch-oriented; others require on-line, real-time capabilities. A mail order house may be able to group its processing in batches. On the other hand, a bank may need real-time processing for its teller terminals.

The firm that must process a large number of card records requires a system that can manipulate large numbers of cards quickly. If many reports are generated, or long print outs involved, the system must have good line printer capacity. If a firm's processing requires a variety of complex sorts and mathematical operations to be performed on a relatively small number of records, a large CPU capacity with limited input/output facilities is adequate. The volume of storage for files affects selection too. For example, the Federal Internal Revenue Service needs many secondary storage facilities—tape drives, disk drives, etc.—to store millions of tax records.

In selecting a business system, the following must be considered:

1. Expansibility
2. File type and size
3. Kind of problems processed
4. Speed
5. On-line, real-time needs
6. Installation and engineering costs
7. Programming costs
8. Personnel training costs

Comparison of Methods

These characteristics are the criteria used in our comparison of the three types of data processing systems.

MANUAL DATA PROCESSING. Manual data processing methods are relatively low cost for processing a small volume of data. Manual systems are flexible and easily changed, revised, or altered. Installation costs are low, and little specialized equipment is necessary. Operators can be easily trained to perform calculations, file, prepare reports, etc.

Manual data processing is practical for firms with a low volume of data to be processed. It is suitable for one-time problems. Since no programming time or effort is involved, the staff can begin processing the data with little preplanning, testing, or debugging.

UNIT RECORD PROCESSING. Unit record data processing is relatively economical for processing moderate amounts of data. A single unit record machine may lease for $100 to several hundred dollars per month; an entire system for $800 to $1,000 per month, or more. Card-oriented computers, such as the IBM 360/20 or UNIVAC 1004, lease for several thousand dollars per month. Unit record systems are flexible and are easily changed or modified.

Unit record machines, or card-oriented computers, are not, however, suitable for high-volume processing. They would be inefficient for a firm needing a great deal of file storage area and would be unable to meet real-time processing needs.

Unit record equipment is economical to service and does not require an air conditioned or other specialized environment. It is easier to train operators to run unit record equipment than to train a skilled programmer.

ELECTRONIC DATA PROCESSING. Computers range in size from small machines that lease for under $2,000 per month to large systems that lease for several hundred thousand dollars. These systems are expensive and are practical only if fully utilized a large part of each day.

Computer systems are fast and if a high volume of data is processed, the cost is relatively low. These systems are suitable for large firms that have a

COMPUTER HELPS SPOT FOREIGN OBJECT IN EYE

Two Kansas doctors recently developed a way to quickly and accurately determine the location of a foreign object in the eye, by using a computer. Dr. Thomas J. Cusack, radiologist at Kansas University Medical Center, said the method is a simplification of a technique developed by William Sweet in 1898. Sweet's method uses X-ray pictures of the eye taken from several different angles. It requires sophisticated mathematics, geometry, and graphing to locate the object by triangulation.

The use of the computer in the Kansas method eliminates the calculations by the radiologist. The result is a much faster, more accurate localization of the foreign body.

Of such eye cases, Cusack said, "Chances are that a radiologist would do this type of thing about once a year. Besides the radiologist's being out of practice, there is much time lost in searching for the seldom-used graph paper and instruction sheets used in Sweet's method."

He said the formerly cumbersome figuring is done more quickly and accurately by computer. "The computer will not forget how to do it. The possibility of misinterpreting the instructions or drawing the lines wrong is eliminated."

Once a computer is programmed for the method, it can even instruct the radiologist how to make the necessary measurements on the X-ray pictures.

SOURCE   Abstracted from "Computer Used to Spot Foreign Object in Eye." *Los Angeles Times*, June 7, 1972, Part IA, p. 7.

great number of calculations to be performed and need a large storage capacity. They are also suited to real-time processing.

Computers are inefficient for one-time data processing problems. In these instances the manual or unit record systems are more useful. In the time it would take one programmer to write a program for a simple data processing problem, a manual operator could perform the job and have the results ready. But this advantage is soon lost if there is much data to be processed or the job is to be run several times.

Computer systems require trained console operators, specialized maintenance staff, and skilled programmers. Computer systems also require special environmental and plant conditions. Air conditioning, special floors, and furniture are a few of the factors involved here.

HARDWARE SELECTION

Another major task of the feasibility study is the selection and specification of hardware for the proposed system. If computers are involved, the job becomes even more complicated and technical. The major elements weighed when selecting a computer are

1 Vendor capability

2 Equipment capability

Vendor Capability

Computers are complex machines and need support and maintenance by a team of experts for proper functioning. With this in mind, the systems analyst looks at a vendor's abilities in many areas when selecting a particular brand or make of computer. He evaluates the vendor's reputation and past performance, his thoroughness and attitude in responding to proposals, his capabilities, the size of his maintenance staff, the number and skill of his systems programmers, and the extent of his supporting services. Figure 20.3 is a checklist of important criteria in choosing a vendor.

EXPERIENCE AND STABILITY. A major factor in selection of a vendor is his experience in the data processing field and his ability to handle the particular needs of a firm. Some manufacturers have extensive experience in real-time

"5 million dollars or I'll degauss your memory."

©Datamation®

FIGURE 20.3   CHECKLIST FOR VENDOR CAPABILITIES

✓	REPUTATION
✓	PROPOSAL
✓	EXPERIENCE
	PAST PERFORMANCE
✓	MAINTENANCE STAFF
	SUPPORT SERVICES
✓	SOFTWARE
	TRAINING COURSES
	MANUALS
	LOCAL OFFICES

processing, whereas others are batch-processing oriented. Some are specialists in terminal hardware. A number of computer manufacturers have been in business for many years and employ a skilled staff of systems engineers, machinists, technicians, and programmers.

EQUIPMENT SUPPORT.   The support services provided by vendors also vary greatly. Some include full maintenance, repair, and installation services in their purchase or lease fee. Some have large branches located in major cities of the country and provide training courses, operating manuals, and extensive help in adapting to a new system.

PROGRAM SUPPORT.   To gain the maximum benefits from a computer and other complicated data processing equipment, a firm must have sound programming support from the vendor. Some manufacturers provide complete program packages, including operating systems, compilers, and utility programs. Others offer extensive programming libraries, including scientific and commercial subroutine packages.

     An important element in the selection of a computer is the choice of compilers. Some manufacturers have a large number of compilers available for each make or model of machine; others have only one or two compilers available.

Equipment Capability   Another major criteria in the selection of a computer is the machine's physical capabilities.

     Equipment capability is generally related to cost. The higher the cost, the greater the processing speed or storage capacity of the computer.

Sometimes there is a trade-off, and a business systems analyst has to choose between high core storage capacity and high processing speed. For a given dollar amount he can get one or the other, but not both. He must decide which aspect is most important to his system. Figure 20.4 is a checklist of equipment capabilities.

FIGURE 20.4   CHECKLIST FOR EQUIPMENT CAPABILITIES

✓	CPU PERFORMANCE
✓	I/O PERFORMANCE
	PRIMARY STORAGE
✓	SECONDARY STORAGE
✓	OVERALL EVALUATION
	MAINTENANCE
✓	EXPANSIBILITY
	MULTIPROCESSING

CPU PERFORMANCE.   Several measures are used to compare CPU performances. The core storage capacities, cycle time, and number of instructions processed per second are major factors. Table 20.1 compares different models of the IBM/360 system. A business systems analyst considers the following elements when rating CPU performance:

- Word size
- Instruction cycle time
- Addition time
- Number of programmable registers
- Number of input/output channels
- Core storage capacity
- Arithmetic capability
- Physical size and characteristics

I/O PERFORMANCE.   The capabilities of the I/O devices are deciding factors in selecting peripheral equipment. Slow or insufficient card readers or line printers can cause a computer to become I/O bound. Under such conditions the amount of work processed during a shift would be far less than the maximum expected. Some of the measures compared are

- Number of cards read per minute
- Number of cards punched per minute

TABLE 20.1   IBM SYSTEM/360 COMPARISON

MODEL	CPU CYCLE TIME IN MICROSECONDS[a]	MAIN STORAGE READ/WRITE IN MICROSECONDS	STORAGE CAPACITY IN BYTES	SELECTOR CHANNELS AVAILABLE
30	0.75	1.5	8K–65K	2
40	0.625	2.5	16K–262K	2
50	0.5	2.0	65K–524K	3
65	0.2	0.75	131K–1048K	6
75	0.2	0.75	262K–1048K	6

[a]UNIT	FRACTION OF A SECOND	DECIMAL EQUIVALENT
Second		1.0
Millisecond	one thousandth	0.001
Microsecond	one millionth	0.000001
Nanosecond	one billionth	0.000000001

- Number of lines printed per minute
- Size and number of characters displayed on a video screen
- Speed at which data can be transmitted between CPU and I/O devices
- Number of terminals that can be operated at one time

SECONDARY STORAGE PERFORMANCE.   The capacity of secondary storage devices is an important factor, particularly in a system that depends on data accessed from storage. If a large number of files must be kept on-line for access by the CPU, adequate secondary storage facilities must be provided. The elements studied in comparing secondary storage devices are

- Number of disk drives on the system
- Number of tape drives on the system
- Data cell and data drum storage capacity
- Density of media (bytes per inch on tape)
- Capacity in bytes per device

OVERALL SYSTEM PERFORMANCE.   Several additional elements must be evaluated in a comparison of computer systems. Business systems analysts must know what provisions have been made for peripheral devices. Can the computer support a plotter or graphic display devices? Can it handle paper tape? Can the system remote process? Can it multiprogram (run several jobs at one time)?

Other important questions concern a computer's core storage capacity and utilization. Some computers have fixed zones, called partitions, separating core storage modules. The partitions cannot be adjusted or changed, even if one module is overloaded and another is not. Some computers are designed for dynamic allocation of core storage. The CPU can assign core storage modules to different functions as needed by the problem program.

Sometimes a test or "benchmark" program is used to compare machines. The same program will be tested on several different computers to determine the different time and cost benefits.

KEY TERMS

Feasibility study
Preliminary study
Task force committee

Ongoing committee
Project director
Investigative study

EXERCISES

1. Why is it important to measure business system performance?
2. List and discuss six important elements measured in evaluating system performance.
3. What are the three main phases of the feasibility study? What is the purpose of each?
4. Discuss three approaches for selecting personnel to implement a feasibility study.
5. What questions does the investigative study analyze? Give several examples.
6. Describe the support provided by some vendors when a firm plans a new business system.
7. Describe the kinds of findings presented in the final report and how they are used by management.
8. How do the needs of file-oriented firms differ from calculation-oriented firms? Give three examples of each.
9. When selecting a system, what characteristics are considered? How are they important?
10. Contrast the suitability of manual, unit record, and computer data processing methods for a medium-sized firm.
11. Summarize the major points a firm must evaluate when selecting hardware.
12. List and discuss six items that must be evaluated when judging computer capabilities.
13. What elements are evaluated when comparing input/output equipment capabilities.
14. Use your phone directory to determine what computer equipment vendors serve your local community.
15. As an individual assignment, make an appointment with a computer equipment vendor. Discuss the services, support, and help his firm provides clients.

The Data 21 Processing Department

Early data processing units were outgrowths of accounting departments and were primarily related to the financial, accounting, and payroll needs of the company. As these units developed efficient methods of processing large amounts of data and acquired specialized machines, it soon became obvious that they could serve the entire business in a multitude of ways. Today, the data processing department is a service unit providing an orderly flow of data to all areas and activities of a firm. It assists management, employees, customers, and others by preparing vital internal and external data. Figure 21.1 illustrates the relationship of the data processing department to other central service units in a firm.

STRUCTURE OF DATA PROCESSING DEPARTMENT

The size and complexity of data processing departments vary with the kind and size of the business they serve. For a small firm, a few data processing employees, operating a small computer or a limited amount of EAM equipment, may be sufficient. Medium-sized organizations may employ from 5 to 20 individuals and operate both unit record equipment and a computer. Large firms, on the other hand, may employ many thousands of people in data processing and operate a computer network that ties together several large computers in many parts of the country.

433

FIGURE 21.1   RELATIONSHIP OF DATA PROCESSING AND
OTHER CENTRAL SERVICES

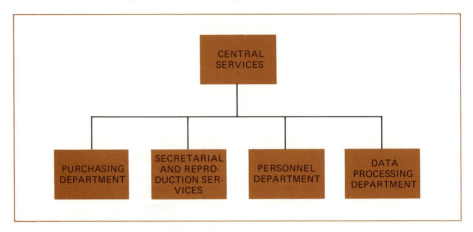

There is a difference between the jobs of the systems programmers and analysts discussed in this chapter and the business systems analysts discussed previously. Systems analysts are concerned with programming the operating systems and compilers of the computer. The business systems analyst is concerned with solving problems related to the organization of the business enterprise. Sometimes the data processing department handles both functions. In this case, the organization chart will look like Figure 21.2.

Small Data Processing Department

The smallest and simplest organization is one in which one or two employees are responsible for data processing operations. In a small firm, these individuals serve as combination programmers, computer operators, keypunch operators, systems analysts, and managers.

But data processing is a complex field and different skills are required of the programmer and the systems analyst. The skills that make a good computer operator differ from those required of EAM operators. Because of this, there is a need for specialization within the data processing department.

Figure 21.3 shows a typical organization chart for a small data processing department, with four specialized employees: a programmer, an input/output operator (including keypunch operators), a computer operator, and a manager.

As the workload demands, one employee may help another in his work. This is feasible because the computer is small and the programming is not too complex.

The relatively low volume of work processed by a small business usually limits the need for programming languages to only a few, easily handled by one or two programmers. Little or no systems programming, such as modifying the operating system of a computer or altering compilers, is done.

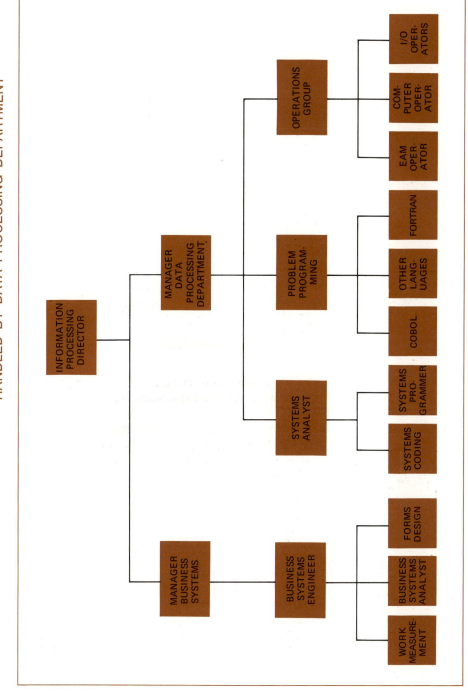

FIGURE 21.2 ORGANIZATION CHART OF BUSINESS SYSTEMS FUNCTIONS HANDLED BY DATA PROCESSING DEPARTMENT

FIGURE 21.3   ORGANIZATION CHART OF SMALL DATA
                        PROCESSING DEPARTMENT

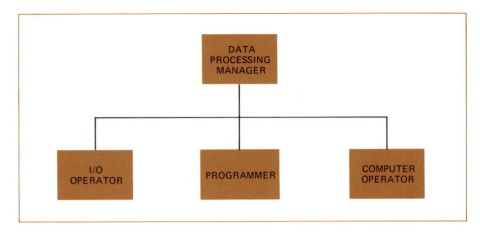

Medium-Sized
Data Processing
Department

More and more medium-sized firms are using computerized data processing systems. Insurance companies, manufacturers, sales agents and brokers, advertising agencies, and other moderately sized companies employ from 5 to 20 employees in their data processing departments.

The increase in size permits more specialization within the department. Figure 21.4 is an organization chart of a medium-sized company. The department is headed by a data processing manager who spends most of his time supervising employees and guiding the operation of the department. Under him are a staff of programmers, business systems analysts, and EAM and computer operators.

The function of the business systems analyst has been touched upon in the previous chapter. His duties include the study of business systems and an analysis of data flow problems and the recommendation for solutions. He reduces the solutions to discrete steps and often records them as flowcharts. He designs forms, records, and files and specifies procedures and equipment.

The programmer's task is to convert the business systems analyst's flowcharts and instructions into a running program. Occasionally, the business systems analysis and coding is done by the same individual.

If the firm needs to program in more than one language, several programmers, each proficient in a different language, may be employed and assigned to different types of problems. One or more keypunch operators may be assigned to each programmer. The punched programs are turned over to a computer operator for running.

The computer and EAM operators run the computers, unit record machines, and other equipment. They feed jobs to the computer and operate the console. In a smaller firm, the programmer may operate the console himself.

FIGURE 21.4   ORGANIZATION CHART OF MEDIUM-SIZED DATA PROCESSING DEPARTMENT

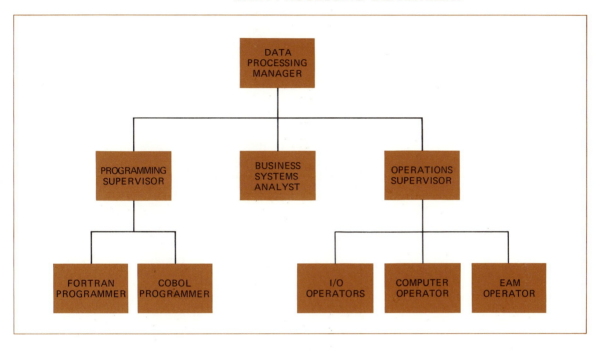

Usually the computer operator receives the programs punched and ready to run. He loads cards, mounts tapes, removes print outs, etc. In some firms, he may be required to operate the EAM equipment as well.

If the workload merits 24-hour operation, an operation supervisor may be in charge, with three shift supervisors under him.

Large Data Center   A data center in a large firm may employ from a dozen to several hundred workers and occupy an entire floor of a large office building. Figure 21.5 is an organization chart of a data processing department in a large business firm.

There may be dozens of keypunch operators, supervisors, systems analysts, systems engineers, programmers, business systems analysts, operators, clerks, librarians, and documentation specialists. The larger the company, the greater the specialization that can take place in the data processing department. With specialization comes greater efficiency and output. Since large firms process a high volume of work, the department can also be put on a 24-hour operating schedule, which further maximizes equipment utilization.

SYSTEMS GROUP.   The systems group is responsible for planning and expanding the operating system and computer control programs and for altering compilers. They are also responsible for the maintenance and development of all systems software. The systems group employs systems analysts, systems programmers, and librarians.

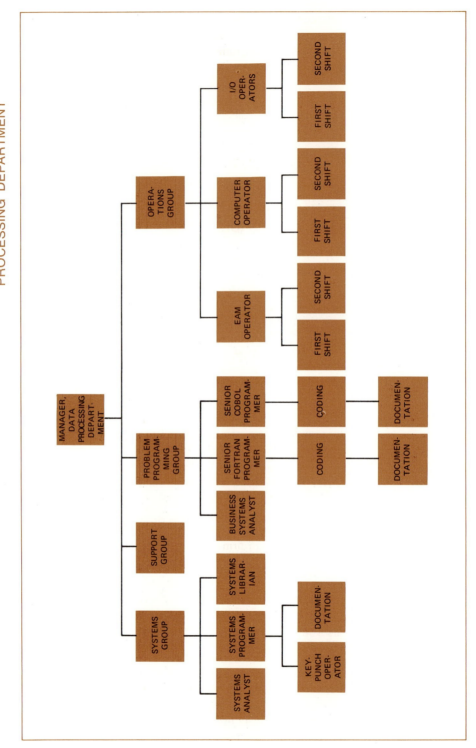

FIGURE 21.5   ORGANIZATION CHART OF LARGE DATA PROCESSING DEPARTMENT

PROGRAMMING GROUP. Some companies need to process a wide variety of problems in business, engineering, mathematics, graphics, and research. They employ programmers with specialized abilities in such languages as COBOL, FORTRAN, RPG, and Assembler.

With more personnel available the functions usually performed by the programmer can be further specialized and assigned to different individuals. Documentation and keypunching can be assigned to specialists. Even the job of programming instructions can be reduced to different levels. A senior programmer may lay out the overall program and assign separate sections of the program to other programmers for coding. Finally, the parts are assembled into a running program and it is documented by another specialist.

OPERATIONS GROUP. The operation function is also divided into specialized activities. Large computer centers often operate EAM facilities alongside of computers. Some have several sizes and types of computers available in one installation.

These firms employ several supervisors to coordinate the operations group. Their staff may be assigned to operate a particular computer, input or output device, the computer console, or tape and disk drives, etc.

SUPPORT GROUP. Large firms employ a large support staff for the data processing department. The greater volume of programming increases the need for tape and program librarians, mathematicians, statisticians, technicians, clerk typists, supervisors, etc.

Personnel
Requirements

Personnel needs are usually dictated by the volume and type of programming done by a firm, as well as its kind, size, and degree of sophistication. The personnel department and the data processing manager use job description outlines as a guide when considering applications for employment.

The number of positions needed in each department is obtained from a review of reports and records. Obviously, a firm requiring a great deal of keypunching or data input will employ more keypunch operators and supervisors than firms that do more systems design and programming. The latter will need coders, programmers, and systems analysts.

To staff the positions in the department, the personnel department and data processing manager usually follow several routine procedures. Applicants are first interviewed and screened by the personnel department. They fill out applications for employment, giving pertinent data such as previous employment, experience, and education. The personnel department may also test the applicant to evaluate his mental capacity and performance. Then the applicant is interviewed by the data processing manager or supervisor. The results are evaluated and a selection made.

The data processing manager or supervisor introduces the new employee to the job. Usually the employee takes a training or indoctrination course or is placed under close supervision for a period of time. Some firms use periodic employee evaluation procedures to advance employees in status, pay, and responsibility.

In-service training is another responsibility of data processing management. As new equipment is acquired, or new procedures installed, retraining programs, seminars, and courses may be offered to employees to enable them to adjust to the new operations with a minimum of delay and inconvenience.

CENTRALIZED VERSUS DECENTRALIZED DATA PROCESSING

A major question facing a firm's top-level management is whether data processing facilities should be centralized or decentralized. Figure 21.6 shows these two systems. Should one large computer be purchased to serve the needs of the entire firm? Or would several smaller computers, located in different branches or cities be more adequate?

The answer depends on the firm's needs, its volume of data processing, as well as other factors. Generally, a high volume of centralized data processing operations justifies a large computer installation. In this way a firm has the advantage of operating one large computer, with its greater power, speed, and storage capacity. Security problems are minimized at the same time.

With decentralized data processing, on the other hand, decisions can be made closer to the source. Since they will usually be concerned with a smaller part of the total enterprise, they are less subject to gross error. But decentralizing can often mean difficulties in standardizing procedures and coordinating data processing functions.

ACCESSIBILITY AND SECURITY

The modern data center is often considered a support unit whose services extend across many organization and division lines. This concept raises several questions regarding management and control of the data processing center. Where does the data center fit into the organization chart? Who is to have control? What security measures should be instituted? What jobs are suitable and acceptable for run? What jobs are to be given highest priority? Who should schedule jobs?

Accessibility of the Computer

Computer installations must be fully utilized if they are to be run economically. This is particularly important in large data centers with expensive, high-capacity hardware and a highly skilled supporting staff. Close attention to scheduling and priorities is important. For this reason, few large data centers permit hands-on operation of large computers. They prefer to control access, use, and scheduling of the machine for maximum efficiency.

FIGURE 21.6   (A) CENTRALIZED AND (B) DECENTRALIZED DATA
            PROCESSING FACILITIES

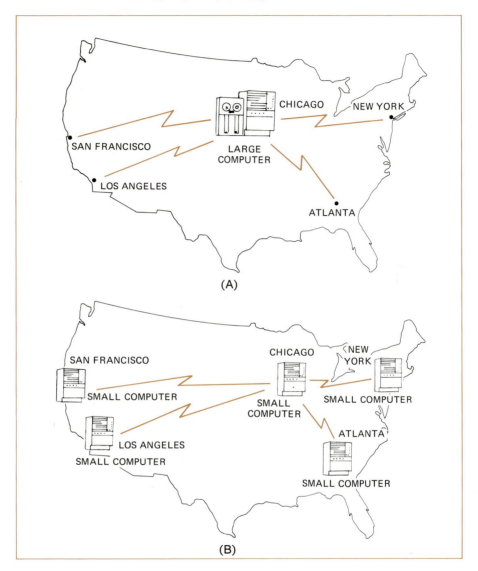

DATA PROCESSING REQUISITION FORM.   A special form is often used to
enable the data center to account for all jobs and to monitor flow and type of
work processed. A sample data processing requisition is shown in Figure
21.7. The form must be completed for each job processed and includes such
information as the name of the person submitting the job, a charge number,
approximate CPU time, number of pages of output, and the person who

FIGURE 21.7   DATA PROCESSING REQUISITION FORM

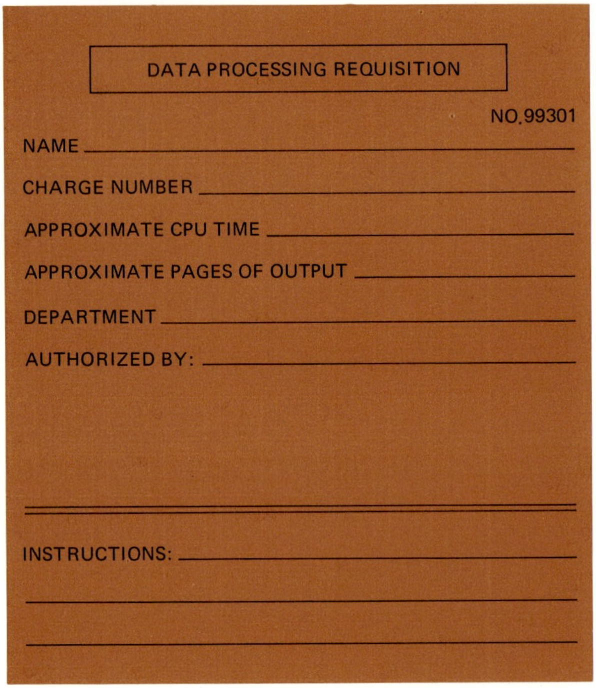

| DATA PROCESSING REQUISITION |
| NO. 99301 |

NAME _____

CHARGE NUMBER _____

APPROXIMATE CPU TIME _____

APPROXIMATE PAGES OF OUTPUT _____

DEPARTMENT _____

AUTHORIZED BY: _____

_____

INSTRUCTIONS: _____

_____

_____

authorized job. Space is provided for details and special instructions to the staff.

COST CONTROL.   Another difficulty encountered in implementing a computer installation is costs. Without effective means of controlling the use of resources and scheduling of work, data processing costs may far exceed estimates. Cost control programs are instituted at most installations to see that resources and computers are utilized in the most effective way. Scheduling and priority systems are used to maximize throughput, reduce costs, and to increase turnaround time. (Turnaround time is the time it takes for a job to be processed by the data center and the results returned to the proper department.)

For example, short-run jobs (those with five minutes or less of compile and run time) are given greater priority in some data centers and are run during prime hours. Longer jobs, requiring more than five minutes of compilation and execution time, may be run during off hours or the late evening shift. This policy results in a faster turnaround time for most jobs and better utilization of the night staff and facilities.

The goals of cost control are to

❶ Gain most efficient use of data processing facilities

❷ Gain most efficient use of data processing staff

❸ Reduce costs

❹ Account for each job processed and charge it to the proper department

❺ Maximize services offered

Security and Disaster Protection In many firms, the data center has become the central depository for the firm's most important records, statistics, data, and files. The loss of these records and data could threaten the existence of the firm.

FIGURE 21.8 DOUBLE-DOOR ENTRY CONTROL SYSTEM (Concealed detectors identify persons carrying magnets, other metallic objects, or tape reels equipped with special labels. Doors automatically trap unauthorized persons.)

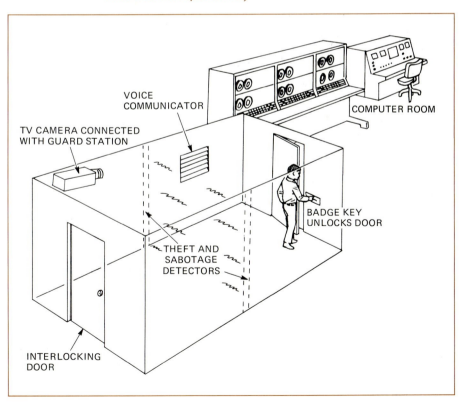

VOICE COMMUNICATOR

TV CAMERA CONNECTED WITH GUARD STATION

COMPUTER ROOM

BADGE KEY UNLOCKS DOOR

THEFT AND SABOTAGE DETECTORS

INTERLOCKING DOOR

COMPUTER EXONERATED

The Tenth Circuit Court of Appeals in Denver ruled a company is responsible for the actions of its computer because "a computer operates only in accordance with the information and directions supplied by its human programmers." State Farm Mutual Insurance Company claimed it was not liable in an accident that occurred the same day a policy was automatically renewed by its computer system because the insured's check had arrived after the accident and the retroactive renewal had been issued in error. The judge ruled the reinstatement was a direct result of the errors and oversights of State Farm agents and employees and ". . . the fact that the actual processing of the policy is carried out by an unimaginative mechanical device can have no effect on the company's responsibilities for these errors and oversights."

SOURCE "Computer Exonerated," Benchmarks, *Datamation*, May 1972, p. 153.

The data center is subject to both internal and external hazards. Earthquakes, fires, and other natural disasters are external threats. Theft, vandalism, fraud, and unauthorized use of data constitute internal dangers which threaten security.

It is essential to protect the security of important records and data. Much of the information stored in a data center is irreplaceable. Money from insurance policies may replace equipment, but this money may not be able to undo the damage if records are lost or tampered with.

Several measures are taken to reduce these security and disaster threats. They include screening personnel, physical plant security, back-up copies of files and provisions for substitute computers in emergencies.

SCREENING PERSONNEL. Extensive security and personnel investigations are made on employees who will work in the data center. Security bonds are sometimes required of these personnel.

PHYSICAL PLANT PROTECTION. In an effort to provide maximum security for the computer installation, data centers use several techniques to deter unauthorized entry. These include burglar alarms, keycard door locks, and security police. Other measures include the installation of closed-circuit television, anti-sabotage devices, and ultrasonic and audio detection systems. Figure 21.8, shown on the previous page, illustrates a double-door entry control system.

"THIS GENTLEMAN SAYS THAT HIS SEAT IS ALREADY TAKEN"

BACK-UP FILES.   Since it is virtually impossible to protect against all natural and physical calamities, back-up files and computers are often used. Back-up files are duplicate files maintained in another building or at a remote location. The files may be transmitted or updated by telephone communications link. Some duplicate files are shipped to storage facilities.

Back-up computers are used to reduce the problem of disruption in service. Important programs and operating routines are written to run on several different computers. Arrangements are made with other companies, service bureaus, or other branches of the firm to run the jobs on their computers in the event of trouble.

UNAUTHORIZED USE OF FILES.   Special labels, passwords, etc. are used to limit access to certain files. Elaborate software and hardware systems have been developed which prevent unauthorized users from gaining access to data files.

KEY TERMS

Systems programmer
Systems analyst
Centralized data processing

Decentralized data processing
Turnaround time

EXERCISES
1. Briefly trace the changing role of the data processing department in the business enterprise. What will likely be its future role?
2. Briefly describe the typical organization and personnel involved in a small data processing department.
3. Briefly describe the typical organization and personnel involved in a medium-sized data processing department.
4. Briefly describe the typical organization and personnel involved in a large data processing department.
5. What are the advantages and disadvantages of centralized versus decentralized data processing facilities.
6. What is meant by accessibility to the computer, and why is it important to the business firm?
7. What are the goals of cost control? Describe a common cost control procedure.
8. List the major security threats to a data processing installation.
9. Discuss some common security measures which help eliminate or reduce security threats.
10. What is the function of the data processing requisition form?
11. Visit your data center or one in a private business firm. Discuss their data processing organizational structure. Draw a simplified flowchart of the organizational structure.

PART SEVEN

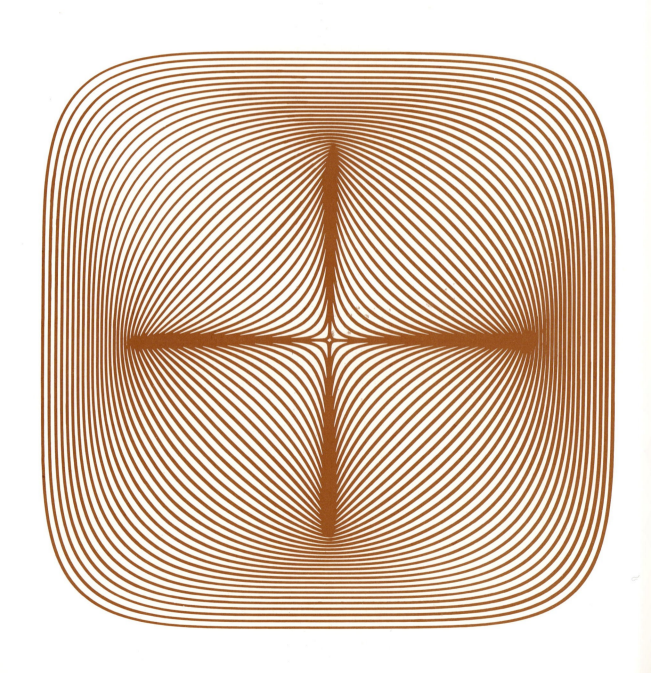

Teleprocessing and Computer Utilities

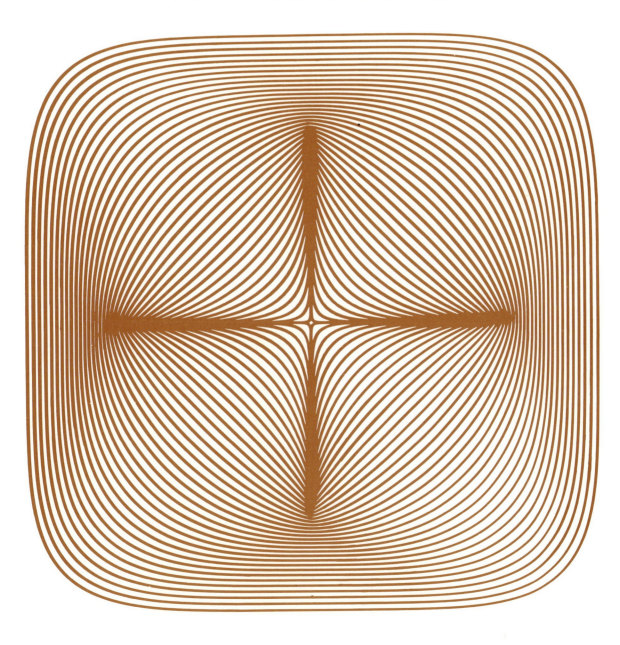

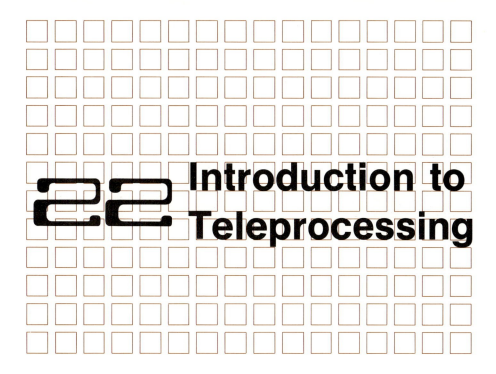

Introduction to Teleprocessing
22

Teleprocessing is a method of processing data in which the input and output devices are in a different location from the computer. Teleprocessing is the result of the synthesis of the techniques and principles of both electronic data processing and telecommunications. Telecommunications is the science of moving data through wires, radio waves, or microwave transmission circuits. In teleprocessing, these methods are used to transmit data between the input/output devices and the CPU.

Teleprocessing involves a network of one or more computers and one or more terminals. A teleprocessing system may be as simple as one terminal connected to a computer by telephone lines, or as complex as a network of computers tied to hundreds of terminals throughout the country.

Figure 22.1 illustrates a simple teleprocessing system, with capabilities for input, output, processing, and storage. The input/output devices and the CPU are connected by a communications link.

A communications link is the physical means of connecting locations for the purpose of transmitting and receiving information. It is the circuitry that ties two devices together and permits data to flow between them.

HISTORY OF TELEPROCESSING

Early telegraph systems often used paper tape to store and transmit information. This laid the groundwork for teleprocessing. Before World War II,

FIGURE 22.1   TELEPROCESSING SYSTEM

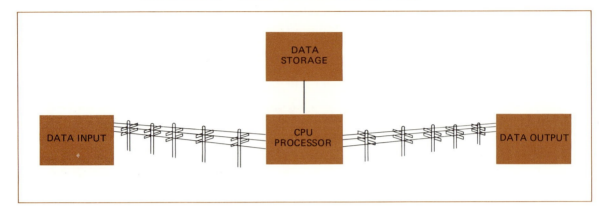

teleprocessing was limited to transmitting data punched in paper tape to calculators several hundred miles away for processing. The results were punched into paper tape and transmitted back to the receiving station.

One of the first significant applications of teleprocessing, developed by the military after World War II, was the teleprocessing system called SAGE (Semi-Automatic Ground Environment) in which telephone lines tied several remote terminals to a CPU. The availability of real-time data increased the military's ability to make rapid, accurate judgments for air defense strategies.

The practicality of the military teleprocessing system was evident. Business firms began to use teleprocessing as a tool for solving business data processing problems. One early successful system was SABRE (Semi-Automatic Business Research Environment), which processed airline reservations. A listing of available seats was stored in a central computer. Terminals were placed in airline ticket offices. Ticket agents could query the system to learn the number of unsold seats on any given flight. This reliable and highly successful method of handling seat reservations pointed the way toward other teleprocessing applications.

Today, teleprocessing is invaluable to businesses with large inventories or costly remote data flow problems and is used for such tasks as credit checking, hotel and motel reservations, inventory control, auto license verification, controlling shipments in transit, sales reports, order entry, and ticket sales.

EXAMPLES OF TELEPROCESSING SYSTEMS

Teleprocessing systems are flexible arrangements of machines, programs, and communications equipment. A system may have one or many terminals.

A single CPU may serve all needs of the system, or several CPU's may be linked together. Users may be located within the same building, or separated by thousands of miles.

Simple System

Figure 22.2 illustrates the simplest teleprocessing system. One CPU with batch processing capability serves one remote terminal. Jobs can be entered and outputted on the batch I/O device at the CPU site. At the same time, the system can handle queries and input from the remote terminal. In this example, the terminal in the sales department is tied to the CPU by hard wires (that is, the terminal is wired directly to the CPU).

In a variation of this arrangement the computer could be located in the accounting department with additional terminals in other parts of the building.

More Complex System

A more complex teleprocessing system is shown in Figure 22.3. Here, the computer is located in the firm's main office. Each branch in the same city

FIGURE 22.2 SIMPLE TELEPROCESSING SYSTEM

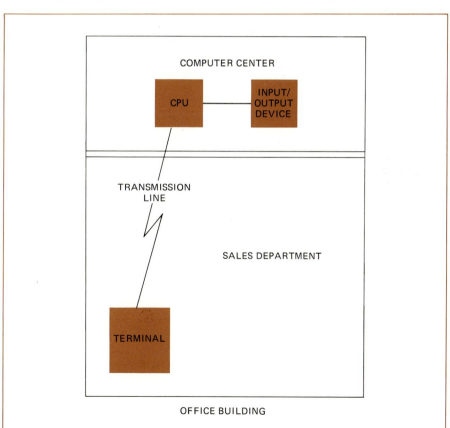

FIGURE 22.3   MORE COMPLEX TELEPROCESSING SYSTEM

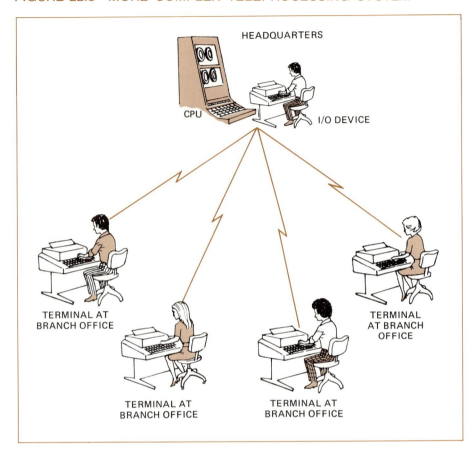

has a terminal. The remote terminals are tied to the computer through telephone lines. Data can be entered or output at the computer site or at any of the remote terminals on the line. With this system, each branch office has computer capacity available, without requiring the actual installation of a machine.

Complex
Network

The firm in Figure 22.4 has one large computer in its home office. Each branch, located in a major city, has several terminals connected to it from outlying areas. This enables each local branch to serve several terminals on one transmission line.

Figure 22.5 illustrates a similar arrangement, except that two computers are on the system. Since the computers are tied on-line, it is possible to use either or both to process data from any remote terminal. This teleprocessing system allows the computer network to handle overloads and breakdowns more efficiently. Either computer serves as a back-up in the event of a CPU

FIGURE 22.4   NATIONAL TELEPROCESSING SYSTEM

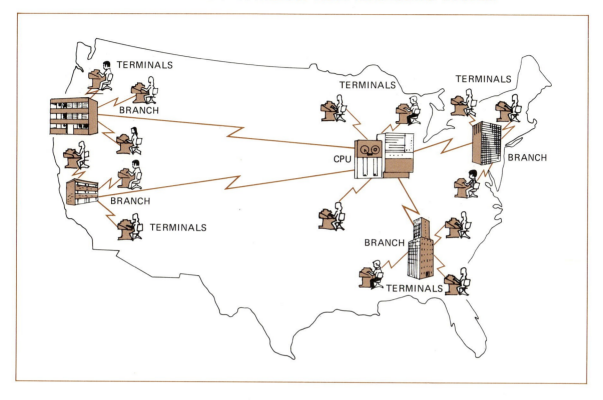

failure. In the system in Figure 22.4 a failure of the central CPU would cause the entire system to go down.

If a large volume of processing is to be done, the network shown in Figure 22.6 may be preferred. In this example, several computers are on-line with a number of terminals around the country. Thus, overloads are handled more efficiently and greater reserve capacity is on-line. Systems with more than one CPU on-line are called *multiprocessing* systems.

THE BASIC TELEPROCESSING SYSTEM

Elements in the Teleprocessing System

The basic teleprocessing system involves several elements or components:

1. Data entry
2. Data transmission
3. Data processing
4. Data storage
5. Data inquiry

Data entry is the operation of inputting data to the system through a network of remote terminals. Data is sent to the CPU through the data

FIGURE 22.5   NATIONAL TELEPROCESSING NETWORK WITH TWO CPU'S

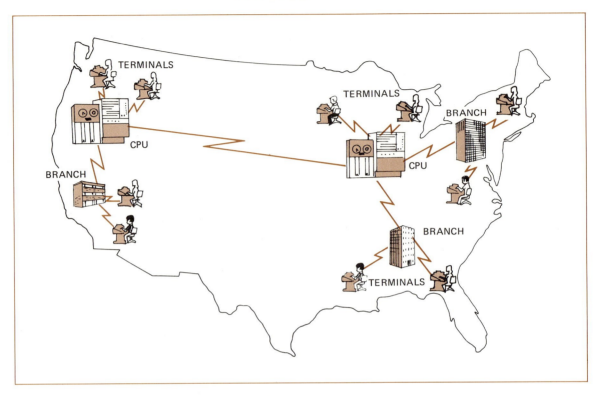

transmission system. Data processing is performed in the CPU. Files and programs are kept in data storage accessible to the CPU. Data inquiry is made from remote terminals to the master file.

Data Entry   The method of data entry depends on the type of teleprocessing system, the needs of the firm, and the time element.

Some teleprocessing systems, as shown in Figure 22.7, are essentially nothing more than data input systems. All data comes in to a central computer through a system of remote input terminals. Data processing and output take place at the central computer location. No output goes to the remote terminals. These systems do not bring the resources of the computers or results of the output to the terminals, but use each remote terminal as a data entry point.

Systems such as these are useful when a home office wants to collect data from local units and do all processing and outputting in the central office. An example would be a centralized billing system. All sales from branches would be entered on terminals and the data transmitted to the main office. There, bills, invoices, and other accounting data would be prepared, and statements would be mailed out to customers.

FIGURE 22.6   COMPLEX NATIONAL TELEPROCESSING SYSTEM

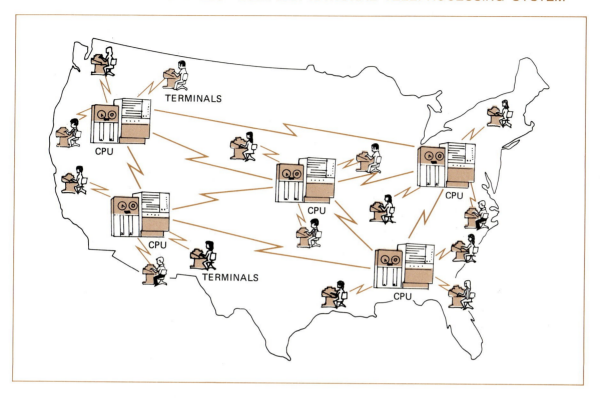

MODES OF DATA ENTRY.   There are four major modes of data entry.
1. *Off-Line Data Preparation—On-Line Data Entry.*   In this mode, data is
collected off-line and sent to the CPU in a batch for processing. For
example, data may be collected throughout the day and recorded on
punched cards, magnetic tape, or paper tape. When data is ready for entry,
or at the close of the working day, an operator would place the tape or
cards on a terminal, signal the computer to prepare for data input, and
begin transmission. Off-line data entry might be used to run a payroll or a
statistical procedure.
2. *On-Line Data Preparation—On-Line Data Entry.*   In this mode, data is
keyboarded and transmitted to the central computer at the time the
transaction occurs. A signal from the remote terminal initiates the
transmission. No intermediate storage device, such as paper or magnetic
tape, is used. However, a buffer is sometimes placed in the system to see
that characters are fed to the CPU with the proper timing.
    Bank teller terminals use this mode. The data is sent to the CPU at the
instant the teller enters the details of the transaction on the terminal.
3. *Computer-Accessed Data Entry.*   In this mode, the computer is
programmed to call the terminal when the CPU is ready to receive the
data. This mode differs from those above in that the computer rather than

FIGURE 22.7   SIMPLE DATA ENTRY SYSTEM

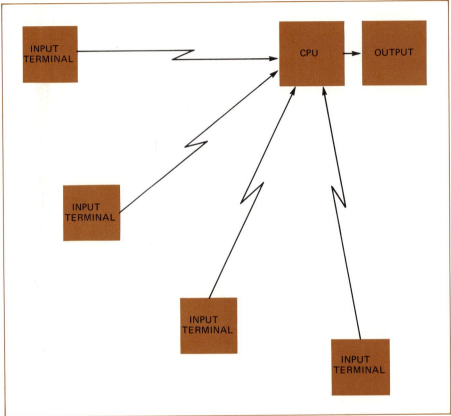

the terminal operator initiates the transmission. Data is gathered, entered, and stored in the terminal over a period of time. When the CPU is ready to receive and process the data, it signals the terminal to begin transmission. The terminal then sends the CPU all the data it is holding in storage.

Applications of this mode include billing, payroll, and inventory systems. Data is collected and entered in the terminal during the working day. The CPU receives and processes the data at the end of the working day, when its workload is smaller, or at periods when the transmission lines are not in heavy use.

4. *Shared Data Input.* In this mode, several remote terminals are connected to the CPU through one transmission line. The arrangement is similar to a telephone party line. A terminal can go on-line and send data *only* when the line is not being used by another terminal.

Data Transmission   One of the essential elements in a teleprocessing system is the transmission of data between terminals and CPU or between several CPU's. The data is usually transmitted over telephone, telegraph, or leased lines, or through micro or radio wave circuits. The selection of the transmission mode for a teleprocessing system depends on the needs of the firm and the available computer hardware and related equipment.

DATA TRANSMISSION LINES.   Communication lines for teleprocessing systems are priced according to their ability to transmit data, which is determined by type of circuit and grade of line or volume of data that can be fed from point to point.

Circuits Used. Three types of circuits are in common use as shown in the figure on the left. They are

❶ Simplex circuits

❷ Half-duplex circuits

❸ Full-duplex circuits

SIMPLEX
ONE WAY ONLY

In the simplex circuit, data can flow in only one direction. A line either receives data or transmits data. It cannot do both, and is, therefore, a limited means of data transmission. A terminal coupled to a simplex line that only transmits data is called a send-only terminal. A terminal coupled to a simplex line that only receives data is called a receive-only terminal.

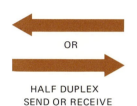

OR

HALF DUPLEX
SEND OR RECEIVE
ALTERNATELY

A half-duplex line, on the other hand, can receive and transmit data, but can do only one at a time. The half-duplex line can be shifted from one direction of data flow to the other by the CPU or the terminal, but its utility is still limited. If a terminal is transmitting data over a half-duplex line, the computer cannot interrupt the input flow to send back an important message. It must wait until the terminal shifts the line to the receive mode before delivering the information. The half-duplex line is the most widely used because it handles most communication needs at a reasonable cost.

FULL DUPLEX
SEND AND RECEIVE
SIMULTANEOUSLY

A full-duplex circuit is obviously the most efficient because it allows a two-way transmission of data to occur simultaneously. Suppose an operator is entering data through a terminal to the computer and is unaware that the system's storage capacity has reached its limit. With a full-duplex circuit, the computer can signal the terminal to stop inputting data before the system becomes overloaded.

Speed of Data Transmission. Communication lines are also classified by the volume of data they can transmit. The greater the number of characters transmitted per second, the higher the grade of line. The lower the volume, the lower the grade.

The standard measure of data transmission speed is *bits per second* (*bps*). (The term baud is sometimes inaccurately applied here. Baud refers to a measure in the teletype industry.) The higher the bps or line capacity, the more data it can move per given interval of time.

Three grades of lines are used for data transmission:

❶ Narrow band line

❷ Voice grade line

❸ Wide band line

COMPUTERS AND FOOD

HARVESTING THE CROPS

At Rutgers University's Department of Agricultural Engineering, a computer is being used to find out how much force is needed to shake ripe fruit from trees while leaving the unripe ones on the branches. Present automated fruit harvesting methods, such as ultrasonic and mechanical tree shaking and air blasting, do not accurately control the amount of force necessary. The Rutgers' researchers are employing a small analog computer to simulate fruit trees and to learn their reactions to varying forces.

IT AIN'T CHICKEN FEED

"If it ain't got corn or soybean meal in it, it ain't chicken feed." Many old timers will tell you that you can't grow healthy chickens without these ingredients. But experiments with birds at the University of Maryland proved you could.

Poultry scientists asked the University's computer to come up with a low-cost ration that would supply all known food essentials for chickens. The machine was fed a list of 50 ingredients and the market price of each. It was then programed to analyze 56 requirements that the feed must meet and select the cheapest mix that would meet the specifications. The result: ground wheat and blood meal—an unlikely mix!

SOURCE   Abstracted from "Computers and Food," by George C. Tolis, *Computer Usage*, Vol. 3, No. 2, Spring 1968.

The narrow band line usually has a maximum transmission speed of 300 bps. These lines are less than voice grade in quality and are not widely used. They are, however, more economical to lease than other grades.

Voice grade, or voice band, lines can transmit more than 300 bps. They are called voice grade because they are commonly used for ordinary telephone conversations.

Wide band lines are capable of transmitting data at 18,000 bps or higher. Of the three lines available from the telephone company these lines have the greatest capacity for moving data and are the most expensive to lease.

Thus, we see that the most versatile and expensive line would be a full-duplex, wide band line. A simplex, narrow band would be less expensive, but more limited in use.

CHANNELS.   A channel is the path between each terminal and its CPU. A CPU that services 30 terminals simultaneously would require 30 channels. With appropriate equipment it is possible to transmit up to 45 channels of information over one communication line. Specialized data transmission equipment must be installed to make multiple channels available on a single line. But regardless of the number of channels on the same circuit, the user pays only the basic charge for a single line.

COUPLERS. A coupler is a device used to connect a terminal or a CPU to a telephone line. These devices are also called modems (MOdulator-DEModulators) or interface facilities.

As keys are depressed on the terminal keyboard, the coupler converts the characters into pulses suitable for transmission over the telephone line. At the computer, another coupler converts the pulses back to a form suitable for processing in the CPU.

Couplers may be either hard wired or acoustic. A hard-wired coupler is permanently connected to the telephone line and the data transmission device. It forms a direct physical and electronic path between the elements on the circuit. Couplers at the CPU end of a system are usually hard wired.

©Datamation®

Acoustic couplers are not permanently connected to either the CPU, terminal, or the telephone line. This has the advantage of allowing a terminal to be connected to any telephone line in the field. Acoustic couplers convert signals from the terminal into an audible tone for transmission over ordinary telephone lines.

Data Processing

The full potential of teleprocessing was not realized until two major developments in technology occurred: the designing of computers capable of multiprogramming and real-time processing.

MULTIPROGRAMMING. A multiprogramming system consists of a computer capable of executing several jobs at one time. At any given moment, the computer may be compiling several jobs, executing several others, and handling the inquiries and transactions of others.

A major capability of a multiprogramming computer is its ability to interrupt the processing of one or more jobs and to execute higher priority work first. When a multiprogramming computer receives an interrupt message from a high-priority job, it will temporarily store all data being processed at that moment. It will execute and output the job with the higher priority and then return to the original jobs at the point where it left off.

REAL-TIME PROCESSING. Real-time processing means that transactions are processed by a computer as they occur, and results are available to the user immediately. Data is input and output via on-line devices.

Figure 22.8 illustrates a real-time system terminal developed by Burroughs Corporation. Today, many computer manufacturers market real-time computer systems capable of multiprogramming. They can service many remote terminals on a real-time basis and, at the same time, handle batch processing jobs fed from on-site devices.

REMOTE JOB ENTRY. Teleprocessing brings the power of the computer to users in remote locations. Via remote job entry, they can process data in much the same way as in batch job processing. The difference is that the input/output devices are located away from the CPU. Data in the remote job entry (RJE) system is input to a computer and output from it via an elaborate terminal system consisting of card readers, card punches, line printers, typewriters, keyboards, etc.

The terminal transmits data from cards, tape, or keyboard to the CPU. Programs including job control cards and data decks are input in this way. The data is processed by the CPU and the results sent back to the remote terminal for output on the line printer, punch, etc. With remote job entry, a user thousands of miles away from a computer can maintain large files, or prepare the monthly billing or the firm's payroll, as if he were at the CPU site.

Data Storage

Data storage is an essential part of teleprocessing, since each user stores his master files, programs, etc. at the CPU site. The computer must be able to access files quickly in order to properly service a group of remote terminals.

FIGURE 22.8 BURROUGHS CORPORATION REAL-TIME SYSTEM

Large secondary storage systems of magnetic tape, disk, and drum must be maintained for all computers used for time-sharing applications.

Data Inquiry   Some teleprocessing systems, designed only to output data are called inquiry systems. (See Figure 22.9.) Remote users can only request the computer to output information from a file accessible to the CPU. They cannot update or add data to a file. File maintenance and data input are done at the site of the CPU.

FIGURE 22.9   DATA OUTPUT (INQUIRY) SYSTEM

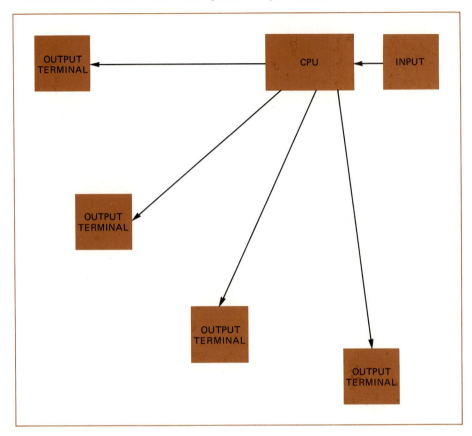

Examples of data inquiry systems include stock market quotation and inventory inquiry systems. In these systems, the user queries the computer about the status of a given file. Usually he cannot change or update the information in the file.

If the system is modified to permit file maintenance and data input from the terminals, it is called a remote processing system.

Files can be queried by

❶ Telephone inquiry with audio response
❷ Keyboard inquiry and response
❸ Keyboard inquiry with video display

TELEPHONE INQUIRY WITH AUDIO RESPONSE.   Audio response terminals are sometimes used to output data from a teleprocessing system. The user calls the system and inputs a key number, such as part number or item number. The computer then accesses the master file and locates the requested record. It assembles a verbal message, which is fed back over the telephone line to the terminal. The user receives a spoken reply to his query over the telephone.

KEYBOARD INQUIRY AND RESPONSE. In this mode, the operator keyboards a part number, name, or other descriptive information. The computer processes the inquiry and transmits the results to the remote terminal for output.

KEYBOARD INQUIRY WITH VIDEO DISPLAY. In this mode, the user keyboards in the descriptive data and the computer processes his request. The results of the processing are sent back to the terminal and displayed on a video screen.

Figure 22.10 illustrates the output from a real-time application, displayed on a Burroughs B9353 Input and Video Display System.

ADVANTAGES AND LIMITATIONS OF TELEPROCESSING

Teleprocessing is a flexible and fast means of accessing files. It eliminates the necessity of physically carrying data to the computer center and its remote entry capabilities make real-time applications from the field possible.

FIGURE 22.10   OUTPUT FROM BURROUGHS B9353 INPUT
AND VIDEO DISPLAY SYSTEM

```
TELLER NUMBER    SECURITY    REQUEST    TRANSACTION
    014             6           0            42

        NAME                        SOC. SEC. NO.
A. BANK CUSTOMER                     224-26-4524
MRS. BANK CUSTOMER                   377-38-1723
1761 ROSLYN ROAD
BURROUGHSVILLE, U. S. A.        ZIP  48152

                                        RECD    REL.
APPLICATION    ACCT. NO.    STATUS    ALERT    LOCN    ACCT.    BALANCE

   DDA        225-220-2      OPEN       ::      0563    4082     1,987.36
   ILN        3259-8360      OPEN               0784    0000        97.36
   SAV        438-897-0      OPEN               0028    1086       739.02
   MTG        77869-3-2      OPEN        #      1006    0093    17,549.32


::  -  HOLD ON THE ACCOUNT
 #  -  ESCROW BALANCE DEFICIENT
```

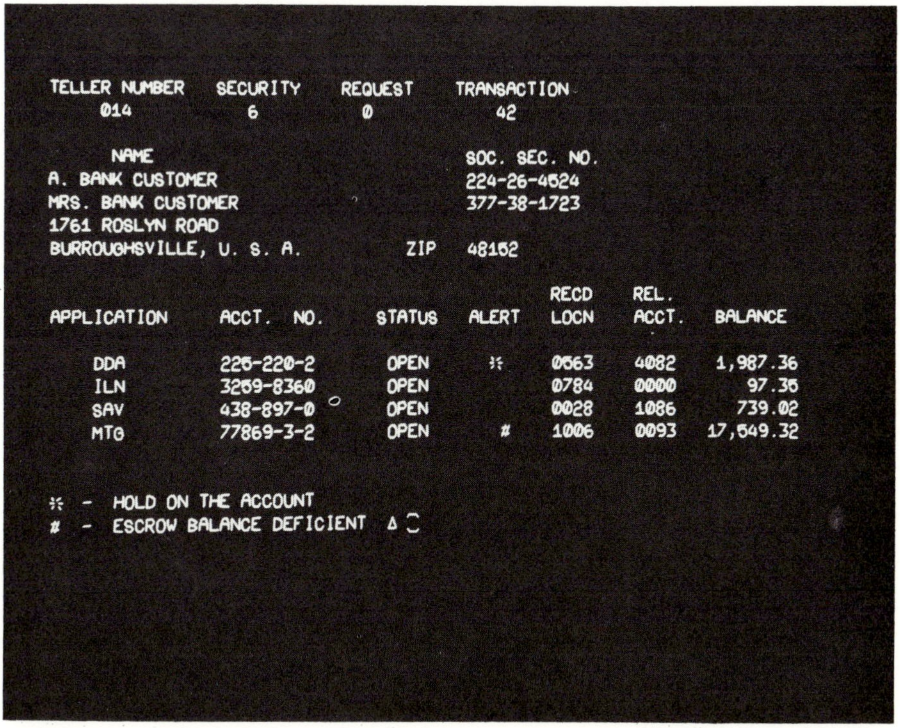

Teleprocessing enables many users to share the same system at the same time, thus reducing cost and giving each user greater computer capability than if he were to purchase his own machine.

Teleprocessing permits more efficient use of computers, since users can take advantage of the time difference between the East and West Coasts. For example, users in the East can process jobs on computers in California before the working day begins in the West. And conversely, western users can use New York computers after the working day in the East has ended.

Teleprocessing has its limitations. Since all parts of the system are bound by a communications link, expensive tie lines, interconnecting lines, telephone lines, etc. must be installed. Additional equipment and complex programming are also involved.

Cost and accounting procedures must be designed to handle a large volume of users. Records must be kept so that each user can be charged for CPU time and storage used. Job control procedures must be set up to handle jobs coming in from all users. Security measures must be available to prevent unauthorized users from querying or accessing files.

Finally, teleprocessing is subject to communications failures. A downed line, or interruption in the transmission between the CPU and terminal causing loss of data, is an ever-present problem.

TELEPROCESSING HARDWARE

Survey Some of the specialized hardware that make up the basic teleprocessing system are described below.

IBM 1030 DATA COLLECTION SYSTEM. This system, shown in Figure 22.11, consists of two, free-standing units: a keyboard with provisions for a card reader or badge reader and a line printer. The keyboard input device has 12 columns of keys. An operator can enter data at the rate of 60 characters per second. It is suitable for use in a manufacturing plant, warehouse, storeroom, etc.

IBM 1050 DATA COMMUNICATIONS SYSTEM. This system, shown in Figure 22.12, provides the user with a full range of input/output services from a remote terminal and includes a keyboard, line printer, card punch/reader and paper tape.

Data is entered via the manual keyboard, card reader, or paper tape and is relayed to the CPU for processing. Leased lines, telephone lines, or other wire systems are used to connect the remote input device and the CPU. The results are fed back to the terminal and printed out on a line printer or card punch.

IBM 1092 and 1093 PROGRAMMED KEYBOARDS. This flexible keyboard entry system, shown in Figure 22.13, contains a bank of 100 blank

FIGURE 22.11   IBM 1030 DATA COLLECTION SYSTEM

FIGURE 22.12   IBM 1050 DATA COMMUNICATIONS SYSTEM

FIGURE 22.13   IBM 1092 PROGRAMMED KEYBOARD

programmable keys. A plastic sheet, called a keymat, is laid over the board to identify each key.

A special sensing device on the keyboard can identify up to 48 different keymats. Thus, for example, one keymat may identify columns used for inventory records. Another may contain payroll column identification. A third may give a code designation to each key for use in entering data from an oil refinery or manufacturing plant.

Data is entered by keying information directly on the keyboard. From there it is relayed to the CPU. After entry of the data, another keymat can be laid over the keyboard and the terminal used for an entirely different application.

The IBM 1093 Keyboard is coupled via a voice grade telephone line to the CPU. Another keyboard unit, the IBM 1092 Programmed Keyboard, may be attached to the 1093 to increase its capacity.

IBM 2740 COMMUNICATIONS TERMINAL. This device, illustrated in Figure 22.14, is designed to be used both as a remote data entry keyboard and as a stand-alone typewriter. In the stand-alone mode, the machine resembles an IBM "Selectric" typewriter and is used for letters, correspondence, reports, etc. In the remote data entry mode, data can be fed to a computer or to other 2740's on the same line.

The machine is also used for data output. The terminal prints out the characters received from the CPU or other 2740's with a rapidly moving, round type element. This type element can be easily changed and a different type style or size inserted in its place. The machine will print with carbon or linen ribbon suitable for high-quality executive correspondence. The terminal can also be used for interactive programming, with such languages as BASIC and APL.

FIGURE 22.14   IBM 2740 COMMUNICATIONS TERMINAL

VERNITRON VDT-4 DATAPORT.   This system, shown in Figure 22.15, is a two-way teleprocessing terminal that sends and receives data. It consists of two parts: a portable teleprinter and an acoustic coupler.

It is connected to the computer via an ordinary voice grade telephone line. It is a full-duplex system, which allows the operator to enter data from the keyboard while the device receives signals from the CPU.

Up to 300 characters per second can be transmitted on the system. The unit is portable and small enough to be placed on a table or desk. The

FIGURE 22.15   VERNITRON VDT-4 DATAPORT

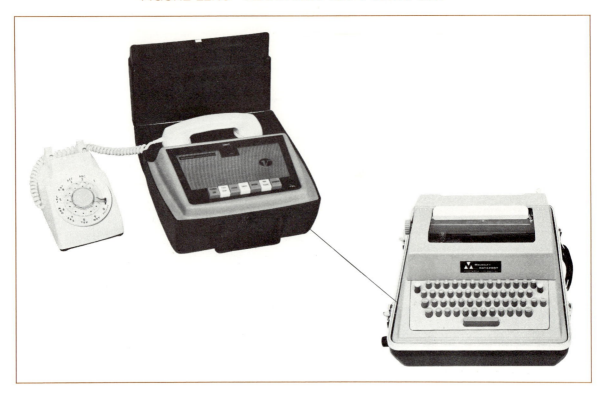

terminal is plugged into a 120-V AC line and the handset of a telephone placed in the cradle of the acoustic coupler. No hard wires or physical circuitry are required to connect the Dataport to the telephone line.

Paper is fed from a roll on the teleprinter. As keys are struck, the characters are printed out on the teleprinter and the corresponding electronic image of the letter is relayed to the CPU. Data being output by the CPU is printed out on the same teleprinter.

ADS DATA TRANSMISSION SYSTEM 660. The 660 Multiplexer is designed to provide up to 45 channels of communication over a single voice grade phone line. Two 660 Multiplexers are in the system, one connected to each end of the line, as shown in Figure 22.16. The multiplexer on one end sets up channels to transmit the data coming from the terminals. The multiplexer at the other end of the line separates the data back into separate paths and feeds it to the CPU.

This arrangement provides an efficient, low-cost means of coupling 45 terminals on-line to a computer using only a single voice grade line.

FIGURE 22.16   DATA TRANSMISSION SYSTEM WITH 660 ADS MULTIPLEXER

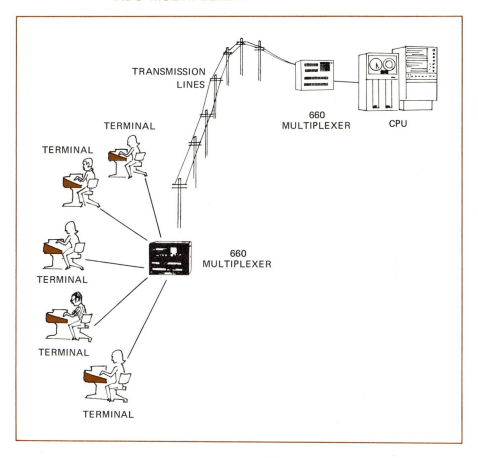

KEY TERMS

Teleprocessing
Telecommunications
Simplex circuits
Half-duplex circuits
Full-duplex circuits
Send-only terminal
Receive-only terminal
Narrow band line
Voice grade line

Wide band line
Channel
Modem
Hard-wired coupler
Acoustic coupler
Multiprocessing
Real-time processing
Remote job entry

EXERCISES

1. Define teleprocessing and explain how it differs from conventional or local processing.
2. Summarize the five major elements in the basic teleprocessing system.
3. How does on-line data entry differ from off-line? Give several examples of data entry applications suitable to each.
4. List the three kinds of transmission circuits in use and explain how they differ.
5. How do narrow band, voice grade, and wide band lines differ?
6. What are the advantages of an acoustic coupler? Suggest several applications for portable terminals with acoustic couplers.
7. Define multiprogramming and explain how it is important to teleprocessing.
8. How does remote job entry processing differ from real-time processing? Give examples of processing jobs suitable to each.
9. Summarize the major advantages and disadvantages of teleprocessing.
10. Visit a stockbroker's office, business firm, or small engineering company that uses teleprocessing. Determine what kinds of equipment are on-line, their applications, and the advantages of the system.

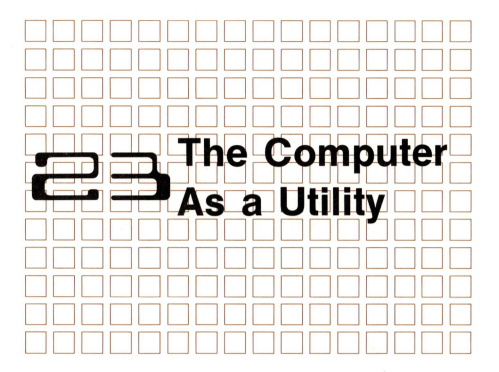

23 The Computer As a Utility

A computer utility is a firm that provides data processing facilities to other organizations. Computer utilities sell their services on a measured basis for profit. Services may be provided either at the user's facilities or at the data center installation.

Computer utilities have existed for many years. Between 1940 and 1950, computer manufacturers provided these services in order to demonstrate and sell new equipment; such services were viewed as a means of enhancing the sales department.

IBM was one of the first firms to develop a full range of utility services, including back-up support, training, testing, and demonstrations to customers. In 1956, a U. S. Justice Department decision held that IBM must divest itself of its service bureau operation. An independent organization, The Service Bureau Corporation (SBC), evolved from this branch of IBM.

Many other firms then entered the computer utility marketplace. Large service utilities were established by General Electric, Tymshare, Control Data, Call A Computer, Computer Sciences Corporation, Comshare, Remote Computing Corporation, etc. Emphasis soon changed from sales enhancement to providing a full range of data processing services to all users on a competitive basis.

The computer utility industry is continuing to grow. It has been estimated that over $1.8 billion was spent for utility services in 1969, and an annual growth rate of 15 to 30% is expected during the 1970's.[1]

[1] *Datamation,* "The Changing Role of the Service Bureau," March 1970, p. 52.

UTILITY-SITE SERVICES

Firms that provide a large volume of utility services are often called service bureaus. These firms operate a fully equipped data center and employ a staff of programmers, operators, and technicians to assist customers.

Some services provided at the utility site are described below. The data, source documents, and records required for processing must be brought to the data center; the results are either picked up by messenger or mailed back to the customer.

Keypunching and Verifying

Many computer utilities employ a large staff of keypunch and verifying operators. They convert raw data or source documents to punched cards or magnetic tape. The customer brings the source documents or records to the center to be keypunched and verified. The cards or tapes generated are processed on the computer, or sent back to the user's site for processing. These services are often used by small firms who do not have enough keypunch operators and machines, or who need help during peak overload periods.

Programming, Testing, and Debugging

Most utilities employ a staff of skilled programmers, proficient in many languages. Other companies buy the services of these programmers when they need a new program developed. They find it more economical to pay a utility to design, code, test, and debug a new program, than to have their own on-site staff do it. Once a program is running, it can be used routinely on the firm's own computer.

Unit Record Services

EAM rooms equipped with a variety of unit record machines are often available at the utility site. Card sorters, reproducing punches, and interpreters are provided for short-run jobs. Operators may be present to assist the customer, or the EAM center may allow hands-on use of equipment.

Production Runs

A major portion of the utility's business is handling production runs. Production runs are jobs run on a computing system to maintain files, produce output such as reports, or any other data necessary for the normal operations of a business firm. They are usually repetitive jobs, run at regular intervals. Raw data is manipulated by programs that have been previously tested for accuracy.

A firm with no computer may rely upon a utility for all of its data processing needs. Raw data is sent to the utility to be keypunched and processed. The utility then sends back reports, ledgers, and updated account records, and handles all mailing of invoices, statements, etc.

Consulting

Because of the highly specialized nature of data processing, many firms buy advice in the selection of equipment and programming software. Utilities have a consulting staff available to help customers with systems analysis, computer selection, systems evaluation, performance measurement, cost comparison, etc. Consultants are also sometimes called to aid in equipment and systems modification.

A firm can bring its data processing problem to the utility for help in finding the solution. The utility's engineers and analysts study the situation, visit the customer's facilities, interview employees, and analyze data flow in the organization. They develop a package for their customers containing algorithms and flowcharts for an improved data flow system.

USER-SITE SERVICES

Teleprocessing and time sharing have extended the usefulness of computer utilities to the remote business enterprise. Teleprocessing provides the communications link between the computer and the remote firm. Time sharing allows many users to share the facilities of the remote computer at the same time. In this system, the computer is on-line with many terminals simultaneously, switching from one to another for a fraction of a second. Each user appears to be in sole control of the computer and processes his own job without awareness of the other users on-line. All data entry and output is handled remotely. It is unnecessary for the user to physically move cards, tapes, or raw data back and forth between his site and the data center. The topics below give some indication of the services available at the user's site.

Interactive Programming

Major utility firms offer a wide selection of both interactive programming, and batch processing languages. Interactive programming, using languages such as BASIC, APL, and PL/I, is particularly suited to remote processing. In addition, most utilities offer the usual batch processing languages such as FORTRAN, COBOL, and ALGOL.

Some programmers prefer to develop, write, and debug a new program on an interactive terminal. After it is running, it is used for production runs on the customer's on-site computer. These programmers find they can write and debug a program on-line much faster than through batch processing procedures. The immediate feedback of results saves many hours or days in program development.

On-Line Libraries and Routines

Utilities also offer applications programs. These programs handle such common business data processing procedures as payroll, accounting, inventory control, statistics, financial management, and engineering applications. Some of these programs are proprietary in nature and were developed at extensive cost to the utility. However, they are put on-line for use by customers with no additional charge.

To use one of these programs, the programmer calls the routine into active storage by keyboarding a few instructions and then enters his data. No additional programming is needed.

On-Line Text Editing

Many businesses write reports, manuals, and bulletins that require editing during preparation. On-line text editing is one of the services offered by many utilities. (See Chapter 18 for a discussion of text editing and ATS, a text editing language.)

The basic text for the document is entered on the remote terminal keyboard at the user's site and stored on-line at the utility. It is transmitted to the utility's computer as a string of characters. From his terminal, the user can make revisions, changes, or alterations in the text, and instruct the computer to print out a new draft on his remote printer. A document may go through several revisions before the final copy is printed out on the terminal.

Basic Terminal Support

Engineering, aerospace, research, and other firms that use mathematics or extensive calculations in their operations often use services offered by a utility. These firms lease from one to several dozen terminals connected to the utility by acoustic or hard-wired couplers. The terminals are placed at strategic locations in the offices and are used as super calculators to solve mathematical problems. (See Figure 23.1.) These terminals combine the capacity of a sophisticated computer with the convenience of a desk-top calculator.

Remote Job Entry (RJE)

A major part of the service provided by utilities consists of handling batch processing jobs transmitted from remote job entry terminals.

These terminals allow users to enter data in the form of punched cards, paper tape, or magnetic tape and transmit it to the CPU for processing. The results of the processing are printed out on a remote line printer, or punched into paper tape.

In fact, many firms rely entirely on utilities for their production runs, with data input and output being transmitted through terminals. All programs, routines, and files are stored at the utility. Only data on current transactions has to be transmitted for processing. Reports, invoices, statements, ledgers, journals, etc. are returned.

Information Retrieval

Large utilities provide users with extensive storage capacity for data files. The diversity and capacity of this storage equipment usually exceeds the facilities available at most on-site systems. Hence firms with large data files often store them on- or off-line at utilities, rather than tie up space or working capacity at their own data processing facility.

DATA BANK

A data bank is a generalized collection of data that can be queried by users on a system. A data bank can be maintained either at the utility or user site. But since data banks store large files and require fast access time, the utility site may be preferred.

FIGURE 23.1 IBM REMOTE TERMINAL

Data Base   The heart of the data bank is the data base—files generated and input at the start of the system and updated and revised as necessary. (See Figure 23.2.)

FIGURE 23.2 DATA BANK SERVICES

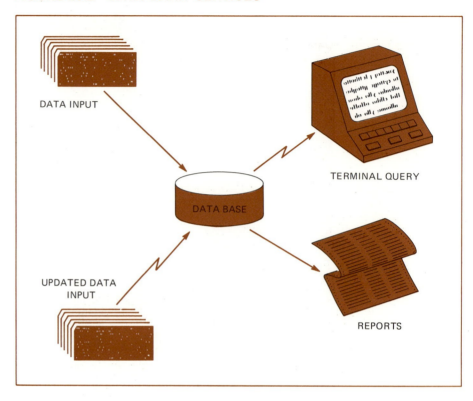

The steps involved in developing and implementing a data base include

1 Definition of data in the base
2 Structuring of files and input media
3 Structuring of query procedures and output media
4 Inputting of raw data to build base
5 Opening of system to users
6 Continual updating of data by inputting new information

Information drawn from many sources within the company may be placed in a data bank. Some common items included are

- Sales information
- Order backlog
- Customer buying patterns
- Current selling prices
- Shipping information and costs

- Supply of raw materials
- Cost of materials
- Equipment and plant capacity
- Financial data
- Personnel data

These items are supplied by departments as raw data input, and new data is continually input to keep the file current.

Query and Output   Data in the data bank can be retrieved from output stations, called query terminals, located at convenient points in the user's office. (See Figure 23.3.) For example, a savings and loan association that queries a data bank hundreds of times in a working day may have terminals at each teller's window, at loan desks, and in executive offices. The data base is accessed by entering a key word called a descriptor on the terminal. Output may be hard-copy reports printed on a line printer, a display on a video terminal, or a message given on an audio response unit.

Advantages   The data bank provides management with a comprehensive storehouse of generalized information, which can be useful in decision making. It permits

FIGURE 23.3   QUERYING FILE STORED AT UTILITY

COMPUTER JOB BANK

A computerized job bank in Van Nuys, California, will list all openings within commuting distance of the San Fernando Valley and make them available almost instantly to job hunters. The computerized operation is expected to enable state employment offices that do not have the equipment or manpower to share new job orders with all Human Resources Development offices in an area.

All the benefits of the computer will not go to employees, however. Employers have long wanted to list vacancies with one administrator at one telephone number and HRD thinks the job bank will meet this need.

Anyone seeking employment can check the job bank screen to see what is available. Work will be classified in such groups as industrial, domestic, or mechanical, by duties, wages, and hours. Employers will not be listed by name, however, so that HRD can control the number of applicants.

Other government and private agencies will have access to the HRD computer, with the restriction that they obtain permission from the HRD administrators before contacting employers.

Interviewers now spend a lot of time on clerical work; with the new system, they will spend their days talking with job-seekers and employers. The labor market will also be easier to define. When a new industry is planned for the Valley, HRD will be able to describe the skills, ages, and experience of potential employees. More accurate statistical information also is expected to make job-training programs more effective by pinpointing labor shortages.

SOURCE Abstracted from "New Plan to Make Job Hunting Easier," by Pat Bryant, *Los Angeles Times*, Part 9, June 8, 1972.

users to generate specialized reports by restructuring existing data rather than opening new files.

OTHER UTILITY SERVICES

Included in the range of data processing facilities offered by most computer utilities are training and instructional services.

Utilities prepare manuals on how to use their services, the contents of their applications libraries, and how to call out and use routines. They supply language manuals, programming hints, debugging and editing instructions, etc. Most utilities provide users with a variety of supporting documentation on programs, including manuals, user guides, directions, etc. They may also provide instructional slides, filmstrips, and video and tape recordings, and offer courses, lectures, seminars, and in-service training programs.

UTILITY VERSUS IN-HOUSE COMPUTERS

Reasons for Using Utilities   A business firm buys services from a computer utility for several reasons. Among them are the cost savings in data processing and the greater capacity and speeds of the computing systems available. The major elements considered are

FREQUENCY OF NEED.   If a firm does not have a sufficient number of data processing jobs to justify an on-site installation, a utility may be the best answer. The cost of maintaining an on-site computer, related equipment, and required staff may be higher than the cost of comparable services from a utility.

"HE INSISTS ON A SECOND OPINION"

BACK-UP RESOURCE. Utilities can provide a back-up service for a firm's equipment. The utility ensures that service will not be interrupted in the event of computer failure within the company.

VOLUME OF DATA AND STORAGE. It is often most economical to install a small computer at the user's site and buy overflow capacity from a utility. The bulk of the work is run on-site, but when overflow conditions occur, the utility handles the excess volume. This results in lower operating costs since the firm can manage with a smaller computer and fewer staff.

TYPE OF JOB. If a firm needs to process a large, one-time job, it may be more economical to buy time from a utility than to tie up its own on-site installation.

PROCESSING SPEED NEEDED. Many utilities have large, high-speed computers capable of processing long, complex jobs quickly. A problem can be solved on these machines much faster than on a smaller, on-site machine.

TRIAL INSTALLATIONS. A firm may buy time on a utility in order to test a computer system. Using the facilities available at the utility gives the firm an opportunity to make comparisons and judge the practicality of a system before making a large financial investment in it.

SPECIAL PROGRAMS AND SERVICES. Some utilities offer a variety of special programs and applications packages to customers. (This has been discussed in Chapter 14.) These may not be available on a user's own computer, or could be costly to develop.

Advantages
Deciding whether to lease their own equipment or buy services from a utility is one of the most difficult decisions a business firm may have to make. There are advantages and limitations to both practices.

Buying utility services frees working capital for employment elsewhere in the business. Equipment costs as well as the expenses for building alterations are avoided. In addition, a firm that purchases all of its computing services from a utility need not be concerned about updating and modernizing facilities. The responsibility for learning about new hardware and software falls on the utility. Similarly, the problem of liquidating obsolete equipment is avoided.

Usually a large utility company can more profitably operate sophisticated, large-capacity computing systems than the average firm.

The wide selection of applications programs available from utilities makes it unnecessary for each user to write all new software; the user's efforts can be directed toward designing specialized programs.

Buying services from a utility gives a firm increased flexibility. A business can vary the amount of computer power at its disposal to efficiently meet changes in data processing demands. Increased computer capacity can be achieved quickly with a request for more terminals. Conversely, a business does not have to maintain more data processing capacity than it needs.

Many firms prefer to buy their computing services from utilities because of the systems support provided. It relieves them of the technical and implementation problems involved in expanding a system and installing new equipment.

Limitations   When a firm buys service from a utility, it is relying on outsiders to handle one of its most vital assets, its business data. If security is broken, or the utility fails to produce services as promised, a company may be in real trouble.

A firm that owns or leases its own computing equipment can schedule and set priority for its own work. When it buys services from a utility, its work may not be assigned the priority it expected. If the utility becomes overloaded, a customer's reports, billing, or other processing may be delayed, causing a critical problem for the firm.

Remote processing requires complex teleprocessing and communications equipment. They are subject to problems in addition to those faced by all computer installations. Telephone lines and communications links can develop trouble that results in transmission failures.

AN EXAMPLE OF A LARGE UTILITY ORGANIZATION

Today, large and small computer utilities provide a full range of data processing service to large and small businesses throughout the country. One large utility, Cybernet, is described below to illustrate the scope of such organizations and the range of services offered.

Cybernet   Cybernet is the computer utility service of Control Data Corporation. The system consists of more than 30 data centers in the United States and a dozen international centers. Over 10,000 miles of communications lines link the system together (as shown in Figure 23.4).

Cybernet has a network of five Control Data 3300 Computers and eight Control Data 6600 Computers, located in major cities of the country. A communications network, composed of voice grade and wide band lines link the CPU's in this system.

Customers gain access to the computing system via a terminal installed in their office as shown in Figure 23.5. Telephone lines are used to tie remote terminals to the data centers. Several types of terminal systems with differing capacities are available. Card readers, video display terminals, plotters, magnetic tape and paper tape drives, line printers, etc. can be connected to the system. A small 12K computer can be installed in the user's office to further expand the system's applications.

A large staff of programmers, systems engineers, computer operators,

FIGURE 23.4   CYBERNET NETWORK

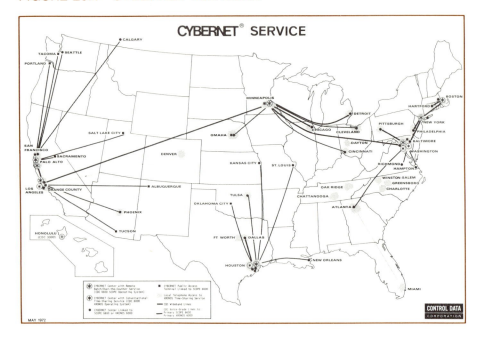

FIGURE 23.5   CYBERNET REMOTE ACCESS TERMINAL

librarians, communications specialists, managers, and marketing people are employed. Both batch processing services and real-time, conversational programming are available to remote users.

Cybernet has many languages available on its system, including BASIC, COBOL, and FORTRAN. Many applications programs are on-line, providing data analysis, linear programming, structural analysis, mathematical and electronic-circuitry programming, and simulations and modeling.

KEY TERMS

Computer utility	Information retrieval
Service bureau	Data bank
Production run	Data base
On-line programming	Discriptor
On-line libraries and routines	Query terminal
On-line text editing	

EXERCISES

1. List four utility services commonly available at the user's site.
2. List four utility services commonly available at the utility site.
3. How do time-sharing services differ from remote batch processing?
4. Discuss five reasons why a firm might purchase services from a utility.
5. Briefly trace the history of the computer utility. What are its prospects for the future?
6. Summarize the size, scope, and services offered by a large utility such as Cybernet.
7. What is basic terminal support? Who uses it and for what purposes?
8. What are "production runs"? Give two examples.
9. List and discuss four limitations and four advantages of the utility.
10. Select one utility service discussed in this chapter. Describe it briefly and suggest an application for a medium- to small-sized company.
11. Select one utility service discussed in this chapter. Describe it briefly and suggest an application of this service for a large company.

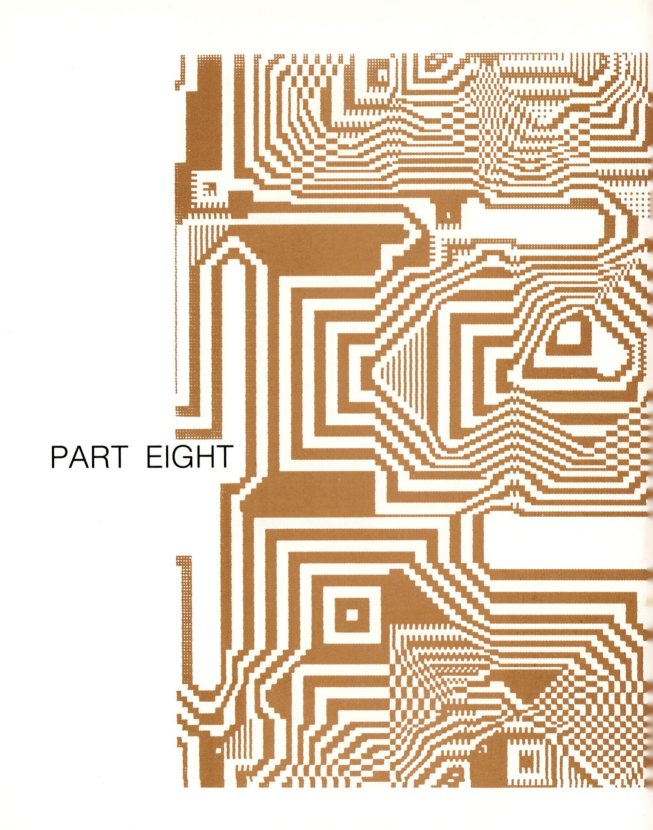

PART EIGHT

applied
business
systems

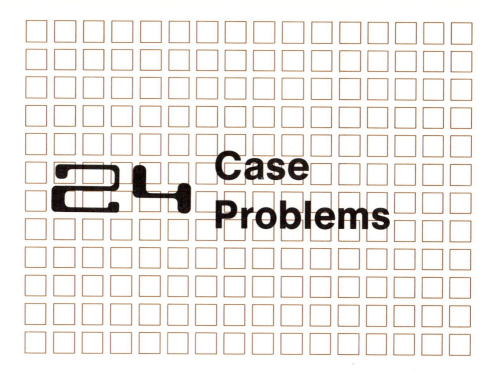

24 Case Problems

This chapter relates the theories and principles discussed in previous chapters to real-life, day-to-day situations. The examples are drawn from actual case histories of firms that developed electronic data processing systems to solve problems or improve services.

Each case is presented from the user's viewpoint. It is assumed that a business systems analyst has studied the situation, planned a solution, and directed its implementation.

Each example states the background of the firm and gives size, location, markets, product, and other pertinent data. Then it either outlines the old data flow system and its weaknesses, or describes existing conditions and explains why they were unsatisfactory.

The solution to the problem is given next in a description of the new business system. Procedural changes are explained, new software and hardware are discussed. Finally, the benefits gained from the implementation of the new system are summarized.

In reviewing the cases in this chapter, you should keep two points in mind. First, the benefits of a new system are usually measured in terms of profits, income, or return on investment of the entire company. Implementing a new system may double or triple EDP costs, but increase profit.

The benefits realized may also be nonmonetary, such as improved customer relations, a better corporate image, or higher employee morale. These benefits may be at the cost of higher data processing expenditures.

Second, this chapter discusses successful case histories. It is quite possible that other firms, with different management, product lines, personnel, etc. may not experience similar results.

INVENTORY–WAREHOUSE PROBLEM

Alchemy Chemical Corporation

Alchemy Chemical is a large supplier of industrial chemicals and equipment. It markets thousands of chemicals and reagents, glassware, microscopes, laboratory apparatus, and testing instruments.

Alchemy has its headquarters in a large urban city. Twenty smaller branches, located in eight other cities, serve various geographic areas. (See Figure 24.1.) A team of salesmen call upon customers to inform them of new products, solicit business, and take orders.

Orders are either phoned into the branch or carried by hand to the sales desk. Under the old system, written orders were prepared at the sales desk and given to the shipping department, where goods were picked, wrapped,

FIGURE 24.1   ALCHEMY CHEMICAL CORPORATION

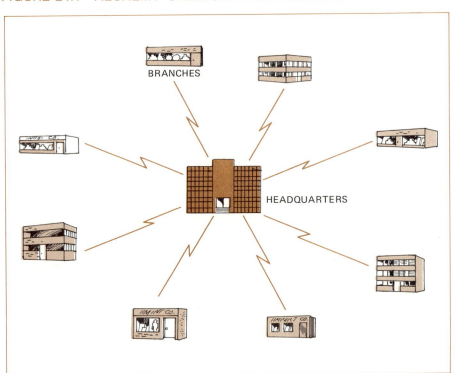

and shipped. If an item was not in stock, it was ordered from another branch and shipped directly to the customer.

Each branch warehouse stocked about 75,000 different items. When an order was received, the item was checked against inventory by manually pulling the proper card from a file, which contained the names of all goods and their current inventory.

THE PROBLEM   The inventory system was costly and inefficient. Many clerks were required to maintain the 75,000 inventory cards. Items were often out of stock because the order clerk did not complete the inventory card in time. Cards were sometimes misfiled, or errors were made while updating the records. When cards were misfiled or lost, several hours were wasted in taking a physical inventory. Often salesmen had to keep customers waiting on the phone while a clerk checked stock.

Since the data on the inventory cards was hard to summarize, management did not have sufficient or current information. Turnover on each item in stock was hard to determine.

THE SOLUTION   A computer system was installed in the Alchemy headquarters and two video display terminals were installed in each branch, one at the order desk and another in the sales department. Telephone lines linked the computer at the head office with the terminals at the branches.

A data base, consisting of inventory information from all branches, was gathered and recorded on magnetic disks. This file included part number of each item in stock, current inventory, price information, and the name of the supply source. This file could be updated by any of the sales desks or warehouses. In addition, the file was structured to display a warning when items were low in stock and should be reordered.

Under this new system, the salesman calls the branch office to place an order. An order clerk, seated before the video terminal in the sales department, queries the data bank by keying in the part number and quantity ordered. The terminal immediately responds with a display showing the quantity in stock, cost, and other data. As items are sold or removed from stock, the inventory is updated from the sales desk and warehouse. The stock available in each branch warehouse can be queried from any terminal. Figure 24.2 contrasts the old inventory system with the new computerized method.

The computer is programmed to print out management reports at weekly intervals. These reports give the current inventory of all items in stock and turnover factor. Reports summarize sales by product line, branch, and supplier.

BENEFITS   With the new system, Alchemy's customers benefit from faster information; as a result service and sales have increased and the company has realized greater profits.

Management has more complete information and control of inventory. The

FIGURE 24.2   ALCHEMY FLOWCHART

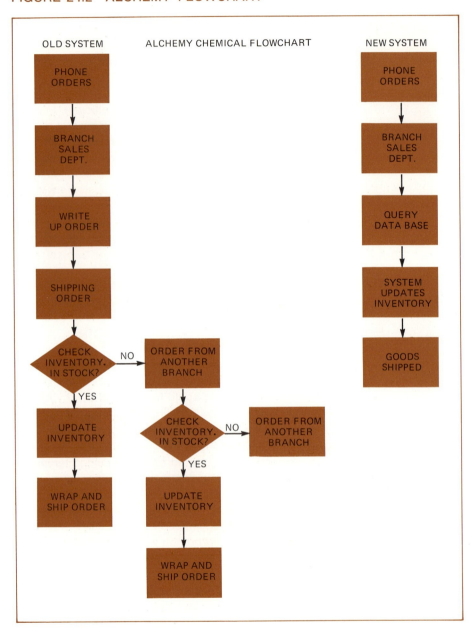

turnover rate of each item in stock is known. Fewer runouts occur, since the system prepares a report listing the low items, supplier, and time required for order to be received.

SALES MANAGEMENT INFORMATION PROBLEM

Babbage Office Machines and Supplies

Babbage sells adding machines, desk calculators, and office photocopy equipment. The product line also includes desks, chairs, filing cabinets, and other office equipment.

A general sales manager, who coordinates the sales efforts of the entire firm, is employed at the home office. (See Figure 24.3.) Several branch sales offices are located in other cities. Each branch is headed by a sales manager who oversees its activities. Each branch hires its own salesmen. The general sales manager frequently visits the individual units to conduct sales meetings, review reports, and guide and coordinate the sales activities.

Under the old system, branch salesmen called on customers and phoned in orders. Orders were also received directly from the customers by phone or mail. Each salesman completed a weekly sales report giving his total calls for the week and the amount and type of goods sold.

FIGURE 24.3   BABBAGE OFFICE MACHINES AND SUPPLIES

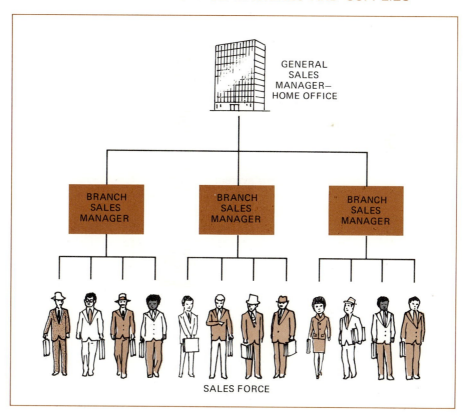

THE PROBLEM   The problem was a lack of current information and incomplete sales and marketing information. The salesmen often neglected to turn in their weekly reports on time and to complete them accurately. Much time was lost locating and organizing records. The general sales manager had little time to plan sales and marketing strategies.

Because of inadequate data and incomplete reports from the salesmen, it was hard to distinguish the best-selling products from those that were not moving. It was difficult to identify the salesmen who were doing a successful job and those who needed help. Often sales information would not be ready until after the close of the period thus delaying reports to the home office. With inadequate or nonexistent information, management could not make intelligent decisions or even determine where changes or improvements were required.

THE SOLUTION   A computerized system was installed in the home office and an off-line terminal in each branch. The typewriter-like terminal is coupled to the computer by calling the home office on the telephone. The phone handset is placed on the coupler connecting the terminal to the computer. Data, keyboarded on the terminal, is fed to the computer.

As orders are written up at the branch, items are removed from stock and shipped. At the end of each day, the sales data is transmitted to the bank at the home office. The salesman prepares a log of his total calls for the week and it is regularly transmitted to the data bank. Figure 24.4 contrasts the old and new systems.

The system is programmed to print out sales reports. The Branch Sales Profile, printed each day for the branch sales manager, lists sales by amount, salesman, and product. Slow moving items and large single sales are extracted and reported separately.

A report is also printed at the home office for the general sales manager. He can also query the system about any branch and thus review the current status of a branch before a visit.

BENEFITS   With the new system, the branch sales manager has sales figures and related information available promptly. He knows which products are selling and which salesmen are effective.

The reports prepared at the home office enable the general sales manager to spot overall problems faster and give him a better picture of the entire operation. His visits to the branches are more effective, since both he and the branch sales managers have common statistics for decision making. Time can be spent planning and developing new marketing strategies, instead of reviewing incomplete reports.

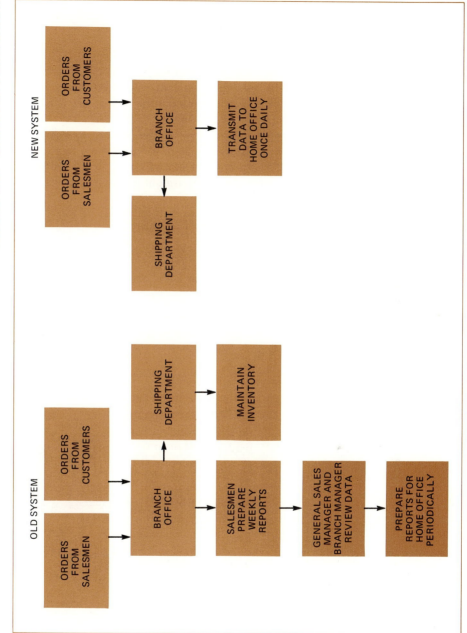

FIGURE 24.4 BABBAGE FLOWCHART

DISTRIBUTION PROBLEM

Volta Parts Company

Volta is located in the suburb of a large city. It manufactures electronic parts, components, testing equipment, and instruments, which are sold to customers throughout the country. Customers are concentrated in several large cities. (See Figure 24.5.)

Customers require very fast service on replacement parts. All orders arrive at the main plant by airmail or long distance telephone. Orders are filled promptly and wrapped or crated for shipment. Each evening, Volta ships about 300 packages (total weight about 10,000 lbs) by truck lines or rail.

THE PROBLEM   The use of ground carriers is both slow and expensive. The preferred mode would be air freight. But the great number of small packages make the cost prohibitive.

THE SOLUTION   The solution to Volta's problem was the installation of a computer programmed to output information on the best way to consolidate and direct

FIGURE 24.5   VOLTA PARTS COMPANY

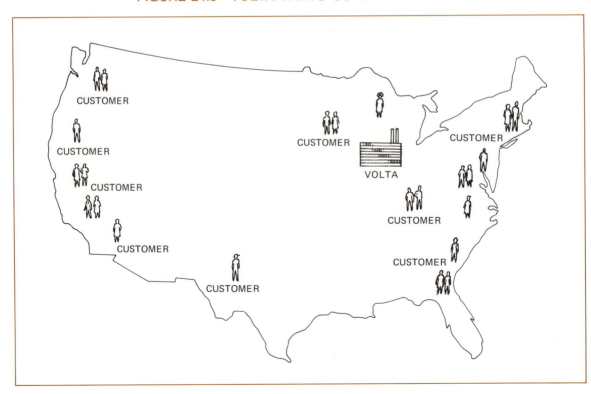

shipments. With the new system, data on shipping information, data on customers, shipper tariffs and schedules, etc. are stored in the computer. Data regarding goods ready for shipment are entered during the day. At the end of each day, the computer prints out a schedule indicating the most efficient way to group packages for shipping.

All packages going to each of five major cities are put in one large crate and sent air freight. Upon arrival at their destination, the large crates are opened and individual packages are delivered to the customer via local carriers. (This is done by the local carrier at no charge.) Shipments to smaller communities are sent by the most efficient ground transportation. Figure 24.6 contrasts the old and new systems.

BENEFITS   Using the computer to help consolidate and plan shipments, Volta can take advantage of reduced air freight rates.

FIGURE 24.6   VOLTA FLOWCHART

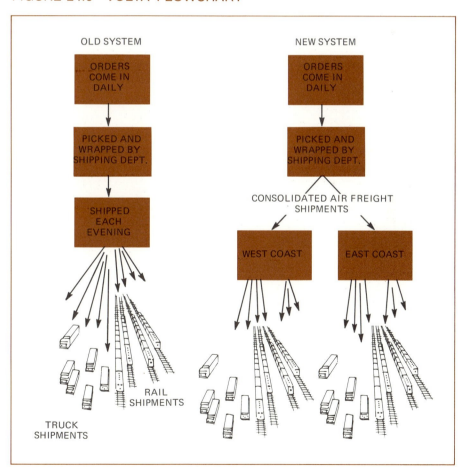

The computer provides management with several reports. It prints out cost reports and a comparison of shipping rates using different media. Customers get faster service at the same rate, because with air freight, shipping time has been reduced from an average of 15 days to 4 days.

PERSONNEL INFORMATION PROBLEM

Bleriot Airparts Company

Bleriot's twelve plants produce airframe parts and guidance and radar equipment. (See Figure 24.7.) Each plant has its own personnel department responsible for hiring and selecting employees, including engineers, scientists, designers, technicians, clerks, and typists. The plants range in size from about 75 employees to more than 1,500.

Each employee's personnel record includes such data as age, military service, health history, previous employer, special training courses taken, education, special abilties and skills, language skills, and marital status.

FIGURE 24.7 BLERIOT AIRPARTS COMPANY

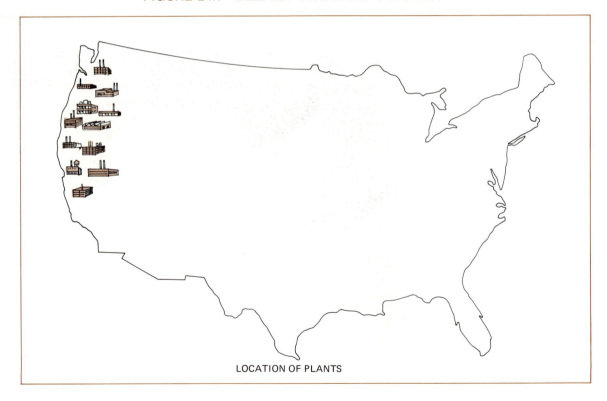

LOCATION OF PLANTS

THE PROBLEM Bleriot has a labor pool of about 10,000 people, who range from those with limited skills such as file clerks or typists to those with highly specialized knowledge such as aerospace engineers.

Bleriot is expanding into a more diverse line of equipment and products. These new lines are developed by "project groups," a staff of technicians, engineers, typists, etc. assigned to a particular problem. Bleriot must find the best staff for these new project groups.

The personnel department in the plant planning a project had to review 10,000 personnel files to identify employees with requisite skills, who could be transferred to the new group. This method was slow, and employees who could do the job best were often overlooked. As a result, Bleriot would hire new personnel for a group, and then later discover an employee with the required skills.

THE SOLUTION A computer was already available in the data processing department. A master file, including all of the pertinent information for each employee, was developed. A computer program was designed and written to process personnel records in the file. Under the new system, the personnel

FIGURE 24.8 BLERIOT FLOWCHART

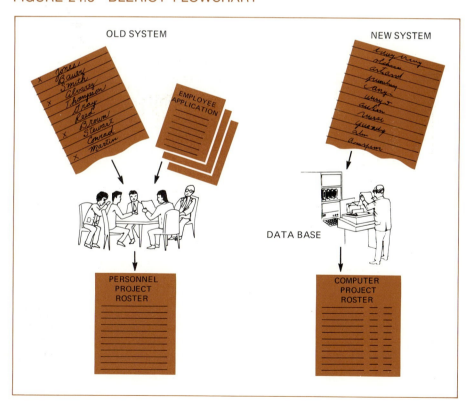

department, or a project director, can query the files with the list of requirements and the computer will output a list of employees who can fill the position. Queries are fed to the computer via a terminal or other input device. Figure 24.8 contrasts the old method with the new system.

BENEFITS   The new system is not only economical, but it has boosted employee morale because it enables them to increase their job mobility. Since fewer new employees are being hired, the costs for training and indoctrination programs are reduced.

     Management can get a closer look at employees. They are aware of the mix of personnel with specialized skills, language skills, security clearance, and special training. The system gives valuable information regarding medical-safety hazards and is useful in planning security, recruiting, and training programs.

CONSUMER CREDIT PROBLEM

Central City Merchants Association

The Central City Merchants Association is composed of a group of retail merchants located in a large midwestern city. Members include department stores, appliance dealers, garages, clothing stores, and furniture stores. (See Figure 24.9.)

     Each merchant extends credit to customers. Before reform, credit standing was learned by checking records kept by each merchant and calling the Association headquarters for a review of their files. (The Association's files include information on delinquent accounts, pending lawsuits, bad check passers, etc.) While the merchant waited on the phone, an Association clerk would search through several lists and file folders for the customer's name. If no negative credit information was found, he reported that the customer had a good credit rating.

THE PROBLEM   The major limitations of the credit system were its high cost of maintenance and the delays in reporting important credit information. All credit data was recorded manually in files and searched by hand. It sometimes required several hours or more to check a name and clear credit if a suit were pending or if special instructions were noted in the file. The merchant had to either wait for clearance from the Association or extend credit without it and run the risk of a loss.

     In some instances, customers would run up large bills at several stores at one time, or issue bad checks in payment for merchandise. It often took several weeks before this information filtered back to the Association's credit office and was recorded in the file. In the meantime, the merchant might extend even more credit or accept bad checks as payment.

FIGURE 24.9 CENTRAL CITY MERCHANTS ASSOCIATION

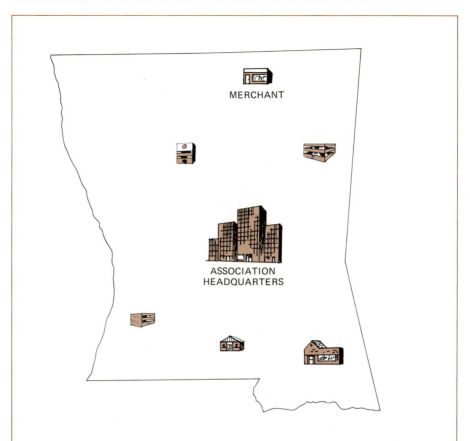

MERCHANT

ASSOCIATION
HEADQUARTERS

THE SOLUTION   The Association solved its problem by implementing a computerized consumer credit system. A computer was installed in the Association office. A master file containing all credit information was recorded on magnetic disk. Included were the names of accounts, delinquencies, bad check passers, etc. Several clerks were assigned the task of maintaining the master file and entering new credit data. The master file was updated promptly to guarantee accurate credit ratings.

With the new system, several clerks are assigned to handle phone queries from the merchants. A clerk keyboards credit request information on a video display terminal connected to the computer. The computer searches the master file and displays any data pertaining to that customer on the video terminal. The clerk then relays this credit information to the merchant. It now takes only a few minutes to process a query. Figure 24.10 contrasts the old and new systems.

FIGURE 24.10   CENTRAL CITY FLOWCHART

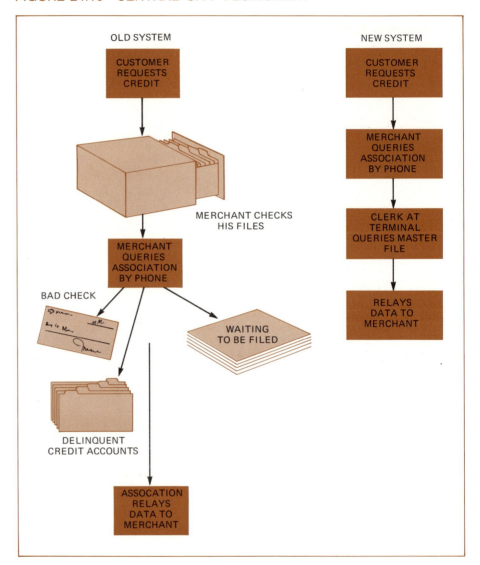

BENEFITS   The immediate benefits of the new system were the reduction in credit losses suffered by the merchants, improved customer relations, and, in some cases, an increase in sales. With credit information relayed immediately, delays in accepting checks and processing new orders are avoided. The incidences of accepting bad checks are substantially reduced.

Other benefits appeared later. As the bulk of credit data went on-line, costs for maintaining the credit check system were reduced and fewer clerks were required.

BANK TELLER PROBLEM

Trustworthy Bank

Trustworthy Bank is a medium-sized banking firm located in a northern state. It provides full banking facilities for its users, including loans, escrow and note collection service. There are 15 branches with a total of 150 teller windows in operation on an average business day. (See Figure 24.11.) Each branch employs from 4 to 12 tellers.

At the end of the day, deposits, debits, and credits were processed in a batch system on the firm's computer. To process a deposit, for example, the teller stamped the customer's deposit slip and entered the amount in his deposit book. Each day, the teller checked the contents of her drawer against the paperwork for that day. Later the deposits were sent to the main branch for posting to accounts. Reports and audits were handled at the main branch after all data was in. Withdrawals in excess of a minimum amount routinely required verifying the customer's balance.

THE PROBLEM   This system had several inadequacies. Since data was not processed until the end of the day, phone queries to check balances and authorize withdrawals from accounts had to be made frequently. If clerks at the data

FIGURE 24.11   TRUSTWORTHY BANK

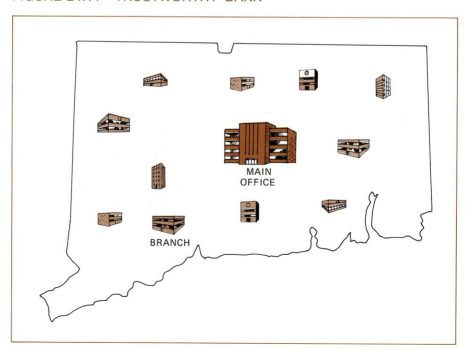

center were busy, the customer had to wait at the window until the withdrawal was cleared.

Each teller spent a good deal of time at the end of each day reconciling the day's cash flow. Without an hourly record of transactions, auditing of teller windows was difficult and reports for management could not be prepared until all posting was completed.

THE SOLUTION   Trustworthy Bank installed a group of real-time teller terminals, coupled on-line to its computer in the main branch. A teller can query a data bank at

FIGURE 24.12   TRUSTWORTHY FLOWCHART

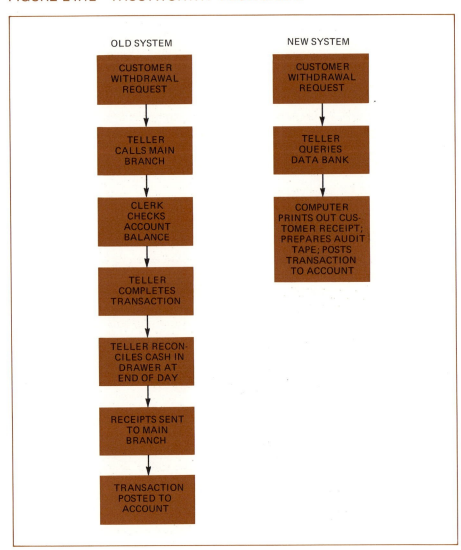

any time during the day. All deposits and withdrawals are posted immediately from the terminal as they occur.

For example, when a customer makes a withdrawal, the teller keys in the account number and the amount of the transaction. The computer accesses the customer's account in the data bank and determines whether there are sufficient funds to cover the withdrawal. A receipt for the customer, showing the teller number, amount of withdrawal, and other data is printed out by the terminal. As the withdrawal is entered in the data bank, an audit tape is prepared giving a complete record of the transaction. Figure 24.12 contrasts the old and new systems used at Trustworthy Bank.

BENEFITS   The new system has benefited both Trustworthy and its customers. Since all transactions are handled on-line, tellers can query the account balance immediately to update passbooks and customers can make large withdrawals or cash checks without delay. Transactions now take less time and tellers can serve more customers per hour. As a result, some of the tellers have been reassigned to other duties and, therefore, labor costs have been reduced.

The audit tapes generated by each teller terminal facilitate the general audit. In addition, the computer prints out management reports that list the number of checks cashed and deposits received by each branch, total the cash in and out, and give the net cash.

TAX SERVICE PROBLEM

Loophole Tax Service

Loophole Tax Service operates a group of 42 income tax offices. During peak periods, Loophole employs extra tax consultants to staff additional temporary offices. (See Figure 24.13.) Each year the firm processes thousands of federal and state tax returns for clients.

The consultants interviewed clients and noted figures regarding their tax liability. After the client left the consultant reviewed the figures and calculated the tax liability, payments, etc. with an adding machine.

The figures were given to a typist who completed the tax forms. The forms were reviewed by the consultant and then given to the client.

THE PROBLEM   This system was slow and inefficient. Consultants wasted time on routine calculations, such as adding up itemized deductions. Many typists were required to prepare the forms. This work was slow since figures had to be carefully positioned on the forms. Sometimes important items were overlooked or errors crept into calculations.

One of the greatest difficulties was the rush during the tax season, especially just before the tax forms were due. Typists and consultants were at their busiest, increasing overtime costs and chances of errors. Unfortunately, many last-minute clients had to be turned away.

FIGURE 24.13 LOOPHOLE TAX SERVICE

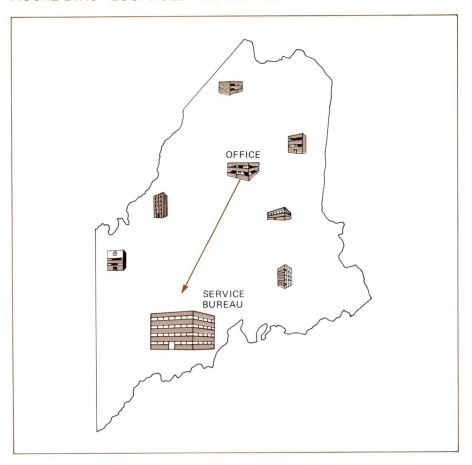

THE SOLUTION   The solution to Loophole's problem was to buy computer time and software from a service bureau. On a piecework price arrangement, the service bureau does all keypunching, processing, and preparing of finished tax returns.

With the new system, a standard data sheet is used by all consultants to record data obtained during the client interview. The consultant pencils in such things as tax liability, deductions, and exemptions in the spaces provided. The forms are then given to the service bureau and the data keypunched into cards. These cards are fed to the computer with the service bureau's tax preparation program. The line printer is loaded with a multi-part, three-carbon form, imprinted with the standard tax form. The computer performs all calculations and prints out the results in the proper areas on the tax forms. The forms are returned to Loophole. One copy is for the client; one for the government; and the third is for Loophole's records. Figure 24.14 contrasts the old and new systems.

FIGURE 24.14 LOOPHOLE FLOWCHART

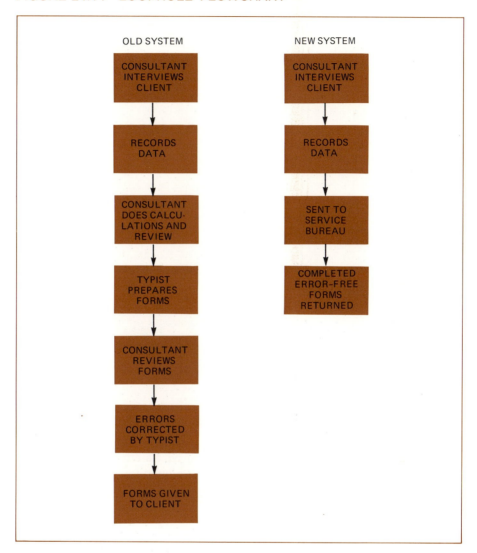

OLD SYSTEM

CONSULTANT
INTERVIEWS
CLIENT

RECORDS
DATA

CONSULTANT
DOES CALCU-
LATIONS AND
REVIEW

TYPIST
PREPARES
FORMS

CONSULTANT
REVIEWS
FORMS

ERRORS
CORRECTED
BY TYPIST

FORMS GIVEN
TO CLIENT

NEW SYSTEM

CONSULTANT
INTERVIEWS
CLIENT

RECORDS
DATA

SENT TO
SERVICE
BUREAU

COMPLETED
ERROR-FREE
FORMS
RETURNED

BENEFITS   With the new system, Loophole Tax Service has been able to reduce costs and errors and handle more clients during the busy tax season. Since the computer performs all routine calculations, fewer clerical and mathematical errors occur. Important items are less likely to be overlooked, since the computer flags omissions, or any items that appear to be excessive or in error.

The system has substantially reduced the amount of time a consultant spends on each return and he can now serve many more clients. Labor costs

CHECKMATE

An electronic David trounced a Goliath-like computer in an intramural chess match at Columbia University in New York City. A Data General Supernova computer (32,768 bytes of memory) needed only 25 moves to checkmate an IBM System 360/91 (two million bytes), one of the largest computer systems in the world.

The Supernova's chess program written by Professor Monroe Newborn and George Arnold, a student, is written in Assembler language and uses a technique that determines the best move by searching between four and eight half-moves ahead, selectively analyzing about 1,000 terminal positions. A move is determined in about one minute—well within chess tournament rules.

Professor Newborn noted that having exclusive use of the smaller computer, along with running the program on-line, helps offset the greater speed and capacity of the larger machine.

The game lasted more than 90 minutes, but the Supernova gained a decided advantage on the sixth move, when the System 360/91, playing white, blundered and traded a knight for a pawn. One of the authors of the program noted that the huge computer saw the correct move—bishop takes bishop—but it did not realize that exchanging bishops would save the knight. He said once the big computer decided it could not save the knight, it decided to pick up a pawn.

The Supernova is now being prepared for the U.S. Computer Chess Championship competition.

SOURCE "Supernova Checkmates 360/91 in Columbia University Chess Match," *Data General News*, April 1972, Vol. 4, No. 2, p. 3.

have fallen since far fewer typists are employed. Loophole's customers benefit because computer-printed tax forms are much neater than manually typed forms.

SMALL BUSINESS FIRM PROBLEM

Adam Smith Manufacturing Company

Adam Smith is the president of a small company that has been in business for 16 years. Thirty-three people are employed by the company, which manufactures small precision parts. (See Figure 24.15.)

Six clerical employees are needed to handle data processing and paperwork. They process the weekly payroll, mail out over 300 checks per month to suppliers and vendors, prepare 2,000 invoices per month, and prepare statements for their several hundred accounts. In addition, Smith must keep many records, including ledgers, accounts payable, and accounts receivable. He must send out collection letters to overdue accounts. Current operating figures, such as sales analysis, projections, and inventory records, are needed for management decision making.

THE PROBLEM   The six employees handling the paperwork faced many problems. When the workload was very heavy, they often mailed out invoices and statements late and made errors. Records were not maintained, and data flow and reports were inadequate.

    Smith felt that inefficiencies in paperwork and data processing prevented his company from expanding and increasing earnings.

THE SOLUTION   Smith presented his problem to several computer companies. They suggested a systems approach to his business. Smith leased a computer for $1,500 per

FIGURE 24.15   ADAM SMITH MANUFACTURING COMPANY

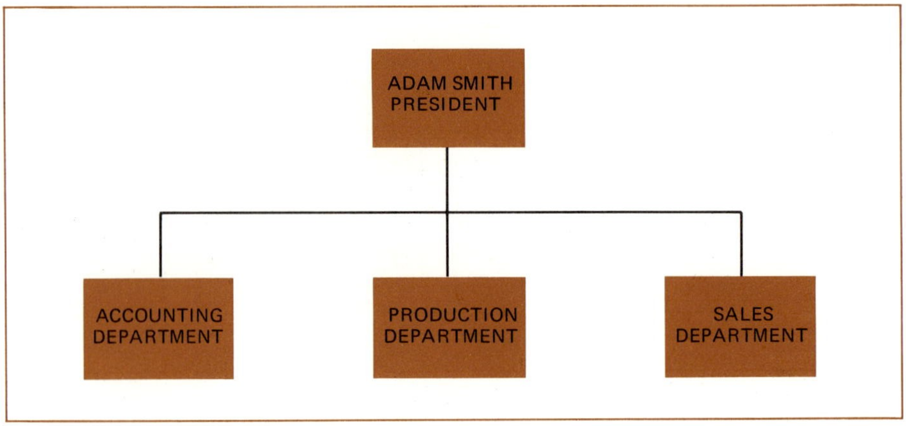

month and, with the help of the manufacturer's systems engineers, shifted the bulk of his data processing to the new system.

Some ready-made programs were available from the computer systems library to process the payroll, invoicing, inventory, etc. These programs were implemented by the systems engineers with only a few minor changes and program modifications. Figure 24.16 contrasts the old system with the new one.

BENEFITS   Smith had hoped the new system would reduce his payroll costs. But this did not materialize. Instead, he hired a computer programmer/operator and transferred four of his employees from the accounting department to the sales and production departments.

Smith has been able to increase his sales 20%, while costs are up only 5%. As a result, capacity and profit have increased substantially. The computer system handles the entire payroll and accounts receivable, and issues the company checks. It prepares earnings reports and government forms and handles the general ledgers and accounts payable.

Invoicing procedures have improved. Smith has a better picture of his cash flow and more adequate information on inventory. Collections have improved, since bills are mailed out promptly and delinquent accounts called to his attention sooner. The computer prepares the collection letters, which used to be typed by a secretary.

Smith has discovered added benefits. His production foreman found that several other computer programs available from the manufacturer were of value in the development and production of new products. These programs save the foreman and his staff about 50 hours each month. They are run during off hours, when the computer is not busy on other work. Smith feels this totally unexpected benefit has an economic value of several hundred dollars per month.

FIGURE 24.16 ADAM SMITH FLOWCHART

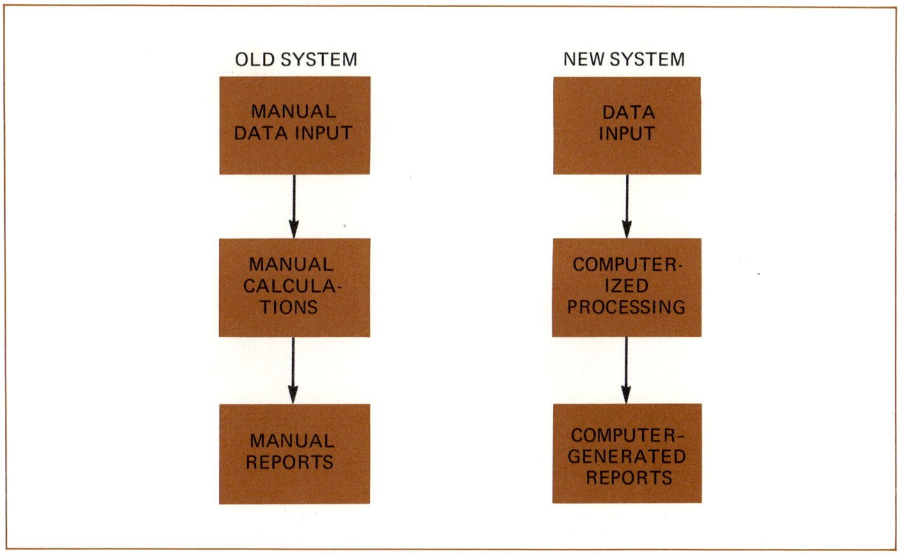

REAL ESTATE MANAGEMENT PROBLEM

Makemoney Consultants

Makemoney is a real estate and investment management consulting service. It offers investment, brokerage, site acquisition, and property management services to investors and landowners. Clients rely on Makemoney to analyze investment transactions and offer advice regarding land and building purchases. A staff of sales consultants deals directly with the clients. Analysts, statisticians, and forecasters work in the office preparing reports and data. (See Figure 24.17.)

THE PROBLEM The previous data processing system at Makemoney involved the preparation of estimates and typewritten reports. These required many hours of laborious manual calculations and a considerable amount of repetitive figuring. A full-time staff of ten employees was needed to figure rates of return, profit on real estate transactions, investment projections, and routine statistical work. During peak periods, errors occurred more frequently, and the analysts and statisticians sometimes fell behind in their work.

Because it is a small company, Makemoney could not afford to purchase or lease a computer large enough to handle its work, but it had a clear need for computerized data processing.

THE SOLUTION Makemoney arranged to purchase computing time and software from a local time-sharing company. Two typewriter terminals connected by existing

FIGURE 24.17   MAKEMONEY CONSULTANTS

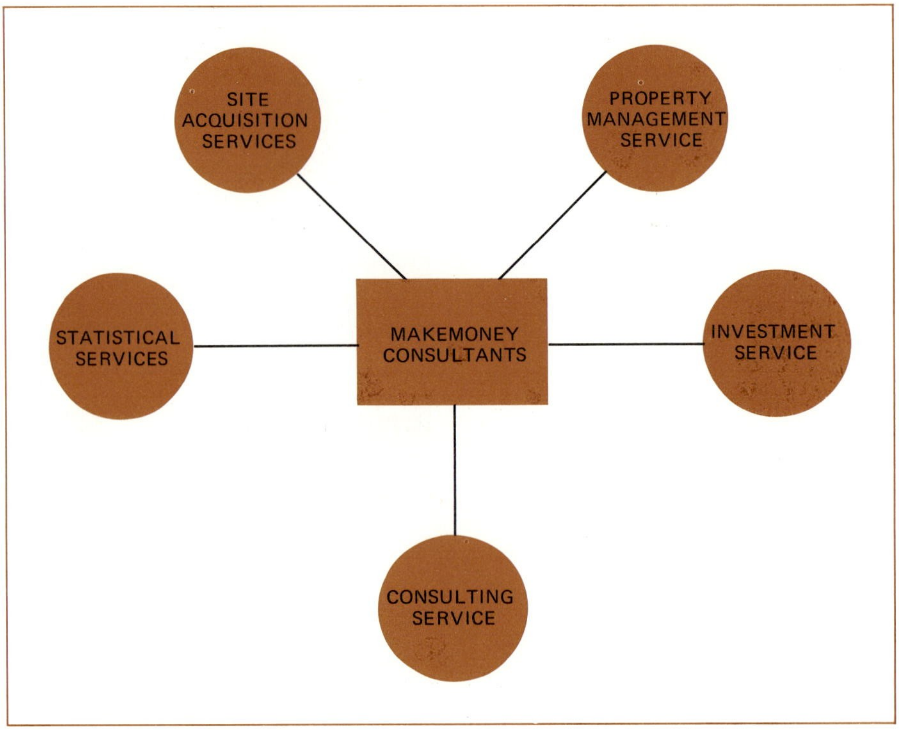

telephone lines to the time-sharing computer were installed. The terminals lease for about $100 per month each, and the charges for computing time from the company average $600 per month.

The time-sharing company has a variety of programs available for its customers. Makemoney uses a group of financial, real estate, money handling, interest, and statistical programs to service its needs. It also uses software to process cash flow, trend analysis, profit and loss statements, etc. These programs are on-line, ready for use, and Makemoney is able to use them with little or no changes.

Several employees are assigned the task of inputting and processing data on the terminals. The results are given to the sales consultants who, in turn, review the information with their clients. Figure 24.18 contrasts the old and new systems.

BENEFITS   With its new computer system, Makemoney is able to give its clients more accurate, complete, and prompt consulting services. The sales consultants can quickly advise clients concerning land transactions, enabling clients to act faster and take advantage of lower market prices.

With the computer processing all calculations, projections, and estimates,

FIGURE 24.18   MAKEMONEY FLOWCHART

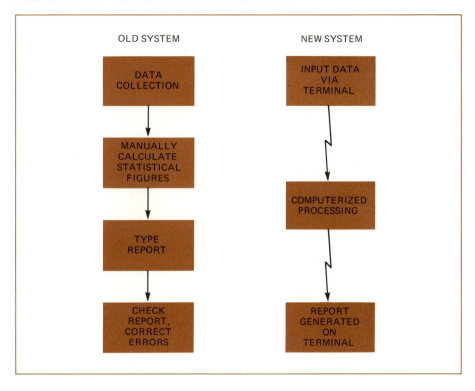

statisticians and analysts no longer fall behind during peak periods. The reports printed out by the terminals in Makemoney's office are neat and accurate. Makemoney can give them directly to their clients without any retyping or correction.

Makemoney was able to promote several of its analysts and statisticians to sales consultants. The new business they bring in far exceeds the cost of the time-sharing service. As a result, Makemoney is doing about a 20% greater volume of business, with little increase in operating costs. As Makemoney continues to expand, the installation of extra teletype terminals will handle the increased volume of work.

EXERCISES   Answer the questions below for each of the nine cases presented in this chapter.
1. Prepare a list of hardware the firm might use in implementing the new system.
2. What computer language would be most valuable to the firm?
3. What proprietary programs, if any, might be used?
4. What further changes or improvements would you suggest?

APPENDIX

Employment Opportunities in Data Processing

INDUSTRY GROWTH AND NEEDS

Electronic data processing offers interesting, satisfying career opportunities for men and women who have the necessary skills, training, and experience. The growth rate of data processing exceeds most other American industries and is expected to continue to increase very rapidly through the 1970's.

Despite the entrance of 50,000 new people each year,[1] a shortage of 50,000–100,000 employees exists.

Types of Jobs Data processing is a diverse field employing individuals in business establishments, government, schools and universities, and private institutions. Most individuals in data processing are employed in the business area in the following categories: manufacturing, public utilities (transportation, communications), wholesale trade, retail trade, finance (real estate, insurance), and services.

Job opportunities exist in relatively small as well as large firms, in different geographic areas, and in communities of all sizes.

As more firms acquire EDP systems, more jobs will be created for those with the necessary skills, knowledge, and abilities. Other jobs related to manual accounting, such as hand-posting in ledgers, filing, and operating a comptometer, are being absorbed in EDP.

Job environments differ widely. Some individuals work in relative isolation

[1] *Datamation,* December 1969, p. 181.

515

in a private office. Others travel thousands of miles each year and meet hundreds of people. Some jobs require a high degree of manual dexterity; others, virtually none. Some require years of study in mathematics or electronics; for others, a practical knowledge of selling and marketing principles is basic.

SALARIES.   Salaries vary according to job classification, years of experience, and training. They vary also with the geographic area, need for individuals with a given specialty, and current business and economic conditions. As a rule, salaries paid in data processing are above the national average and reflect the degree of training and experience. As in any business, however, a surplus of applicants in a particular job category will affect salaries.

WORKING CONDITIONS AND BENEFITS.   Generally, employment in the data processing industry requires little physical effort. Since most firms house their data processing equipment in modern, air-conditioned quarters, EDP employees, as a rule, work in newer, better equipped, and more comfortable quarters than other clerical and office workers.

Some firms offer fringe benefits such as educational allowances. Company health plans, profit sharing, bonus programs, and liberal vacation benefits are common in this industry.

SKILLS AND APTITUDES.   Generally, the specific job determines the skills and aptitudes required. The student should talk to his school counselor or guidance officer and review aptitude test scores and interest measures to evaluate his capabilities.

Age, sex, and racial differences are no bar to employment or success in EDP. Both men and women are employed in jobs with equal status within the industry, and advancement is based on capabilities and performance.

EDUCATION AND TRAINING

Schools and Colleges
Schools, colleges, and universities offer a variety of courses in data processing.

INDIVIDUAL COURSES.   Short courses may last from six or ten weeks to one year. They usually cover a specific, but limited, skill. A course in COBOL or FORTRAN programming is an example.

Another course may train the student to be a computer console operator for a particular brand and size of computer or to operate a single machine such as the keypunch or VariTyper.

These short courses permit the student to enter the industry with a minimum of his time and money devoted to training and preparation.

However, for advancement and greater opportunity, additional academic coursework, training, and supervised on-the-job instruction are usually required.

COMPREHENSIVE PROGRAMS—COMMUNITY COLLEGES. Many community colleges offer two-year programs that either grant the student an A.A. degree, or a certificate of proficiency in data processing. Either of these is valuable on entry into the job market.

The emphasis in coursework varies. Some community colleges stress data processing for business and industry with the curriculum designed to suit students for employment in insurance, banking, manufacturing companies, and in government. Other schools stress equipment and hardware and provide coursework in practical operations and maintenance. The student may, for example, be taught how to service keypunches and tape readers, and be given instruction in electronics and electromechanical theory and practice, computer logic, arithmetic and mechanics, including trouble shooting, testing, and repairing computer systems.

Still other colleges offer strong mathematically oriented computer courses, which stress numerical methods and the mathematical elements of computer programming.

Graduates of a two-year course may qualify as beginning programmers, salesmen, or in computer maintenance or installation. Or the student may transfer to a university and pursue additional coursework and a B.S. or B.A. degree.

COLLEGES AND UNIVERSITIES. As in the two-year programs, EDP curriculums vary greatly in the four-year schools and universities. Since EDP is relatively new, there are no universally accepted core courses. Most programs have been developed to meet special needs or the employment demands of firms in a given community.

Most four-year schools offer courses in programming languages and an introduction to data processing. Business schools offer undergraduate and graduate work in business management and systems analysis. Other programs develop information systems technology, business systems analysis, or computer technology.

Many universities offer graduate work—leading to M.B.A. degrees—in electronic data processing, computer science, and business administration.

Home Study Courses

Several equipment manufacturers and private schools offer comprehensive home study courses in basic computer systems, programming, and systems engineering. These programs utilize programmed instruction, film strips, audio and video tapes, self-testing, and supervised reading.

Firms such as IBM maintain customer education centers offering coursework in basic systems, programming languages, and applications. They provide packaged home study courses, examinations, and advisory services, and give certificates of completion.

Manufacturers
Training Programs

Some firms provide customers with training programs designed primarily for in-service training of employees, or for orientation to their services.

Manufacturers' courses cover engineering, manufacturing, project management, and systems programming. Courses offered by time-sharing firms teach users how to operate remote terminals and cover programming languages.

Certificate in
Data Processing

A Certificate of Proficiency is awarded by the Data Processing Management Association (DPMA) to individuals who pass a written examination. The examination is offered annually at over 100 schools and colleges throughout the country and is open to those who have five years experience in data processing.

The certificate is an asset when seeking employment in the data processing field. It certifies that the holder has a broad educational background and practical knowledge of data processing. The student interested in more details should contact the association at 505 Busse Highway, Park Ridge, Illinois, 60068.

The educational background recommended by the DPMA provides a balanced coverage of essentials. The following abstract of their study outline lists the main topics of study. It should be noted that the list is extensive and covers advanced mathematical and systems theory. All jobs in data processing do not require such extensive preparation, however.

1. Data processing equipment. The student should understand the basic principles of data processing equipment and its evolution. He should have a knowledge of computer components and their functions and how data is fed in and out of a computer. In addition, a knowledge of data transmission, unit record equipment, and basic office machines is useful.
2. Computer programming and software. An understanding of computer programming, compilers, methods of addressing, loops, subroutines, sorts, and memory systems is necessary. Some familiarity with the common programming languages is required. Particular stress should be on COBOL and FORTRAN.
3. Principles of management. The student should understand the fundamentals of general management and organization principles, management techniques, corporate organization structure, and data processing management practice.
4. Quantitative methods. A foundation in quantitative methods is essential for the specialist. He should understand basic principles of accounting, cost acounting, and internal control and auditing. In addition, the student should have a knowledge of mathematical notation, computations and set theory, the mathematics of finance and accounting, linear programming, operations research, and statistics.
5. Systems analysis and design. The student should understand the principles of systems analysis, hardware evaluation techniques, systems design and implementation. His study should cover system input, output, file organization, documentation, system maintenance, and the operation of real-time and time-sharing systems.

JOB DESCRIPTIONS

Jobs in data processing may be classified in many ways: for example, by necessary skills, salary, or industry group.

The Dictionary of Occupational Titles (D.O.T.), available in most school and public libraries, gives a thorough description of the various job categories. These volumes outline in detail the duties, skills, and aptitudes necessary for performance of each job.

Occupational Guides published by state employment offices are another useful source of job descriptions. These guides usually outline job duties, working conditions, employment, pay and hours, promotion, and training, and provide information about where to find additional data.

Many large-scale employers, such as state and local government, school districts and private firms, publish job availability and employment bulletins, which discuss job descriptions, requirements, salary, and how to apply for the job.

Major Data Processing Opportunities

The following list of jobs and their descriptions is an overview of the diverse nature of the industry.

KEYPUNCH OPERATOR. The keypunch operator uses key-driven machines to record data as punched holes in cards. Keypunch operators usually work in large rooms, with many other employees. Operating noise is thus a factor and should be considered by anyone sensitive to sound.

Speed, accuracy, and concentration are essential. Operators must be able to accept instruction and cooperate with fellow workers. This job is primarily sedentary; hours are good; and work may be available around the clock. Innovations in data input methods and equipment may affect job availability and some of the skills required of keypunch operators.

TABULATING MACHINE OPERATOR. The "tab" operator works with unit record equipment such as sorting machines, collators, reproducing punches, interpreters, and tabulators. This electromechanical equipment analyzes, classifies, tabulates, and reproduces data. It is programmed by manually wiring control panels. Since most machines are card-fed devices, a "tab" operator must be able to carry stacks of cards from one machine to another.

With the growth of EDP, the reliance upon unit record equipment has diminished to some extent. Unit record installations are primarily found in the small to medium-sized firm, or in firms that operate unit record equipment as well as electronic computers.

The "tab" operator should enjoy working with machines, have good eyesight, and be able to lift from 20 to 60 lbs. of punched cards. The employment outlook for this group is less optimistic because of the trend toward EDP.

PROGRAMMERS.   A programmer's responsibilities range from planning and flowcharting a problem to coding (writing the instructions for the computer) and debugging it (locating errors in programs). Generally, he plans the solution of a stated clerical, administrative, or statistical problem.

The programmer must determine what information should be entered in the program and in what form, the mathematical and logical operations the computer must perform, and the output. Sometimes the work is divided into several groups: one person does the research and early planning of the program; another, the actual coding of the instructions.

The programmer may consult personnel from other departments about their clerical and data processing needs. He must learn what information or reports are required, how the information is to be used, and what source documents are available. After analyzing these details, he develops a general plan and writes a set of instructions for the computer.

Working conditions are good, and jobs are available in a variety of establishments. The long-range employment outlook is optimistic and will parallel the growth for skilled office employees. As new programming languages enter the industry, some new skills and retraining may be necessary.

SYSTEMS ANALYST.   The systems analyst studies business problems and formulates procedures for solving them, using EDP equipment. He develops a set of guidelines that the programmer converts into computer instructions. The work involves analyzing subject matter and identifying conditions and criteria required to automate a procedure. He specifies the number and type of records, files, and documents to be used. He outlines actions to be taken by personnel and computers in sufficient detail for programming. He presents recommendations and proposed procedures to management. He frequently uses drawings, flowcharts, and diagrams. He coordinates the development of test problems and participates in trial runs of new and revised systems. He recommends equipment changes to obtain more effective overall operations.

The employment outlook for this group is good. As more firms begin to utilize data processing, there will be an increased need for individuals who can diagnose business data problems and propose solutions.

DIGITAL COMPUTER OPERATOR (Console Operator).   The console operator monitors and operates the control console of the computer. He determines the procedures to be followed from the programmer's instruction sheet for the run. He readies the equipment, loads the computer with tape, reels, disks, or cards, and starts the run. During a run, he may manipulate dozens of switches and observe the status of the machine through lights on the console. If the computer stops, or signals an error, he must try to locate the source of the trouble. He communicates with the computer by typing instructions on a console typewriter, or receives messages on a video screen.

Console operators may operate a variety of auxiliary equipment. These machines may convert data from tape to card, or from tape to the printed page. Other auxiliary communication equipment ties together computers at different points, through leased or telephone lines.

The console operator may work alone on a single computer, or with several others in a computer installation. Many firms operate their computers around the clock, using second and third shifts. The need for console operators is basic to the industry and should grow in the next decade.

Improvements in computers and programming languages have simplified, rather than complicated, machine operations. Because of these changes, machines are often less complex to operate than a decade or two ago. As a result, those studying for careers in computer console operations and even programming, will discover that it is now easier to qualify for these openings.

LIBRARIAN, DOCUMENTATION SPECIALIST. This occupational category supports the activities of the programmers and systems engineers. Librarians catalog and file data, reports, programs, and documentation on programs. Documentation specialists write up the details and specifications on running programs. They prepare notes, drawings, and textual statements regarding the program flow, format of input and output records, etc. Tape librarians file and catalog magnetic tape, disks, and even tab cards in large computer installations.

Librarians usually work alone or in small groups. They must be able to write clearly, and file and catalog tape, disks, and programs.

DATA PROCESSING MANAGER, DIRECTOR. This individual is responsible for the overall output and operations of the data processing department. The Director coordinates the activities of the computer installation with those of other departments and organizations and must provide uninterrupted service to the firm. As an administrator, he supervises the other employees in the data processing department and must plan work loads, staffing, selection and training, and promotion. A manager must remain aware of new equipment and systems and be able to communicate well, both verbally and in writing.

The employment outlook for managers is good and will increase as more firms adopt EDP methods.

SALES AND MARKETING. A wide variety of positions are open in the sales and marketing of computers, terminals, time-sharing services, and related hardware. Those engaged in this job classification demonstrate equipment, analyze needs, and make recommendations regarding new devices and services.

The sales staff for time-sharing companies calls upon both large and small businesses, demonstrates computer terminals and software services. The hours and working conditions vary greatly with the kind of equipment or service sold and the employer. Some travel may be involved, and often the salesman will plan his own workday and routing. The successful sales person must have a good grasp of data processing fundamentals, enjoy being with people, and like selling.

CUSTOMER ENGINEERING AND MAINTENANCE.   Customer engineers are employed by computer manufacturers to call upon firms using their systems. They help the customer make the most efficient use of the available equipment.

The installer often travels to new installations and remains with the account until the system is in operation and performing properly.

Maintenance people visit computer installations at regular intervals to perform preventative maintenance procedures or to service the equipment. They clean, lubricate, and adjust machines, and perform routine diagnostic tests on computers, line printers, card punches, etc.

The employment outlook for this group is good and will grow as more machines go into service. Technical skills and a knowledge of electronics and hardware are required. Many smaller firms that make computer components and supporting equipment also hire technicians, installers, maintenance people, and engineers.

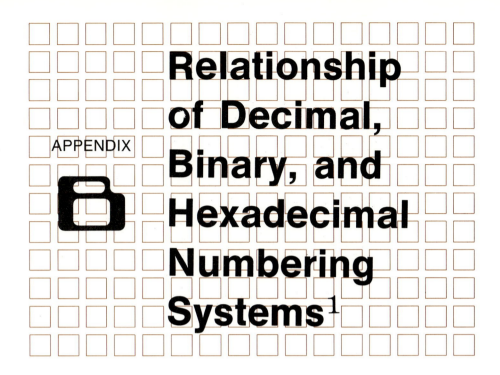

Relationship of Decimal, Binary, and Hexadecimal Numbering Systems[1]

APPENDIX

DECIMAL	HEXA-DECIMAL	BINARY	DECIMAL	HEXA-DECIMAL	BINARY	DECIMAL	HEXA-DECIMAL	BINARY
0	00	0000 0000	21	15	0001 0101	42	2A	0010 1010
1	01	0000 0001	22	16	0001 0110	43	2B	0010 1011
2	02	0000 0010	23	17	0001 0111	44	2C	0010 1100
3	03	0000 0011	24	18	0001 1000	45	2D	0010 1101
4	04	0000 0100	25	19	0001 1001	46	2E	0010 1110
5	05	0000 0101	26	1A	0001 1010	47	2F	0010 1111
6	06	0000 0110	27	1B	0001 1011	48	30	0011 0000
7	07	0000 0111	28	1C	0001 1100	49	31	0011 0001
8	08	0000 1000	29	1D	0001 1101	50	32	0011 0010
9	09	0000 1001	30	1E	0001 1110	51	33	0011 0011
10	0A	0000 1010	31	1F	0001 1111	52	34	0011 0100
11	0B	0000 1011	32	20	0010 0000	53	35	0011 0101
12	0C	0000 1100	33	21	0010 0001	54	36	0011 0110
13	0D	0000 1101	34	22	0010 0010	55	37	0011 0111
14	0E	0000 1110	35	23	0010 0011	56	38	0011 1000
15	0F	0000 1111	36	24	0010 0100	57	39	0011 1001
16	10	0001 0000	37	25	0010 0101	58	3A	0011 1010
17	11	0001 0001	38	26	0010 0110	59	3B	0011 1011
18	12	0001 0010	39	27	0010 0111	60	3C	0011 1100
19	13	0001 0011	40	28	0010 1000	61	3D	0011 1101
20	14	0001 0100	41	29	0010 1001	62	3E	0011 1110

[1]From *IBM System 360 Reference Data*, X20-1703, pp. 7–10.

DECIMAL	HEXA-DECIMAL	BINARY	DECIMAL	HEXA-DECIMAL	BINARY	DECIMAL	HEXA-DECIMAL	BINARY
63	3F	0011 1111	109	6D	0110 1101	155	9B	1001 1011
64	40	0100 0000	110	6E	0110 1110	156	9C	1001 1100
65	41	0100 0001	111	6F	0110 1111	157	9D	1001 1101
66	42	0100 0010	112	70	0111 0000	158	9E	1001 1110
67	43	0100 0011	113	71	0111 0001	159	9F	1001 1111
68	44	0100 0100	114	72	0111 0010	160	A0	1010 0000
69	45	0100 0101	115	73	0111 0011	161	A1	1010 0001
70	46	0100 0110	116	74	0111 0100	162	A2	1010 0010
71	47	0100 0111	117	75	0111 0101	163	A3	1010 0011
72	48	0100 1000	118	76	0111 0110	164	A4	1010 0100
73	49	0100 1001	119	77	0111 0111	165	A5	1010 0101
74	4A	0100 1010	120	78	0111 1000	166	A6	1010 0110
75	4B	0100 1011	121	79	0111 1001	167	A7	1010 0111
76	4C	0100 1100	122	7A	0111 1010	168	A8	1010 1000
77	4D	0100 1101	123	7B	0111 1011	169	A9	1010 1001
78	4E	0100 1110	124	7C	0111 1100	170	AA	1010 1010
79	4F	0100 1111	125	7D	0111 1101	171	AB	1010 1011
80	50	0101 0000	126	7E	0111 1110	172	AC	1010 1100
81	51	0101 0001	127	7F	0111 1111	173	AD	1010 1101
82	52	0101 0010	128	80	1000 0000	174	AE	1010 1110
83	53	0101 0011	129	81	1000 0001	175	AF	1010 1111
84	54	0101 0100	130	82	1000 0010	176	B0	1011 0000
85	55	0101 0101	131	83	1000 0011	177	B1	1011 0001
86	56	0101 0110	132	84	1000 0100	178	B2	1011 0010
87	57	0101 0111	133	85	1000 0101	179	B3	1011 0011
88	58	0101 1000	134	86	1000 0110	180	B4	1011 0100
89	59	0101 1001	135	87	1000 0111	181	B5	1011 0101
90	5A	0101 1010	136	88	1000 1000	182	B6	1011 0110
91	5B	0101 1011	137	89	1000 1001	183	B7	1011 0111
92	5C	0101 1100	138	8A	1000 1010	184	B8	1011 1000
93	5D	0101 1101	139	8B	1000 1011	185	B9	1011 1001
94	5E	0101 1110	140	8C	1000 1100	186	BA	1011 1010
95	5F	0101 1111	141	8D	1000 1101	187	BB	1011 1011
96	60	0110 0000	142	8E	1000 1110	188	BC	1011 1100
97	61	0110 0001	143	8F	1000 1111	189	BD	1011 1101
98	62	0110 0010	144	90	1001 0000	190	BE	1011 1110
99	63	0110 0011	145	91	1001 0001	191	BF	1011 1111
100	64	0110 0100	146	92	1001 0010	192	C0	1100 0000
101	65	0110 0101	147	93	1001 0011	193	C1	1100 0001
102	66	0110 0110	148	94	1001 0100	194	C2	1100 0010
103	67	0110 0111	149	95	1001 0101	195	C3	1100 0011
104	68	0110 1000	150	96	1001 0110	196	C4	1100 0100
105	69	0110 1001	151	97	1001 0111	197	C5	1100 0101
106	6A	0110 1010	152	98	1001 1000	198	C6	1100 0110
107	6B	0110 1011	153	99	1001 1001	199	C7	1100 0111
108	6C	0110 1100	154	9A	1001 1010	200	C8	1100 1000

DECIMAL	HEXA-DECIMAL	BINARY		DECIMAL	HEXA-DECIMAL	BINARY		DECIMAL	HEXA-DECIMAL	BINARY
201	C9	1100 1001		220	DC	1101 1100		239	EF	1110 1111
202	CA	1100 1010		221	DD	1101 1101		240	F0	1111 0000
203	CB	1100 1011		222	DE	1101 1110		241	F1	1111 0001
204	CC	1100 1100		223	DF	1101 1111		242	F2	1111 0010
205	CD	1100 1101		224	E0	1110 0000		243	F3	1111 0011
206	CE	1100 1110		225	E1	1110 0001		244	F4	1111 0100
207	CF	1100 1111		226	E2	1110 0010		245	F5	1111 0101
208	D0	1101 0000		227	E3	1110 0011		246	F6	1111 0110
209	D1	1101 0001		228	E4	1110 0100		247	F7	1111 0111
210	D2	1101 0010		229	E5	1110 0101		248	F8	1111 1000
211	D3	1101 0011		230	E6	1110 0110		249	F9	1111 1001
212	D4	1101 0100		231	E7	1110 0111		250	FA	1111 1010
213	D5	1101 0101		232	E8	1110 1000		251	FB	1111 1011
214	D6	1101 0110		233	E9	1110 1001		252	FC	1111 1100
215	D7	1101 0111		234	EA	1110 1010		253	FD	1111 1101
216	D8	1101 1000		235	EB	1110 1011		254	FE	1111 1110
217	D9	1101 1001		236	EC	1110 1100		255	FF	1111 1111
218	DA	1101 1010		237	ED	1110 1101				
219	DB	1101 1011		238	EE	1110 1110				

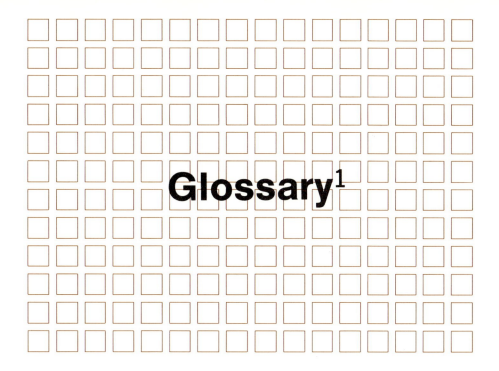

Glossary[1]

ABSOLUTE ADDRESS An address that is permanently assigned by the machine designer to a storage location. A pattern of characters that identifies a unique storage location without further modification. Synonymous with machine address, specific address.

ACCESS TIME The time interval between the instant at which data is called for from a storage device and the instant delivery begins. The time interval between the instant at which data is requested to be stored and the instant at which storage is started.

*ACTIVITY A term to indicate that a record in a master file is used, altered, or referred to.

ADDRESS An identification as represented by a name, label, or number for a register, location in storage, or any other data source or destination, such as the location of a station in a communication network.

ALGOL *Algo*rithmic *L*anguage. A language primarily used to express computer programs by algorithms.

ALGORITHM A prescribed set of well-defined rules or processes for the solution of a problem in a finite number of steps.

ALPHAMERIC See *alphanumeric*.

---

[1] All unmarked entries are reproduced with permission from the *American National Standard Vocabulary for Information Processing*. Copyright © 1970 by American National Standards Institute, copies of which may be purchased from the American National Standards Institute at 1430 Broadway, New York, New York 10018.

ALPHANUMERIC   Pertaining to a character set that contains letters, digits, and usually other characters such as punctuation marks. Synonymous with alphameric.

ANALOG COMPUTER   A computer in which analog representation of data is mainly used. A computer that operates on analog data by performing physical processes on these data. Contrast with *digital computer*.

*ANALOG DATA   Data represented in a continuous form, as contrasted with digital data represented in a discrete (discontinuous) form. Analog data is usually represented by means of physical variables, such as voltage, resistance, and rotation.

*ANSI   American National Standards Institute. Formerly ASA and USASI.

*APL   *A Programming Language.* A mathematically oriented language.

ARITHMETIC UNIT   The unit of a computing system that contains the circuits that perform arithmetic operations.

ARRAY   An arrangement of elements in one or more dimensions.

ASCII   American National Standard Code for Information Interchange. The standard code, using a coded character set consisting of seven-bit coded characters (eight bits including parity check), used for information interchange among data processing systems, communication systems, and associated equipment. The ASCII set consists of control characters and graphic characters. Synonymous with USASCII.

ASSEMBLE   To prepare a machine language program from a symbolic language program by substituting absolute operation codes for symbolic operation codes and absolute or relocatable addresses for symbolic addresses.

*ASSEMBLER LANGUAGE   A symbolic programming language that uses symbolic operation codes and addresses. The translation of these codes into machine language is called an assembly.

*ATS   *Administrative Terminal System.* A text processing language.

*AUDIO RESPONSE UNIT   A device that outputs information, recorded on a magnetic storage media, using the spoken word.

AUXILIARY STORAGE   A storage that supplements another storage. In flowcharting, an off-line operation performed by equipment not under control of the central processing unit.

BACKGROUND PROCESSING   The automatic execution of lower priority computer programs when higher priority programs are not using the system resources. Contrast with *foreground processing*.

*BACK-UP SYSTEM   Standby facilities such as a computer or files, for use in case of damage, loss, or overloading.

*BASE   The number of characters used in a digital numbering system.

*BASIC   *Beginners All-Purpose Symbolic Instruction Code.* A programming language used in time sharing.

BATCH PROCESSING   Pertaining to the technique of executing a set of programs such that each is completed before the next program of the set is started. Loosely, the execution of programs serially. Pertaining to the sequential input of computer programs or data.

*BAUDOT CODE   A code for the transmission of data in which five equal-length bits represent one character.

BCD (BINARY CODED DECIMAL NOTATION)   Positional notation in which the individual decimal digits expressing a number in decimal notation are each represented by a binary numeral.

*BCDIC (BINARY CODED DECIMAL INTERCHANGE CODE)   An extension of the BCD numeric code, consisting of six intelligence channels and one parity check-bit channel. Up to 64 different characters can be transmitted.

*BINARY NOTATION   A fixed-base notation where the base is two.

*BIT   Contraction of "Binary digit," the smallest unit of information in a binary system. A bit may be either one or zero.

*BLANK-COLUMN DETECTION   A unit record procedure that detects unpunched or uncoded columns.

BLOCK   A set of things, such as words, characters, or digits, handled as a unit. A collection of contiguous records recorded as a unit. Blocks are separated by block gaps and each block may contain one or more records.

*BLOCKING   Combining two or more records into one block.

*BPS (BITS PER SECOND)   In serial transmission, the instantaneous bit speed within one character, as transmitted by a machine or a channel.

BRANCH   A set of instructions that are executed between two successive decision instructions. To select a branch as above. Loosely, a conditional jump.

BUFFER   A routine or storage used to compensate for a difference in rate of flow of data, or time of occurrence of events, when transmitting data from one device to another.

BUG   A mistake or malfunction.

BYTE   A sequence of adjacent binary digits operated upon as a unit and usually shorter than a computer word.

*CARD PUNCH   A device to record information in cards by punching holes in the cards to represent letters, digits, and special characters.

*CARD READER   A device that senses and translates into internal form the holes in punched cards.

*CATHODE RAY TUBE DISPLAY   A device that presents data in visual form by means of controlled electron beams. The data display produced by the device above.

CENTRAL PROCESSING UNIT (CPU)   A unit of a computer that includes circuits controlling the interpretation and execution of instructions. Synonymous with *main frame*.

CHAIN PRINTER   A printer in which type slugs are carried by the links of a revolving chain.

CHANNEL   A path along which signals can be sent, for example, data channel, output channel. The portion of a storage medium that is accessible to a given reading or writing station, for example, track, band. In communication, a means of one-way transmission.

*CHANNEL ADDRESS   The code that refers to a particular circuit that connects the CPU to an I/O device.

*CHANNEL SCHEDULER   In the Disk and Tape Operating Systems (DOS and TOS), that part of the supervisor that controls all input/output operations.

CHARACTER   A letter, digit, or other symbol that is used as part of the organization, control, or representation of data. A character is often in the form of a spatial arrangement of adjacent or connected strokes.

CHARACTER SET   A set of unique representations called characters, for example, 26 letters of the English alphabet, 0 and 1 of the Boolean alphabet, the set of signals in the Morse code alphabet, the 128 characters of the ASCII alphabet.

CHECK BIT   A binary check digit, for example, a parity bit.

*CLASSIFY   To arrange into classes of information according to a system or method.

CLOCK   A device that generates periodic signals used for synchronization. A device that measures and indicates time. A register whose content changes at regular intervals in such a way as to measure time.

CLOSED SHOP   Pertaining to the operation of a computer facility in which most productive problem programming is performed by a group of programming specialists rather than by the problem originators. The use of the computer itself may also be described as closed shop if full time trained operators, rather than user/programmers serve as the operators. Contrast with *open shop*.

COBOL   *Common Business-Oriented Language*. A business data processing language.

*CODASYL   *Conference of Data Systems Languages*. The group of users and manufacturers of data processing systems that developed and maintain the COBOL language.

*CODING   The operation of converting instructions into language commands that can be processed by a computer.

COLLATE   To combine items from two or more ordered sets into one set having a specified order not necessarily the same as any of the original sets. Contrast with *merge*.

COLUMN   A vertical arrangement of characters or other expressions. Loosely, a digit place.

COMMUNICATION LINK   The physical means of connecting one location to another for the purpose of transmitting and receiving data.

COMPILE   To prepare a machine language program from a computer program written in another programming language by making use of the overall logic structure of the program, or generating more than one machine instruction for each symbolic statement, or both, as well as performing the function of an assembler.

COMPILER   A program that compiles.

COMPUTER   A data processor that can perform substantial computation, including numerous arithmetic or logic operations, without intervention by a human operator during the run.

*COMPUTER UTILITY An organization that provides data processing consultation, services, and time-share support to another firm, usually via remote processing facilities.

CONSOLE That part of a computer used for communication between the operator or maintenance engineer and the computer.

*CONSTANT A fixed or invariable value or data item.

*CONTROL PROGRAM See *operating system*.

*CONTROL UNIT In a digital computer, those parts that effect the retrieval of instructions in proper sequence, the interpretation of each instruction, and the application of the proper signals to the arithmetic unit and other parts in accordance with this interpretation.

*CORE STORAGE A form of high-speed storage, using magnetic cores.

COUNTER A device such as a register or storage location used to represent the number of occurrences of an event.

*COUPLER See *modem*.

*CYLINDER The group of data tracks accessed simultaneously by a set of read and write heads on a disk storage device.

DATA A representation of facts, concepts, or instructions in a formalized manner suitable for communication, interpretation, or processing by human or automatic means. Any representation, such as characters or analog quantities, to which meaning is, or might be, assigned.

DATA BANK A comprehensive collection of libraries of data. For example, one line of an invoice may form an item, a complete invoice may form a record, a complete set of such records may form a file, the collection of inventory control files may form a library, and the libraries used by an organization are known as its data bank.

*DATA BASE See *data bank*.

*DATA CELL DRIVE A random-access storage device that holds millions of characters on strips of magnetic material. The strips are filed in groups called cells.

*DATA COLLECTION The act of bringing data from one or more points to a central point.

*DATA CYCLE The fundamental data processing sequence of operations, composed of input, processing, and output.

*DATA DECK That portion of a job which contains the data or information to be processed by the program.

*DATA FLOW The data path through a problem solution.

*DATA INQUIRY One element of a teleprocessing system in which remote files can be accessed by a request for information.

*DATA MANAGEMENT A general term that collectively describes those functions of the control program that provide access to data sets, enforce data storage conventions, and regulate the use of input/output devices.

*DATA MANIPULATION   See *data processing*.

DATA PROCESSING   The execution of a systematic sequence of operations performed upon data. Synonymous with *information processing*.

*DATA TRANSMISSION   The sending of data from one part of a system to another part.

DEBUG   To detect, locate, and remove mistakes from a routine or malfunctions from a computer. Synonymous with *troubleshoot*.

*DECIMAL NOTATION   A fixed-base notation, where the base is ten.

DECISION   A determination of future action.

*DECISION TABLE   A tabular form showing the alternative conditions and actions that may take place in a program.

DECODER   A device that decodes. A matrix of logic elements that selects one or more output channels according to the combination of input signals present.

DETAIL FILE   See *transaction file*.

*DETAIL PROGRAM FLOWCHART   Flowchart which shows a step-by-step diagram of each detail involved in the solution of a problem. Synonymous with *micro* or *detail flowchart*.

*DIAGNOSTIC MESSAGE   Messages printed out by the computer during compilation or execution of a program, pertaining to the diagnosis or isolation of errors in the program.

*DIGIT ROW   One of the horizontal rows of bits on a punched card, generally referring to the rows 1 to 9.

DIGITAL COMPUTER   A computer in which discrete representation of data is mainly used. A computer that operates on discrete data by performing arithmetic and logic processes on these data. Contrast with *analog computer*.

*DIGITAL DATA   Data represented in discrete, discontinuous form, as contrasted with analog data represented in continuous form. Digital data is usually represented by means of coded characters, for example, numbers, signs, symbols, etc.

DIRECT ACCESS   See *random access*.

DISK   Alternate spelling for disc. See *magnetic disc*.

*DISK PACK   A direct access storage device containing magnetic disks on which data is stored. Disk packs are mounted on a disk storage drive.

DISPLAY   A visual presentation of data.

DOCUMENT   A medium and the data recorded on it for human use, for example, a report sheet, a book. By extension, any record that has permanence and that can be read by man or machine.

DOCUMENTATION   The creating, collecting, organizing, storing, citing, and disseminating of documents, or the information recorded in documents. A collection of documents or information on a given subject.

*DOS   Disk Operating System.

DUMP   To copy the contents of all or part of a storage, usually from an internal storage into an external storage.

*EAM   *Electrical Accounting Machine.* Pertaining to data processing equipment that is predominantly electromechanical, such as keypunch, mechanical sorter, collator, and tabulator.

*EBCDIC   *Extended Binary Coded Decimal Interchange Code.* A coding system widely used in modern computers, which can represent up to 256 characters. Consists of 8-bit coded characters and a 9th parity bit.

EDIT   To modify the form or format of data, for example, to insert or delete characters such as page numbers or decimal points.

ELECTRONIC DATA PROCESSING (EDP)   Data processing largely performed by electronic devices. Pertaining to data processing equipment that is predominately electronic, such as an electronic digital computer.

*END-OF-FILE MARK   A code that signals that the last record of a file has been read.

END-OF-TAPE MARKER   A marker on a magnetic tape used to indicate the end of the permissible recording area, for example, a photo-reflective strip, a transparent section of tape, or a particular bit pattern.

*END PRINTING   A form of interpreting in which large letters, approximately $\frac{1}{4}''$ high, are printed on the end of a punched card, at right angles to the zone and digit rows.

ERROR   Any discrepancy between a computed, observed, or measured quantity and the true, specified, or theoretically correct value or condition.

*EVEN PARITY   A checking system in which a binary digit is added to an array of bits to make the sum of the bits even.

*EXECUTE   To carry out an instruction or perform a routine.

*EXECUTION CYCLE   The phase in the CPU operating cycle during which an instruction is performed or carried out.

*FEASIBILITY STUDY   A planning study, made to evaluate the aspects of implementing a new system, or modifying an existing one. The study involves consideration of such elements as cost, time, labor.

FIELD   In a record, a specified area used for a particular category of data, for example, a group of card columns used to represent a wage rate or a set of bit locations in a computer word used to express the address of the operand.

FILE   A collection of related records treated as a unit. For example, one line of an invoice may form an item, a complete invoice may form a record, the complete set of such records may form a file, the collection of inventory control files may form a library, and the libraries used by an organization are known as its data bank.

*FILE LABEL   A unique name assigned to a file to identify its contents.

FILE MAINTENANCE   The activity of keeping a file up to date by adding, changing, or deleting data.

*FILE PROTECTION RING   A plastic ring placed around the hub of a reel of magnetic tape to allow data to be written on the tape. It is a means of error prevention.

FIXED-POINT REPRESENTATION   A positional representation in which each number is represented by a single set of digits, the position of the radix point being fixed with respect to one end of the set, according to some convention.

*FIXED-LENGTH RECORD   Pertaining to a file in which all records are constrained to be of equal, predetermined length.

FLIP FLOP   A circuit or device containing active elements, capable of assuming either one or two stable states at a given time.

FLOATING-POINT REPRESENTATION   A number representation system in which each number, as represented by a pair of numerals, equals one of those numerals times a power of an implicit fixed positive integer base where the power is equal to the implicit base raised to the exponent represented by the other numeral.

FLOWCHART   A graphical representation for the definition, analysis, or solution of a problem in which symbols are used to represent operations, data, flow, equipment, etc.

FOREGROUND PROCESSING   The automatic execution of the programs that have been designed to preempt the use of the computing facilities. Usually a real-time program.

FORMAT   The arrangement of data.

FORTRAN   *For*mula *Tran*slating system. A language primarily used to express computer programs by arithmetic formulas.

FULL DUPLEX   In communications, pertaining to a simultaneous two-way independent transmission in both directions. Synonymous with duplex.

FUNCTION   A specific purpose of an entity or its characteristic action. In communications, a machine action such as a carriage return or line feed.

*GANG PUNCH   To punch all or part of the information from one punched card into succeeding cards.

GATE   A device having one output channel and one or more input channels, such that the output channel state is completely determined by the input channel states, except during switching transients. A combinational logic element having at least one input channel.

GENERAL-PURPOSE COMPUTER   A computer designed to handle a wide variety of problems.

GENERATOR   A controlling routine that performs a generate function, for example, report generator, I/O generator.

*GRAPHIC OUTPUT   Symbols output from a system. Includes plots, drawings, curves, and lines.

*GROUPING   Combining records into a unit to conserve storage space or reduce access time.

HALF DUPLEX   In communications, pertaining to an alternate, one way at a time, independent transmission.

*HARD COPY   See *document*.

HARDWARE   Physical equipment, as opposed to the program or method of use, for example, mechanical, magnetic, electrical, or electronic devices. Contrast with *software*.

HEADER CARD A card that contains information related to the data in cards that follow.

*HEXADECIMAL NOTATION A numeration system with a base of sixteen.

HOLLERITH Pertaining to a particular type of code or punched card utilizing 12 rows per column and usually 80 columns per card.

*HOLLERITH CARD See *punched card*.

*HOUSEKEEPING Operations or routines that do not contribute directly to solution of the problem but do contribute directly to the operation of the computer.

INDEX An ordered reference list of the contents of a file or document together with keys or reference notations for identification or location of those contents. To prepare a list as in the above. A symbol or numeral used to identify a particular quantity in an array of similar quantities. To move a machine part to a predetermined position, or by a predetermined amount, on a quantized scale.

*INFORMATION See *data*.

INFORMATION PROCESSING See *data processing*.

INFORMATION RETRIEVAL The methods and procedures for recovering specific information from stored data.

INITIALIZE To set counters, switches, and addresses to zero or other starting values at the beginning of, or at prescribed points in, a computer routine.

INPUT Pertaining to a device, process, or channel involved in the insertion of data or states, or to the data or states involved.

*INPUT/OUTPUT Commonly called I/O. A general term for the equipment used to communicate with a computer. The data involved in such communication. The media carrying the data for input/output.

*INPUT/OUTPUT CONTROL PROGRAM (IOCS) A control program designed to schedule the flow of data into and out of the computer system.

INSTRUCTION A statement that specifies an operation and the values or locations of its operands.

*INSTRUCTION CYCLE The phase in the CPU operating cycle during which an instruction is called from storage and the required circuitry to perform that instruction is set up.

*INTEGER A natural, or whole number.

*INTELLIGENCE CHANNEL In communications, a pathway for meaningful, or useful information (as contrasted with the check-bit channel which transmits parity information).

*INTEGRATED CIRCUIT A combination of interconnected circuit elements inseparably associated on, or within, a continuous substrate.

*INTERACTIVE LANGUAGE A language designed to allow the programmer to communicate with the computer during the execution of the program.

*INTERACTIVE PROGRAM A computer program that permits data to be entered, or the course of programming flow to be changed, during its execution.

INTERPRETER A computer program that translates and executes each source language statement before translating and executing the next one. The device that prints on a punched card the data already punched in the card.

INTER-RECORD GAP (IRG) An area on a data medium used to indicate the end of a block or record.

INTERRUPT To stop a process in such a way that it can be resumed.

JOB A specified group of tasks prescribed as a unit of work for a computer. By extension, a job usually includes all necessary computer programs, linkages, files, and instructions to the operating systems.

*JOB CONTROL LANGUAGE A language for communicating with the computer to identify a job or describe its requirements to the operating system.

*JOB STREAM The flow of cards, or records input to a computer system, containing the job control statements, source program, and data deck.

K An abbreviation for the prefix kilo, that is, 1000, in decimal notation. Loosely, when referring to storage capacity, two to the tenth power, 1024 in decimal notation.

KEY One or more characters within an item of data that are used to identify it or control its use.

KEYPUNCH A keyboard-actuated device that punches holes in a card to represent data.

LABEL One or more characters used to identify a statement or an item of data in a computer program.

LANGUAGE A set of representations, conventions, and rules used to convey information.

LIBRARY A collection of organized information used for study and reference. A collection of related files.

LIBRARY ROUTINE A proven routine that is maintained in a program library.

LINE PRINTER A device that prints all characters of a line as a unit.

LINEAR PROGRAMMING In operations research, a procedure for locating the maximum or minimum of a linear function of variables which are subject to linear constraints.

*LISTING To print every item of input data. Loosely, a print out of all cards or records in a program or file.

*LOAD-POINT MARK A marker on a magnetic tape used to indicate the beginning of the permissible recording areas. For example, a photo-reflective strip, a transparent section of tape, or a particular bit pattern.

LOGICAL RECORD A collection of items independent of their physical environment. Portions of the same logical record may be located in different physical records.

*LONGITUDINAL PARITY CHECK In magnetic tape, on a tape in which each lateral row of bits represents a character, the last character placed in a block and which is used for checking parity of each track in the block in the longitudinal direction.

LOOP A sequence of instructions that is executed repeatedly until a terminal condition prevails.

MACHINE LANGUAGE   A language that is used directly by a machine.

*MAGNETIC CORE   A configuration of magnetic material that is used to concentrate an induced magnetic field to retain a magnetic polarization for the purpose of storing data, or for its nonlinear properties as in a logic element. It may be made of such material as iron, iron oxide, or ferrite and in such shapes as wires, tapes, toroids, rods, or thin film.

MAGNETIC DISC   A flat, circular plate with a magnetic surface on which data can be stored by selective magnetization of portions of the flat surface.

MAGNETIC DRUM   A right circular cylinder with a magnetic surface on which data can be stored by selective magnetization of portions of the curved surface.

MAGNETIC INK CHARACTER RECOGNITION   The machine recognition of characters printed with magnetic ink. Abbreviated MICR.

MAGNETIC TAPE   A tape with a magnetic surface on which data can be stored by selective polarization of portions of the surface. A tape of magnetic material used as the constituent in some forms of magnetic cores.

MAIN FRAME   Same as *central processing unit*.

MANAGEMENT INFORMATION SYSTEM   Management performed with the aid of automatic data processing. An information system designed to aid in the performance of management functions. Abbreviated MIS.

*MANUAL DATA PROCESSING   Data processing procedures using pencil, paper, adding machine, calculator, etc.

*MARK SENSE   To mark a position on a punched card with an electrically conductive pencil, for later conversion to machine punching.

MASTER FILE   A file that is either relatively permanent, or that is treated as an authority in a particular job.

MATCH   To check for identity between two or more items of data.

MATHEMATICAL MODEL   A mathematical representation of a process, device, or concept.

MATRIX   In mathematics, a two-dimensional rectangular array of quantities. Matrices are manipulated in accordance with the rules of matrix algebra. In computers, a logic network in the form of an array of input leads and output leads with logic elements connected at some of their intersections. By extension, an array of any number of dimensions.

MEMORY   See *storage*.

MERGE   To combine items from two or more similarly ordered sets into one set that is arranged in the same order. Contrast with *collate*.

*MICRO FLOWCHART   See *detail program flowchart*.

*MICROSECOND   One-millionth of a second.

*MILLISECOND   One-thousandth of a second.

*MINICOMPUTER   A small, desk-top, digital computer, with a CPU, at least one I/O device, and primary storage capacity of 4K bytes.

MNEMONIC SYMBOL A symbol chosen to assist the human memory, for example, an abbreviation such as "mpy" for "multiply."

MODEM *Mo*dulator-*Dem*odulator. A device that modulates and demodulates signals transmitted over communications facilities.

*MONITOR PROGRAM See *operating system*.

MULTIPLEX To interleave or simultaneously transmit two or more messages on a single channel.

*MULTIPLEXER CHANNEL Feeds data between a group of slow speed input/output devices and the CPU.

MULTIPROCESSING Pertaining to the simultaneous execution of two or more computer programs or sequences of instructions by a computer or computer network. Loosely, parallel processing.

MULTIPROGRAMMING Pertaining to the concurrent execution of two or more programs by a computer.

*NANOSECOND One-thousand-millionth of a second.

OBJECT PROGRAM A fully compiled or assembled program that is ready to be loaded into the computer.

*OCTAL REPRESENTATION Pertaining to the numeration system with a base of eight.

*ODD PARITY A checking system in which a binary digit is added to an array of bits to make the sum of the bits odd.

OFF LINE Pertaining to equipment or devices not under control of the central processing unit.

*OFF-LINE SYSTEM In teleprocessing, that kind of system in which human operations are required between the original recording function and the ultimate data processing function. This includes conversion operations as well as the necessary loading and unloading operations incident to the use of point-to-point or data gathering system.

ONLINE Pertaining to equipment or devices under control of the central processing unit. Pertaining to a user's ability to interact with a computer.

*ON-LINE SYSTEM In teleprocessing, a system in which the input data enters the computer directly from the point of origin and/or in which output data is transmitted directly to where it is used.

*OP CODE See *operation code*.

OPEN SHOP Pertaining to the operation of a computer facility in which most productive problem programming is performed by the problem originator rather than by a group of programming specialists. The use of the computer itself may also be described as open shop if the user/programmer also serves as the operator, rather than a full-time trained operator. Contrast with *closed shop*.

OPERAND That which is operated upon. An operand is usually identified by an address part of an instruction.

OPERATING SYSTEM Software which controls the execution of computer programs and which may provide scheduling, debugging, input/output control, accounting, compilation, storage assignment, data management, and related services.

OPERATION CODE A code that represents specific operations.

OPTICAL CHARACTER RECOGNITION Machine identification of printed characters through use of light-sensitive devices. Abbreviated OCR.

*OUTPUT Data that has been processed. The state or sequence of states occurring on a specified output channel. The device or collective set of devices for taking data out of a device. A channel for expressing a state of a device or logic element. The process of transferring data from an internal storage to an external storage.

*OVERLAP To do something at the same time that something else is being done; for example, to perform input/output operations while instructions are being executed by the central processing unit.

PARALLEL Pertaining to the concurrent or simultaneous occurrence of two or more related activities in multiple devices or channels.

PARITY CHECK A check that tests whether the number of ones (or zeros) in an array of binary digits is odd or even.

PERIPHERAL EQUIPMENT In a data processing system, any unit of equipment, distinct from the central processing unit, which may provide the system with outside communication.

*PERT *Program Evaluation and Review Technique.* A systems analysis technique used to find the most efficient scheduling of time and resources when producing a complex project or product.

*PHOTOTYPESETTER An output device that prints out characters using a photographic imaging system.

*PHYSICAL RECORD A record from the standpoint of the manner or form in which it is stored, retrieved, and moved—that is, one that is defined in terms of physical qualities.

*PICOSECOND One-thousandth of a nanosecond.

*PL/I *Programming Language I*, a high-level programming language.

*PLOT To map or diagram. To connect the point-by-point coordinate values.

*PORT-A-PUNCH A hand-held device that allows the operator to manually punch out pre-cut holes. Used to encode data while in the field in machine-readable form.

*POL See *problem-oriented language*.

*PRIMARY STORAGE The main internal storage.

PROBLEM-ORIENTED LANGUAGE A programming language designed for the convenient expression of a given class of problems.

*PROBLEM PROGRAM See *source program*.

PROCESSOR In hardware, a data processor. In software, a computer program that includes the compiling, assembling, translating, and related functions for a specific programming language, COBOL processor, FORTRAN processor.

*PRODUCTION RUN A computer run, involving actual data, as contrasted with a test run, using data for checking purposes.

PROGRAM A series of actions proposed in order to achieve a certain result. Loosely, a routine. To design, wire, and test a program.

*PROGRAM FLOWCHART A step-by-step diagram, showing each discrete procedure and element in the solution of the problem.

*PULSE TRAIN The resulting electronic impulses which transmit encoded information.

PUNCHED CARD A card punched with a pattern of holes to represent data. A card as above, before being punched.

PUNCHED TAPE A tape on which a pattern of holes or cuts is used to represent data.

*QUEUE A waiting line formed by items in a system waiting for service—for example, customer at a bank teller window or messages to be transmitted in a message switching system. To arrange in, or form, a queue.

RANDOM ACCESS Pertaining to the process of obtaining data from, or placing data into, storage where the time required for such access is independent of the location of the data most recently obtained or placed in storage. Pertaining to a storage device in which the access time is effectively independent of the location of the data.

*READ/WRITE HEAD That part of a magnetic tape drive which records electronic pulses on magnetic tape, or reads data from tape.

REAL TIME Pertaining to the actual time during which a physical process transpires. Pertaining to the performance of a computation during the actual time that the related physical process transpires in order that results of the computation can be used in guiding the physical process.

RECORD A collection of related items of data, treated as a unit. For example, one line of an invoice may form a record; a complete set of such records may form a file.

RECORD LENGTH A measure of the size of a record, usually specified in units such as words or characters.

REGISTER A device capable of storing a specified amount of data, such as one word.

REMOTE ACCESS Pertaining to communication with a data processing facility by one or more stations that are distant from that facility.

*REMOTE JOB ENTRY (RJE) A system of hardware and software that enables jobs to be input, processed, and output via remote terminals.

*REPORTING Data outputted in a form usable to man, for example, information transferred from magnetic tape to printed payroll checks.

*REPORT PROGRAM GENERATOR (RPG) A computer language used for processing large data files.

*REPRODUCE To prepare a duplicate of stored information, especially for punched cards, punched paper tape, or magnetic tape.

ROUTINE An ordered set of instructions that may have some general or frequent use.

ROW A horizontal arrangement of characters or other expressions.

RUN A single, continuous performance of a computer program or routine.

SEARCH To examine a set of items for one or more having a desired property.

*SECONDARY STORAGE Auxiliary storage.

*SECTOR A pie-shaped portion or area on the surface of a magnetic disk storage device.

*SELECTOR CHANNEL Feeds data between a single high-speed input/output device and the CPU.

*SEQUENCE CHECKING (CHECKING SEQUENCE) A unit record procedure that determines whether all records in a file are ordered in a series, or according to rank or time.

*SEQUENTIAL ACCESS Pertaining to the sequential or consecutive transmission of data to or from storage. Pertaining to the process of obtaining data from or placing data into storage where the time required for such access is dependent upon the location of the data most recently obtained or placed in storage. Synonymous with serial access.

SERIAL Pertaining to the sequential or consecutive occurrence of two or more related activities in a single device or channel. Pertaining to the sequencing of two or more processes. Pertaining to the sequential processing of the individual parts of a whole, such as the bits of a character or the characters of a word, using the same facilities for successive parts.

SIMULATION To represent certain features of the behavior of a physical or abstract system by the behavior of another system.

SOFTWARE A set of computer programs, procedures, and possibly associated documentation concerned with the operation of a data processing system, for example, compilers, library routines, manuals, circuit diagrams. Contrast with *hardware*.

SORT To segregate items into groups according to some definite rules. Same as order.

*SOURCE DOCUMENT A record prepared at the time, or place, a transaction takes place. These documents serve as the source for data to be input to the computer system.

SOURCE PROGRAM A computer program written in a source language.

SPECIAL-PURPOSE COMPUTER A computer that is designed to handle a restricted class of problems.

*SPOOLING A process of writing output data on a temporary storage device (usually a magnetic drum) until an output unit is available.

*STANDARD CHARACTER SET The limited collection of letters, numbers, and characters used to encode a program in a given language.

STATEMENT In computer programming, a meaningful expression or generalized instruction in a source language.

STORAGE Pertaining to a device into which data can be entered, in which they can be held, and from which they can be retrieved at a later time. Loosely, any device that can store data. Synonymous with *memory*.

STORAGE PROTECTION An arrangement for preventing access to storage for either reading or writing, or both.

STORED PROGRAM COMPUTER   A computer controlled by internally stored instructions that can synthesize, store, and in some cases, alter instructions as though they were data, and that can subsequently execute these instructions.

SUBROUTINE   A routine that can be part of another routine.

*SUBSYSTEM   A part of a larger system, which in itself forms an organized whole.

*SUMMARY PUNCH   A card-punching machine which can be connected to an accounting machine to punch totals or balance cards. To punch summary information in cards.

*SUPERVISOR   A routine or routines executed in response to a requirement for altering or interrupting the flow of operation through the central processing unit, or for performance of input/output operations, and, therefore, the medium through which the use of resources is coordinated and the flow of operations through the central processing unit is maintained. Hence, a control routine that is executed in supervisor state.

SYMBOLIC ADDRESS   An address expressed in symbols convenient to the computer programmer.

SYSTEM   An assembly of methods, procedures, or techniques united by regulated interaction to form an organized whole. An organized collection of men, machines, and methods required to accomplish a set of specific functions.

*SYSTEM ANALYSIS   The analysis of an activity to determine precisely what must be accomplished and how to accomplish it.

*SYSTEM FLOWCHART   A diagram that shows the data flow in an entire organization or system. It specifies the work stations, operations to be performed, communications links, etc.

*SYSTEM GENERATION   The procedure of designing, organizing, and setting up an operating system to meet the needs of a specific organization.

*SYSTEM LIBRARY   The collection of all cataloged data sets at an installation.

TELECOMMUNICATIONS   Pertaining to the transmission of signals over long distances, such as by telegraph, radio, or television.

*TELEPROCESSING   A form of information handling in which a data processing system utilizes communication facilities.

TERMINAL   A point in a system or communications network at which data can either enter or leave.

*THROUGHPUT   A measure of system efficiency; the rate at which work can be handled by a system.

TIME SHARING   Pertaining to the interleaved use of the time of a device.

*TOS   Tape Operating System.

TRACK   The portion of a moving storage medium, such as a drum, tape, or disc, that is accessible to a given reading head position.

*TRAILER RECORD A record that follows one or more records and contains data related to those records.

TRANSACTION FILE A file containing relatively transient data to be processed in combination with a master file. For example, in a payroll application, a transaction file indicating hours worked might be processed with a master file containing employee name and rate of pay.

*TRANSISTOR A small solid-state, semi-conducting device, ordinarily using germanium, that performs nearly all the functions of an electronic tube, especially amplification.

TROUBLE-SHOOT See *debug*.

*TURNAROUND TIME The elapsed time between submission of a job to a computing center and the return of results.

*TYPE BAR A linear type element containing all printable symbols.

*UNIT RECORD Historically, a card containing one complete record. Currently, the punched card.

*UPDATE To modify a master file with current information according to a specified procedure.

*USASCII *United States of America Standard Code for Information Interchange.* Code consisting of seven intelligence channels and an eighth check-bit channel.

VARIABLE A quantity that can assume any of a given set of values.

VARIABLE-LENGTH RECORD Pertaining to a file in which the records are not uniform in length.

VERIFY To determine whether a transcription of data or other operation has been accomplished accurately. To check the results of keypunching.

*VOLUME That portion of a single unit of storage media which is accessible to a single read-write mechanism.

*WIRING CONTROL PANEL Device used to program unit record equipment. Consists of a frame with rows of hubs. The hubs are connected in various patterns using jumper wires.

WORD A character string or a bit string considered as an entity.

WORD LENGTH A measure of the size of a word, usually specified in units such as characters or binary digits.

WRITE To record data in a storage device or a data medium. The recording need not be permanent, such as the writing on a cathode ray tube display device.

X PUNCH A punch in the second row from the top on a Hollerith punched card. Synonymous with eleven-punch.

Y PUNCH A punch in the top row of a Hollerith punched card. Synonymous with twelve-punch.

ZONE PUNCH A punch in the eleven, twelve, or zero row of a Hollerith punched card.

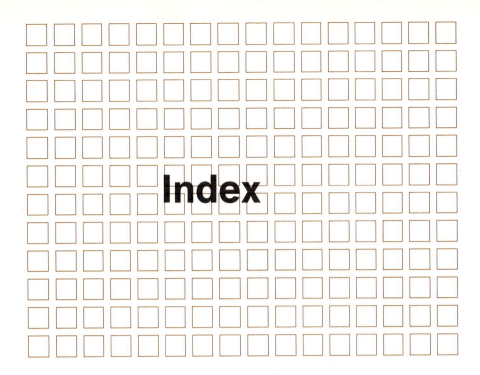

Index

(Page numbers in italics refer to illustrations.)

CREDITS

CHAPTER 1

1.1 (A) Reprinted from *Computer Decisions,* ©️ 1970, Hayden Publishing Co., Inc. **(B)** Copyright *Computerworld,* Newton, Mass. 02160. **1.2** *Economic Almanac—Business Facts Book, 1966–67,* National Industrial Conference Board. **1.3** Courtesy of UNIVAC Division, Sperry Rand Corp. **1.4** Courtesy of Burroughs Corp. **1.5** Courtesy of Burroughs Corp. **1.6** Courtesy of Westinghouse Electric Corp. **1.7** Courtesy of Texas Instruments, Inc. **1.8** Reprinted from *Computer Decisions,* ©️ 1970, Hayden Publishing Co., Inc.

CHAPTER 2

2.2 From the Planning Research Corporation Collection. **2.3** From the Planning Research Corporation Collection. **2.4** From the Planning Research Corporation Collection. **2.5** From the Planning Research Corporation Collection. **2.6** From the Planning Research Corporation Collection. **2.7** Courtesy of the Bettmann Archive, Inc. **2.8** From the Planning Research Corporation Collection. **2.9** From the Planning Research Corporation Collection. **2.10** From the Planning Research Corporation Collection. **2.11** From the Planning Research Corporation Collection. **2.12** Courtesy of UNIVAC Division, Sperry Rand Corp. **2.13** Courtesy of IBM Corp. **2.14** Courtesy of IBM Corp. **2.15** Courtesy of IBM Corp. **2.16** Reprinted by permission from *Reference Manual, IBM 519 Document-Originating Machine,* ©️ 1961 by International Business Machines Corporation. **2.17** Courtesy of Scan-Data Corp. **2.18** Courtesy of Scan-Data Corp. **2.20** Courtesy of IBM Corp. **2.21** Courtesy of Teletype Corp. **2.22** Harbrace photo.

CHAPTER 3

3.5 Reprinted by permission from *IBM Data Recorder Operator's Guide,* ©️ 1971 by International Business Machines Corporation. **3.9** Courtesy of IBM Corp. **3.10** Courtesy of IBM Corp. **3.11** Courtesy of UNIVAC Division, Sperry Rand Corp. **3.12** Courtesy of IBM Corp. **3.13** Courtesy of IBM Corp. **3.14** Courtesy of IBM Corp.

CHAPTER 4

4.11 Harbrace photo. **4.12** Courtesy of UNIVAC Division, Sperry Rand Corp. **4.14** Courtesy of IBM Corp.

CHAPTER 5

5.8 Reprinted by permission from *Reference Manual, IBM 519 Document-Originating Machine,* Ⓒ 1961 by International Business Machines Corporation. **5.10** Courtesy of IBM Corp. **5.11** Reprinted by permission from *Reference Manual, IBM 519 Document-Originating Machine,* Ⓒ 1961 by International Business Machines Corporation. **5.12** Reprinted by permission from *Reference Manual, IBM 519 Document-Originating Machine,* Ⓒ 1961 by International Business Machines Corporation. **5.14** Courtesy of IBM Corp. **5.15** Reprinted by permission from *Reference Manual, IBM 557 Alphabetic Interpreter,* Ⓒ 1959 by International Business Machines Corporation. **5.17** Courtesy of IBM Corp.

CHAPTER 6

6.3 Courtesy of IBM Corp. **6.5** Courtesy of UNIVAC Division, Sperry Rand Corp. **6.6 (A)** and **(B)** Courtesy of Burroughs Corp. **6.9** Courtesy of Digital Equipment Corp. **6.10** Courtesy of IBM Corp. **6.11** Courtesy of UNIVAC Division, Sperry Rand Corp. **6.12** Courtesy of IBM Corp. **6.13** Courtesy of Burroughs Corp. **6.14** Photograph courtesy of the Xerox Corp. **6.15** Courtesy of UNIVAC Division, Sperry Rand Corp.

CHAPTER 7

7.3 Courtesy of IBM Corp. **7.5** Courtesy of IBM Corp. **7.6** Courtesy of IBM Corp. **7.8** Courtesy of Thom McAn Shoe Co. **7.9** Courtesy of IBM Corp. **7.11** Courtesy of IBM Corp. **7.12** Courtesy of Data Action Co. **7.13** Courtesy of Data Action Co. **7.14** Courtesy of Computer Machinery Corp.

CHAPTER 8

8.5 Reprinted by permission from *Introduction to IBM Data Processing Systems,* Ⓒ 1970 by International Business Machines Corporation. **8.6** Reprinted by permission from *Introduction to IBM Data Processing Systems,* Ⓒ 1970 by International Business Machines Corporation. **8.7** Reprinted by permission from *Introduction to IBM Data Processing Systems,* Ⓒ 1970 by International Business Machines Corporation. **8.8** Reprinted by permission from *Introduction to IBM Data Processing Systems,* Ⓒ 1970 by International Business Machines Corporation. **8.9** From *A B C's of Teletype Equipment,* Teletype Corp. **8.10** Reprinted by permission from *IBM System/360 Component Description, 2400 Series Magnetic Tape,* Ⓒ 1970 by International Business Machines Corporation.

CHAPTER 9

9.1 (A) Courtesy of IBM Corp. **(B)** Courtesy of UNIVAC Division, Sperry Rand Corp. **(C)** Courtesy of Energy Conversion Devices, Inc. **(D)** From *Electronics,* Sept. 28, 1970. **9.2** Reprinted by permission from *Introduction to IBM Data Processing Systems,* Ⓒ 1970 by International Business Machines Corporation. **9.3** Reprinted by permission from *Introduction to IBM Data Processing Systems,* Ⓒ 1970 by International Business Machines Corporation. **A** (p. 197) Reprinted by permission from *Introduction to IBM Data Processing Systems,* Ⓒ 1970 by International Business Machines Corporation.

CHAPTER 10

10.1 (B) Harbrace photo. **10.2** Harbrace photo. **10.3** Reprinted by permission from *IBM 729, 7330, and 727 Magnetic Tape Units, Principles of Operation,* by International Business Machines Corporation. **10.4** Reprinted by permission from *Introduction to IBM Data Processing Systems,* Ⓒ 1970 by International Business Machines Corporation. **10.5** Reprinted by permission from *Introduction to IBM Data Processing Systems,* Ⓒ 1970 by International Business Machines Corporation. **10.6** Harbrace photo. **10.7** Harbrace photo. **10.8** Courtesy of IBM Corp. **10.9** Courtesy of IBM Corp. **10.10** Reprinted by permission from *Introduction to IBM Data Processing Systems,* Ⓒ 1970 by International Business Machines Corporation. **10.11** Courtesy of IBM Corp. **10.12 (A)** Courtesy of IBM Corp. **(B)** Reprinted by permission from *IBM System/360 Component Description, 2841 and Associated,* Ⓒ 1966 by International Business Machines Corporation. **10.13** Courtesy of IBM Corp. **10.14** Reprinted by permission from *IBM System/360 Disk Operating System, System Control and System Service Programs,* ©️ 1971 by International Business Machines Corporation.

CHAPTER 11

11.1 Harbrace photo. **11.2** Reprinted by permission from *Introduction to IBM Data Processing Systems,* ©️ 1970 by International Business Machines Corporation. **11.3** Reprinted by permission from *IBM 1403, Printer Component Description,* by International Business Machines Corporation. **11.4** From "Typesetting" by Gerard O. Walter, ©️ May, 1969 by Scientific American, Inc. All rights reserved. **11.5** Harbrace photo. **11.6** Courtesy of IBM Corp. **11.7** Harbrace photo. **11.8** Courtesy of IBM Corp. **11.9** Harbrace photo. **11.10** Courtesy of UNIVAC Division, Sperry Rand Corp. **11.11** Courtesy of Hazeltine Corp. **11.12** Courtesy of University Computing Co. **11.13** Courtesy of IBM Corp. **11.14** Courtesy of VariTyper Division, Addressograph Multigraph Corp. **11.15** Courtesy of University Computing Co.

CHAPTER 12

12.5 Harbrace photo. **12.7 (A)** Courtesy of Internal Revenue Service, U. S. Government. **12.8** Reprinted by permission from *IBM Data Processing Techniques,* ©️ 1962 by International Business Machines Corporation. **12.9 (A)** Reprinted by permission from *IBM Data Processing Techniques,* ©️ 1962 by International Business Machines Corporation.

CHAPTER 14

14.1 Courtesy of University Computing Co.

CHAPTER 18

18.1 Reprinted by permission from *An Introduction to PL/I: Student Text,* by International Business Machines Corporation. **18.2** Reprinted by permission from *PL/I (F) Programmer's Guide, IBM System/360,* ©️ 1972 by International Business Machines Corporation. **18.7 (A)** Reprinted by permission from *IBM APL/360 Primer,* ©️ 1969 by International Business Machines Corporation. **(B)** Courtesy of University Computing Co. **18.9** Courtesy of Teletype Corp. **18.11 (A)** and **(B)** Courtesy of Proprietary Computer Systems, Inc.

CHAPTER 21

21.8 Courtesy of Infosystems (formerly Business Automation).

CHAPTER 22

22.8 Courtesy of Burroughs Corp. **22.10** C. F. Rank Commercial Photography. **22.11** Courtesy of IBM Corp. **22.12** Courtesy of IBM Corp. **22.13** Courtesy of IBM Corp. **22.14** Courtesy of IBM Corp. **22.15** Courtesy of Vernitron Corp. **22.16** Courtesy of American Data Systems.

CHAPTER 23

23.1 Courtesy of IBM Corp. **23.3** Courtesy of Tymshare, Inc. **23.4** Courtesy of Control Data Corp. **23.5** Courtesy of Control Data Corp.

Cartoons in Chapters 1–10, 12–14, 17–23 are reprinted with permission of *Datamation*®, copyright Technical Publishing Co., Barrington, Ill. 60010, 1972. Cartoon in Chapter 11 reprinted by permission of Publishers-Hall Syndicate. Cartoon in Chapter 15 reprinted by permission of Newspaper Enterprise Association. Cartoon in Chapter 16 reprinted by permission of Job Market Publications.

Computer art for part openings: Part One, Lloyd Sumner—Computer Creations; Part Two, Allen Bernholtz Consultants Inc.; Part Three, Lloyd Sumner—Computer Creations; Part Four, Allen Bernholtz Consultants Inc.; Part Five, Lloyd Sumner—Computer Creations; Part Six, Ken Knowlton; Part Seven, California Computer Products Inc.; Part Eight, Ken Knowlton.

B 3
C 4
D 5
E 6
F 7
G 8
H 9
I 0
J 1